THE ECONOMICS BOOK

THE ECONOMICS BOOK

DK LONDON

PROJECT ART EDITORS
Anna Hall, Duncan Turner

SENIOR EDITORS
Janet Mohun, Rebecca Warren

EDITOR
Lizzie Munsey

US EDITOR
Kate Johnsen

MANAGING ART EDITOR
Michelle Baxter

MANAGING EDITOR
Camilla Hallinan

PUBLISHER
Sarah Larter

ART DIRECTOR
Philip Ormerod

ASSOCIATE PUBLISHING DIRECTOR
Liz Wheeler

PUBLISHING DIRECTOR
Jonathan Metcalf

ILLUSTRATIONS
James Graham

PICTURE RESEARCH
Louise Thomas

PRODUCTION EDITOR
Ben Marcus

PRODUCTION CONTROLLER
Sophie Argyris

original styling by

STUDIO8 DESIGN

DK DELHI

SENIOR ART EDITOR
Ivy Roy

ART EDITOR
Arijit Ganguly

ASSISTANT ART EDITORS
Sanjay Chauhan, Kanika Mittal

CONSULTANT ART DIRECTOR
Shefali Upadhyay

SENIOR EDITOR
Anita Kakar

EDITORS
Rupa Rao, Priyaneet Singh

DEPUTY MANAGING EDITOR
Alka Thakur

EDITORIAL MANAGER
Rohan Sinha

DTP MANAGER
Balwant Singh

DTP DESIGNERS
Vishal Bhatia, Bimlesh Tiwary

produced for DK by
TALLTREE LTD

MANAGING EDITOR
David John

COMMISSIONING EDITOR
Sarah Tomley

SENIOR DESIGNER
Ben Ruocco

SENIOR EDITORS
Rob Colson, Deirdre Headon

First American Edition, 2012

Published in the United States by
DK Publishing
4th floor, 345 Hudson Street
New York, New York 10014

07 08 09 10 11   10 9 8 7 6 5 4 3 2 1
001 - 186345 - Feb/2018

Copyright © 2012, 2018
Dorling Kindersley Limited
A Penguin Random House Company

Published in Great Britain by
Dorling Kindersley Limited.

A catalog record for this book is available
from the Library of Congress.

ISBN: 978-1-4654-7391-2

DK books are available at special
discounts when purchased in bulk
for sales promotions, premiums,
fund-raising, or educational use.
For details, contact: DK Publishing
Special Markets, 375 Hudson Street,
New York, New York 10014 or
SpecialSales@dk.com.

Printed and bound in China.

A WORLD OF IDEAS:
SEE ALL THERE IS TO KNOW
www.dk.com

CONTRIBUTORS

NIALL KISHTAINY, CONSULTANT EDITOR

Niall Kishtainy teaches at the London School of Economics and specializes in economic history and development. He has worked for the World Bank and the United Nations Economic Commission for Africa.

GEORGE ABBOT

George Abbot is an economist who worked in 2012 on Barack Obama's presidential reelection campaign. He previously worked with Compass, the influential UK think tank, on strategic documents such as *Plan B: A New Economy for a New Society*.

JOHN FARNDON

John Farndon is the author of many books on contemporary issues and the history of ideas, including overviews of the booming economies of China and India.

FRANK KENNEDY

Frank Kennedy worked for over 25 years in investment banking in the City of London as a top-ranked investment analyst and as a managing director in capital markets, where he led a European team advising financial institutions. He studied economic history at the London School of Economics.

JAMES MEADWAY

Economist James Meadway works at the New Economics Foundation, an independent British think tank. He has also worked as a policy adviser for the UK Treasury.

CHRISTOPHER WALLACE

Christopher Wallace is Head of Economics at the UK's prestigious Colchester Royal Grammar School. He has been teaching economics for more than 25 years.

MARCUS WEEKS

Marcus Weeks studied philosophy and worked as a teacher before embarking on a career as an author. He has contributed to many books on the arts and popular sciences.

CONTENTS

INDUSTRIAL AND ECONOMIC REVOLUTIONS
1820–1929

WAR AND DEPRESSIONS
1929–1945

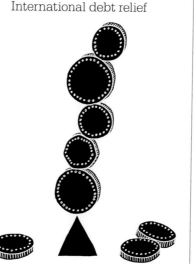

INTRODU

F ew people would claim to know very much about economics, perhaps seeing it as a complex and esoteric subject with little relevance to their everyday lives. It has been generally felt to be the preserve of professionals in business, finance, and government. Yet most of us are becoming more aware of its influence on our wealth and well-being, and we may also have opinions—often quite strong ones—about the rising cost of living, taxes, government spending, and so on. Sometimes these opinions are based on an instant reaction to an item in the news, but they are also frequently the subject of discussions in the workplace or over the dinner table. So to some extent, we do all take an interest in economics. The arguments we use to justify our opinions are generally the same as those used by economists, so a better knowledge of their theories can give us a better understanding of the economic principles that are at play in our lives.

Economics in the news

Today, with the world in apparent economic turmoil, it seems more important than ever to learn something about economics. Far from occupying a separate section of our newspaper or making up a small part of the television news, economic news now regularly makes the headlines. As early as 1997, the US Republican political campaign strategist Robert Teeter noted its dominance, saying, "Look at the declining television coverage [of politics]. Look at the declining voting rate. Economics and economic news is what moves the country now, not politics."

Yet how much do we really understand when we hear about rising unemployment, inflation, stock market crises, and trading deficits? When we're asked to tighten our belts or pay more taxes, do we know why? And when we seem to be at the mercy of risk-taking banks and big corporations, do we know how they came to be so powerful or understand the reasons for their original and continued existence? The discipline of economics is at the heart of questions such as these.

The study of management

Despite the importance and centrality of economics to many issues that affect us all, economics as a discipline is often viewed with suspicion. A popular conception is that it is dry and academic, due to its reliance on statistics, graphs, and formulas. The 19th-century Scottish historian Thomas Carlyle described economics as the "dismal science" that is "dreary, desolate, and, indeed, quite abject and distressing." Another common misconception is that it is "all about money," and while this has a grain of truth, it is by no means the whole picture.

So, what is economics all about? The word is derived from the Greek word *Oikonomia*, meaning "household management," and it has come to mean the study of the way we manage our resources, and more specifically, the production and exchange of goods and services. Of course, the business

> " In economics, hope and faith coexist with great scientific pretension and also a deep desire for respectability.
> **John Kenneth Galbraith**
> **Canadian-US economist (1908–2006)** "

of producing goods and providing services is as old as civilization, but the study of how the process works in practice is comparatively new. It evolved only gradually; philosophers and politicians have expressed their opinions on economic matters since the time of the ancient Greeks, but the first true economists to make a study of the subject did not appear until the end of the 18th century.

At that time the study was known as "political economy," and had emerged as a branch of political philosophy. However, those studying its theories increasingly felt that it should be distinguished as a subject in its own right and began to refer to it as "economic science." This later became popularized in the shorter form of "economics."

A softer science
Is economics a science? The 19th-century economists certainly liked to think so, and although Carlyle thought it dismal, even he dignified it with the label of science. Much economic theory was modeled on mathematics and even physics (perhaps the "-ics" ending of "economics" helped to lend it scientific respectability), and it sought to determine the

laws that govern how the economy behaves, in the same way that scientists had discovered the physical laws underlying natural phenomena. Economies, however, are man-made and are dependent on the rational or irrational behavior of the humans that act within them, so economics as a science has more in common with the "soft sciences" of psychology, sociology, and politics.

Economics was perhaps best defined by British economist Lionel Robbins. In 1932, he described it in his *Essay on the Nature and Significance of Economic Science*

The first lesson of economics is scarcity: there is never enough of anything to satisfy all those who want it. The first lesson of politics is to disregard the first lesson of economics.
Thomas Sowell
US economist (1930–)

as "the science which studies human behavior as a relationship between ends and scarce means which have alternative uses." This broad definition remains the most popular one in use today.

The most important difference between economics and other sciences, however, is that the systems it examines are fluid. As well as describing and explaining economies and how they function, economists can also suggest how they ought to be constructed or can be improved.

The first economists
Modern economics emerged as a distinct discipline in the 18th century, in particular with the publication in 1776 of *The Wealth of Nations*, written by the great Scottish thinker Adam Smith. However, what prompted interest in the subject was not so much the writings of economists as the enormous changes in the economy itself with the advent of the Industrial Revolution. Previous thinkers had commented on the management of goods and services within societies, treating questions that arose as problems for moral or political philosophy. But with the arrival of factories and mass producers of goods came a new »

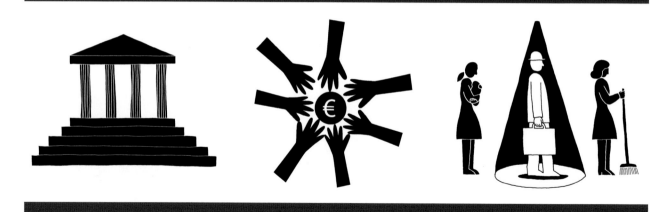

era of economic organization that looked at the bigger picture. This was the beginning of the so-called market economy.

Smith's analysis of the new system set the standard with a comprehensive explanation of the competitive market. Smith suggested that the market is guided by an "invisible hand," where the rational actions of self-interested individuals ultimately give the wider society exactly what it needs. Smith was a philosopher, and the subject of his book was "political economy" —it stretched beyond economics to include politics, history, philosophy, and anthropology. After Smith a new breed of economic thinkers emerged who chose to concentrate entirely on the economy. Each of these built upon our understanding of the economy—how it works and how it should be managed—and laid the foundations for the various branches of economics.

As the discipline evolved, economists identified specific areas to examine. One approach was to look at the economy as a whole, either at a national or international level, which became known as "macroeconomics." This area of economics takes in topics such as growth and development, measurement of a country's wealth

in terms of output and income, and its policies for international trade, taxation, and controlling inflation and unemployment. In contrast, what we now call "microeconomics" looks at the interactions of individual people and firms within the economy: the business of supply and demand, buyers and sellers, markets and competition.

New schools of thought

Naturally, there were differences of opinion among economists, and various schools of thought evolved. Many welcomed the prosperity that the modern industrial economy

Economics is, at root, the study of incentives: how people get what they want, or need, especially when other people want or need the same thing.
Steven D. Levitt
Stephen J. Dubner
US economists (1967– and 1963–)

brought and advocated a "hands-off" or laissez-faire approach to allow the competitive market to create wealth and stimulate technological innovation. Others were more cautious in their estimation of the market's ability to benefit society and identified failings of the system. They thought these could be overcome by state intervention and argued for a role for governments in providing certain goods and services and in curbing the power of the producers. In the analysis of some, notably the German philosopher Karl Marx, a capitalist economy was fatally flawed and would not survive.

The ideas of the early "classical" economists such as Smith were increasingly subjected to rigorous examination. By the late 19th century economists educated in science were approaching the subject through the disciplines of mathematics, engineering, and physics. These "neoclassical" economists described the economy in graphs and formulas, and proposed laws that governed the workings of the markets and justified their approach.

By the end of the 19th century economics was beginning to develop national characteristics: centers of economic thinking had

grown as university departments were established, and there were distinguishable differences between the major schools in Austria, Britain, and Switzerland, particularly on the desirability of some degree of state intervention in the economy.

These differences became even more apparent in the 20th century, when revolutions in Russia and China brought almost a third of the world under communist rule, with planned economies rather than competitive markets. The rest of the world, however, was concerned with asking whether the markets alone could be trusted to provide prosperity. While continental Europe and Britain argued about degrees of government intervention, the real battle of ideas was fought in the US during the Great Depression after the Wall Street Crash of 1929.

In the second half of the 20th century the center of economic thought shifted from Europe to the US, which had become the dominant economic superpower and was adopting ever more laissez-faire policies. After the collapse of the Soviet Union in 1991, it seemed that the free market economy was indeed the route to economic success, as Smith had predicted. Not everyone

agreed. Although the majority of economists had faith in the stability, efficiency, and rationality of the markets, there were some who had doubts, and new approaches arose.

Alternative approaches

In the late 20th century new areas of economics incorporated ideas from disciplines such as psychology and sociology into their theories, as well as new advances in mathematics and physics, such as game theory and chaos theory. These theorists also warned of weaknesses in the capitalist system. The increasingly severe and frequent financial crises that took place at the beginning of the 21st century reinforced the feeling that there was something fundamentally wrong in the system; at the same time scientists concluded that our ever-increasing economic wealth came at a cost to the environment in the form of potentially disastrous climate change.

As Europe and the US begin to deal with perhaps the most serious economic problems they have ever faced, new economies have emerged, especially in Southeast Asia and the so-called BRIC countries (Brazil, Russia, India, and China). Economic power is once

again shifting, and no doubt new economic thinking will evolve to help manage our scarce resources.

One prominent casualty of the recent economic crises is Greece, where the history of economics started, and where the word "economics" comes from. In 2012, protesters in Athens pointed out that democracy also comes from the Greeks but is in danger of being sacrificed in the search for a solution to a debt crisis.

It remains to be seen how the world economy will resolve its problems, but, armed with the principles of economics outlined in this book, you will see how we got into the present situation, and perhaps begin to see a way out. ∎

The purpose of studying economics is …to learn how to avoid being deceived by economists.
Joan Robinson
UK economist (1903–83)

LET TRA
BEGIN
400 BCE—1770 CE

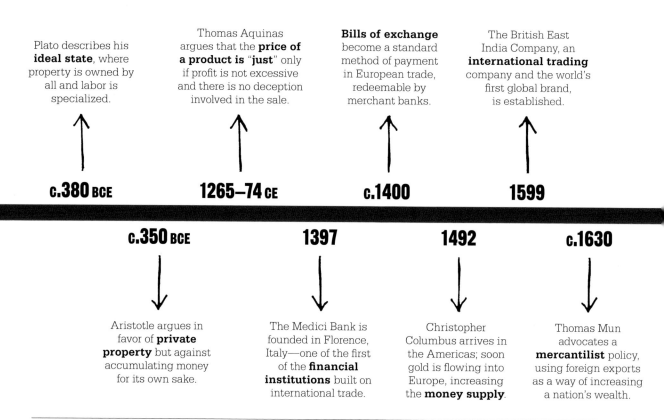

Plato describes his **ideal state**, where property is owned by all and labor is specialized.

Thomas Aquinas argues that the **price of a product is "just"** only if profit is not excessive and there is no deception involved in the sale.

Bills of exchange become a standard method of payment in European trade, redeemable by merchant banks.

The British East India Company, an **international trading** company and the world's first global brand, is established.

c.380 BCE   **1265–74 CE**   **c.1400**   **1599**

c.350 BCE   **1397**   **1492**   **c.1630**

Aristotle argues in favor of **private property** but against accumulating money for its own sake.

The Medici Bank is founded in Florence, Italy—one of the first of the **financial institutions** built on international trade.

Christopher Columbus arrives in the Americas; soon gold is flowing into Europe, increasing the **money supply**.

Thomas Mun advocates a **mercantilist** policy, using foreign exports as a way of increasing a nation's wealth.

As civilizations evolved in the ancient world, so too did systems for providing goods and services to populations. These early economic systems emerged naturally as various trades and crafts produced goods that could be exchanged. People began to trade, first by bartering and later with coins of precious metal, and trade became a central part of life. The business of buying and selling goods operated for centuries before it occurred to anyone to examine how the system worked.

The ancient Greek philosophers were among the first to write about the topics that came to be known collectively as "economics." In *The Republic*, Plato described the political and social makeup of an ideal state, which he said would function economically, with specialty producers providing products for the common good. However, his pupil Aristotle defended the concept of private property, which could be traded in the market. These are arguments that have continued to the present day. As philosophers Plato and Aristotle thought of economics as a matter of moral philosophy: rather than analyzing how an economic system worked, they came up with ideas for how it should work. This kind of approach is said to be "normative"—it is subjective and looks at "what ought to be" the case.

The normative approach to economics continued into the Christian era, as medieval philosophers such as Thomas Aquinas (p.23) attempted to define the ethics of private property and trading in the marketplace.

Aquinas considered the morality of prices, arguing for the importance of "just" prices, where no excessive profit was made by the merchant.

The ancients lived in societies where labor was composed largely of slaves, and medieval Europe ran on a feudal system—where peasants were protected by local lords in exchange for labor or military service. So the moral arguments of these philosophers were somewhat academic.

Rise of the city-states

A major change occurred in the 15th century, as city-states developed in Europe and became wealthy through international trade. A new, prosperous class of merchants replaced the feudal landowners as the important players in the economy, and they worked hand-in-

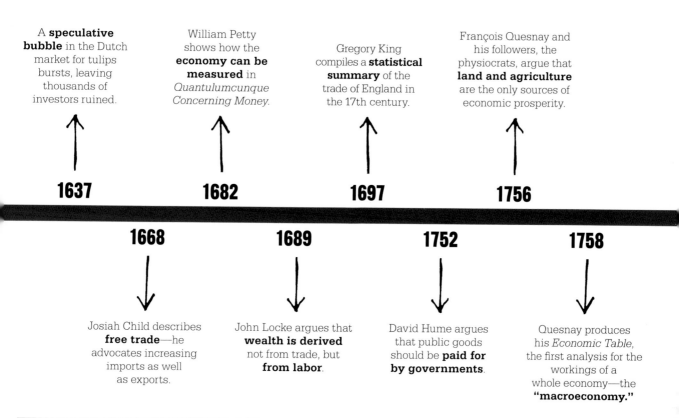

A **speculative bubble** in the Dutch market for tulips bursts, leaving thousands of investors ruined.

William Petty shows how the **economy can be measured** in *Quantulumcunque Concerning Money*.

Gregory King compiles a **statistical summary** of the trade of England in the 17th century.

François Quesnay and his followers, the physiocrats, argue that **land and agriculture** are the only sources of economic prosperity.

1637 **1682** **1697** **1756**

1668 **1689** **1752** **1758**

Josiah Child describes **free trade**—he advocates increasing imports as well as exports.

John Locke argues that **wealth is derived** not from trade, but **from labor**.

David Hume argues that public goods should be **paid for by governments**.

Quesnay produces his *Economic Table*, the first analysis for the workings of a whole economy—the **"macroeconomy."**

hand with dynasties of bankers, who financed their trading and voyages of discovery.

New trading nations replaced small-scale feudal economies, and economic thinking began to focus on how best to control the exchange of goods and money from one country to another. The dominating approach of the time, known as mercantilism, was concerned with the balance of payments—the difference between what a country spends on imports and what it earns from exports. Selling goods abroad was seen as good because it brought money into the country; importing goods was seen as damaging because money flowed out. To prevent a trade deficit and protect domestic producers against foreign competition, mercantilists advocated the taxing of imports.

As trade increased, it moved beyond the hands of individual merchants and their backers. Partnerships and companies were set up, often with government backing, to oversee large trading operations. These firms began to be split into "shares" so they could be financed by many investors. Interest in buying shares grew rapidly in the late 17th century, leading to the establishment of many joint-stock companies and stock exchanges, where the shares could be bought and sold.

A new science

The huge increase in trading also prompted a renewed interest in the working of the economy and led to the beginnings of the discipline of economics. Emerging at the beginning of the 18th century, the so-called Age of Enlightenment,

which prized rationality above all, took a scientific approach to "political economy." Economists attempted to measure economic activity and described the working of the system, rather than looking only at moral implications.

In France a group of thinkers known as the physiocrats analyzed the flow of money around the economy and effectively produced the first macroeconomic (whole-economy) model. They placed agriculture rather than trade or finance at the heart of the economy. Meanwhile, political philosophers in Britain shifted the emphasis away from mercantilist ideas of trade, and toward producers, consumers, and the value and utility of goods. The framework for the modern study of economics was beginning to emerge. ■

PROPERTY SHOULD BE PRIVATE
PROPERTY RIGHTS

IN CONTEXT

FOCUS
Society and the economy

KEY THINKER
Aristotle (384–322 BCE)

BEFORE
423–347 BCE Plato argues in
The Republic that rulers should
hold property collectively for
the common good.

AFTER
1–250 CE In classical Roman
law the sum of rights and
powers a person has over a
thing is called *dominium*.

1265–74 Thomas Aquinas
argues that owning property is
natural and good, but private
property is less important than
the public good.

1689 John Locke states that
what you create by your own
labor is yours by right.

1848 Karl Marx writes the
Communist Manifesto,
advocating the complete
abolition of private property.

We learn about ownership
and personal property
from our earliest
childhood tussles over toys. This
concept is often taken for granted,
yet there is nothing inevitable
about the idea. Private property
is fundamental to capitalism. Karl
Marx (p.105) noted that the wealth
generated by capitalism presents
societies with "an immense
collection of commodities" that are
privately owned and may be traded
for profit. Businesses are also
privately owned and operated for
profit in a free market. Without the
idea of private property, there is no
potential for personal gain—there is
no reason even to enter the market.
There is, in effect, no market.

Types of property
"Property" encompasses a wide
range of things, from material
goods to intellectual property (such
as patents or written text). It has
entered realms that even free
market economists would not
defend, such as slavery—where
people were viewed as commodities.
Historically, material property
has been organized three different
ways. First, everything can be held
in common and used by everyone
as they wish, on the basis of mutual
trust and custom. This was the case
in tribal economies, and it is still
practiced by the Huaorani people of
the Amazon. Second, property can
be held and used collectively; this
is the essence of the communist
system. Third, property can be held
in private, with each person free to
do with it as they choose. This is the
concept at the heart of capitalism.
Modern economists tend to
justify private property on pragmatic
grounds, arguing that the market
simply can't operate without some
division of resources. Earlier
thinkers made more of a moral case

Defending private ownership is
important in capitalist countries. This
house in Warsaw, Poland, is the most
secure home ever built; it turns into a
steel cube at the touch of a button.

See also: Markets and morality 22–23 ▪ Provision of public goods and services 46–47 ▪ Marxist economics 100–05 ▪ Definitions of economics 171

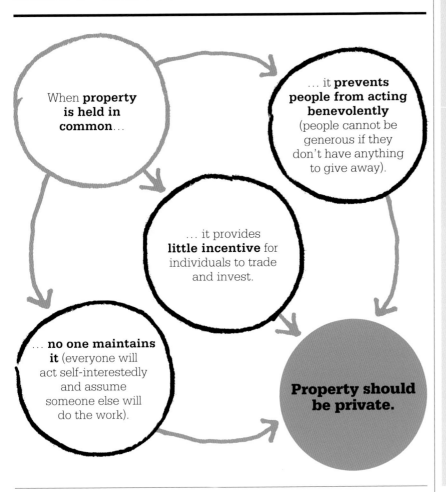

When **property is held in common**…

… it **prevents people from acting benevolently** (people cannot be generous if they don't have anything to give away).

… it provides **little incentive** for individuals to trade and invest.

… **no one maintains it** (everyone will act self-interestedly and assume someone else will do the work).

Property should be private.

How private?

In every modern society some things are shared as collective property, such as streets and parks. Others, such as cars, are private property. Property rights, or legal ownership, normally confers on the owner exclusive rights over a particular resource, but this is not always the case. The owner of a house in a historic district, for instance, might not be allowed to knock it down and replace it with a skyscraper or a factory, or even change the use of the current building. The governments of every country in the world reserve the right to override private ownership when this is deemed necessary, for reasons varying from the needs of infrastructure to national safety issues. Even in the US, a staunchly capitalist nation, the government may force a property owner to relinquish his or her rights. However, the 14th amendment to the Constitution softens this blow by stating that the owner must be compensated with the market price.

for private property. The Greek philosopher Aristotle argued that "property should be private." He pointed out that when property is held in common, no one takes responsibility to maintain and improve it. Moreover, people can only become generous if they have something to give away.

A right to property

In the 17th century all land and housing in Europe was effectively owned by monarchs. The English philosopher John Locke (1632–1704), however, spoke out for individual rights, saying that as God gave us dominion over our own bodies, we also have dominion over the things we make. The German philosopher Immanuel Kant (1724–1804) later argued that private property is a legitimate expression of the self.

Another German philosopher, however, rejected the notion of private property entirely. Karl Marx insisted that the concept of private property is nothing but a device by which the capitalist expropriates the labor of the proletarian, keeps him in slavery, and excludes him. The proletariat is effectively locked out of the select group that controls all wealth and power. ▪

> It is clearly better that property should be private, but the use of it common; and the special business of the legislator is to create in men this benevolent disposition.
> **Aristotle**

WHAT IS A JUST PRICE?

MARKETS AND MORALITY

Many people know what it is like to be exploited or "ripped off" by a vendor, such as when buying overpriced ice-creams at a tourist venue. Yet according to prevailing economic theory, there is no such thing as a rip-off. The price of anything is simply the market price—the price people are prepared to pay. For market economists there is no moral dimension to price at all—pricing is simply an automatic function of supply and demand. Merchants who appear to be overcharging are simply pushing the price to its limits. If they push their price further than people are

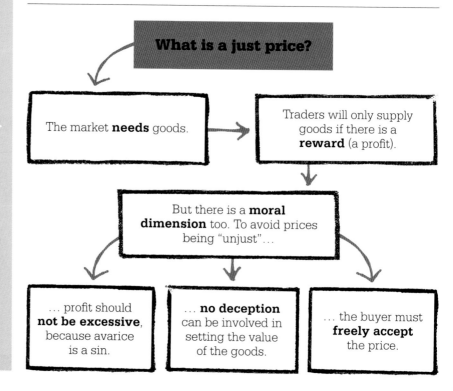

What is a just price?

The market **needs** goods. → Traders will only supply goods if there is a **reward** (a profit).

But there is a **moral dimension** too. To avoid prices being "unjust"…

… profit should **not be excessive**, because avarice is a sin.

… **no deception** can be involved in setting the value of the goods.

… the buyer must **freely accept** the price.

See also: Property rights 20–21 ▪ Free market economics 54–61 ▪ Supply and demand 108–13 ▪ Economics and tradition 166–67

Thomas Aquinas

St. Thomas Aquinas was one of the greatest scholars of the Middle Ages. He was born in Aquino, Sicily, in 1225, to an aristocratic family, and began his education at the age of five. At the age of 17 he decided to leave worldly wealth behind and join an order of poor Dominican monks. His family was so shocked that they kidnapped him on his way to join the order and held him captive for two years. His determination, however, remained unbroken, and eventually the family gave in, letting him go to Paris, where he came under the tutelage of the scholar monk Albert the Great (1206–80). Aquinas studied and taught in France and Italy, and in 1272, founded a *studium generale* (a type of university) in Naples, Italy. His many philosophical works were hugely influential in paving the way to the modern world.

Key works

1256–59 *Disputed Questions on Truth*
1261–63 *Summa contra Gentiles*
1265–73 *Summa Theologica*

Medieval communities felt strongly about the prices merchants charged. In 1321, William le Bole of London was punished for selling underweight bread by being dragged through the streets.

prepared to pay, people stop buying, so the merchants are forced to bring down their prices. Market economists consider the marketplace to be the only way to establish price, as nothing—not even gold—has an intrinsic value.

A price freely accepted

The idea that the marketplace should set prices seems to contrast sharply with the view expressed by Sicilian scholar Thomas Aquinas in his *Summa Theologica*, one of the first studies of the marketplace. For Aquinas, a scholar monk, price was a deeply moral issue. Aquinas recognized avarice as a deadly sin, but at the same time he saw that if a merchant is deprived of the profit incentive, he would cease to trade, and the community would be deprived of goods it needed.

Aquinas concluded that a merchant may charge a "just price," which includes a decent profit, but excludes excessive profiteering, which is sinful. This just price is simply the price the buyer freely agrees to pay, given honest information. The vendor is not obliged to make the buyer aware of facts that might lower the price in the future, such as the shiploads of cheap spice due to dock shortly.

The issues of price and morality are very much alive today, since both economists and the public discuss "the just price" of a CEO's bonus or the minimum wage. Free market economists, who reject interference in the market, and those who advocate government intervention—whether for moral or economic reasons—continue to argue about the rights and wrongs of imposing restrictions on pricing. ∎

> ❝ No man should sell a thing to another man for more than its worth. ❞
> **Thomas Aquinas**

YOU DON'T NEED TO BARTER WHEN YOU HAVE COINS
THE FUNCTION OF MONEY

IN CONTEXT

FOCUS
Banking and finance

KEY EVENT
Kublai Khan adopts fiat money in the Mongol Empire during the 13th century.

BEFORE
3000 BCE In Mesopotamia the shekel is used as a unit of currency: a unit of barley of a certain weight equals a certain value of gold or silver.

700 BCE The oldest known coins are made on the Greek island of Aegina.

AFTER
13th century Marco Polo brings promissory notes from China to Europe, where they are used by Italian bankers.

1696 The Bank of Scotland is the first commercial operation to issue bank notes.

1971 President Nixon cancels the convertibility of the US dollar to gold.

In many parts of the world people are increasingly moving towards a cashless society in which goods are bought with credit cards, electronic transfers, and mobile-phone chips. But dispensing with cash does not mean that money is not used. Money remains at the heart of all our transactions.

The disturbing effects of money are well known, inciting everything from miserliness to crime and warfare. Money has been used as a tribute (sign of respect), in religious rites, and for ornamentation. "Blood money" is paid as recompense for murder; brides are bought with "bride money" or given away with dowries to enrich their husbands. Money lends status and power to individuals, families, and nations.

A barter economy
Without money, people could only barter. Many of us barter to a small extent, when we return favors. A man might offer to mend his neighbor's broken door in return for a few hours of babysitting, for instance. Yet it is hard to imagine these personal exchanges working on a larger scale. What would happen if you wanted a loaf of bread and all you had to trade was

The Tiwa tribal people of Assam, India, exchange goods through barter during the Jonbeel Mela, an age-old festival to preserve harmony and brotherhood between tribes.

your new car? Barter depends on the double coincidence of wants, where not only does the other person happen to have what I want, but I also have what he wants.

Money solves all these problems. There is no need to find someone who wants what you have to trade; you simply pay for your goods with money. The seller can then take the money and buy from someone else.

See also: Financial services 26–29 ▪ The quantity theory of money 30–33 ▪ The paradox of value 63

Money is transferable and deferrable—the seller can hold on to it and buy when the time is right. Many argue that complex civilizations could never have arisen without the flexibility of exchange that money allows. Money also gives a yardstick for deciding the value of things. If all goods have a monetary value, we can know and compare every cost.

Different kinds of money

There are two kinds of money: commodity and fiat. Commodity money has intrinsic value besides its specified worth, for example when gold coins are used as currency. Fiat money, first used in China in the 10th century, is money that is simply a token of exchange with no value other than that assigned to it by the government. A paper bank note is fiat money.

Many paper currencies were initially "promises to pay" against gold held in reserve. In theory dollars issued by the US Federal Reserve could be exchanged for their gold value. Since 1971, the value of a dollar has no longer been convertible to gold and is set entirely by the US Treasury, without reference to its gold reserves. Such fiat currencies rely on people's confidence in a country's economic stability, which is not always assured. ▪

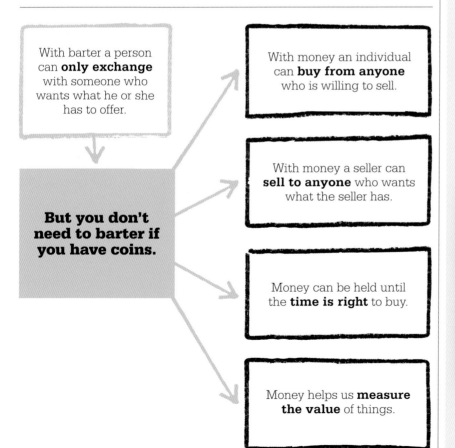

With barter a person can **only exchange** with someone who wants what he or she has to offer.

But you don't need to barter if you have coins.

With money an individual can **buy from anyone** who is willing to sell.

With money a seller can **sell to anyone** who wants what the seller has.

Money can be held until the **time is right** to buy.

Money helps us **measure the value** of things.

Shelling out

Wampum were strings of white and black shell beads treasured by the indigenous North Americans of the Eastern Woodland tribes. Before the European settlers arrived in the 15th century, wampum was used mainly for ceremonial purposes. People might exchange wampum to record an agreement or to pay tribute. Its value came from the immense skill involved in making it, and in its ceremonial associations.

When Europeans arrived, their tools revolutionized wampum making, and Dutch colonizers mass-produced the beads by the million. Soon, they were using wampum to trade and buy things from the native peoples, who had no interest in coins, but valued wampum. Wampum soon became a currency with an accepted exchange rate. In New York eight white or four black wampum equaled one stuiver (a Dutch coin of the time). The use and value of wampum diminished in the 1670s.

This Shawnee shoulder bag is decorated with wampum beads, which developed into a currency for some North American tribes.

MAKE MONEY FROM MONEY
FINANCIAL SERVICES

IN CONTEXT

FOCUS
Banking and finance

KEY THINKERS
The Medici family
(1397–1494)

BEFORE
13th century Scholastic
writers condemn usury.

AFTER
1873 British journalist Walter
Bagehot urges the Bank of
England to act as "lender of last
resort" to the banking system.

1930 The Bank for International
Settlements is founded in
Basel, Switzerland, leading
to international rules
of banking regulation.

1992 US economist Hyman
Minsky publishes *The
Financial Instability
Hypothesis*, which has proved
useful in explaining the
2007–08 financial crisis.

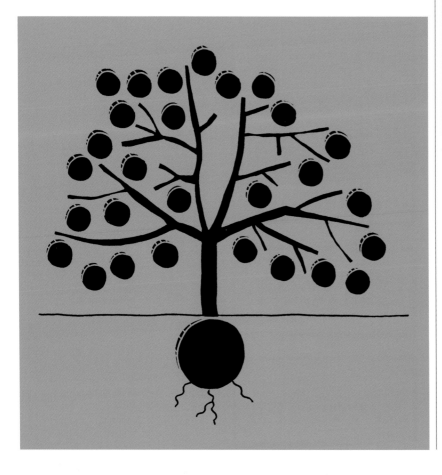

Humans have long engaged
in borrowing and lending.
There is evidence that
these activities took place 5,000
years ago in Mesopotamia (present-
day Iraq) at the very dawn of
civilization. But modern banking
systems did not emerge until the
14th century in northern Italy.

The word "bank" comes from
the Italian word for the "bench" on
which the bankers sat to conduct
business. In the 14th century the
Italian peninsula was a land of city-
states that benefited from the
influence and revenue of the papacy
in Rome. The peninsula was ideally
located for trade between Asia,
Africa, and the emerging nations

See also: Public companies 38 ▪ Financial engineering 262–65 ▪ Market uncertainty 274–75 ▪ Financial crises 296–301 ▪ Bank runs 316–21

of Europe. Wealth began to accumulate, especially in Venice and Florence. Venice relied on sea power: institutions were created there to finance and insure voyages. Florence focused on manufacturing and trade with northern Europe, and here merchants and financiers came together at the Medici Bank.

Florence was already home to other banking families, such as the Peruzzi and the Bardi, and to different types of financial bodies—from pawnbrokers, who lent money secured by personal belongings, to local banks that dealt in foreign currencies, accepted deposits, and lent to local businesses. The bank founded by Giovanni di Bicci de' Medici in 1397 was different.

The Medici Bank financed long-distance trade in commodities such as wool. It differed from existing banks in three ways. First, it grew to a great size. In its heyday under the founder's son, Cosimo, it ran branches in 11 cities, including London, Bruges, and Geneva. Second, its network was decentralized. Branches were managed not by an employee but by a local junior partner, who shared in the profits. The Medici family in Florence were the senior partners, watching over the network, earning most of the profit, and retaining the family trademark, which symbolized the bank's sound reputation. Third, branches took in large deposits from wealthy savers, multiplying the lending that could be given out for a modest amount of initial capital, and so multiplying the bank's profits.

Economics of banking
These elements of the Medici success story correspond to three economic concepts highly relevant

to banking today. The first is "economies of scale." It is expensive for an individual to draw up a single legal loan contract, but a bank can draw up 1,000 such contracts at a fraction of the "per-contract" cost. Dealings in money (cash investments) are suitable for economies of scale. The second is "diversification of risk." The Medicis lowered the risk of bad lending by spreading their lending geographically. Moreover, because the junior partners shared in profits and losses, they needed to lend wisely—in effect they took on some of the Medici risks. The third concept is "asset transformation." Merchants might want to deposit earnings or borrow money. One »

Merchant bankers of the late 14th century arranged deposits and loans but also converted foreign currencies and watched over the circulation for signs of forged or forbidden coins.

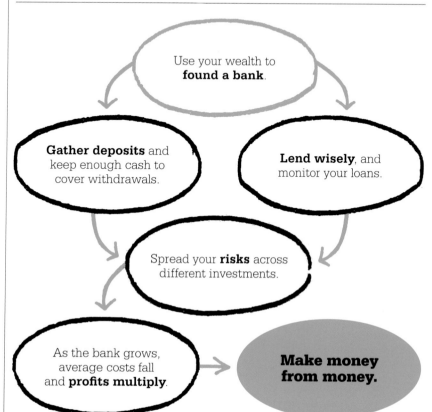
Use your wealth to **found a bank**.

Gather deposits and keep enough cash to cover withdrawals.

Lend wisely, and monitor your loans.

Spread your **risks** across different investments.

As the bank grows, average costs fall and **profits multiply**.

Make money from money.

merchant might want a safe place to store his gold, from where he can withdraw it quickly if necessary. Another might want a loan—which is riskier for the bank and may tie up money for a longer time. So the bank came to stand between the two needs: "borrowing short, and lending long." This suited everybody —the depositor, the borrower, and of course the bank, which used customer deposits as borrowed money ("leverage"), to multiply profits and make a high return on its owners' invested capital.

However, this practice also makes the bank vulnerable—if a large number of depositors demand their money back at the same time (in "a run on the bank"), the bank may be unable to provide it because it will have used the depositors' money to make long-term loans, and it retains only a small fraction of depositors' money in ready cash. This risk is a calculated one, and the advantage of the system is that it usefully connects savers and borrowers.

Financing long-distance trade was a high-risk business in 14th-century Europe. It involved time and distance, so it suffered from what has been called the "fundamental problem of exchange" —the danger that someone will run off with the goods or the money after a deal has been struck. To solve this problem, the "bill of exchange" was developed. This was a piece of paper witnessing a buyer's promise to pay for goods in a specific currency when the goods arrived. The seller of the goods could also sell the bill immediately to raise money. Italian merchant banks became particularly skilled at dealing in these bills, creating an international market for money.

By buying the bill of exchange, a bank was taking on the risk that the buyer of the goods would not pay up. It was therefore essential for the bank to know who was likely to pay up and who was not. Lending—indeed finance in general—requires specialized, skilled knowledge, because a lack of information (known as "information asymmetry") can result in serious problems. The borrowers least likely to repay are the ones most likely to ask for loans; and once they have received a loan, there are temptations not to repay. A bank's most important function

Bills of exchange, such as this one from 1713, later developed into the common bank check. All types promise to pay the bearer a specific amount of money on a certain date.

is its ability to lend wisely, and then to monitor borrowers to deter "moral hazard"—when people succumb to the temptation not to repay and default on the loan.

Geographical clusters
Banks often cluster together in the same place to maximize information and skill. This explains

Granting mortgages to "subprime" borrowers (people unable to repay) led to a wave of house repossessions and the financial crisis of 2007–08.

A 21st-century banking crisis

The global financial crisis, which began in 2007, has led to rethinking about the nature of banking. Leverage, or borrowed money, lay at the heart of the crisis. In 1900, about three-quarters of the assets of a bank might be financed by borrowed money. In 2007, the proportion was often 95–99 percent. The banks' enthusiasm for placing financial bets on future movements in the market, known as derivatives, magnified this leverage and the risks it carried.

Significantly, the crisis followed a period of banking deregulation. A variety of financial innovations seemed lucrative in a rising market. However, they led to poor lending standards by two groups: those providing housing loans to poor US families, and bond investors overly reliant on the advice of credit rating agencies. These are the issues faced by all banks since the Medicis: poor information, financial incentives, and risk.

> A banker is a fellow who lends you his umbrella when the sun is shining, but wants it back the minute it begins to rain.
> **Mark Twain**
> US author (1835–1910)

the development of financial districts in large cities. Economists call this phenomenon "network externalities," which refers to the fact that, as a cluster starts to form, all the banks benefit from the network of deepening skills and information. Florence was one such cluster. The City of London, with its goldsmiths and shipping experts, became another. In the early 1800s the remote northern inland province of Shanxi became China's leading financial center. Today, the internet creates new ways of clustering online.

The benefit of specialization explains why there are so many different types of banks—covering savings, mortgages, car loans, and so on. The form a bank takes can also address information problems. Mutual societies and credit unions, for instance, which are effectively owned by their customers, first arose in the 19th century to increase trust between the bank and its

The City of London is home to a dense cluster of banks built over medieval streets. Today it is the world's largest center for foreign-exchange trading and cross-border bank lending.

customers at a time of social change. Because the members of these organizations checked up on each other, and the managers had good local knowledge, they could provide the long-term loans that their customers needed. In some countries, such as Germany, they thrived. The Dutch bank Rabobank is an example of a cooperative model, as is Bangladesh's "micro-finance" Grameen Bank, which makes many loans of small amounts.

However, clustering can also lead to risky competition and crowdlike behavior. It is especially important for banks to have a good reputation because they have an asset transformation role—they transform deposits into loans—and their loan-assets are riskier, longer, and less easy to turn into cash (less "liquid") than their deposit-liabilities.

Bad news can lead to panics. Bank failures can have severe consequences for other banks, and for government and society, as witnessed in the failure of Creditanstalt Bank in Austria in 1931, which led to a run on the German mark, UK sterling, and then the US dollar, triggering further bank runs and contributing to the Great

Depression. As a result banks need to be regulated, and most countries have strict rules about who can form a bank, the information they must disclose, and the scope of their business activities.

Finance broadly

Banking is just the largest part of finance, but all finance is about connecting people who have more money than they need with people who need more money than they have—and will use it productively. Stock exchanges connect these needs directly, through equities (shares conferring ownership of a company), bonds (lending that can be traded), or other instruments.

These exchanges are either physical places, such as the New York Stock Exchange, or regulated markets where trading takes place through phone calls and computers, like the international bond market. The clustering created by exchanges makes these long-term investments more liquid: they can easily be sold and turned into money. Savings can also be pooled to lower transaction costs and diversify risks. Mutual funds, pension funds, and insurance companies all perform this role. ∎

MONEY CAUSES INFLATION

THE QUANTITY THEORY OF MONEY

IN CONTEXT

FOCUS
The macroeconomy

KEY THINKER
Jean Bodin (1530–96)

BEFORE
1492 Christopher Columbus arrives in the Americas. Silver and gold flow into Spain.

AFTER
1752 David Hume states that the money supply has a direct relationship to the price level.

1911 Irving Fisher develops a mathematical formula to explain the quantity theory of money.

1936 John Maynard Keynes says that the velocity of money in circulation is unstable.

1956 Milton Friedman argues that a change in the amount of money in the economy can have a predictable effect on people's incomes.

In 16th-century Europe prices were rising inexplicably. Some said that rulers were using an old practice of "debasing" currencies by minting coins with ever-smaller amounts of gold or silver in them. This was true. However, Jean Bodin, a French lawyer, argued that something much more significant was also happening.

In 1568, Bodin published his *Response to the Paradoxes of Malestroit*. The French economist Jean de Malestroit (?–1578) had blamed the price inflation solely on currency debasement, but Bodin showed that prices were rising sharply even when measured in pure silver. He argued that an

See also: The function of money 24–25 ■ The Keynesian multiplier 164–65 ■
Monetarist policy 196–201 ■ Inflation and unemployment 202–03

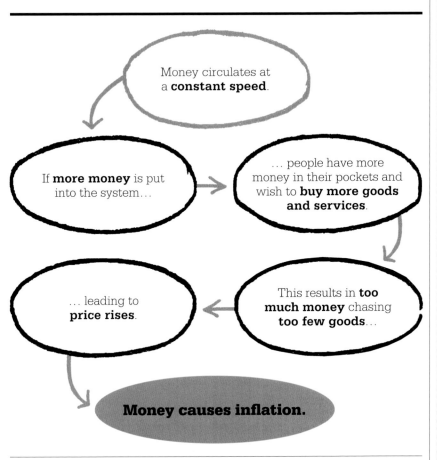

Money circulates at
a **constant speed**.

If **more money** is put
into the system…

… people have more
money in their pockets and
wish to **buy more goods
and services**.

This results in **too
much money** chasing
too few goods…

… leading to
price rises.

Money causes inflation.

Jean Bodin

The son of a master tailor,
Jean Bodin was born in 1530
in Angers, France. He was
educated in Paris, and went
on to study at the University
of Toulouse. In 1560, he
became a king's advocate in
Paris. Bodin's scholarship (he
read law, history, politics,
philosophy, economics, and
religion) attracted royal favor,
and between 1571 and 1584,
he served as aide to the
powerful Duke of Alençon.

In 1576, he married
Françoise Trouilliart and
succeeded his brother-in-law
as the king's procurator in
Laon, northern France.
In 1589, King Henry III was
assassinated, and religious
civil war broke out. Bodin
believed in tolerance, but in
Laon was forced to declare for
the Catholic cause, until the
victorious Protestant King,
Henry IV, took control of the
city. Bodin died of the plague,
aged 66, in 1596.

Key works

1566 *Method for the Easy
Comprehension of History*
1568 *Response to the
Paradoxes of Malestroit*
1576 *Six Books of a
Commonwealth*

abundance of silver and gold was
to blame. These precious metals
were entering Spain from its new
colonies in the Americas and then
spreading throughout Europe.

Bodin's calculations of the
increase in coinage were
remarkably accurate. Later
economists concluded that prices
in Europe quadrupled during the
16th century, at the same time as
the amount of physical silver and
gold circulating in the system
tripled; Bodin had estimated the
increase in precious metals at more
than 2.5 times. He also highlighted
other factors behind the inflation: a
demand for luxuries; a scarcity of
goods for sale due to exports and

waste; greedy merchants able to
restrict the supply of goods through
monopolies; and, of course, the
rulers adulterating the coins.

The money supply

Bodin was not the first to point
to the new influence of American
treasure and the effect of the
abundance or scarcity of money
on price levels. In 1556, a Spanish
theologian named Martín de
Azpilcueta (better known as
Navarrus) had come to the same
conclusion. However, Bodin's essay
also discussed the demand for and
the supply of money, the operation
of these two sides of an economy,
and how disturbances to the »

supply of money led to inflation. His thorough study is considered the first important statement of the quantity theory of money.

The reasoning behind this theory is partly based on common sense. Why is the price of a cup of coffee in a rich part of town so much higher than in a poor area? The answer is that customers in the rich part have more money to spend. If we consider the population of a whole country and double the money in people's pockets, it is natural that they will want to use their increased spending power to buy more goods and services. But goods and services are always in limited supply, so there will be too much money chasing too few goods, and prices will rise.

This chain of events shows the important relationship between the quantity of money in an economy and the general price level. The quantity theory of money states that a doubling of the supply of money will result in a doubling in the value of transactions (or income or expenditure). In the theory's more extreme form, a doubling of money will lead to a doubling of prices, but not real value. Money will be neutral in its effect on the real, relative value of goods and services—for example, on how many jackets can be bought for the price of a computer.

Real price, nominal price

After Bodin, many economists developed his idea further. They came to recognize that there is a distinct separation between the real side of the economy and the nominal, or money, side. Nominal prices are simply money prices, which can change with inflation. This is why economists focus on real prices—on what quantity of a thing (jackets, computers, or time spent working) has to be given up in return for another kind of thing, no matter what the nominal price is. In the extreme quantity theory, changes in the money supply may influence prices, but it has no effect on the real economic variables, such as output and unemployment. What is more, economists realized that money is itself a "good" that people want to own for its spending power.

> The abundance of gold and silver… is greater in this kingdom today than it has been in the last 400 years.
> **Jean Bodin**

However, the money they want is not nominal money, but "real money"—money that can buy more.

Fisher's equation

The fullest statement of the quantity theory of money was made by the US economist Irving Fisher (1867–1947), who used the mathematical formula $MV = PT$. Here "P" is the general level of prices, and "T" is the transactions that take place in a year, so PT (Prices ×

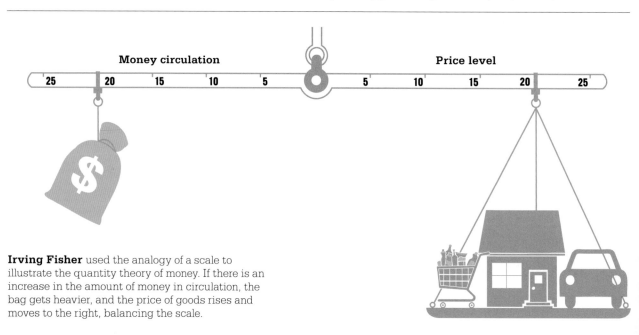

Irving Fisher used the analogy of a scale to illustrate the quantity theory of money. If there is an increase in the amount of money in circulation, the bag gets heavier, and the price of goods rises and moves to the right, balancing the scale.

This painting by Dutch master Pieter Bruegel (1559) shows vagrants rubbing shoulders with the rich during Lent. Steep price rises in the 15th century led to much hardship among the poor, a rise in vagrancy, and peasant revolts.

Transactions) is the total value of transactions occurring annually. "M" is the supply of money. But because PT is a total flow of goods, while M represents a stock of money that can be used over and over again, the equation needs something to represent the circulation of money. This circular flow, which causes money to rotate through the economy—like the spinning drum of a washing machine—is "V", the velocity of money.

This equation becomes a theory when we make assumptions about the relationships between the letters, which economists do in three ways. First, V, the velocity of money, is assumed to be constant, since the way in which we use money is part of habit and custom and does not change much from year to year (our washing machine drum spins at a steady rate). This is the key assumption behind the quantity theory of money. Second, it is assumed that T, the quantity of transactions in an economy, is driven solely by consumers' demand and producers' technology, which together determine prices. Third, we allow

that there can be one-time changes to M (the supply of money), such as the flow of New World treasure into Europe. With V (velocity) and T (transactions) fixed, it follows that a doubling of money will lead to a doubling of prices.

Combined with the difference between nominal and real, the quantity theory of money has led to the notion that money is neutral in its effect on the economy.

Challenge and restatement

But is money really neutral? Few believe that it is neutral in the short run. The immediate effect of more money in the pocket is for it to be spent on real goods and services. John Maynard Keynes (p.161) said it was probably neutral in the long run, but in the short run it would affect real variables such as output and unemployment. Evidence also suggests that money velocity (V) is not constant. It seems to rise in booms when inflation is high and falls in recessions when inflation is low.

Keynes had other ideas that challenged the quantity theory of money. He proposed that money

is used, not just as a medium of exchange, but also as a "store of value"—something you can keep, either for buying goods, for security in case of hard times in the future, or for future investments.

Keynesian economists argue that these motives are affected less by income or transactions (PT in the formula) than by interest rates. A rise in the interest rate will lead to a rise in the velocity of money.

In 1956, US economist Milton Friedman (p.199) defended the quantity theory of money, arguing that an individual's demand for real money balances (where money buys more) depends on wealth. He claimed that it is people's incomes that drive this demand.

Today, central banks print money electronically and use it to buy government debt in a process known as quantitative easing. Their aim has been to prevent a feared fall in the money supply. So far, the most visible effect has been to reduce interest rates on government debt. ∎

> 66
> Inflation is always and everywhere a monetary phenomenon.
> **Milton Friedman**
> 99

PROTECT US FROM FOREIGN GOODS

PROTECTIONISM AND TRADE

IN CONTEXT

FOCUS
Global economy

KEY THINKER
Thomas Mun (1571–1641)

BEFORE
c.1620 Gerard de Malynes
argues that England should
regulate foreign exchange to
stop the nation's gold and
silver from going abroad.

AFTER
1691 English merchant Dudley
North argues that the main
spur to increased national
wealth is consumption.

1791 US Treasury Secretary
Alexander Hamilton argues for
protection of young industries.

1817 British economist David
Ricardo argues that foreign
trade can benefit all nations.

1970s US economist
Milton Friedman insists
that free trade helps
developing countries.

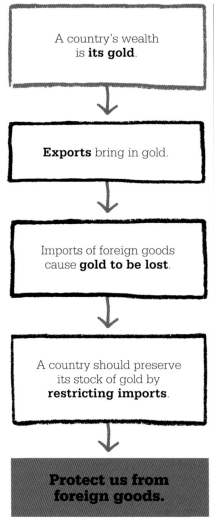

A country's wealth
is **its gold**.

Exports bring in gold.

Imports of foreign goods
cause **gold to be lost**.

A country should preserve
its stock of gold by
restricting imports.

**Protect us from
foreign goods.**

For the last half century many economists have championed free trade. They argue that only by removing restrictions on trade (such as tariffs) can goods and money flow freely around the world and global markets develop without inhibition. Some disagree, arguing that where there is a huge imbalance of trade between two countries, it can impact jobs and wealth.

A mercantilist view
The argument over free trade dates back to the mercantilist era, which began in Europe in the 16th century and continued until the late 18th century. With the rise of Dutch and English seaborne trade, wealth began to shift from southern Europe toward the north.

This was also the age when nation-states began to emerge, along with the idea of the wealth of the nation, which was measured by the amount of "treasure" (gold and silver) it possessed. Mercantilists believed that the world drew from a "limited pot," so the wealth of each nation depended on ensuring a favorable "balance of trade," in which more gold flows into the nation than out. If an excess of gold

See also: Comparative advantage 80–85 ▪ International trade and Bretton Woods 186–87 ▪ Market integration 226–31 ▪ Dependency theory 242–43 ▪ Global savings imbalances 322–25

flows out, the nation's prosperity declines, wages fall, and jobs are lost. England sought to cut the outflow of gold by imposing sumptuary laws, which aimed to limit the consumption of foreign goods. For instance, laws were passed restricting the types of fabric that could be used for clothes, reducing the demand for fine foreign cotton and silk.

Malynes and Mun

Gerard de Malynes (1586–1641), an English expert on foreign exchange, believed that the outflow of gold should be restricted. If too much flowed out, he argued, the value of English currency would fall.

However, the century's greatest mercantilist theorist, Englishman Thomas Mun, insisted that what matters is not the fact that payments are made abroad, but how trade and payments finally balance out. Mun wanted to boost exports and cut imports through more frugal consumption of domestic produce. However, he saw no problem in spending gold abroad if it was used to acquire goods that were then reexported for a larger sum, ultimately returning more gold to the country than had initially been spent. This would boost trade, provide work for the shipping industry, and increase England's treasure.

Free trade agreements

In the 18th century Adam Smith (p.61) was to disagree with this view. What matters, he insisted in *The Wealth of Nations*, is not the wealth of individual nations but the wealth of all nations. Nor is the pot fixed; it can grow over time—but only if trade between

nations is unrestricted. If left free, Smith insisted, the market would always grow to enrich all countries eventually.

For the last half century Smith's view has dominated, because most Western economists argue that restrictions on trade between nations hobble their economies. Today, free trade areas such as the EU (European Union), ASEAN (Association of Southeast Asian Nations), and NAFTA (North American Free Trade Agreement) are the norm, while global organizations such as the World Trade Organization (WTO) and the International Monetary Fund (IMF) urge countries to reduce tariffs and other trade barriers to allow foreign firms to enter their domestic markets. The creation of barriers to foreign trade is criticized now as protectionism.

However, some economists are concerned that exposure to large global businesses has the potential to damage developing countries who are unable to nurture infant industries behind protective

French farmers demonstrated on tractors in Paris, 2010, to denounce a sharp fall in grain prices after import quotas were liberalized.

barriers, as the US, Britain, Japan, and South Korea did before they became economically powerful. China, meanwhile, pursues a trade policy that in many ways echoes Mun's thinking by running large trade surpluses and building up a huge reserve of foreign exchange. ▪

Thomas Mun

Born in 1571, Thomas Mun grew up in a family of wealthy London merchants. His father died when he was three, and his mother married Thomas Cordell, who became a director of the East India Company, Britain's largest trading company. Mun began trading as a merchant in the Mediterranean. In 1615, he became a director of the East India Company. His ideas were developed originally to defend the company's export of large

amounts of silver, on the grounds that this generated reexport trade. In 1628, the company appealed to the British government to protect their trade against Dutch competition. Mun represented their case to Parliament. He had amassed a considerable fortune by the time he died in 1641.

Key works

1621 *A Discourse of Trade*
c.1630 *England's Treasure by Foreign Trade*

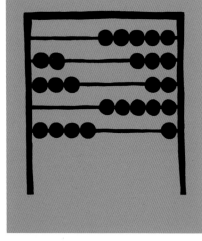

THE ECONOMY CAN BE COUNTED
MEASURING WEALTH

IN CONTEXT

FOCUS
Economic methods

KEY THINKER
William Petty (1623–87)

BEFORE
1620 English scientist Francis
Bacon argues for a new
approach to science based
on the collection of facts.

AFTER
1696 English statistician
Gregory King writes his
great statistical survey of
England's population.

1930s Australian economist
Colin Clark invents the idea of
gross national product (GNP).

1934 Russian-US economist
Simon Kuznets develops
modern national income
accounting methods.

1950s British economist
Richard Stone introduces
balanced, double-entry
national accounting.

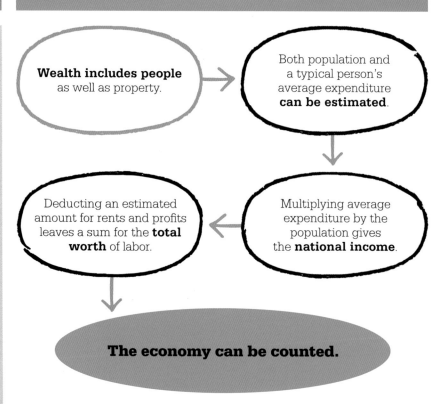

Wealth includes people as well as property.

Both population and a typical person's average expenditure **can be estimated**.

Multiplying average expenditure by the population gives the **national income**.

Deducting an estimated amount for rents and profits leaves a sum for the **total worth** of labor.

The economy can be counted.

Today we take it for granted that the economy can be measured, and its expansions and contractions accurately quantified. But this was not always the case. The idea of measuring the economy dates back to the 1670s and the pioneering work of English scientist William Petty. His insight was to apply the new empirical methods of science to financial and political affairs—to use real world data rather than relying on logical reasoning. He decided to express himself only "in terms of number, weight, or

See also: The circular flow of the economy 40–45 ▪ Testing economic theories 170 ▪ The economics of happiness 216–19 ▪ Gender and economics 310–11

measure." This approach helped form the basis of the discipline that would become known as economics.

In his 1671–2 book *Political Arithmetick*, Petty used real data to show that, contrary to popular belief, England was wealthier than ever. One of his groundbreaking decisions was to include the value of labor as well as land and capital. Although Petty's figures are open to dispute, there is no doubting the effectiveness of his basic idea. His calculations included population size, personal spending, wages per person, the value of rents, and others. He then multiplied these figures to give a total figure for the nation's total wealth, creating accounts for an entire nation.

Similar methods were developed in France by Pierre de Boisguilbert (p.334) and Sébastien le Prestre (1633–1707). In England Gregory King (1648–1712) analyzed

The Battle of La Hogue was fought in 1692 during the Nine Years' War. English statistician Gregory King calculated how long each country involved could afford to fight.

the economies and populations of England, Holland, and France. He calculated that none had the finances to continue the war they were then engaged in—the Nine Years' War—beyond 1698. His figures might have been correct, because the war ended in 1697.

Measures of progress

Statistics are now at the heart of economics. Today, economists generally measure gross domestic product (GDP)—the total value of all the goods and services exchanged for money within a country in a particular period (usually a year). However, there is still no definitive way of calculating national accounts, although efforts have been made to standardize methods.

Economists have now begun to broaden the measurement of prosperity. They have formulated new measures such as the genuine progress indicator (GPI), which includes adjustments for income distribution, crime, pollution, and the happy planet index (HPI), a measure of human well-being and environmental impact. ▪

William Petty

Born in 1623 to a humble family in Hampshire, England, William Petty lived through the English Civil War and rose to high positions in both the Commonwealth government and then the restored monarchy. As a young man he worked for the English political philosopher Thomas Hobbes in Holland. After returning to England, he taught anatomy at Oxford University. A great believer in the new science, he found universities uninspiring, so left for Ireland, where he made a monumental land survey of the entire country.

In the 1660s he returned to England and began the work on economics for which he is now known. For the remainder of his life he moved between Ireland and England, both physically and in the focus of his work. Petty is regarded as one of the first great political economists. He died in 1687, aged 64.

Key works

1662 *Treatise of Taxes and Contributions*
1671–2 *Political Arithmetick*
1682 *Quantulumcunque Concerning Money*

LET FIRMS BE TRADED
PUBLIC COMPANIES

IN CONTEXT

FOCUS
Markets and firms

KEY THINKER
Josiah Child (1630–99)

BEFORE
1500s Governments grant merchants the monopoly of trade within specific regions.

1552–71 The Bourse in Antwerp and Royal Exchange in London are set up for shareholders to buy and sell stock in joint-stock companies.

AFTER
1680 London stock "brokers" meet in Jonathan's Coffee House to arrange share deals.

1844 The Joint Stock Companies Act in the UK allows firms to be incorporated more quickly and easily.

1855 The idea of limited liability protects investors in joint-stock companies from scams such as the South Sea Bubble of 1720 (p.98).

Merchant ships have always raised funds for voyages by promising a share of profits. In the 1500s the rewards could be huge, but these high-risk ventures tied up money for years before a profit was realized. The answer was to share the risk, and so joint-stock companies were formed, where investors injected money into a company in return for becoming joint holders of its trading stock, and a right to a proportional share of the profits.

East India Company

An early joint-stock company, formed in 1599, was the East India Company (EIC), launched to develop trade between Britain and the East Indies. Its rights to free trade were so ably defended by the "father of mercantilists," London merchant Josiah Child, that it became a global phenomenon. By the time of his death the company had about 3,000 shareholders, subscribed to a stock of more than $14 million,

and was borrowing a further $28 million on bonds. Its annual sales raised up to $10 million.

The idea of the public limited company—in which shareholders are protected from liability beyond their investment—developed from joint-stock companies. The selling of shares is an important way of raising funds. Some argue that shareholders' power to sell shares leads to a lack of commitment, but the joint-stock company remains at the heart of capitalism. ∎

The high-risk, high-reward potential of merchant shipping was shared by joint-stock companies. Vessels such as the *John Wood*, seen here in Bombay in the 1850s, brought home the goods.

See also: Economic equilibrium 118–23 ▪ Corporate governance 168–69 ▪ Institutions in economics 206–07

WEALTH COMES FROM THE LAND
AGRICULTURE IN THE ECONOMY

In recent years bankers have sometimes been characterized as parasites, living off wealth created by the labor of others. François Quesnay (p.45), a French farmworker's son and one of the great minds of the 18th century, might recognize this description.

Quesnay argued that wealth lies not in gold and silver, but springs from production—the output of the farmer or manufacturer. He argued that agriculture is so valuable because it works with nature—which multiplies the farmer's effort and resources—to produce a net surplus. Manufacturing, on the other hand, is "sterile" because the value of its output is equal to the value of the input. However, later theorists showed that manufacturing can also produce a surplus.

The natural order
Quesnay's championing of the value of agriculture was influential, leading to the development of the French school of physiocrat thinkers who believed in the primacy of the "natural order" in the economy.

If we knew the economics of agriculture, we would know much of the economics of being poor.
Theodore Schultz
US economist (1902–98)

Many economists, including Theodore Schultz, have argued that agricultural development is the foundation for progress in poor countries. In 2008, the World Bank reported that growth in the agricultural sector contributes more to poverty reduction than growth in any other sector. But economists today also recognize that diversification into industry and services, including finance, is vital for long-term development. ∎

See also: Demographics and economics 68–69 ▪ The labor theory of value 106–07 ▪ The emergence of modern economies 178–79 ▪ Development economics 188–93

MONEY AND GOODS FLOW BETWEEN PRODUCERS AND CONSUMERS

THE CIRCULAR FLOW OF THE ECONOMY

IN CONTEXT

FOCUS
The macroeconomy

KEY THINKER
François Quesnay
(1694–1774)

BEFORE
1664–76 English economist William Petty introduces the concepts of national income and expenditure.

1755 Irish merchant banker Richard Cantillon's *Essay*, first published in France, discusses the circulation of money from the city to the countryside.

AFTER
1885 Karl Marx's *Capital* describes the circulation of capital using a model inspired by Quesnay.

1930s Russian-American economist Simon Kuznets develops modern national income accounting.

Madame de Pompadour (the mistress of Louis XV) installed Quesnay at Versailles as her physician. To him her lifestyle must have epitomized the lavish surplus of landowners' wealth.

I n economics one can think small—microeconomics—or one can think as large as the entire system: this is the study of macroeconomics. In 18th-century France a group known as the physiocrats tried to think big—they wanted to understand and explain the whole economy as a system. Their ideas form the foundation of modern macroeconomics.

The physiocrats

Physiocracy is an ancient Greek word meaning "power over nature." The physiocrats believed that nations gained their economic wealth from nature, through their agricultural sector. Their leader, François Quesnay, was surgeon and physician to King Louis XV's mistress, Madame de Pompadour. His complicated model of the economy was thought by some to reflect the circulation of blood in a human body.

The mercantilist approach (pp.34–35) dominated economic thinking at the time. Mercantilists thought the state should behave like a merchant, growing business, acquiring gold, and actively interfering with the economy through taxes, subsidies, controls, and monopoly privileges. The physiocrats took the opposite view: they argued that the economy was naturally self-regulating and needed only to be protected from bad influences. They favored free trade, low taxes, secure property rights, and low government debt. Where the mercantilists said that wealth came from treasure, Quesnay and his followers viewed it as being rooted in what modern economists call the "real" economy —those sectors that create real goods and services. They believed that agriculture was the most productive of these sectors.

The physiocrats were influenced by the thinking of an earlier French landowner, Pierre de Boisguilbert. He said that agriculture is superior to manufacturing, and consumables are more valuable than gold. He said the more goods consumed, the more money moves in the system, making consumption the driving force in the economy. He also said that a little money in the hands of the poor (who spend it) is worth far more to the economy than in the hands of the rich (who hoard it). The movement, or circulation, of money is all-important.

The Economic Table

The physiocratic system of circulation was set out in Quesnay's *Economic Table*, which was published and revised several times between 1758 and 1767. This is a diagram that illustrates, through a series of crossing and connecting lines, the flow of money and goods between three groups in society: landowners, farmers, and artisans. The goods are agricultural and manufactured products (produced by the farmers and artisans). Although Quesnay used corn as his example of an agricultural product, he said that this category could include anything produced from the land, including mining products.

Quesnay's model is best understood through an example. Imagine each of the three groups starts with $2 million. The landowners produce nothing. They spend their $2 million equally between farming and artisan products, and consume all of them. They receive $2 million in rent from the farmers—which the farmers can just afford, since they are the only group to produce a surplus—and so the landowners end up back where they started. The farmers are the productive group. From a starting point of $2 million they produce $5 million worth of agricultural products, over and above what they consume themselves. Of this $1 million worth is sold to landowners for their consumption. They sell $2 million worth to artisans, half for consumption and half as raw materials for the goods the artisans will produce. This leaves $2 million worth to be used toward next year's growing season. In terms of production they are back where they started. However, they also have $3 million from sales, of which they spend

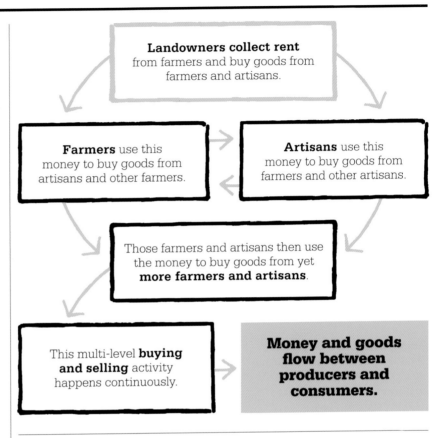

Landowners collect rent from farmers and buy goods from farmers and artisans.

Farmers use this money to buy goods from artisans and other farmers.

Artisans use this money to buy goods from farmers and other artisans.

Those farmers and artisans then use the money to buy goods from yet **more farmers and artisans**.

This multi-level **buying and selling** activity happens continuously.

Money and goods flow between producers and consumers.

$2 million on rent and $1 million on artisan goods (tools, agricultural implements, and so on).

Quesnay referred to any group outside the land-based farmers and landowners as "sterile," because he believed that they could not produce a net surplus. The artisans, in this instance, use their starting amount of $2 million to produce $2 million worth of manufactured goods over and above what they consume themselves. These are sold equally to landowners and farmers. But

Quesnay's Economic Table shows the zigzag flow of wealth between farmers, landowners, and artisans. It was the first attempt to explain the workings of a national economy.

they spend their entire revenue on agricultural products: $1 million for their own consumption, and $1 million on raw materials. They have consumed everything they have.

Quesnay's model does more than present end-of-year results—it also shows how money and goods circulate through the year and demonstrates why this is so important. The sale of products between the various groups continues to generate revenue, which is then used to buy more products, which produces yet more revenue. A "multiplier effect" occurs (in Quesnay's diagram it appeared as a zigzag series of lines), similar to that presented »

> ❝
> Let the sum total
> of the revenues be
> annually returned into
> and along the entire
> course of circulation.
> **François Quesnay**
> ❞

by John Maynard Keynes (p.161) in the 1930s, when he pointed out the beneficial effects of a government spending money in a depressed economy.

Analyzing the economy

The kinds of questions Quesnay asked, and the way he went about answering them, anticipated modern economics. He was one of the first to attempt to uncover general abstract laws that govern economies, which he did by breaking economies down into their constituent parts and then rigorously analyzing the relationships between the parts. His model included inputs, outputs, and the interdependencies of different sectors. Quesnay suggested that these might exist in a state of equilibrium, an idea that was later developed by Léon Walras (p.120), becoming one of the foundations of economic theorizing.

Quesnay's approach to quantifying economic laws makes his *Economic Table* possibly the first empirical macroeconomic model. The numbers in his Table were the result of a close study of the French economic system, giving them a firm empirical basis. This study indicated that farming technology was sufficient for farmers to generate a net surplus of at least 100 percent. In our example this is what they achieve —starting with $2 million of corn, they receive this back plus a net surplus of $2 million, which is then paid in rent. Modern economists use these kinds of empirical results to think about the impact of policy changes, and Quesnay used his Table for a similar purpose. He argued that if farmers had to pay too much tax, either directly or indirectly, they would cut back their capital investment in farming technology, and production would fall below the level needed for the economy to thrive. This led the physiocrats to argue that there should be only one tax: on the rental value of land.

Based on his empirical findings, Quesnay made a host of other policy recommendations, including investment in agriculture, the spending of all revenue, no hoarding, low taxes, and free trade. He thought capital was especially important because his entrepreneur-farmers needed to borrow cheaply in order to pay for land improvements.

Classical ideas

Quesnay's idea of sectors being productive or unproductive has reappeared throughout the history of economic thought as economists consider industry versus services, and the private sector versus the government. His sole focus on agriculture may look narrow to modern eyes, since it is now understood that wealth generation from industry and services is vital to an economy's growth. However, his emphasis on the "real" side of the economy was an important step towards modern economic thinking. He most obviously anticipated modern national income accounting, which is used to assess nations' macroeconomic performance. This income accounting is based on the circular flow of income and expenditure

According to the physiocrats, investment in agriculture was key to ensuring the national wealth of France. Free export was a way of sustaining demand and restricting merchant power.

The interdependence of consumers and producers was first illustrated by Quesnay. Consumers rely on producers for goods and services, who in turn rely on the consumers for sales and labor.

Goods and services

Consumer expenditure

Wages, rent, dividends

Households

Firms

Labor

around the economy. The value of the total product of an economy is equal to the total income earned —a notion that was an important part of Quesnay's theory. In the 20th century much of the analysis of macroeconomies has revolved around the Keynesian multiplier (pp.164–65). Keynes showed how government spending could stimulate further spending in a "multiplier effect." This idea has obvious links to

This system... is, perhaps, the nearest approximation to truth that has yet been published on the subject of political economy.
Adam Smith

Quesnay's circular flow, with its susceptibility to expansion and stagnation.

Perhaps most importantly, Quesnay's concepts of surplus and capital became key to the way that the classical economists analyzed economic growth. A typical classical model focuses on three factors of production: land, labor, and capital. Landowners receive rent and spend wastefully on luxuries; laborers accept a low wage, and if it rises, they produce more children. However, entrepreneurs earn profit and re-invest it productively in industry. So profit drives growth, and economic performance depends on sectors of the economy generating surpluses. Thus, Quesnay anticipated later ideas about the growth of economies and inspired Karl Marx (p.105), who produced his own version of the *Economic Table*. Marx said of Quesnay that "never before had thinking in political economy reached such heights of genius." ∎

François Quesnay

Born near Paris, France, in 1694, François Quesnay was the son of a plowman and the eighth of 13 children. At the age of 17 he began an apprenticeship in engraving, but then transferred to the university, graduating from the college of surgeons in 1717.

He made his name as a surgeon and specialized in treating the nobility; in 1749, he moved to the royal palace at Versailles, near Paris, as physician to Madame de Pompadour. In 1752, he saved the king's son from smallpox and was awarded a title and enough money to buy an estate for his own son.

His interest in economics began in the early 1750s, and in 1757 he met the Marquis de Mirabeau, with whom he formed *les Economistes*—the physiocrats. He died in 1774.

Key works

1758 *Economic Table*
1763 *Rural Philosophy* (with Marquis de Mirabeau)
1766 *Analysis of the Arithmetic Formula for the Economic Table*

PRIVATE INDIVIDUALS NEVER PAY FOR STREET LIGHTS
PROVISION OF PUBLIC GOODS AND SERVICES

IN CONTEXT

FOCUS
Decision making

KEY THINKER
David Hume (1711–76)

BEFORE
c.500 BCE In Athens indirect taxes are used to finance city festivals, temples, and walls. Occasional direct taxes are levied at times of war.

1421 The first patent is granted to Italian engineer Filippo Brunelleschi to protect his invention of hoisting gear for barges.

AFTER
1848 *The Communist Manifesto* advocates collective ownership of the means of production by the workers.

19th century Public street lighting is introduced in Europe and America.

1954 US economist Paul Samuelson develops a modern theory of public goods.

Street lights are an example of a **public good** because…

… it is difficult to stop people from **benefiting** from street lighting.

… one person's **use of street lighting** does not diminish another's enjoyment of it.

Private firms do not provide street lights since they can't **stop non-payers** from using them.

Essential public goods are usually provided by the government, because…

… **private individuals never pay for street lights.**

Even within a well-functioning market economy, there are areas in which markets fail. One important example of market failure is in the provision of public goods—goods that are to become freely available to all, or where it would be difficult to prevent their use by non-payers. These goods, which include things such as national defense, are difficult for a private firm or individual to

See also: Free market economics 54–61 ▪ External costs 137 ▪ Markets and social outcomes 210–13

Lighthouses are a public good from which it is hard to exclude non-payers, and which many people can use at the same time. They are invariably provided collectively.

supply profitably. This problem, known as "free-riding" (where consumers enjoy the goods without paying for them) means that there is no profit incentive. However, there is a demand for these goods, and because private markets may not be able to satisfy this demand, public goods are usually provided by governments and funded through taxation.

A failure of the market to provide these goods was recognized by the philosopher David Hume in the 18th century. Influenced by Hume, Adam Smith (p.61), an ardent advocate of the free market, conceded that a government's role was to provide those public goods that it would not be profitable for individuals or firms to produce.

There are two distinguishing characteristics of public goods that cause them to be undersupplied by the markets: non-excludability, meaning that it is difficult to prevent people who don't pay for the goods from using them; and

non-rivalry, meaning that one person's consumption of the good does not diminish the ability of others to consume it. A classic example is street lighting; it would be almost impossible to exclude non-payers from enjoying its benefits, and no individual's use of it detracts from that benefit to other users.

As industrial economies developed in the 19th century, countries had to overcome the problem of free-riding in areas such as intellectual property. Intangible goods, such as new knowledge and discoveries, have the attributes of non-excludability and non-rivalry, and so are at risk of being undersupplied by the market. This could discourage the development of new technologies unless they can be protected in some way. To do this, countries developed laws granting patents, copyright, and trademarks to protect the returns from new knowledge and inventions. Most economists acknowledge that government has a responsibility to provide public goods, but debate continues about the extent of that responsibility. ▪

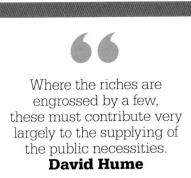

Where the riches are engrossed by a few, these must contribute very largely to the supplying of the public necessities.
David Hume

David Hume

The epitome of the "Scottish Enlightenment," David Hume was one of the most influential British philosophers of the 18th century. He was born in Edinburgh in 1711, and from an early age showed signs of a brilliant mind: he entered Edinburgh University at the age of 12, studying first law and then philosophy.

In 1734, Hume moved to France, where he set out his major philosophical ideas in *A Treatise of Human Nature*. He then devoted much of his time to writing essays on literary and political subjects and struck up a friendship with the young Adam Smith, who had been inspired by his writings. In 1763, Hume was given a diplomatic role in Paris, where he befriended the revolutionary French philosopher Jean-Jacques Rousseau. He settled in Edinburgh again in 1768, where he lived until his death in 1776, aged 65 years.

Key works

1739 *A Treatise of Human Nature*
1748 *An Enquiry Concerning Human Understanding*
1752 *Political Discourses*

THE AGE OF REAS

1770–1820

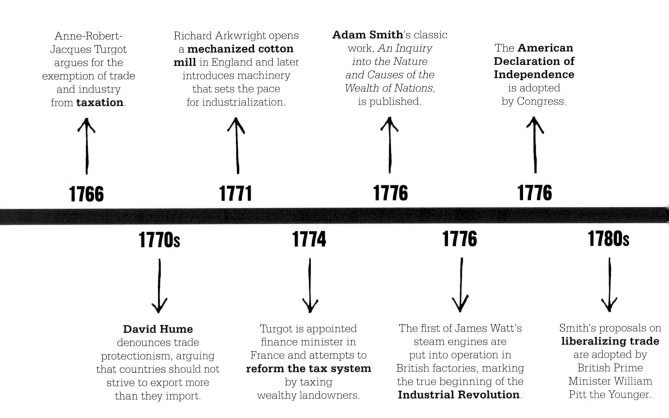

Anne-Robert-Jacques Turgot argues for the exemption of trade and industry from **taxation**.

Richard Arkwright opens a **mechanized cotton mill** in England and later introduces machinery that sets the pace for industrialization.

Adam Smith's classic work, *An Inquiry into the Nature and Causes of the Wealth of Nations*, is published.

The **American Declaration of Independence** is adopted by Congress.

1766   **1771**   **1776**   **1776**

1770s   **1774**   **1776**   **1780s**

David Hume denounces trade protectionism, arguing that countries should not strive to export more than they import.

Turgot is appointed finance minister in France and attempts to **reform the tax system** by taxing wealthy landowners.

The first of James Watt's steam engines are put into operation in British factories, marking the true beginning of the **Industrial Revolution**.

Smith's proposals on **liberalizing trade** are adopted by British Prime Minister William Pitt the Younger.

Toward the end of the 18th century much of the world was undergoing enormous political change. The so-called Age of Reason produced scientists whose discoveries were leading to new technologies that would transform the way goods were produced. At the same time political philosophers had inspired revolutions in France and North America that would have a profound effect on the social structures of both the Old and the New Worlds. In the field of economics a new scientific approach was overturning the old mercantilist view of an economy driven by protected trade and reliant on exports as a means of preserving its wealth. By the end of the Napoleonic wars in 1815, Europe, and Britain in particular, had begun to industrialize on an unprecedented scale. A fresh approach was needed to describe and meet the demands of this rapidly emerging economic new world.

Rational economic man
The economist who rose most successfully to this new challenge was a Scotsman, Adam Smith (p.61). His background in the philosophy of British Enlightenment thinkers, such as John Locke and David Hume (p.47), led him to approach the subject initially as one of moral philosophy. However, in his famous book of 1776, *The Wealth of Nations*, he presented a comprehensive analysis of the market economy and how it contributed to the economic welfare of the people. Central to his thesis was the concept of "rational economic man." Smith argued that individuals made economic decisions on the basis of reason and in their own self-interest, not for the good of society. When they were allowed to act in this way in a free society with competitive markets, an "invisible hand" guided the economy for the benefit of all. This was the first detailed description of a free market economy, which Smith advocated as the means of ensuring prosperity and freedom. It is generally regarded as a milestone in the development of economics as a discipline. The approach to economics that Smith helped to establish is often referred to as "classical" economics. His analysis of a competitive market economy was essentially a

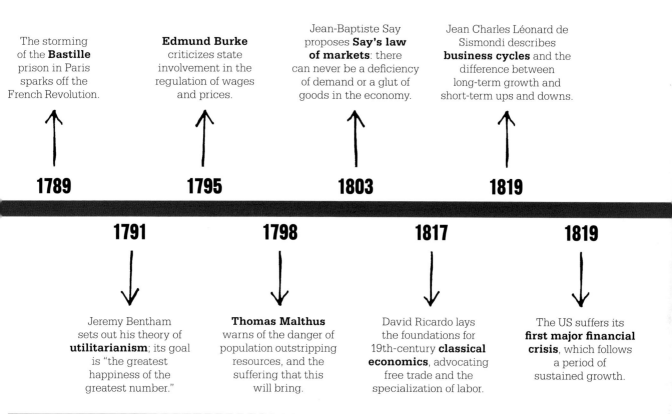

The storming of the **Bastille** prison in Paris sparks off the French Revolution.

1789

Edmund Burke criticizes state involvement in the regulation of wages and prices.

1795

Jean-Baptiste Say proposes **Say's law of markets**: there can never be a deficiency of demand or a glut of goods in the economy.

1803

Jean Charles Léonard de Sismondi describes **business cycles** and the difference between long-term growth and short-term ups and downs.

1819

1791

Jeremy Bentham sets out his theory of **utilitarianism**; its goal is "the greatest happiness of the greatest number."

1798

Thomas Malthus warns of the danger of population outstripping resources, and the suffering that this will bring.

1817

David Ricardo lays the foundations for 19th-century **classical economics**, advocating free trade and the specialization of labor.

1819

The US suffers its **first major financial crisis**, which follows a period of sustained growth.

description of what we now know as capitalism. However, *The Wealth of Nations* was far more than a description of the economy as a whole, or "macroeconomics." It also examined issues such as the division of labor and its contribution to growth, and what factors were involved in giving value to goods. The publication of Smith's work coincided with the start of the Industrial Revolution in Britain, a period of rapidly accelerating economic growth and prosperity aided by dynamic new technology and innovation. Smith's ideas found a willing audience, eager to understand how the economy worked and how best to take advantage of it. His work was hugely influential, raising many of the questions that needed to be addressed in managing the

economy of an industrialized society. In particular Smith addressed the place of government in a capitalist society, arguing for a limited role for the state.

Ending protectionism

British political economist David Ricardo (p.84) was one of the most influential of Smith's followers. A staunch advocate of free trade, Ricardo put the final nail in the coffin of protectionism when he showed how all countries, even those that were less productive, could benefit from free trade. He also cast a critical eye over the ways that government spending and borrowing affected the economy. Another of Smith's followers was Thomas Malthus (p.69), a British clergyman and scholar famous today for his

gloomy predictions of the suffering that would ensue from a population growing faster than resources could feed it. Many of Smith's ideas were also taken up by the French physiocrat school, most notably Anne-Robert-Jacques Turgot (p.65) and François Quesnay (p.45), who argued for a fair system of taxation, and Jean-Baptiste Say (p.75), who first described the relationship between supply and demand in a market economy.

Not everyone agreed with Smith's analysis, of course, and in the 19th century there was soon to be a strong reaction against the notion of a completely free market capitalist economy, but the classical economists of the early industrial period raised questions that remain at the center of economics today. ∎

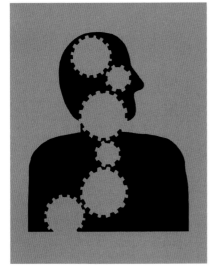

MAN IS A COLD, RATIONAL CALCULATOR

ECONOMIC MAN

IN CONTEXT

FOCUS
Decision making

KEY THINKER
Adam Smith (1723–90)

BEFORE
c.350 BCE Greek philosopher
Aristotle claims that innate
self-interest is the primary
economic motivator.

1750s French economist
François Quesnay claims that
self-interest is the motivation
behind all economic activity.

AFTER
1957 US economist Herbert
Simon argues that people are
not able to acquire and digest
all available information about
every topic, so their rationality
is "bounded" (limited).

1992 US economist Gary
Becker receives the Nobel
Prize for his work on rational
choice in the fields of
discrimination, crime,
and human capital.

As individuals we are **self-interested**.

↓

We aim to improve our **personal well-being** by consuming goods and services and achieving goals.

↓

We make decisions by **collecting information and calculating** which actions will help us achieve our aims without being too costly.

↓

Man is a cold, rational calculator.

Most economic models are underpinned by the assumption that humans are essentially rational, self-interested beings. This is *Homo Economicus*, or "economic man." The idea—which applies equally to men and women—assumes that every individual makes decisions designed to maximize their personal well-being, based on a level-headed evaluation of all the facts. They choose the option that offers the greatest utility (satisfaction) with the least effort. This idea was first expounded by Adam Smith (p.61) in his 1776 work, *The Wealth of Nations*.

Smith's central belief was that human economic interaction is governed mainly by self-interest. He argued that "it is not from the benevolence of the butcher, the brewer, or the baker that we can expect our dinner, but from their regard to their own interest." In making rational decisions suppliers seek to maximize their own profit; the fact that this supplies us with our dinner matters little to them.

Smith's ideas were developed in the 19th century by the British philosopher John Stuart Mill (p.95). Mill believed people were beings

See also: Free market economics 54–61 ▪ Economic bubbles 98–99 ▪ Economics and tradition 166–67 ▪ Markets and social outcomes 210–13 ▪ Rational expectations 244–47 ▪ Behavioral economics 266–69

who desire to possess wealth, by which he meant not just money, but a wealth of all things good. He saw individuals as motivated by the will to achieve the greatest well-being possible, while at the same time expending the least possible effort to achieve these goals.

Costs and benefits

Today, the idea of *Homo Economicus* is referred to as rational choice theory. This says that people make all kinds of economic and social decisions based on costs and benefits. For example a criminal thinking of robbing a bank will weigh the benefits (increased wealth, greater respect from other criminals) against the costs (the chances of getting caught and the effort involved in planning the heist) before deciding whether to commit the crime.

Economists consider actions to be rational when they are taken as a result of a sober calculation of costs and benefits in relation to reaching a goal. Economics may have little to say about the goal itself, and some goals may appear to be quite irrational to most people. For example, while to most of us it may seem a dangerous decision to inject the human body with unverified performance-enhancing drugs, for numerous athletes—in the context of the desire to be the best—the decision may be a rational one.

Some people have questioned whether the idea of *Homo Economicus* is realistic. They argue that it does not allow for the fact that we cannot weigh every relevant factor in a decision—the world is too complex to collect and evaluate all the relevant facts needed to calculate costs and benefits for every action. In practice we often make quick decisions based on past experience, habit, and rules of thumb.

The theory also falters when there are conflicting long- and short-term goals. For instance someone might buy an unhealthy burger to stave off immediate hunger, despite knowing that this is an unhealthy choice. Behavioral

Monks who lead a life of fasting and prayer, denying worldly goods in the expectation of an afterlife, act rationally within their beliefs, regardless of what others may think of their goal.

economists have begun to explore the ways in which humans act differently from *Homo Economicus* when making choices. The idea of "economic man" may not be entirely accurate for explaining individual behavior, but many economists argue that it remains useful in analyzing the actions of profit-maximizing firms. ∎

Parents' investments in children, especially through education, are an important source of an economy's capital stock, according to Becker.

Family economics

US economist Gary Becker (1930–) was one of the first to apply economics to areas usually thought of as sociology. He argues that decisions relating to family life are made by weighing costs and benefits. For example he views marriage as a market and has analyzed how economic characteristics influence the matching of partners. Becker also concluded that family members will help each other, not out of love, but out of self-interest in the hope of a financial reward. He believes that investment in a child is motivated by the fact that it often produces a better rate of return than traditional retirement savings. However, children cannot be legally forced to take care of their parents, so they are brought up with a sense of guilt, obligation, duty, and love, which effectively commits them to helping their parents. For this reason it can be argued that the welfare state damages families by reducing their need for interdependence.

THE INVISIBLE HAND OF THE MARKET BRINGS ORDER

FREE MARKET ECONOMICS

According to the Scottish thinker Adam Smith, the West had embarked on a great revolution before the 18th century, with nations changing from agrarian, or agricultural, societies to commercial ones. During the Middle Ages towns had developed, and they were slowly joined up by roads. People brought goods and fresh produce to the towns, and the markets—with their buying and selling—became a part of life. Scientific innovation produced reliable, agreed-upon units of measurement, along with new ways of doing things, and centralized nation-states formed from the mix of principalities that had dotted Europe. People enjoyed a new freedom and had begun to exchange goods for their own personal gain, not merely for that of their overlord.

Smith asked how the actions of free individuals could result in an ordered, stable market—where people could make, buy, and sell what they wanted without enormous waste or want. How was this possible without some kind of guiding hand? In his great work of 1776, *The Wealth of Nations*, he provided the

Mandeville's *Fable of the Bees*
explored the idea that when people
act out of self-interest, they benefit
the whole of society, like the self-interested
behavior of bees benefits the hive.

answer. Man, in his freedom, rivalry, and desire for gain, is "led by an invisible hand to promote an end, which was no part of his intention" —he inadvertently acts on behalf of the wider interest of society.

Laissez-faire economics

The idea of "spontaneous order" was not new. It was proposed in 1714 by the Dutch writer Bernard Mandeville in his poem *The Fable of the Bees*. This told the story of a beehive that was thriving on the "vices" (self-interested behavior) of its bees. When the bees became virtuous (no longer acting in their own self-interest but trying to act for the good of the hive), the beehive collapsed. Smith's notion of self-interest was

Covent Garden Market in London
is pictured here in 1774. Smith thought
markets were key to making society fair.
With the freedom to buy and sell, people
could enjoy "natural liberty."

not a vicious one. He saw humans as having an inclination to "truck and barter" (bargain and exchange) and to better themselves. Humans, in his view, were social creatures who act with moral restraint, using "fair play" in competition.

Smith believed that governments should not interfere with commerce, a view that was also held by other Scottish thinkers around him, including the philosopher David Hume (p.47). An earlier French writer, Pierre de Boisguilbert, used the phrase *laisse faire la nature* ("leave nature alone"), by which he meant "leave business alone." The term "laissez-faire" is used in economics to advocate minimal government. In Smith's view government did have an important role, supplying defense, justice, and certain "public goods" (pp.46–47) that private markets were unlikely to provide, such as roads.

Smith's vision was essentially optimistic. The English philosopher Thomas Hobbes had earlier argued that without strong authority, human life would be "nasty, brutish, and short." British economist Thomas Malthus (p.69) looked at the market and predicted mass starvation as a direct result of increased wealth. After Smith, Karl Marx (p.105) would predict that the market leads to revolution. Smith, however, saw society as perfectly functional, and the entire economy as a successful system, an imaginary machine that worked. He mentioned the "invisible hand" only once in his five volume work, but its presence is often felt. Smith described how his system of "perfect liberty" could have positive outcomes. First, it provides the

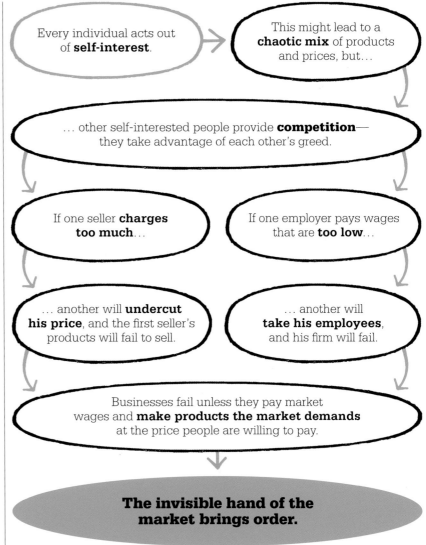

goods that people want. If demand for a product exceeds its supply, consumers compete with each other to drive the price up. This creates a profit opportunity for producers, who compete with each other to supply more of the product.

This argument has stood the test of time. In an essay in 1945, titled *The Use of Knowledge in*

Society, the Austrian economist Friedrich Hayek (p.177) showed how prices respond to individuals' localized knowledge and desires, leading to changes in the amounts demanded and supplied in the market. A central planner, Hayek said, could not hope to gather up so much dispersed information. It is widely believed that communism » collapsed in Eastern Europe because central planning failed to deliver the goods that people wanted. Some criticisms of Smith's first point have been raised, such as the fact that the market might only provide the goods that are wanted by the rich; it ignores the desires of the poor. It also responds to harmful desires—the market can feed drug addiction and promote obesity.

Fair prices

Second, Smith said that the market system generates prices that are "fair." He believed that all goods have a natural price that reflects only the efforts that went into making them. The land used in making a product should earn its natural rent. The capital used in its manufacture should earn its natural profit. The labor used should earn its natural wage. Market prices and rates of return can differ from their natural levels for periods of time, as might happen in times of scarcity.

Smith described the ways in which labor, landowners, and capital (here invested in the horses and plow) work together to keep the economic system moving and growing.

In that case, opportunities for gain will arise, and prices will increase, but only until competition brings new firms into the market and prices fall back to their natural level. If one industry begins to suffer a slump in demand, prices will drop and wages will fall, but as a different industry rises, it will offer higher wages to attract workers. In the long run, Smith says, "market" and "natural" rates will be the same: modern economists call this equilibrium.

Competition is essential if prices are to be fair. Smith attacked the monopolies occurring under the mercantilist system, which demanded that governments should control foreign trade. When there is only one supplier of a good, the firm that supplies it can permanently hold the price above its natural level. Smith said that if there are 20 grocers selling a product, the market is more competitive than if there are just two. With effective competition and low barriers to entry into a market—which Smith also said was essential—prices tend to be lower. Much of this underlies mainstream economists' views

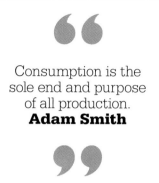

about competition, although dissenters, such as Austrian-American economist Joseph Schumpeter (p.149), would later say that innovation can also lower prices, even where there appears to be little competition. As inventors come forward to provide higher quality products at lower prices, they blow away existing firms in a storm of creative destruction.

Fair incomes

Smith also argued that market economies provide incomes that are fair and can be spent on goods in a sustainable "circular flow,"

in which money paid in wages circulates back into the economy when the worker pays for goods, only to be paid back out in wages to repeat the process. Capital invested in production facilities helps to increase labor productivity, which means that employers can afford to pay higher wages. And if employers can afford to pay more, they will because they have to compete with each other for workers.

Turning to capital, Smith said that the amount of profit that capital can expect to earn through investments is roughly equal to the rate of interest. This is because employers compete with each other to borrow funds to invest in profitable opportunities. Over time the rate of profit in any particular field falls as capital accumulates and opportunities for profit are exhausted. Rents gradually rise as incomes rise and more land is used.

Smith's realization of the interdependence of land, labor, and capital was a real breakthrough. He noted that workers and landowners tend to consume their incomes, while employers are more frugal, investing their savings in capital stock. He saw that wage rates vary, depending on different levels of "skill, dexterity, and judgment," and that there are two forms of labor: productive (engaged in agriculture or manufacturing) and what he called "unproductive" (supplying services needed to back up the main work). The highly unequal outcomes of today's market system are a long way from what Smith envisioned.

Economic growth
Smith claimed that the invisible hand itself stimulates economic growth. The source of growth is twofold. One is the efficiencies gained through the division of

Demand in a market can change for many reasons. As it does so, the market responds by altering supply. This happens spontaneously—there is no need for a guiding hand or plan in a market that encourages competition among self-interested people.

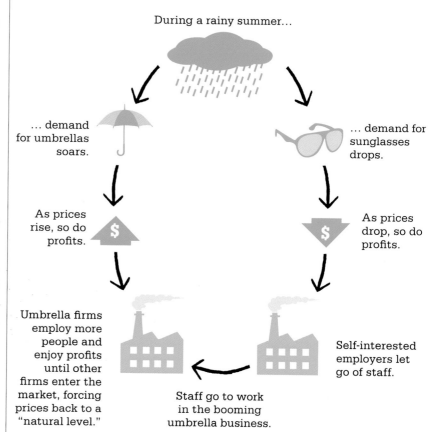

During a rainy summer…

… demand for umbrellas soars.

As prices rise, so do profits.

Umbrella firms employ more people and enjoy profits until other firms enter the market, forcing prices back to a "natural level."

Staff go to work in the booming umbrella business.

… demand for sunglasses drops.

As prices drop, so do profits.

Self-interested employers let go of staff.

labor (pp.66–67). Economists call this "Smithian growth." As more products are produced and consumed, the economy grows, and markets also grow. As markets grow, there are more opportunities for specialization of work.

The second engine of growth is the accumulation of capital, driven by saving and the opportunity for profit. Smith said that growth can be reduced by commercial failures, a lack of resources required to maintain the fixed capital stock, an inadequate money system (there is more growth with paper money than with gold), and a **»**

> It is not from the benevolence of the butcher, the brewer, or the baker that we expect our dinner, but from their regard to their self-interest.
> **Adam Smith**

high proportion of unproductive workers. He claimed that capital is more productive in agriculture than in manufacturing, which is higher than in trade or transport. Ultimately, the economy will grow until it reaches a wealthy, stationary state. In this, Smith underestimated the role of technology and innovation—the Schumpeterian growth described earlier (p.58).

Classical legacy

Smith's system was comprehensive. It considered small (microeconomic) details and the large (macroeconomic) picture. It looked at situations in both the short and long run, and its analysis was both static (the state of trade) and dynamic (the economy in motion). It looked in detail at the class known as workers, distinguishing entrepreneurs such as farmers and factory owners from suppliers of labor. In essence it established the parameters for "classical" economics, which focuses on the factors of production —capital, labor, and land—and

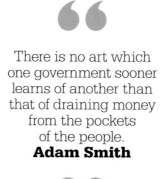

There is no art which one government sooner learns of another than that of draining money from the pockets of the people.
Adam Smith

their returns. Later, free market theory took a different, "neoclassical" form with general equilibrium theory, which sought to show how a whole economy's prices could reach a state of stable equilibrium. Using mathematics, economists such as Léon Walras (p.120) and Vilfredo Pareto (p.133) reframed Smith's claim that the

invisible hand would be socially beneficial. Kenneth Arrow and Gérard Debreu (pp.208–11) showed how free markets do this, but they also showed that the conditions needed were stringent and did not bear much relation to reality.

This was not the end of the story. After World War II the idea of laissez-faire was in hibernation. However, from the 1970s, Keynesian policies, which advocated state intervention in economies, seemed to break down, and laissez-faire enjoyed a strong resurgence. The seeds of this flowering can be found in works on the market economy by Milton Friedman (p.199) and the Austrian School, notably Friedrich Hayek (p.177), who were skeptical about the good that interfering governments can do and argued that social progress would be attained through unfettered markets. Keynesians, too, recognized the power of markets—but for them markets needed to be nudged to work best.

The free market approach enjoyed an important boost from theories in the 1960s and 70s based on the role of rationality and rational expectations (pp.244–47). Public choice theory, for example, depicts government as a group of self-seeking individuals who maximize their own interests and extract money without regard to the social good ("rent-seeking"). New classical macroeconomics uses Smith's assumption that markets always sort themselves out and adds the point that people can see the future implications of any government actions and understand the

Localized markets such as this one in Kerala, India, exhibit all the hallmarks of Smith's free market and demonstrate the natural way in which supply and price adjust to demand.

Adam Smith

The founder of modern economics, Adam Smith was born in Kirkcaldy, Scotland, in 1723, six months after his father's death. A reclusive, absentminded scholar, he went to Glasgow University at the age of 14, then studied at Oxford University for six years before returning to Scotland to take up a professorship in logic at Glasgow University. In 1750, he met and became close friends with the philosopher David Hume.

In 1764, Smith resigned his post at Glasgow to travel to France as tutor to the Duke of Buccleuch, a Scottish aristocrat. In France, he met the physiocrat group of economists (pp.40–45) and the philosopher Voltaire, and he began writing *The Wealth of Nations*. He devoted 10 years to the book before accepting a position as Commissioner of Customs. He died in 1790.

Key works

1759 *The Theory of Moral Sentiments*
1762 *Lectures on Jurisprudence*
1776 *An Inquiry into the Nature and Causes of the Wealth of Nations*

workings of the economic system, so state intervention will not work. Even so, most economists today believe that the market can fail. They focus on disparities in information, held by various participants in a market. George Akerlof referred to this in his *The Market for Lemons* (pp.274–75). Behavioral economists have questioned the whole notion of

> 66
> Human society, when we contemplate it in a certain abstract and philosophical light, appears like a great, an immense machine.
> **Adam Smith**
> 99

Smith didn't foresee the kinds of inequalities that can arise from free markets in their present form. In stock exchanges and money markets notions of "fairness" become almost irrelevant.

rationality (pp.266–69), and see the non-rationality of humans as a reason for markets to fail.

The issue of laissez-faire economics divides economists along political lines. Those on the political Right embrace laissez-faire; those from the Left align themselves with Keynesian intervention. This remains a central debate in economics today.

The financial crisis of 2007–08 has added fuel to this dispute. The free marketeers felt vindicated in their theories about the business cycle, while Keynesians pointed to market failure. US economist Nouriel Roubini (1959–), who predicted the crash, was speaking of those who had distorted Smith's ideas when he said that "decades of free market fundamentalism laid the foundation for the meltdown." ∎

THE LAST WORKER ADDS LESS TO OUTPUT THAN THE FIRST
DIMINISHING RETURNS

IN CONTEXT

FOCUS
Markets and firms

KEY THINKER
Anne-Robert-Jacques Turgot (1727–81)

BEFORE
1759 French economist François Quesnay publishes *Economic Table*—a model that demonstrates the physiocrats' economic theories.

1760s French physiocrat Guérineau de Saint-Péravy's essay on the principles of taxation argues that the ratio of outputs to inputs is fixed.

AFTER
1871 Austrian Carl Menger argues in *Principles of Economics* that price is determined at the margin.

1956 In *A Contribution to the Theory of Economic Growth,* US economist Robert Solow applies the idea of diminishing marginal returns to the growth prospects of countries.

Frenchman Anne-Robert-Jacques Turgot (p.65) was one of a small group of thinkers known as the physiocrats, who believed that national wealth was created from agriculture.

Turgot's twin interests in tax and the output of land led him to develop a theory that explains how the output of each extra worker changes as successive workers are added to the production process. A fellow physiocrat, Guérineau de Saint-Péravy, had said that for each extra worker on the land, the amount of additional output is constant; in other words each extra worker adds the same to production as the last. But in 1767, Turgot pointed out that unprepared soil produces very little when sowed. If the soil is plowed once, output increases; plowed twice, it might quadruple. Eventually, however, the extra work begins to increase output less and less, until additional workers add nothing further to production, because the fertility of the soil is exhausted.

The role of technology
Turgot's idea is that adding more of a variable factor (workers) to a fixed factor (land) will lead to the last worker adding less to output than the first. This has become known as "diminishing marginal returns," and it is one of the most important pillars of modern economic theory. It explains not only why it costs more to produce more, but also why countries struggle to get richer if their population expands without improvements in technology. ∎

The earth's fertility resembles a spring that is being pressed downward… the effect of additional weights will gradually diminish.
A R J Turgot

See also: The circular flow of the economy 40–45 ▪ Demographics and economics 68–69 ▪ Economic growth theories 224–25

WHY DO DIAMONDS COST MORE THAN WATER?

THE PARADOX OF VALUE

IN CONTEXT

FOCUS
Theories of value

KEY THINKER
Adam Smith (1723–90)

BEFORE
1691 English philosopher John Locke connects a commodity's value to its utility (the satisfaction it affords).

1737 Swiss mathematician Daniel Bernoulli poses the "St Petersburg Paradox," examining how players can evaluate options involving chance. The paradox is resolved by applying the concept of marginal utility.

AFTER
1889 Austrian economist Eugen von Böhm-Bawerk develops the subjective theory of value (the value of an object depends on a person's needs rather than the object itself), using the idea of marginal utilities.

In 1769, Anne-Robert-Jacques Turgot (p.65) noted that despite its necessity, water is not seen as a precious thing in a well-watered country. Seven years later Adam Smith (p.61) took this idea further, noting that although nothing is more useful than water, hardly anything can be exchanged for it. Although a diamond has very little value in terms of use, "a very great quantity of other goods may frequently be had in exchange for it." In other words, there is an apparent contradiction between the prices of certain commodities and their importance to people.

Marginal utility

This paradox can be explained with the help of a concept known as marginal utility: the amount of pleasure gained from the last unit of the commodity consumed. In 1889, the Austrian economist Eugen von Böhm-Bawerk explained it through the example of a farmer with five bags of wheat. The farmer's use of the wheat ranges from important—feeding himself—to trivial—feeding birds. If he loses a bag of wheat, he will merely stop feeding the birds. Even though the farmer needs wheat to feed himself, the price he is willing to pay to replace the fifth bag of wheat is low, because it only generates a small amount of pleasure (feeding birds).

Water is abundant, but diamonds are scarce. One extra diamond has a high marginal utility and so commands a much higher price than an extra cup of water. ∎

Diamonds are worth more than water because each one is extremely valuable no matter how many you have, while water becomes less valuable, per unit, as quantities increase.

See also: The labor theory of value 106–07 ▪ Utility and satisfaction 114–15 ▪ Opportunity cost 133

MAKE TAXES FAIR AND EFFICIENT
THE TAX BURDEN

Who bears the burden of tax? The key question of "tax incidence" intrigued the gifted economist Anne-Robert-Jacques Turgot, who was the French Minister of Finance from 1774–76. The question is not as simple as "who should pay tax?" because taxes affect many things, from prices and profits to amounts of goods consumed and incomes received. Changes in these can ripple through the economy in surprising ways. The "burden" of a tax—which is taken to mean a decrease in happiness, welfare, or money—can be shifted from one person or group to another. If you

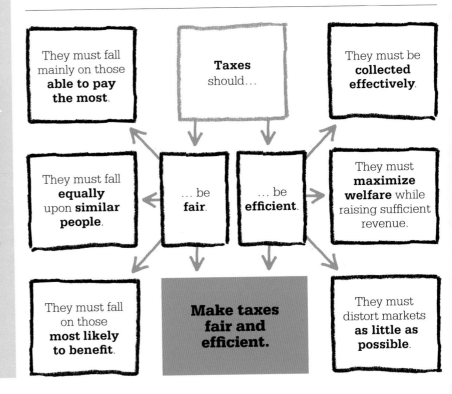

They must fall mainly on those **able to pay the most**.

Taxes should…

They must be **collected effectively**.

They must fall **equally** upon **similar people**.

… be **fair**.

… be **efficient**.

They must **maximize welfare** while raising sufficient revenue.

They must fall on those **most likely to benefit**.

Make taxes fair and efficient.

They must distort markets **as little as possible**.

See also: The circular flow of the economy 40–45 ▪ Efficiency and fairness 130–31 ▪ External costs 137 ▪ The theory of the second best 220–21 ▪ Taxation and economic incentives 270–71

are planning a vacation and a new fuel tax puts the airfare above the level you are prepared to pay, the tax has made you unhappy. The new fuel tax has reduced your welfare, but not necessarily the airline company's profits.

Who should pay taxes?

Turgot argued that taxes interfere with the free market and should be simplified. Powerful groups should not be exempt from taxation, and the details of its implementation matter. His recommendation was for a single tax on a country's net product—the value of its total goods and services minus depreciation.

His thinking was influenced by an early school of economists known as the physiocrats, who believed that only agriculture (land) produces a surplus. Other industries do not produce a surplus and so cannot afford to pay tax—they will always try to pass it on by increasing prices and charges until finally it reaches the landowners. As farmers pay much of their surplus in rent to landowners, who

produce nothing, Turgot argued that the landowners should be taxed on the rent they charged.

Later economists refined the principles of fairness and efficiency that go into an optimal tax system. Fairness includes the idea that those most able to pay should pay the most; that similar people should face similar taxes; and that those who benefit from government spending, such as users of a new bridge, should contribute to it. Efficiency means both effectiveness in collection and maximizing society's welfare while raising the required revenue. Economists argue that efficiency means disturbing the market as little as possible, particularly to avoid blunting incentives for work and investment.

Perfect tax design

The last few decades have seen huge strides in the sophistication of tax design, integrating both fairness and efficiency. "Perfect markets" theory, for example, suggests commodity taxes should be uniform and apply only to "final"

Aristocrats at Versailles were targeted by Turgot's tax reforms of 1776. He suggested they should no longer be exempt from tax, so they arranged his dismissal from office.

goods (for sale to final users); income taxes should be linked to ability rather than income; and taxes on company profits and income from capital should be minimal. "Market failure" analysis, on the other hand, suggests that taxes on undesirables such as pollution increase people's welfare.

In general, tax policies have moved in the directions shown by such theories while paying attention to revenue and political acceptability. ∎

Anne-Robert-Jacques Turgot

Born in Paris, France, in 1727, Turgot was destined for the priesthood until an inheritance in 1751 allowed him to pursue a career in administration. By the late 1760s, he had become friendly with the physiocrats, and later met Adam Smith. From 1761 to 1774, he was the *Intendant* of Limoges, a regional administrator. On the accession of Louis XVI in 1774, Turgot became Minister of Finance and set about making reforms that encouraged free trade. In 1776, he abolished the guilds and ended a government policy that used unpaid, forced

labor to build roads by instituting a road-building tax instead. Louis XVI did not approve and dismissed Turgot from office. His reforms—which some felt might have averted the French Revolution of 1789—were overturned. He died aged 54 in 1781.

Key works

1763 *Taxation in General*
1766 *Reflections on the Production and Distribution of Wealth*
1776 *The Six Edicts*

DIVIDE UP PIN PRODUCTION, AND YOU GET MORE PINS
THE DIVISION OF LABOR

IN CONTEXT

FOCUS
Markets and firms

KEY THINKER
Adam Smith (1723–90)

BEFORE
380 BCE In *The Republic*, the Greek philosopher Plato explains how a city emerges, then grows by exploiting the gains made by dividing labor.

1705 Dutch philosopher Bernard Mandeville coins the term "division of labor" in his *The Fable of the Bees*.

AFTER
1867 Karl Marx argues that division of labor alienates workers and is a necessary evil that will eventually be superseded.

1922 Austrian economist Ludwig von Mises argues that division of labor is not alienating but brings huge benefits, including greater leisure time.

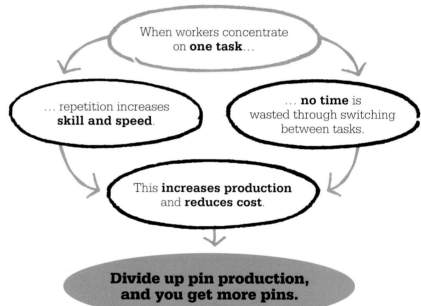

When workers concentrate on **one task**…

… repetition increases **skill and speed**.

… **no time** is wasted through switching between tasks.

This **increases production** and **reduces cost**.

Divide up pin production, and you get more pins.

Whenever people work in a group, they invariably start by deciding who is going to do what. It was the great Adam Smith (p.61) who turned this division of labor into a central economic idea. At the very start of his influential book *The Wealth of Nations*, Smith explains the differences between production when one person carries out the full sequence required to make something, and when several people each do just one task each. Writing in 1776, Smith noted that if one man set about making a pin, going through the many steps involved, he might make "perhaps not one pin in a day." But by dividing the process among several men, with each specializing in a single step, many pins could be

See also: Comparative advantage 80–85 ▪ Economies of scale 132 ▪
The emergence of modern economies 178–79

In a busy stockroom, labor may be divided between porters, inventory clerks, a manager, accountants, distribution specialists, IT workers, and truck drivers.

made in a day. Smith concluded that the division of labor causes "in every art, a proportionable increase of the productive powers of labor."

The engine of growth

Smith was not the first to appreciate the value of the division of labor. About 2,200 years earlier Plato had argued that a state needs specialists, such as farmers and builders, to supply its needs. The Islamic philosopher Al-Ghazali (1058–1111) noted that if we take into account every step involved in making bread, from clearing the weeds in the fields to harvesting the wheat, we would find that the loaf takes its final form with the help of over a thousand workers.

Many early thinkers linked division of labor to the growth of cities and markets. Some thought that the division of labor caused the growth, while others proposed that the growing cities allowed the division of labor.

What was groundbreaking about Smith's idea was that he put division of labor at the heart of the economic system, insisting that it is the engine that drives growth. The more specialized the workers and businesses, the greater the market growth and the higher the returns on investments.

A necessary evil

Karl Marx (p.105) saw the power of this idea but believed that the division of labor was a temporary, necessary evil. Specialization alienates, condemning workers to the dispiriting condition of a machine performing repetitive tasks. He distinguished between the technical division of labor, such as each specialized task in house building, and social division, which is enforced by hierarchies of power and status.

Labor division is the norm within most companies today. Many large corporations now outsource tasks formerly carried out by their own staff to cheaper overseas workers, giving the division of labor a new, international dimension. ▪

Every expansion of the personal division of labor brings advantages to all who take part in it.
Ludwig von Mises

All-American jobs?

When people working in industry worry about the strength of their home economy and rates of employment, they sometimes urge consumers to buy home-produced goods. However, it can be hard to know what is home-produced since division of labor has now become global in scope. For example, Apple is a US company, so consumers might suppose that by buying an iPhone they are contributing to US jobs. In fact, of all the processes involved in making an iPhone, only the product and software design and marketing occur primarily in the US.

Each iPhone is assembled by workers in China, using parts—such as the case, screen, and processor—made by workers in South Korea, Japan, Germany, and six other countries. In addition, each of these parts has been assembled by a range of specialists around the world. The iPhone is a truly global product, made by perhaps tens of thousands of people.

Assembly-line workers in China build computer processors with components made in up to nine different countries.

POPULATION GROWTH KEEPS US POOR
DEMOGRAPHICS AND ECONOMICS

During the 18th century enlightened thinkers began to consider the possibility of improving society's lot through wise social and economic reforms. The British economist Thomas Malthus was a pessimistic voice in this optimistic era, claiming that the growth of populations dooms societies to poverty. Malthus argued that the human sex drive causes faster and faster expansion of the populace. Food production would not keep up because of the law of diminishing returns: as more people work on a fixed amount of land, less and less

Survivors of an earthquake in Pakistan receive food handouts. Malthus opposed any such relief—to assist the destitute would only encourage them to have more children.

output is added. The result is an ever-widening imbalance between the number of people and the supply of food.

However, there is a counteracting force. Malthus saw that malnutrition and disease caused by a more limited food supply would lead to increased mortality and stop the imbalance from getting out of control. Less food to go around would also mean fewer children could be supported, and the birth rate would fall. This would lessen the pressure on land, restoring living standards.

The Malthusian trap
As well as preventing total starvation, changes in birth and death rates stop the population from benefiting from higher living standards for very long. Suppose that the economy has a windfall through the discovery of land. Extra land gives a one-time boost to food production and provides more food per person. People become healthier and the death rate falls. Higher living standards allow for more children. Together, these forces add to population growth. Food production cannot keep up, and the economy reverts to the

See also: Agriculture in the economy 39 ▪ Diminishing returns 62 ▪ The emergence of modern economies 178–79 ▪ Economic growth theories 224–25

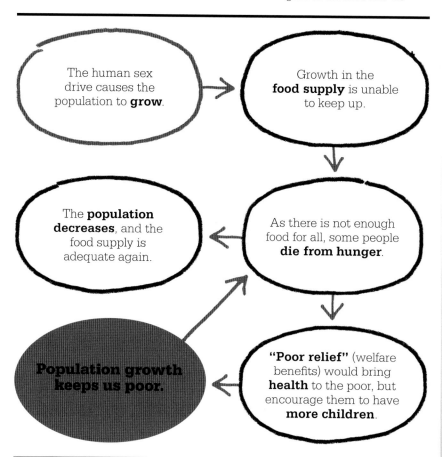

The human sex drive causes the population to **grow**.

Growth in the **food supply** is unable to keep up.

The **population decreases**, and the food supply is adequate again.

As there is not enough food for all, some people **die from hunger**.

Population growth keeps us poor.

"**Poor relief**" (welfare benefits) would bring **health** to the poor, but encourage them to have **more children**.

Thomas Malthus

Thomas Robert Malthus was born in Surrey, England, in 1766, and was given a liberal education by his father, a country squire. His godfathers were the philosophers David Hume and Jean-Jacques Rousseau. He was born with a cleft palate and suffered from a speech defect.

At Cambridge University Malthus was tutored by a religious dissenter, William Frend, before being ordained into the Church of England in 1788. Like his teacher he never shied away from controversy. In 1798, he published his *Essay on the Principle of Population*, the work that would bring him notoriety. In 1805, the new East India College appointed him Professor of Political Economy, a subject not yet taught at universities, which perhaps makes him the first academic economist. Malthus died of heart disease in 1834, aged 68.

Key works

1798 *An Essay on the Principle of Population*
1815 *The Nature of Rent*
1820 *Principles of Political Economy*

original, lower level of living standards. This is called the Malthusian trap: higher living standards are always choked off by population growth. So whatever happens, the economy always reverts to the level of food output that is just enough to support a stable population.

Malthus's vision was one of economic stagnation, with the population eking out a living and its growth being checked by hunger and disease. However, his model—an economy of farmers toiling with simple tools on a fixed amount of land—was already out of step with the times by the turn of the 18th century. New techniques allowed more food to be produced from the same amount of land and labor. New machines and factories allowed more goods to be produced per worker. Technological progress meant that growing populations enjoyed ever-higher living standards. By 2000, Britain had more than three times the population of Malthus's time, with incomes 10 times higher.

Over time, technology has overcome the constraints of land and demographics. Malthus did not foresee this. Today, his ideas are echoed in fears that population levels are pushing against the capacity of the Earth in ways that new technology cannot offset. ▪

MEETINGS OF MERCHANTS END IN CONSPIRACIES TO RAISE PRICES

CARTELS AND COLLUSION

IN CONTEXT

FOCUS
Markets and firms

KEY THINKER
Adam Smith (1723–90)

BEFORE
1290s Wenceslas II, Duke of Bohemia, introduces laws to prevent metal ore traders from colluding to raise prices.

1590s Traders from the Netherlands collaborate in a cartel with a monopoly of the spice trade in the East Indies.

AFTER
1838 French economist Augustin Cournot describes competition in oligopolies.

1890 The first antitrust law is passed in the US.

1964 US economist George Stigler publishes *A Theory of Oligopoly*, examining the problems of maintaining successful cartels.

C ompetition is key to the efficient working of free markets. The presence of several producers in a market drives production and keeps prices down as each competes to attract customers. If there is only a single supplier—a monopoly—it can choose to restrict its output and charge higher prices.

Between these two extremes sits the oligopoly, where a few suppliers—sometimes only two or three—dominate the market for a particular product. Competition between producers in an oligopoly would clearly be in the interests of the consumer, but there is an alternative for the producers that

See also: Effects of limited competition 90–91 ▪ Monopolies 92–97 ▪ The competitive market 126–29 ▪ Markets and social outcomes 210–13 ▪ Game theory 234–41

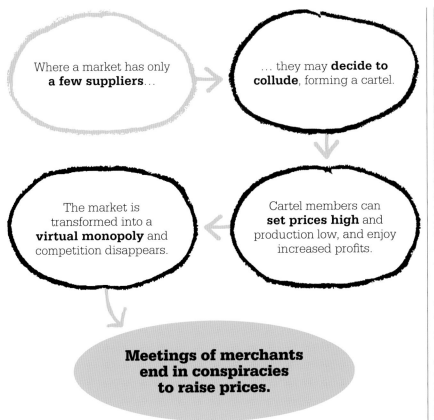

Where a market has only **a few suppliers**...

... they may **decide to collude**, forming a cartel.

Cartel members can **set prices high** and production low, and enjoy increased profits.

The market is transformed into a **virtual monopoly** and competition disappears.

Meetings of merchants end in conspiracies to raise prices.

British Airways was fined $546 million for collusion in 2011, after Virgin Atlantic admitted that the two companies had met six times to discuss proposed price rises.

may be more beneficial to their profit levels: cooperation. If they choose this route and can agree not to undercut one another, they can act collectively like a monopoly and dictate the terms of the market to their own benefit.

Forming cartels

This sort of cooperation between firms is known by economists as "collusion." The price fixing that results makes markets less efficient. Scottish economist Adam Smith (p.61) recognized the importance of self-interest in free markets but was suspicious enough of the motives of suppliers to warn: "People of the same trade seldom meet together, even for merriment and diversion, but the conversation ends in a conspiracy against the public, or in some contrivance to raise prices."

Collaborations between producers have existed for as long as there have been markets, and businesses in many areas of commerce have formed associations to their mutual benefit. In the US in the 19th century these restrictive or monopolistic practices were known as "trusts," but the word "cartel" is now used to describe such collaborations, which operate on a national or international level. The word has gained a negative connotation despite being a notable feature of the German and US economies in the 1920s and 1930s.

In the 20th century the US and the European Union (EU) used legislation to discourage collusion. However, cartels among producers remain a feature of market economies. Collaborations might be a simple agreement between two firms, such as when Unilever and Procter & Gamble colluded to fix the price of laundry detergent in Europe in 2011, or they can take the form of an international trade association, such as the International Air Transport Association (IATA). The IATA's original function was to set prices for fares, which led to accusations of collusion, but it still exists as a representative organization for the airline industry. Cartels can even be formed through cooperation between governments of countries producing a particular commodity, as happened in the case of the Organization of Petroleum Exporting Countries (OPEC), » which was founded in 1960 to coordinate oil prices among member countries.

Challenges for cartels

However, there are problems in setting up and sustaining a cartel, which focus around prices and trust between members. Participants in a cartel cannot simply fix prices. They also have to agree on output quotas to maintain those prices and, of course, the share of the profits. The fewer the members of a cartel, the easier these negotiations are. Cartels are more robust when there are a small number of firms accounting for most of the supply.

The second problem is ensuring that members of a cartel abide by the rules. Producers are attracted to collusion by the prospect of higher prices, but this self-interest is also the weakness of the arrangement. Individual members of a cartel may be tempted to "cheat" by overproducing and undercutting their collaborators. In effect, this is

a version of the prisoner's dilemma (p.238), in which two prisoners can each choose either to remain silent or confess. If both remain silent or both confess, they will receive light sentences; but if only one confesses, he will receive immunity while his partner in crime will get a heavy sentence. The best strategy for each of them is to remain silent (this incurs the shortest jail term), but the temptation is to opt for immunity and confess in the hope that the other does not. The strategies that apply here are equally applicable to cartels, where the rewards for all the players are greater if they collaborate than if they compete but are greatest for any one player who breaks the agreement, while the others suffer as a consequence.

In practice, this is what tends to happen within a cartel, particularly when the quotas are unequally divided. The 12 members of OPEC, for example, meet regularly to agree on output and prices, but these are seldom adhered to. The smaller, less

wealthy members see the chance of gaining some extra profit and exceed their output quota, introducing an element of competitiveness and weakening the power of the cartel as a whole. It only takes one cheat to undermine the operation of a cartel, and the more members in the cartel, the greater the danger of the rules being broken.

Enforcing agreements

Very often, one of a cartel's members—the most powerful in terms of production—emerges as an "enforcer." When the efficacy of OPEC becomes threatened, for instance, by a country such as Angola overproducing to increase its profits, Saudi Arabia, the largest member of the cartel, can take action to stop this. As the largest producer with the lowest production costs it can afford to increase production and lower prices to a level that will punish or may even bankrupt the smaller countries, while only lowering its own profits in the short term. However, in many cases, the temptation to cheat and the reluctance of the enforcer to reduce its profits eventually lead to the break-up of cartels.

Cartels can arrange price-fixing by operating as a virtual monopoly. If no one can offer the consumer a lower price, the one price offered can be much higher than production costs, generating high profits for the cartel.

> We must not tolerate oppressive government or industrial oligarchy in the form of monopolies and cartels.
> **Henry A Wallace**
> **US politician (1888–1965)**

The difficulty in forming and maintaining cartels means that these "conspiracies" are less common than Adam Smith might have expected. In the 1960s US economist George Stigler showed that the natural suspicion of competitors acts against collusion in a cartel, and that cartels are less likely to occur as more firms enter a market. As a result, even in industries where there are only a few large producers, such as for video games consoles and mobile phones, the preference is generally for competition rather than cooperation.

Nevertheless, the few cartels that do exist pose enough of a threat to the market for governments to feel the need to intervene. Public pressure from consumers opposed to price-fixing drove the move to "antitrust" legislation (see right) during the 20th century, outlawing cartels in most countries. Because of the difficulty of proving collusion, many of these laws offer immunity to the first member of a cartel to confess—just as in the prisoner's dilemma—offering yet another incentive to break up the cartel. This tactic was notably successful recently, when Virgin Atlantic Airlines, worried by an investigation

Mobile phone operators in the Netherlands were investigated for suspected cartel practices in 2011, including price-fixing mobile data bundles for prepaid phones.

Economists have their glories, but I do not believe that antitrust law is one of them.
George Stigler

into price-fixing of Atlantic flights, confessed its collusion with British Airways, who were heavily fined.

Government approval

Some libertarian economists, such as Stigler, are skeptical of the need for such laws, given the instability of cartels. Governments are often ambiguous about cartels, seeing some forms of cooperation as potentially desirable. For example, while IATA's price-setting policy was considered collusion, OPEC has sometimes been seen in a more benign light as a trade bloc whose policies lead to stability. The same argument has been put forward in defense of public cartels in certain industries, such as oil or steel, in countries during times of depression. When regulated by governments, cooperation between producers can stabilize production and prices, protect the consumer and smaller producers, and make the industry as a whole more competitive internationally. Public cartels such as these were common in both Europe and the US during the 1920s and 1930s, but mostly disappeared after World War II. National cartels are still a feature of the Japanese economy. ∎

Antitrust laws

Cartels, like monopolies, are generally seen as harmful to the efficiency of free markets and a threat to overall economic well-being. Most governments have attempted to prevent this kind of collusion by legislation in the form of antitrust or competition laws. The first such intervention was in the US in 1890, when the Sherman Act outlawed every contract or conspiracy that restrained interstate or foreign trade. This was followed by further antitrust laws including the Clayton Act in 1914, which prohibited local price cutting to "freeze out" competition. Economists have tended to be skeptical about antitrust legislation, which is, in any case, often difficult to enforce. They point out that cooperation does not always lead to collusive practices, such as price-fixing and bid-rigging, and many believe that much "trust-busting" legislation has been motivated by political pressure rather than economic analysis.

This 1906 cover of a political paper lampoons US politician Nelson Aldrich for building a "web" of tariffs to protect US goods from foreign competition and raise local prices.

SUPPLY CREATES ITS OWN DEMAND
GLUTS IN MARKETS

IN CONTEXT

FOCUS
The macroeconomy

KEY THINKER
Jean-Baptiste Say
(1767–1832)

BEFORE
1820 British economist
Thomas Malthus argues that
underemployment and
overproduction can occur.

AFTER
1936 John Maynard Keynes
states that supply does not
create its own demand—it is
possible for a lack of demand
to cause production to slow,
creating unemployment.

1950 Austrian economist
Ludwig von Mises argues
that Keynes' denial is at the
basis of Keynesian fallacies
about economics.

2010 Australian economist
Steven Kates defends Say's
law and calls Keynesian
economics a "conceptual
disease."

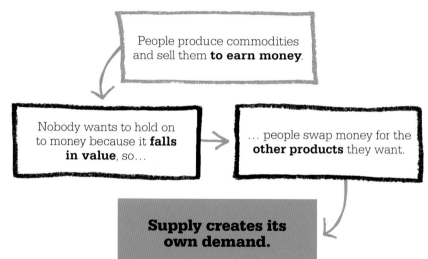

People produce commodities and sell them **to earn money**.

Nobody wants to hold on to money because it **falls in value**, so…

… people swap money for the **other products** they want.

Supply creates its own demand.

In 1776, when Adam Smith wrote *The Wealth of Nations* (pp.54–61), he noted that merchants around him commonly felt there were two reasons why business failed: a scarcity of money or overproduction. He debunked the first of these myths by explaining the role of money in an economy, but it was left to a later French economist, Jean-Baptiste Say, to dismiss the second. His 1803 work, *A Treatise on Political Economy*, is devoted to explaining the impossibility of overproduction.

Say claimed that as soon as a product is made, it creates a market for other products "to the full extent of its own value." This means, for example, that the money a tailor receives when he makes and sells a shirt is then used to buy bread from the baker and beer from the brewer. Say believed that people had no desire to hoard money, and therefore the total value of commodities supplied would equal the total value of goods demanded. The common expression of what is known as Say's law has become

See also: Free market economics 54–61 ▪ Economic equilibrium 118–23 ▪ Depressions and unemployment 154–61

"supply creates its own demand." In fact, Say never used this phrase; it was probably coined in 1921 by the US economist Fred Taylor in his *Principles of Economics*.

The idea was important to Say because if supply creates an equal value of demand, there can never be overproduction, or "gluts," in the economy as a whole. Of course, firms could mistake the level of demand for a commodity and overproduce, but as the Austrian-born US economist Ludwig von Mises (p.147) later said, "the bungling entrepreneur" would soon be driven from that market by losses, and the unemployed resources would be reallocated to more profitable areas of the economy. In fact, it is impossible to overproduce overall, because human wants are far greater than our ability to produce commodities.

Say's law has become a forum for conflict between the classical and the Keynesian economists. The former, such as Say, believe that production, or the supply side of the economy, is the most important factor in growing an economy. Keynesians argue that growth comes only with increased demand.

Why keep money?

In his 1936 masterpiece *The General Theory of Employment*, John Maynard Keynes (p.161) attacked Say's law, focusing on the role of money within the economy. Say had suggested that all money earned is spent on purchasing other commodities. In other words the economy works as if it were based on a system of barter. Keynes, however, suggested that people might sometimes hold money for reasons other than for

buying goods. They might, for instance, want to save some of their income. If these savings were not borrowed by others (such as through a bank) and invested in the economy (as capital for running a business, perhaps), the money would no longer be circulating. As people hold on to their money, demand for goods eventually becomes lower than the value of the goods produced. This state of "negative demand" is known as "demand deficiency," and Keynes said it would lead to pervasive unemployment.

Given the dire state of the world economy during the Great Depression of the early 1930s, Keynes's argument seemed a powerful one, especially when contrasted with a world based on Say's law, which said that unemployment would only occur in some industries for a short time. ▪

Say believed that supply and demand operate through a type of barter. We swap the money we earn for goods we want. In this image meat is bartered for vegetables in an Incan marketplace.

Jean-Baptiste Say

The son of a French Protestant textile merchant, Jean-Baptiste Say was born in Lyons, France, in 1767. At the age of 18 he moved to England, where he spent two years apprenticed to a merchant before returning to Paris to work at an insurance company. He welcomed the French Revolution of 1789, both for its ending of the religious persecution of the protestant Hugenots, and for its removal of an essentially feudal economy, opening up more prospects for commerce.

In 1794, Say became editor of a political magazine in which he promoted the ideas of Adam Smith. In 1799, he was invited to join the French government, but Napoleon rejected some of his views, and Say's work was censored until 1814. During this time he made a fortune by setting up a cotton factory. In his later years he lectured on economics in Paris. He died after a series of strokes in 1832, aged 66.

Key works

1803 *A Treatise on Political Economy*
1815 *England and the English*
1828 *Complete Course of Practical Political Economy*

BORROW NOW, TAX LATER

BORROWING AND DEBT

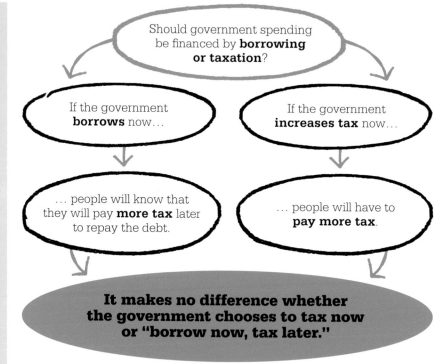

Should government spending be financed by **borrowing or taxation**?

If the government **borrows** now…

If the government **increases tax** now…

… people will know that they will pay **more tax** later to repay the debt.

… people will have to **pay more tax**.

It makes no difference whether the government chooses to tax now or "borrow now, tax later."

Should government spending be financed by borrowing or taxation? This question was first addressed in detail by British economist David Ricardo during Britain's expensive Napoleonic wars against France (1799–1815). In his 1817 book *Principles of Political Economy and Taxation*, Ricardo argued that the method of financing should make no difference. Taxpayers ought to realize that government borrowing today will lead to more taxation in the future. In either case they will be taxed, so they should set aside

See also: Economic man 52–53 ▪ The tax burden 64–65 ▪ The Keynesian multiplier 164–65 ▪ Monetarist policy 196–201 ▪ Saving to spend 204–05 ▪ Rational expectations 244–47

savings that are equivalent to the amount they would have been taxed today in order to meet that eventuality. Ricardo suggested that people understand a government's budget constraints and continue to spend in the same way regardless of its decision to tax or borrow because they know these will ultimately cost them the same. This idea became known as Ricardian equivalence.

Imagine a family with a gambling father who resorts to borrowing from his sons. The father tells his sons that he will let them keep their money this month because he has borrowed from his friend Alex. The happy-go-lucky younger son, Tom, spends his extra cash. The wise older son, James, realizes that next month, Alex's loan will have to be repaid with interest, at which point his father will probably ask him for money. James hides away today's extra cash, knowing he will have to give it to his father in a month. James has recognized that his overall wealth hasn't changed so he has no reason to alter his spending today.

Ricardo was theorizing, and did not suggest that Ricardian equivalence would ever be apparent in the real world. He believed that ordinary citizens suffer from the same fiscal illusion as Tom in our example, and will spend the money on hand. However, some modern economists argue that citizens suffer no such illusions.

The modern debate
The idea reemerged in an article by US economist Robert Barro (1944–) in 1974, and modern analysis has focused on examining the conditions under which people spend regardless of taxation or borrowing.

One assumption is that people are rational decision makers and have perfect foresight; they know that spending now means taxes later. However, this is unlikely to be the case. Borrowing and lending must also take place at identical interest rates without transaction costs.

A further problem is that human life is finite. If people are self-interested, they are unlikely to care about taxes that will be imposed after they die. Barro suggested, however, that parents care about their children and often leave bequests, partly so that their children can pay any tax liabilities that arise after the parents' deaths. In this way individuals factor into their decision making the impact of taxes that they expect to be imposed even after they die.

Government spending
Ricardian equivalence, which is sometimes known as debt neutrality, is a hot topic today because of the high spending, borrowing, and taxation of modern governments. Ricardo's insight has been used by new classical

economists to argue against Keynesian policies—government spending to increase demand and drive growth. They claim that if people know that a government is spending money to lift an economy out of depression, their rational expectations will ensure they anticipate greater taxes in the future so they will not blindly respond to the increased amount of money in the system now. However, the practical evidence—for or against—is inconclusive. ▪

The Greek state was forced to borrow large sums in 2011 to avoid bankruptcy. The civil unrest that followed made it clear that there is a limit to which a government can borrow and tax.

New classical macroeconomics

US economists Robert Barro, Robert Lucas, and Thomas Sargent formed the school of new classical macroeconomics in the early 1970s. Its key tenets are the assumption of rational expectations (pp.244–47) and market clearing—the idea that prices will spontaneously adjust to a new position of equilibrium. New classical theorists claim that this applies in the labor market: wage levels are set through the mutual adjustment of supply (number of people seeking work) and demand (number of people needed). Under this view everyone who wants to work can, if they accept the "going wage." Therefore, all unemployment is voluntary. Rational expectations claims that people look to the future as well as the past when making decisions so they cannot be fooled by a government when it chooses to borrow or tax.

THE ECONOMY IS A YO-YO
BOOM AND BUST

Business cycles are the shift between strong economic growth, described as a boom or expansion period, and periods of economic decline or stagnation. They are often referred to as cycles of boom and bust. The Swiss historian Jean-Charles Sismondi was the first to identify the occurrence of periodic economic crises, but it was the work of a later economist, the Frenchman Charles Dunoyer (1786–1862), who revealed their cyclical form. Sismondi challenged the "market knows best" orthodoxy of Adam Smith (p.61), Jean-Baptiste Say (p.75), and David Ricardo (p.84).

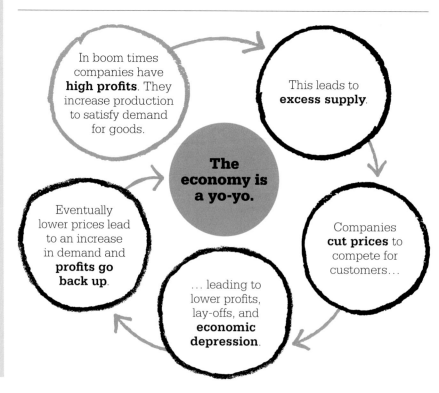

In boom times companies have **high profits**. They increase production to satisfy demand for goods.

This leads to **excess supply**.

The economy is a yo-yo.

Companies **cut prices** to compete for customers…

… leading to lower profits, lay-offs, and **economic depression**.

Eventually lower prices lead to an increase in demand and **profits go back up**.

See also: Free market economics 54–61 ▪ The Keynesian multiplier 164–65 ▪ Financial crises 296–301 ▪ Housing and the economic cycle 330–31

Skyscrapers are often built during times of excessive optimism, a sure sign that the economy is overheating. By the time they are finished, the economy has often crashed.

They believed that if the market is left to its own devices, an economic equilibrium is quickly and easily achieved, leading to full employment. Sismondi thought a sort of equilibrium would eventually be reached, but only after a "frightful amount of suffering."

Before Sismondi published his *New Principles of Political Economy* in 1819, economists had either overlooked short-term economic booms and busts or had attributed them to external events, such as war. Sismondi showed that short-term economic movements are due to the natural results of market forces—overproduction and underconsumption—caused by growing inequality during booms.

Fueling the boom

As economies grow and businesses do well, workers are able to demand wage increases and buy more of the goods they produce. This fuels the economy's boom. As more and more goods are sold, companies expand, hiring more workers to produce more goods. The new workers then have money to buy goods, and the boom continues.

Competition means that all companies will increase production until supply outstrips demand, Sismondi argued. This forces companies to cut prices in order to attract customers, triggering falling profits, falling wages, and lay-offs among the workforce—in other words an economic crash followed by a recession. Companies begin to recover once prices become cheap enough to stimulate demand and credit becomes more available, starting the cycle all over again.

An early crisis that confirmed these economic cycles was the Panic of 1825. This stock-market crash was one of the first documented crises caused solely by internal economic events. It was precipitated by speculative investments in Poyais —a fictional country invented by a con man to attract investments— and the repercussions were felt in markets across the world.

Sismondi argued against the laissez-faire approach of Adam Smith and claimed that government intervention is necessary to regulate the progress of wealth and avoid these periodic crises.

The discovery of these cycles enabled economists to analyze the economy in a new way and to devise strategies for trying to avoid crashes and recessions. Keynes built on Sismondi's and Dunoyer's work to develop his own theories, which were to make up one of the world's dominant economic approaches in the 20th century. ▪

Bull and bear markets

As whole economies grow and contract, markets within them rise and fall. Markets that show sustained price rises are sometimes known as bull markets; those in which prices are falling as bear markets. These labels are usually applied to assets such as shares, bonds, or houses. Bull markets—for example, a rising stock market—often occur during periods of economic growth. Investors become more optimistic about economic prospects and buy shares in companies, so fuelling rising asset values. As the economy falters, the process goes into reverse. Investors become "bearish" and start to sell assets as the market falls. US stocks were in a bull market in the 1990s with the dot-com boom. A major bear market took place during the Great Depression of the 1930s.

> Universal competition, or the effort to always produce more, and always at a lower price… has been a dangerous system.
> **Jean-Charles Sismondi**

TRADE IS BENEFICIAL FOR ALL

COMPARATIVE ADVANTAGE

IN CONTEXT

FOCUS
Global economy

KEY THINKER
David Ricardo (1772–1823)

BEFORE
433 BCE The Athenians impose trade sanctions on the Megarians in one of the first recorded trade wars.

1549 John Hales, an English politician, expresses the widely held view that free trade is bad for the country.

AFTER
1965 US economist Mancur Olson shows that governments respond more to the appeal of a concentrated group than one that is more dispersed.

1967 Swedish economists Bertil Ohlin and Eli Heckscher develop Ricardo's trade theory to examine how a comparative advantage might change over time.

Making a product **entails costs**. One of these costs is time.

Even if Country A can do everything better than Country B, it will profit most by **focusing on the things it does best**. It is too costly to sacrifice time on something it does less well.

This allows Country B, which is good (but not the world's best) at making the products Country A does not make, a chance to make them **without undue competition**.

Both countries benefit from a comparative advantage, which makes the most efficient use of their time and resources.

Overall, **more goods are produced**, giving consumers a wider range of products at lower prices.

Trade is beneficial for all.

The ideas of the renowned 18th-century British economist David Ricardo were clearly shaped by the world he inhabited and by his personal life. He lived in London, England, at a time when mercantilism (pp.34–35) was the dominant economic view. This held that international trade should be heavily restricted. As a result governments introduced policies that aimed to increase exports and decrease imports in an attempt to enrich the nation through an inflow of gold. In England the policy dated back to Elizabethan times. Ricardo thought that in the long run such protectionist policies were more likely to restrict the ability of the country to increase its wealth.

Early trade protection

Ricardo was particularly concerned by the introduction of a British tax known as the Corn Laws. During the Napoleonic Wars (1799–1815) it was not possible to import wheat from Europe so the price of wheat in Britain had risen. As a result of this price increase, many landowners increased the proportion of their lands dedicated to growing crops. However, as the war began to falter in 1812, the price of wheat fell back. As a result, the landowners—who also controlled Parliament— passed the Corn Laws at the end of the war in 1815 to restrict the importation of foreign wheat and place a "floor," a bottom price, on grain.

The laws protected farmers but also pushed the price of bread beyond what poorer people could pay at a time when newly returned soldiers and sailors were unable to find work.

50% **20%**

If Worker A is 20 percent better at making hats but 50 percent better at making shoes, he should focus on shoes. That is the most profitable way to use his time.

Worker B is not better than Worker A at anything, but he is better at making hats than shoes. If he makes hats, he will have a competitive advantage and can trade with Worker A for shoes.

Ricardo vigorously opposed the Corn Laws, despite being a wealthy landowner himself. He claimed that the laws would make Britain poorer, and developed a theory that has become the mainstay for all those wishing to justify free trade between countries.

Comparative advantage

Adam Smith (p.61) had pointed out that the climate differences between Portugal and Britain meant they would benefit from trade. A worker in Portugal could produce more wine than a worker in Britain, who in turn could produce more wool than a worker in Portugal. Any person or state able to produce more per unit

In 1819, a crowd of 80,000 gathered in Manchester, England, to protest against the Corn Laws, which kept the price of wheat high by limiting imports. The protest was brutally suppressed.

of resources than a competitor is said to have an "absolute advantage." Smith said that both Britain and Portugal would profit most by specializing in what they did best and trading the surplus. Ricardo's contribution was to extend Smith's argument to examine whether

countries would benefit from specializing and trading when one party had an absolute advantage in both goods. Would it be worth trading if one country could produce both more wine and more wool per worker than the other country?

Another way of looking at this is to consider whether a person who is better at making both hats and shoes than someone else should split his time between the two jobs or choose one job and then trade with the less-skilled worker, who makes the other product (see diagram, left). Suppose that the superior worker is 20 percent better at making hats, but 50 percent better at making shoes—it will be in the interest of both of them if he works exclusively at making shoes (the product he really excels in), and the inferior man works in making hats (the product he is least bad at making).

The logic behind this argument has to do with the relative costs of making a product in terms of the amount of production time taken or lost. Because the superior worker is so good at making shoes, the cost of his making hats is high—he would »

The increased importation of tires from China (left) led the US to impose trade restrictions in 2009. This, in turn, led to a full-blown trade battle and a deterioration in diplomatic relations.

have to forfeit a lot of valuable shoe production. Although in absolute terms the inferior worker is worse at making shoes and hats than the superior worker, his relative cost when making hats is lower than for the superior worker. This is because he forfeits less shoe production per hat than the superior worker would. The inferior worker is therefore said to have a "comparative advantage" in hats, while the superior worker has a comparative advantage in shoes. When countries specialize in goods for which they have a comparative advantage, more goods are produced in total, and trade delivers more and cheaper goods to both nations.

Comparative advantage resolves a paradox highlighted by Adam Smith—that countries that are inferior at producing goods (they are said to have an "absolute disadvantage" in them) can nonetheless export them profitably.

20th-century advantage
What determines comparative advantage? Swedish economists Eli Heckscher and Bertil Ohlin argued that it comes from countries' relative abundance of capital and labor. Capital-rich countries will have a comparative advantage in capital-intensive products such as machines. Labor-rich countries will have a comparative advantage in labor-intensive products such as farming goods. The result is that countries tend to export goods that use their abundant factor of production; capital-abundant nations such as the US are most likely, therefore, to export manufactured goods. Heckscher and Ohlin's analysis led to another prediction. Not only would trade tend to reduce the differences in prices of goods in different countries, it would also reduce wage differences: the specialization in labor-intensive sectors by labor-abundant economies would tend to push up wage rates, while an effect in the other direction would be seen in the capital-abundant country. So despite the overall increase in the

David Ricardo

Considered one of the world's greatest economic theorists, David Ricardo was born in 1772. His parents moved to England from Holland, and at the age of 14 Ricardo began working for his father, a stockbroker. Aged 21, Ricardo eloped with a Quaker, Priscilla Wilkinson. Religious differences between the families resulted in both sides abandoning the couple, so Ricardo started his own stockbroking firm. He made a fortune betting on a French defeat at Waterloo (1815) by buying English government bonds. Ricardo mixed with notable economists of his day, including Thomas Malthus (p.69) and John Stuart Mill (p.95). He retired from the stock exchange in 1819, and became a member of Parliament. He died suddenly of an ear infection in 1823, leaving an estate worth more than $120 million in real terms today.

Key works

1810 *The High Price of Bullion*
1814 *Essay on the Influence of a Low Price of Corn*
1817 *On the Principles of Political Economy and Taxation*

> The diminution of money in one country, and its increase in another, do not operate on the price of one commodity only, but on the prices of all.
> **David Ricardo**

short run, ultimately there may be losers as well as winners, and consequently opposition to the opening up of trade.

The cries for protectionism are as loud today as they were in Ricardo's time. In 2009, China accused the US of "rampant protectionism" for imposing heavy taxes on imported Chinese car tires. The decision to increase tariffs came after pressure from US workers, who had seen tire imports grow from 14 to 46 million from 2004–08, reducing US tire output, causing factory closures, and creating unemployment. However, the US had previously accused China of unfairly subsidizing its own tire industry, so tensions mounted. China's response was to threaten retaliatory increases in import taxes on US cars and poultry. Tariffs produce effects that ripple through economies. Any protection gained for US tire producers from the tariffs on tires, for example, was counteracted by other negative impacts. Higher tire prices increased the costs of US cars, making them less competitive and reducing the numbers bought by US consumers. The retaliation by China also

damaged US export industries. The jobs of some US tire workers may have been saved, but in the wider economy many more jobs were lost.

Protectionism today

The US economist Mancur Olson has helped to explain why politicians continue to impose policies that are likely to damage the overall economy, even though the costs are widely known. He points out that those against the tariffs—a small number of large domestic producers and their workers—suffer a visible impact from cheap imports. However, the potentially larger number of consumers who have to pay higher prices because of tariffs and those workers in affiliated industries who might lose their jobs through connected impacts are dispersed around the economy.

Contemporary trade

Today, most economists support the basic Ricardian position on trade and, in particular, believe that it helped today's industrialized countries. US economists David Dollar and Aart Kraay have argued that over the last few decades trade has helped developing countries to grow and reduce poverty. They claim that the countries that cut their tariffs have grown faster and have seen less poverty.

Other economists have questioned whether trade always helps developing countries. The US economist Joseph Stiglitz (p.338) argues that developing countries often suffer from market failures and institutional weaknesses that might make a too rapid liberalization of trade costly for them.

There are also contradictions between theory and practice. When the government of India removed tariffs on imports of cheap palm oil from Indonesia, for instance, it had the positive effect of raising the living standards of hundreds of millions of Indians, in line with Ricardo's theory, but it destroyed the livelihoods of 1,000,000 farmers who grew peanuts for oil, which was now passed over for palm oil. In a perfect Ricardian world the peanut farmers would simply transfer into the production of other goods, but in practice they can't because their investment in capital is immobile—a machine that processes peanuts has no other use.

Ricardo's critics argue that in the long run these kinds of impacts might hamper the industrialization and diversification of poorer countries. Moreover, although rich industrialized countries became successful traders, they did not practice free trade when they were first developing. How countries build up comparative advantage over the long run may be more complex than Ricardo's model suggests. Some argue that Europe and then later the Asian Tigers (pp.282–87) built it up through trade protection in which skills were developed before trade opened up. ∎

Goods made in Asia are transported to Western countries in vast container ships. It is estimated that 75 percent of goods in a typical US shopping cart are exported to the US from Asia.

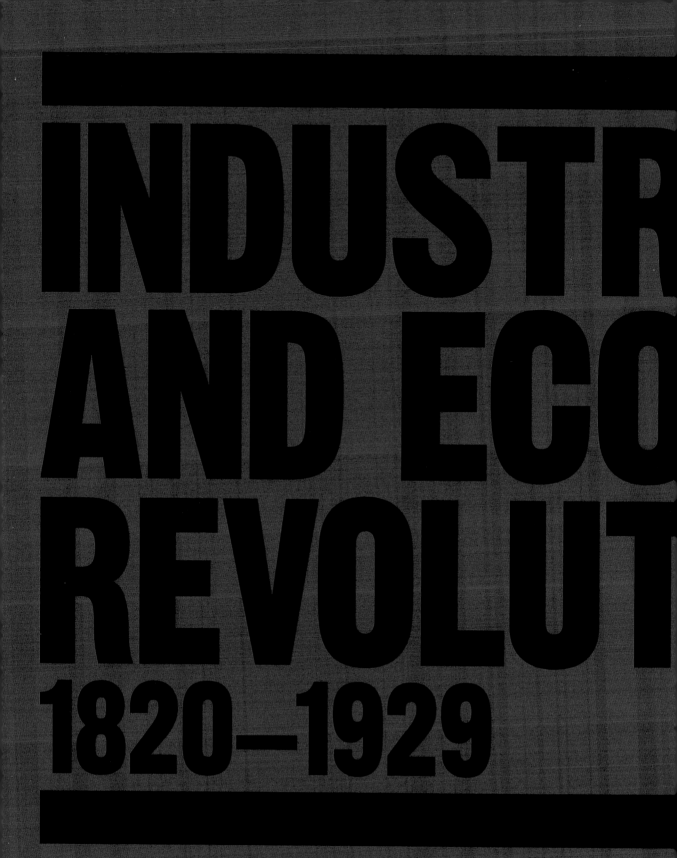

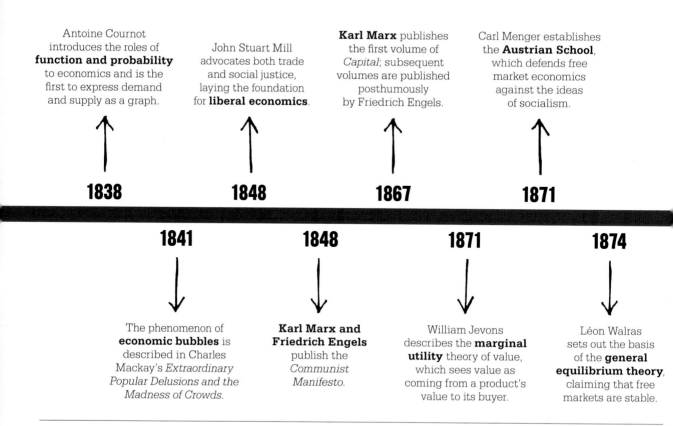

Antoine Cournot introduces the roles of **function and probability** to economics and is the first to express demand and supply as a graph.

John Stuart Mill advocates both trade and social justice, laying the foundation for **liberal economics**.

Karl Marx publishes the first volume of *Capital*; subsequent volumes are published posthumously by Friedrich Engels.

Carl Menger establishes the **Austrian School**, which defends free market economics against the ideas of socialism.

1838   **1848**   **1867**   **1871**

1841   **1848**   **1871**   **1874**

The phenomenon of **economic bubbles** is described in Charles Mackay's *Extraordinary Popular Delusions and the Madness of Crowds*.

Karl Marx and Friedrich Engels publish the *Communist Manifesto*.

William Jevons describes the **marginal utility** theory of value, which sees value as coming from a product's value to its buyer.

Léon Walras sets out the basis of the **general equilibrium theory**, claiming that free markets are stable.

By the early 19th century the effects of the Industrial Revolution were spreading from Britain to Europe and across North America, transforming agricultural nations into industrial economies. The change had been rapid and dramatic, bringing about a fundamental shift in the structure of economies. The focus had shifted from the merchants who traded in goods to the producers, the owners of capital. As well as a new way of thinking about the economy, capitalism also brought with it new social and political issues.

Distorting the market

Most noticeable of the social changes was the emergence of a new "ruling class" of industrialist producers, and a steady growth in the number of firms producing goods, many of which were offering shares of their business for sale in the stock markets. These provided the competitive market that was the focus of the "classical" view of economics, in which the operations of the market are central. However, as market economies developed and grew, new problems began to emerge. For example, as Adam Smith (p.61) had warned in 1776, there was a danger that large producers would dominate the market and operate either as monopolies or as cartels, fixing prices at a high level and keeping production low. Although regulation could prevent such practices, in instances where only a few producers operated, they could easily develop strategies to distort the competitiveness of the market.

Smith had assumed that men behaved rationally in an economy, but this also came into question as investors rushed to buy shares in companies whose worth had been exaggerated. This caused bubbles, contradicting the idea of a stable economy based on reasoned behavior. Despite this, some economists, such as Léon Walras (p.120) and Vilfredo Pareto (p.131), argued that the market economy would always tend toward equilibrium, which would in turn determine the levels of production and prices. Their contemporary Alfred Marshall (p.110) explained supply and demand and how these and prices interact in a system of perfect competition.

The question of price was one that concerned many economists at the time because it affected both

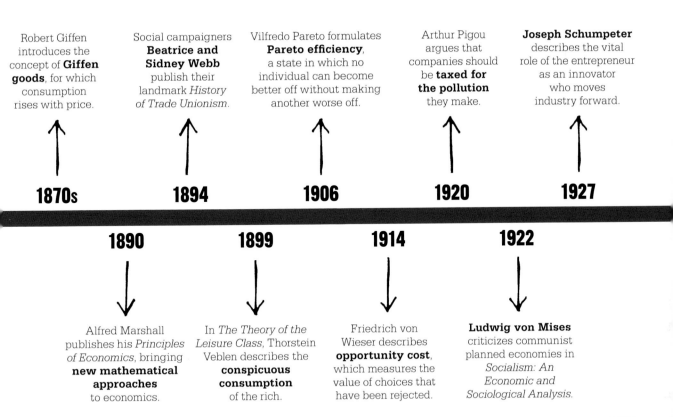

Robert Giffen introduces the concept of **Giffen goods**, for which consumption rises with price.

Social campaigners **Beatrice and Sidney Webb** publish their landmark *History of Trade Unionism*.

Vilfredo Pareto formulates **Pareto efficiency**, a state in which no individual can become better off without making another worse off.

Arthur Pigou argues that companies should be **taxed for the pollution** they make.

Joseph Schumpeter describes the vital role of the entrepreneur as an innovator who moves industry forward.

1870s   1894   1906   1920   1927

1890   1899   1914   1922

Alfred Marshall publishes his *Principles of Economics*, bringing **new mathematical approaches** to economics.

In *The Theory of the Leisure Class*, Thorstein Veblen describes the **conspicuous consumption** of the rich.

Friedrich von Wieser describes **opportunity cost**, which measures the value of choices that have been rejected.

Ludwig von Mises criticizes communist planned economies in *Socialism: An Economic and Sociological Analysis*.

producers and consumers in the new capitalist society. Taking their lead from the moral philosophers of the previous generation, they began to see the value of goods in terms of their utility (the satisfaction they would give), rather than the labor that added value to raw materials. The idea of marginal utility—the gain brought about by the consumption of a particular product—was explained in mathematical terms by William Jevons (p.115).

Marx's theory of value
The theory that the value of a product is determined by the labor involved in producing it still had some adherents, particularly as it concerned not the producers or consumers so much as the workforce producing the goods

for capitalist employers. Looking at value in this light, Karl Marx argued that the inequalities of a market economy amounted to an exploitation of the working class by the owners of capital. In the *Communist Manifesto* and his analysis of capitalism *Capital*, Marx argued for a proletarian revolution to replace capitalism with what he saw as the next stage in economic development: a socialist state in which the means of production are owned by the workers, and an eventual abolition of private property.

Although Marx's ideas were subsequently adopted in many parts of the world, market economies continued to operate elsewhere. Generally, economists continued to defend capitalism as the best means of ensuring

prosperity—although tempered to some extent with measures to compensate for its injustices. Following a mathematical approach to economics that focused on supply and demand, and as a reaction against the ideas of socialism, an Austrian School of economic thought emerged, stressing the creative power of the capitalist system.

The free market economy was soon to receive some hard knocks after the Wall Street Crash of 1929. However, the theories of neoclassical economists, and the Austrian School in particular, later resurfaced as the model for economies in the Western world in the late 20th century and even came to replace most of the world's communist planned economies. ∎

HOW MUCH SHOULD I PRODUCE, GIVEN THE COMPETITION?

EFFECTS OF LIMITED COMPETITION

IN CONTEXT

FOCUS
Markets and firms

KEY THINKERS
Antoine Augustin Cournot
(1801–77)
Joseph Bertrand (1822–1900)

BEFORE
1668 German scientist Johann Becher discusses the impact of competition and monopoly in his *Political Discourse*.

1776 Adam Smith describes how perfect competition maximizes social welfare.

AFTER
1883 French mathematician Joseph Bertrand changes the strategic choices in Cournot's model from quantity to price.

1951 US economist John Nash publishes the general definition of equilibrium for game theory, using Cournot's duopoly as his first example.

By the second half of the 17th century economists had begun to observe the effects in markets of monopolies and of fierce competition. They found that monopolies tended to restrict output to keep prices and profits high. Where there was plenty of competition, prices were driven down to the level of costs, profits were low, and output was high. French economist Antoine Cournot wanted to find out what happened when there were only a few firms selling similar products.

Dueling duopolies
Cournot created his model based on a duopoly of two firms selling identical spring water to consumers. The two firms are not allowed to form a cartel by working together,

If there are just two competing firms (a duopoly) producing **identical** goods…

… each firm knows that the **other firm's output** will affect their own profits.

Each firm reacts by **selecting** its best output given the level of output the other firm chooses (plotted on a reaction curve).

The market will be in a **Cournot equilibrium** where the two reaction curves meet.

This is how much the firm should produce, given the competition.

See also: Cartels and collusion 70–73 ▪ Monopolies 92–97 ▪ The competitive market 126–29 ▪ Game theory 234–41

no other firms can enter the industry (because there are no other natural springs), and each firm has to decide, simultaneously, how many bottles of water to supply.

The total output of the industry is the sum of the two firms' output decisions. Each firm must choose the output that maximizes its profit based on what it thinks the other firm's output will be. If Firm A thinks that Firm B will produce nothing, Firm A will select the low output of a monopolist to maximize profits. On the other hand if Firm A thinks that Firm B will produce a high output, Firm A may choose to produce nothing—because prices would fall too far to make production worthwhile. Cournot represented the decisions of both firms on a "reaction curve." The equilibrium of the market is where the two reaction curves intersect. At this point each firm is selling the most profitable amount given what the other firm is doing. This notion of equilibrium became known as the Nash equilibrium, and it is a central plank of game theory, the branch of modern economics that analyzes strategic interaction between firms and individuals.

Cournot used mathematics to find this equilibrium and prove that the duopolists would choose an output that was higher than would occur in monopoly, but lower than with perfect competition. In other words a few firms would be better for society than a monopolist, but worse than perfect competition.

From this starting point, Cournot extended the model to show how, if the number of firms increases, the industry output reassuringly moves closer to the level expected for perfect competition. Cournot's

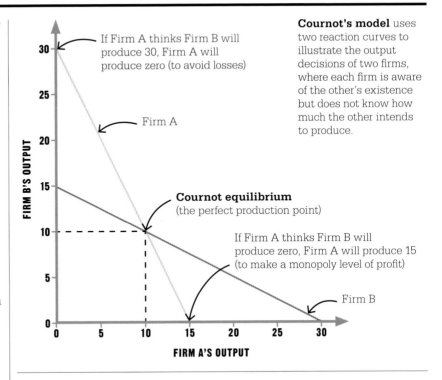

If Firm A thinks Firm B will produce 30, Firm A will produce zero (to avoid losses)

Firm A

Cournot equilibrium
(the perfect production point)

If Firm A thinks Firm B will produce zero, Firm A will produce 15 (to make a monopoly level of profit)

Firm B

Cournot's model uses two reaction curves to illustrate the output decisions of two firms, where each firm is aware of the other's existence but does not know how much the other intends to produce.

model was developed by French economist Joseph Bertrand, who showed that if firms choose by their desired price levels rather than output, the equilibrium for duopolists equals that of perfect competition. This is because any firm that sets a high price will be undercut by another, who will then steal all its buyers. In this way the price will be driven to the most competitive level. ▪

Antoine Cournot

An insatiable reader, Antoine Augustin Cournot was born in France in 1801. Although relatively poor, he studied mathematics at one of the best schools in the country and completed a PhD in engineering. After spending some time as a private tutor and as a secretary for one of Napoleon's generals, he became a university lecturer and then professor. Cournot was plagued by eye problems but managed to publish several works that pioneered the use of mathematics in economics, before going blind. His work was not well received in his lifetime because of its reliance on novel mathematical notation. Today he is regarded as a profound thinker who advanced prophetic ideas.

Key works

1838 *Researches into the Mathematical Principles of the Theory of Wealth*
1863 *Principles of the Theory of Wealth*

PHONE CALLS COST MORE WITHOUT COMPETITION

MONOPOLIES

A monopoly is a situation where one firm has control of a particular market, such as the cell phone market. The firm may be the only supplier of a product or service, or it may have a dominating market share. In many countries a firm is said to have a monopoly if it controls more than 25 percent of a market.

The suggestion that monopolies can cause the price of goods to be higher than they would be if many companies were supplying them has existed for millennia. It dates back at least as far as Aristotle (384–322 BCE), who warned about the problem in a story about the Greek philosopher Thales of Miletus. The public taunted Thales for practicing philosophy, which they said was a useless profession that made no money. To prove them wrong, Thales bought up all the local olive presses in the winter when they were cheap, and then—using his monopoly power—sold them at very high prices in the summer when the presses were needed. In doing so he made himself rich. For Thales the moral was that philosophers could be rich if they wanted. For economists the story warns of the potential power of monopoly.

Market power
In 1848, the English political scientist John Stuart Mill published his *Principles of Political Economy*. It drew together much of the thinking about whether a lack of competition caused prices to rise. The general view was that some industries were likely to tend toward a lack of competition. This trend was created either through artificial means, such as the introduction of a tax by governments on imported goods, or through natural means, as a consequence of firms growing ever larger. Large firms had begun to dominate the market because late 19th-century industry required ever-increasing amounts of capital. The firms that could grow by capturing enough of the market to finance the necessary investment, had the ability to use their market power to drive their smaller competitors out of business and to charge higher prices.

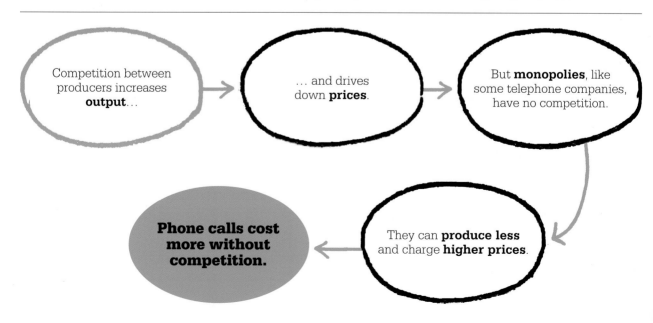

Competition between producers increases **output**…

… and drives down **prices**.

But **monopolies**, like some telephone companies, have no competition.

They can **produce less** and charge **higher prices**.

Phone calls cost more without competition.

See also: Cartels and collusion 70–73 ▪ The competitive market 126–29 ▪ Economies of scale 132 ▪ Creative destruction 148–49

During the Industrial Revolution coal, railways, and water supply all showed a tendency toward concentrated ownership. In mining the ownership of the land was concentrated in just a few hands. In the case of railways and water supply there was no alternative to a limited number of firms offering services because the scale of the infrastructure required was so great that if there were any more than a few firms, no one would be able to cover their costs. Like Adam Smith (p.61) before him, Mill believed that these features of markets did not inevitably lead to monopoly. The most likely outcome was collusion between firms, allowing them to fix high prices. Such arrangements would lead to high costs for consumers in the same way as monopolies.

Monopoly workers

Mill realized that it is not only within the goods market that a lack of competition is able to push prices up. Monopoly effects can emerge in the labor market too. He pointed to the case of goldsmiths, who earned much higher wages than workers of a similar skill because they were perceived to be trustworthy—a characteristic that is rare and not easily provable. This created a significant barrier to entry so that those working with gold could demand a monopoly price for their services. Mill realized that the goldsmiths' situation was not an isolated case. He noted that large sections of the working classes were barred from entering skilled professions because they entailed many years of education and training. The cost of supporting someone through this process was out of reach for most families, so those who could afford it were able to enjoy wages far above what **»**

The railways were an example of a monopoly industry at the time Mill was writing. New lines were expensive and impractical on routes that were already serviced by existing companies.

John Stuart Mill

Born in London in 1806, John Stuart Mill grew up in a wealthy family that was to become a great intellectual dynasty. His father was an overdemanding parent, who educated Mill at home on a difficult and accelerated program that included Greek from the age of three. The aim was for Mill to carry on and develop his father's work on philosophy. The pressure of his upbringing was at least partly responsible for the mental health problems Mill suffered in his early 20s.

One of the great minds of the day, he was willing to speak out in defense of difficult and unpopular causes such as the French Revolution and women's rights. He was also an eloquent opponent of slavery. A 20-year affair with Harriet Taylor, whom he credited with inspiring much of his written work, caused scandal in his own private life. He died in 1873, aged 66.

Key works

1848 *Principles of Political Economy*
1861 *Utilitarianism*
1869 *The Subjection of Women*

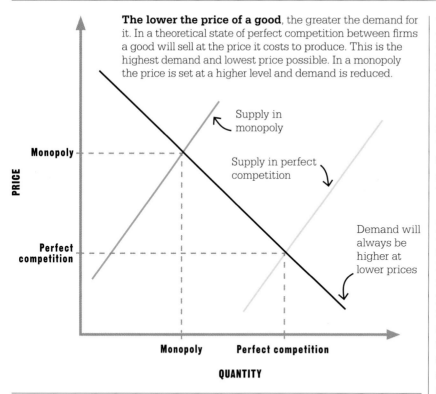

The lower the price of a good, the greater the demand for it. In a theoretical state of perfect competition between firms a good will sell at the price it costs to produce. This is the highest demand and lowest price possible. In a monopoly the price is set at a higher level and demand is reduced.

Supply in monopoly

Supply in perfect competition

Demand will always be higher at lower prices

PRICE

Monopoly

Perfect competition

Monopoly   Perfect competition

QUANTITY

might be expected. Similarly, some historians have viewed the guilds of the medieval era as an example of privileged craftsmen attempting to shut out competition from other workers.

From the late 1890s British economist Alfred Marshall (p.110) rigorously analyzed the effects of monopolies on prices and on consumers' welfare. Marshall was interested in determining whether the higher price and lower output that result from monopolies cause a loss in total welfare for society. In his *Principles of Economics*, Marshall formulated the concept of consumer surplus. This is the difference between the maximum amount that a consumer would be willing to pay for a good and the amount he actually pays. Suppose the consumer buys an apple for 20 cents when he would have been willing to pay 50 cents.

His consumer surplus from the purchase of the apple is 30 cents. In a market with many firms, they compete on price and together supply an amount of apples that generates a certain amount of overall consumer surplus. For an apple sold to the last consumer his

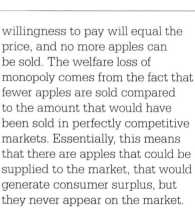

Monopolists, by keeping the market constantly understocked… sell their commodities much above the natural price.
Adam Smith

willingness to pay will equal the price, and no more apples can be sold. The welfare loss of monopoly comes from the fact that fewer apples are sold compared to the amount that would have been sold in perfectly competitive markets. Essentially, this means that there are apples that could be supplied to the market, that would generate consumer surplus, but they never appear on the market.

Advantages of monopoly

Monopolies also create more complex price and welfare effects. Marshall suggested that a monopolist might actually cut its prices to attract customers to its phone network, for example, since people will likely keep using the service once it is connected, even though rival technologies such as cell phones offer alternatives that are at least as good.

Some economists have pointed out that monopolies can have benign effects. In many markets a monopoly would have lower costs than the total costs of a set of smaller firms because a monopolist would spend less on advertising and make full use of economies of scale. For these reasons a monopolist may enjoy higher profits even when its price is lower than would be the case if many firms—with higher costs—were competing. In this case the lower prices might help consumers and help to drive economic growth.

In a similar fashion large firms can attempt to gain monopoly profits, driving out rivals by aggressively cutting prices in the short run. Economists call this predatory pricing. In the long run it can hurt consumers as the market becomes monopolized. However, in the 1950s and 60s US economist William Baumol claimed that it

Operators work the switchboards of the AT&T company in New York in the 1940s. Because of the company's size and dominance, it was considered to be a natural monopoly.

does not matter if there is a monopoly as long as there are no barriers to entering and exiting the market—the mere threat of competition means that the monopoly will set the price at a competitive level. This is because a higher price might attract new entrants to the market, who would take market share from the monopoly. For this reason prices may be no higher under a monopoly than in a market with many competing firms.

Natural monopolies
One argument that began to take shape during Marshall's lifetime is that some monopolies are "natural" because of the enormous cost advantages of having a single firm. Many public utilities are natural monopolies, including telephone networks, gas, and water. The fixed cost of setting up a network of gas distribution pipes is huge, compared to the cost of pumping an extra amount of gas.

This idea led to an acceptance of national monopolies in the public utilities in many countries. Even so, governments began to intervene in these markets to counteract the possible monopoly effects. The problem is that in the case of a natural monopoly, the fixed costs are so high that compelling the firm to charge a competitive price might make the firm unprofitable. Solutions to this problem include the wholesale nationalization of industries or the establishment of regulatory organizations that place limits on price increases, helping consumers but also ensuring the economic viability of the industry.

Mainstream economists argue that monopolized markets fall short of the perfectly competitive ideal. This view has led to government anti-trust policies, which seek to move markets toward competitiveness. This has meant the introduction of measures aimed at preventing monopolies from abusing their market power, including the breakup of monopolies and the banning of mergers of firms that would create monopolies.

The modern Austrian School, including US economist Thomas DiLorenzo (1954–), are critical of this approach. Both argue that real market competition is not the passive behavior of perfectly competitive firms operating in a state of equilibrium. It is about cut-throat rivalry between an often small number of large businesses. Competition takes place through price and non-price competition,

In 1998, the US pharmaceutical industry asserted its monopoly on an AIDS drug by taking legal action against the South African government, which had been buying cheaper, generic versions of the drug.

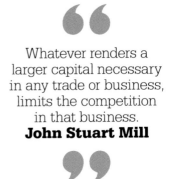

> Whatever renders a larger capital necessary in any trade or business, limits the competition in that business.
> **John Stuart Mill**

through advertising and marketing, and through large firms innovating and creating new products.

Slightly apart from this school of economists, Austrian economist Joseph Schumpeter (p.149) also stressed the dynamic potential of monopoly as firms compete to create new products and dominate entire markets because of the potential profits. What economists agree on is that true competition is good for consumers. It is less certain whether or not monopoly is incompatible with this. In the early 20th century German economist Robert Liefman claimed that "only a peculiar combination of competition and monopoly brings about the greatest possible satisfaction of wants." ∎

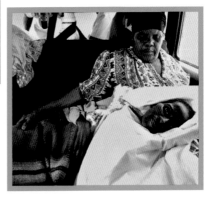

CROWDS BREED COLLECTIVE INSANITY
ECONOMIC BUBBLES

IN CONTEXT

FOCUS
The macroeconomy

KEY THINKER
Charles Mackay (1814–89)

BEFORE
1637 Dutch nurseryman P. Cos publishes *The Tulip Book*, which provides raw data for the future prices of tulips.

AFTER
1947 US economist Herbert Simon writes *Administrative Behavior*, introducing the idea of "bounded rationality"—poor decisions are due to limits in ability, information, and time.

1990 Peter Garber critiques Mackay's work in his essay, *Famous First Bubbles*.

2000 US economist Robert Shiller publishes *Irrational Exuberance*, analyzing the causes and policy interventions that might prevent the occurrence of future economic bubbles.

I n 1841, the Scottish journalist Charles Mackay published *Extraordinary Popular Delusions and the Madness of Crowds*, a classic psychological study of markets and the irrational behavior of people acting in "herds." The book looks at some of the most famous examples of frenzied speculation in history, including Tulipomania (1630s), John Law's Mississippi Scheme (1719–20), and the South Sea Bubble (1720).

Mackay's hypothesis was that crowds acting in a collective frenzy of speculation can cause the prices of commodities to rise far beyond

Hendrik Pot's painting of tulip mania (1640), shows the goddess of flowers riding with drunken, money-weighing men. Other people follow the cart, desperate to keep up with the group.

any intrinsic value they might have. When assets rise in such an uncontrolled way, the situation is called an economic bubble. Like actual bubbles, in an economic bubble prices rise upward but become more and more fragile—and they inevitably burst.

Tulipomania
The Dutch tulip mania of the 1630s is one of the earliest and most notorious instances of an economic bubble. At the beginning of the 17th century tulips from Constantinople became popular with the wealthy of Holland and Germany, and soon everyone wanted them. Tulips were seen to bestow the qualities of wealth and sophistication on their owners, and the Dutch middle class became obsessed with collecting rare varieties. By 1636, the demand for rare species of tulips was so intense that they were traded on Amsterdam's stock exchange.

Many individuals grew suddenly rich. A golden bait hung temptingly out before the people, and everyone—from noblemen to maidservants—rushed to the tulip markets, all imagining that the passion for tulips would last forever. But when the rich stopped planting

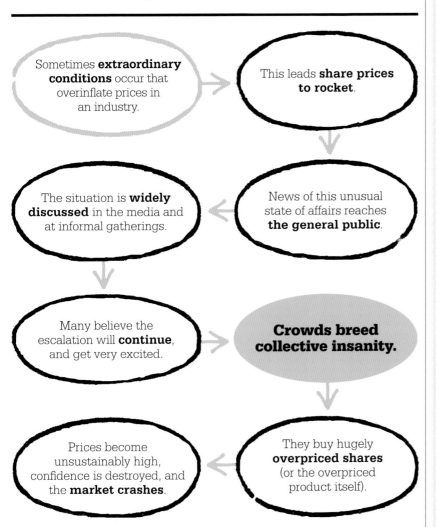

Sometimes **extraordinary conditions** occur that overinflate prices in an industry.

This leads **share prices to rocket**.

The situation is **widely discussed** in the media and at informal gatherings.

News of this unusual state of affairs reaches **the general public**.

Many believe the escalation will **continue**, and get very excited.

Crowds breed collective insanity.

Prices become unsustainably high, confidence is destroyed, and the **market crashes**.

They buy hugely **overpriced shares** (or the overpriced product itself).

tulips, their appeal diminished, and people realized the folly could not continue. Selling became more frantic, confidence plummeted, and the price of tulips collapsed. For those who had borrowed money to invest, it was disastrous.

How bubbles form
US economist Peter Garber claimed that speculators in these situations buy an asset in the full knowledge that the price is far above any "fundamental value" but do so because they expect prices to rise still further before they eventually crash. Since prices cannot rise forever, this involves the irrational belief "that the guy you will sell to is dumber [than you] and will not see the crash coming." However, Garber believes sometimes there are real reasons behind the price rises—such as a fashion for ladies in France to wear rare tulips on their dresses. Nonetheless, in any bubble, the advice remains the same: "Let the buyer beware." ▪

21st-century bubble

The Dotcom Bubble, which burst in March 2000, was the first of the 21st century. It had the classic bubble hallmark of prices being driven purely by speculation rather than by changes in real value (based on output or assets). Investors assumed that the world was about to be changed forever by the internet, so investing in e-commerce seemed to be a once-in-a-lifetime opportunity.

The new companies had no trading history, very low sales, and virtually no profits, yet they attracted hundreds of billions of dollars in investment. The crowd believed that every firm was potentially the next AOL, a firm whose clients jumped from 200,000 to one million in two years, and then climbed at around a million new users each month. Greed overcame fear and people rushed to invest. Between March 2000 and October 2002, more than $7 trillion was wiped off the market value of dotcom shares.

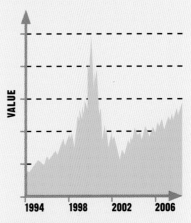

The Dotcom Bubble peaked in 2000. Price rises were so extreme that people everywhere discussed them at dinner tables—a sure sign that a bubble is about to burst.

LET THE RULING CLASSES TREMBLE AT A COMMUNIST REVOLUTION

MARXIST ECONOMICS

IN CONTEXT

FOCUS
Economic systems

KEY THINKER
Karl Marx (1818–83)

BEFORE
1789 Revolution sweeps away the old feudal regime and aristocracy in France.

1816 German thinker Georg Hegel explains his dialectics in *The Science of Logic*.

1848 Revolutions spring up throughout Europe, led by disaffected members of the middle and working classes.

AFTER
1922 The USSR is established on Marxist principles under Vladimir Lenin.

1949 Mao Zedong becomes the founding father of the People's Republic of China.

1989 The fall of the Berlin Wall symbolizes the collapse of Eastern Bloc communism.

Although much of economics is concerned with free market economies, it should not be forgotten that for a large part of the 20th century up to a third of the world was under some form of communist or socialist rule. These states had centralized, or planned, economies. Political philosophers were looking for an alternative to capitalism even as the modern free market economies emerged. However, a truly economic argument for communism was not formulated until the middle of the 19th century, when Karl Marx (p.105) wrote his critique of capitalism.

While Marx's influence is popularly seen as political, he was, perhaps more than anything else, an economist. He believed that the economic organization of society forms the basis for its social and political organization; economics, therefore, drives social change. Marx saw history not in terms of war or colonialism, but as a progression of different economic systems, which gave birth to new forms of social organization.

With the rise of the market came merchants, and with the factory, an industrial proletariat. Feudalism had been replaced by capitalism, which in turn would be supplanted by communism. In his 1848 *Communist Manifesto*, Marx said that this would be brought about by revolution. To explain what he saw as the inevitability of this change, he analyzed the capitalist system and its inherent weaknesses in the three-volume *Das Kapital* (Capital).

However, Marx was not absolutely critical of capitalism. He viewed capitalism as a historically necessary stage

In June 1848, workers in Paris rose up against the government and manned barricades. The uprising was part of a wave of failed revolutions across Europe. It was quickly suppressed.

in economic progress, replacing systems that he considered to be outmoded: feudalism (where peasants were legally tied to their local land-owning lord), and mercantilism (in which governments control foreign trade). He almost admiringly described how it had driven technological innovation and industrial efficiency. But ultimately he believed that capitalism was only a passing stage and an imperfect system whose flaws would inevitably lead to its downfall and replacement.

At the heart of his analysis is the division of society into the "bourgeoisie," a minority who own the means of production, and the "proletariat," the majority who make up the workforce. For Marx this division characterizes capitalism.

Exploiting the workers
With the advent of modern industry the bourgeoisie had effectively become the ruling class, because ownership of the means of

See also: Property rights 20–21 ▪ The labor theory of value 106–07 ▪ Collective bargaining 134–35 ▪
Central planning 142–47 ▪ The social market economy 222–23 ▪ Shortages in planned economies 232–33

production gave them the upper hand over the majority of the population, the proletariat. While workers produced goods and services in return for a wage, the owners of capital—the industrialists and factory owners—sold those goods and services for profit. If, as Marx believed, a commodity's value is based on the labor needed to produce it, capitalists must price the finished goods by first adding the price of labor to the initial commodity cost, then adding profit. In a capitalist system the worker must produce more value than he receives in wages. In this way capitalists extract a surplus value from the workers—this is profit.

To maximize profit, it is clearly in the interests of the capitalist to keep wages at a minimum but also to introduce technology to improve efficiency, often condemning the workforce to degrading or monotonous work, or even unemployment. This exploitation of the workforce, seen by Marx as a necessary feature of capitalism, denies workers both an adequate financial reward and job »

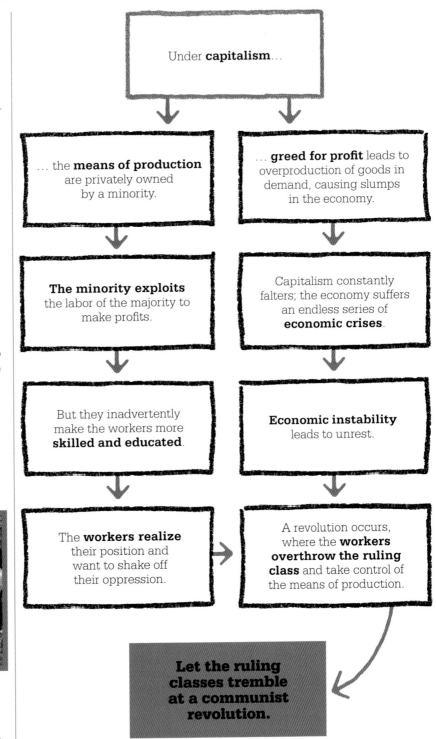

Under **capitalism**...

... the **means of production** are privately owned by a minority.

... **greed for profit** leads to overproduction of goods in demand, causing slumps in the economy.

The minority exploits the labor of the majority to make profits.

Capitalism constantly falters; the economy suffers an endless series of **economic crises**.

But they inadvertently make the workers more **skilled and educated**.

Economic instability leads to unrest.

The **workers realize** their position and want to shake off their oppression.

A revolution occurs, where the **workers overthrow the ruling class** and take control of the means of production.

Let the ruling classes tremble at a communist revolution.

By the mid-19th century new technology and the specialization of labor were making industry more efficient. The result, Marx argued, was an exploited, alienated workforce.

With nothing to lose but his chains, a worker symbolically breaks free of his oppressors in a poster commemorating the 1917 Russian Revolution—an event directly inspired by Marx's ideas.

satisfaction, alienating them from the process of production. Marx argued that this alienation would inevitably lead to social unrest.

Competition and monopoly

Another essential element of capitalism is competition between producers. To compete in a market, a firm must try not only to reduce production costs but also to undercut its competitors' prices. In the process some producers fail and go bankrupt, while others take over an increasing portion of the market. The tendency, as Marx saw it, was toward fewer and fewer producers controlling the means of production and a concentration of wealth in the hands of an ever smaller bourgeoisie. In the long term this would create monopolies that could exploit not only the workers but also consumers. At the same time the ranks of the proletariat would be swelled by the former bourgeoisie and the unemployed.

Marx saw competition as the cause of another failing of the capitalist system: the desire to jump into markets where profits are increasing encourages increased production, sometimes regardless of demand. This overproduction leads not only to waste but also to stagnation and even decline of the whole economy. By its nature capitalism is unplanned and ruled only by the complexities of the market—economic crises are an inevitable result of the mismatch of supply and demand. Therefore, growth in a capitalist economy is not a smooth progression but is interrupted by periodic crises, which Marx believed would become more and more frequent. The hardship created by these crises would be especially felt by the proletariat.

To Marx these apparently insurmountable weaknesses in the capitalist economy would lead to its eventual collapse. To explain how this would come about, he used an idea proposed by the German philosopher Georg Hegel, which showed how contradictory notions are resolved in a process of dialectic: every idea or state of affairs (the original "thesis"), contains within it a contradiction (the "antithesis"), and from this conflict a new, richer notion (the "synthesis") arises.

Marx saw the inherent contradictions within economies – personified in the conflicts between different groups or classes—as driving historical change. He analyzed the exploitation and alienation of the proletariat by the bourgeoisie under capitalism as an example of a social contradiction, where the thesis (capitalism) contains its own antithesis (the exploited workers). The oppression and alienation of the workers, combined with the inherent instability of a capitalist economy lurching from crisis to crisis, would result in massive social unrest. A proletarian revolution was both inevitable and necessary to usher in capitalism's successor in the historical progression (the synthesis)—communism. Marx encouraged revolution in the closing words of the *Communist Manifesto*: "The proletarians have nothing to lose but their chains. They have a world to win. Working men of all countries, unite!"

Revolution

Marx predicted that once the bourgeoisie had been overthrown, the means of production would be taken over by the proletariat. At first this would amount to what Marx called a "dictatorship by the proletariat:" a form of socialism where economic power was in the hands of the majority. However, this would be only a first step toward the abolition of private property in favor of common ownership in a communist state.

> "
> The bourgeoisie... compels all nations, on pain of extinction, to adopt the bourgeois mode of production.
> **Karl Marx**
> **Friedrich Engels**
> "

In contrast to his exhaustive analysis of capitalism, Marx wrote relatively little about the details of the communist economy that would replace capitalism, except that it should be based on common ownership and a planned economy to ensure matching supply and demand. Insofar as it removed all the iniquities and instability of capitalism, he regarded communism as the culmination of a historical progression. His criticism of the capitalist economy was met, unsurprisingly, with hostility. Most economists at the time saw the free market as a means of ensuring economic growth and prosperity, at least for a certain class of people. But Marx was not without his supporters, mainly among political thinkers, and his prediction of communist revolution proved correct—although not where he expected, in industrialized Europe and America, but in rural countries such as Russia and China.

Marx did not live to see the establishment of communist states such as the USSR and the People's Republic of China, and he could not have envisaged the reality of how

In 1959, Fidel Castro's revolutionaries seized power in Cuba. At first primarily a nationalist revolution, it soon became a communist one when Castro allied himself with the Soviet Union.

inefficient such planned economies would be. Today, only a handful of communist-planned economies (Cuba, China, Laos, Vietnam, and North Korea) have survived. There is debate over just how "Marxist" the communism of these states was under the leadership of the likes of Stalin and Mao, but the collapse of communism in the Eastern bloc and the liberalization of the Chinese economy have been seen by many economists as evidence that Marx's theories were flawed.

Mixed economies

In the decades following World War II Western Europe developed a "third way" between communism and capitalism. Many European Union states still operate mixed economies with varying degrees of state intervention and ownership, although some, most notably Great Britain, have moved away from mixed economies toward a more laissez-faire economic policy, where the state plays a smaller role. However, with communism largely discredited, and the collapse of capitalism apparently no nearer than in Marx's time, it would appear that his theory of capitalist dynamism leading to crisis and revolution were wrong. Nevertheless, Marxist economic theory has maintained a following, and recent financial crises have prompted a reappraisal of his ideas. Increasing inequality, concentration of wealth in a few large companies, frequent economic crises, and the "credit crunch" of 2008 have all been blamed on the free market economy. While not going so far as to advocate revolution or even socialism, a growing body of thinkers—not all of them from the political Left—is taking elements of Marx's critique of capitalism seriously. ∎

Karl Marx

Born in Trier, Prussia, in 1818, Karl Marx was the son of a lawyer who had converted from Judaism to Christianity. Marx studied law but became interested in philosophy, in which he gained a PhD from Jena University. In 1842, Marx moved to Cologne and started work as a journalist, but his socialist views soon led to censorship, and he fled to Paris with his wife, Jenny.

It was in Paris that he met the German-born industrialist Friedrich Engels, with whom he wrote the *Communist Manifesto* in 1848. He moved back to Germany briefly the following year, but when the revolutions were quashed, he left for London, where he spent the rest of his life. There, he devoted his time to writing, notably *Capital*, and died in poverty in 1883, despite continual financial assistance from Engels.

Key works

1848 *Manifesto of the Communist Party* (with Friedrich Engels)
1858 *Contribution to the Critique of Political Economy*
1867, 1885, 1894 *Capital: A Critique of Political Economy*

THE VALUE OF A PRODUCT COMES FROM THE EFFORT NEEDED TO MAKE IT
THE LABOR THEORY OF VALUE

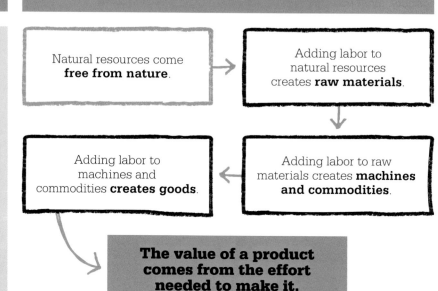

IN CONTEXT

FOCUS
Theories of value

KEY THINKER
Karl Marx (1818–83)

BEFORE
1662 English economist William Petty argues that land is a free gift of nature, and so all capital is "past labor."

1690 English philosopher John Locke argues that workers deserve the fruits of their labors.

AFTER
1896 Austrian Economist Eugen von Böhm-Bawerk publishes *Karl Marx and the Close of his System*, summarizing the criticisms of Marx's labor theory of value.

1942 Radical US economist Paul Sweezy publishes *The Theory of Capitalist Development*, defending Marx's labor theory of value.

Natural resources come **free from nature**.

Adding labor to natural resources creates **raw materials**.

Adding labor to machines and commodities **creates goods**.

Adding labor to raw materials creates **machines and commodities**.

The value of a product comes from the effort needed to make it.

The importance of labor in determining the value of goods has a history that can be traced back to the ancient Greek philosophers. For about 200 years from the mid-17th century, it dominated economic thought. In primitive, preindustrial societies the role of labor in determining the rate at which one good could be exchanged for another was fairly simple. If it took a man a week to make a fishing net, he was unlikely to exchange it for a wooden spoon that had been carved in a morning. However, the issue became much more complicated with the emergence of modern industrial societies in the 18th century. The classical economists Adam Smith (p.61) and David Ricardo (p.84) had each developed a theory of value connected to labor, but it was the German philosopher Karl Marx (p.105) who set out the most famous description of the labor theory of value in his magnum opus *Capital*.

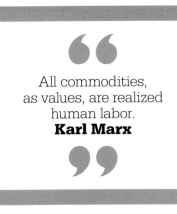

> All commodities, as values, are realized human labor.
> **Karl Marx**

Labor and cost

Marx's idea was that the amount of labor used to produce a good is proportional to its value. The theory is often justified by the following argument. If a haircut involves half an hour of labor, at $40 per hour, the haircut has $20 of value. If it also needs the use of scissors and brushes that cost a total of $60, and lose $1 of their value (through wear) on each haircut, the total value of the haircut is $21. Of the tools the scissors themselves cost $20 because they took 45 minutes of labor to forge from a lump of steel—

costing $12.50—into the pair of scissors. The same reasoning can be applied to explain why the lump of steel cost $12.50, tracing time and costs for producing steel from iron ore. It is possible to trace the expenditure on all the intermediate inputs until we arrive back at the original natural resources, which are free—so all the value has been created by labor.

Marx pointed out that it is too difficult to calculate the value of any good in this way, so value should be determined by the "congealed" lump of labor that the good contains. He also said that value is determined by the "normal" amount of labor we expect its production to take. An inefficient hairdresser may take an hour to cut someone's hair, but the haircut's cost should not then rise by $20. Marx did not deny that supply and demand in the marketplace would influence the value or price of goods in the short run, but said that in the long run the basic structure and dynamics of the value system must come from labor. ∎

When the labor theory of value dominated economic thought, it faced a number of critiques based on paradoxical questions:

If sandcastles are made by labor, why don't they have any value?
Marx's response was that not everything made by labor has value—labor can still be wasted on goods no one wants.

How can an artistic masterpiece be valued from the amount of labor hours used to make it?
The defense to this critique is that a great work of art is an exception to the rule because it is unique. Therefore, there is no average quantity of labor from which to derive a price.

How do vintage wines stored for 10 years increase in value without any additional labor input?
The defense here is that an additional cost does accrue to labor—that of waiting for the wine to mature.

Happiness in work

Karl Marx argued that people are driven by a desire to be connected to other humans, and this is what makes us happy. We show this desire through work.

When a person makes something, that product represents his or her personality. When someone else buys that item, the maker is happy because not only has he or she satisfied the need of another person, but the buyer has also confirmed the "goodness" of the personality of the producer.

Capitalism destroys this essence of humanity, Marx claimed, because it alienates the workers from what they produce. People no longer control their output; they are merely hired to produce a product in which they have had little creative input and are unlikely to consume or even trade. The cooperative nature of society is lost because people are isolated in the competition for jobs. Marx argued that it is this separation from our work that makes us unhappy.

PRICES COME FROM SUPPLY AND DEMAND

SUPPLY AND DEMAND

IN CONTEXT

FOCUS
Theories of value

KEY THINKER
Alfred Marshall (1842–1924)

BEFORE
c.1300 Islamic scholar
Ibn Taymiyyah publishes a
study of the effects of supply
and demand on prices.

1691 English philosopher John
Locke argues that commodity
prices are directly influenced
by the ratio of buyers to sellers.

1817 British economist David
Ricardo argues that prices are
influenced mainly by the cost
of production.

1874 French economist Léon
Walras studies the equilibrium
(balance) in markets.

AFTER
1936 British economist
John Maynard Keynes
identifies economy-wide total
demand and supply.

S upply and demand are
among the fundamental
building blocks of economic
theory. The interplay between the
amount of a product available on
the market and the eagerness of
consumers to buy that product
creates the foundation of markets.

The importance of supply and
demand in economic relationships
was studied as long ago as the
Middle Ages. The medieval
Scottish scholar Duns Scotus
recognized that a price must be fair
to the consumer but must also take
into account the costs incurred in
production and therefore be fair
to the producer. Subsequent
economists studied the effects
of supply-side costs on eventual
prices, and economists such as
Adam Smith (p.61) and David
Ricardo (p.84) linked the price of a
product to the labor required in
its production. This is called the
classical labor theory of value.

In the 1860s new economic
theories began to develop,
challenging these ideas under the
banner of the neoclassical school.
This school of thought introduced
the theory of marginal utility
(pp.114–15), where the satisfaction

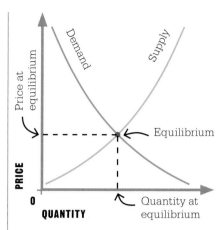
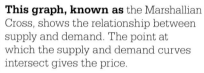

This graph, known as the Marshallian
Cross, shows the relationship between
supply and demand. The point at
which the supply and demand curves
intersect gives the price.

a consumer gains or loses from
having more or less of a product
affects both demand and price.

British economist Alfred
Marshall joined the analysis of
supply with the new neoclassical
approach to demand. Marshall saw
that supply and demand work in
tandem to generate the market
price. His work was important
because he illustrated the varying
dynamics of supply and demand

Alfred Marshall

Born in London, England, in 1842,
Alfred Marshall grew up in the
borough of Clapham before going
to Cambridge University on a
scholarship. There, he studied
mathematics and then
metaphysics, concentrating on
ethics. His studies led him to see
economics as a practical means of
implementing his ethical beliefs.

In 1868, Marshall took up a
lectureship specially created for
him in moral science. His interest
in this continued until a visit to
the US in 1875 made him focus
more on political economy.
Marshall married Mary Paley, his

former student, in 1877 and
became principal of University
College, Bristol, UK. In 1885,
he returned to Cambridge as
professor of political economy, a
post he held until his retirement
in 1908. From about 1890 until
his death in 1924, Marshall was
considered the dominant figure
in British economics.

Key works

1879 *The Economics of Industry*
(with Mary Paley Marshall)
1890 *Principles of Economics*
1919 *Industry and Trade*

See also: The paradox of value 63 ▪ The labor theory of value 106–07 ▪ Economic equilibrium 118–23 ▪ Utility and satisfaction 114–15 ▪ Spending paradoxes 116–17 ▪ Elasticity of demand 124–25 ▪ The competitive market 126–29

> In every case the more of a thing is offered for sale in a market, the lower is the price at which it will find purchasers.
> **Alfred Marshall**

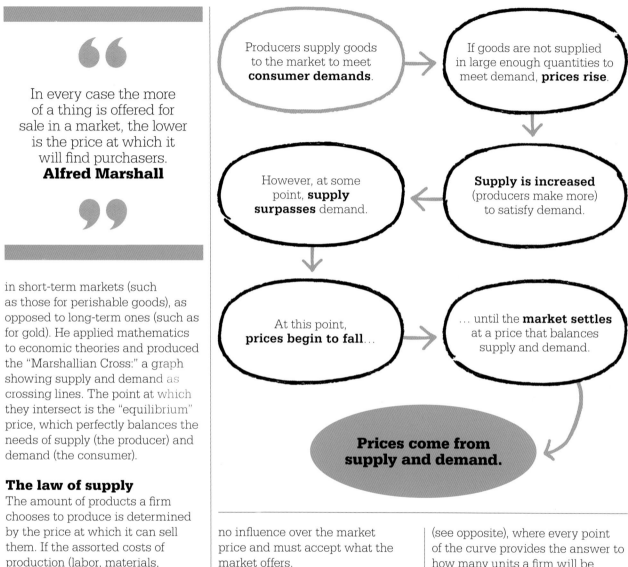

Producers supply goods to the market to meet **consumer demands**.

If goods are not supplied in large enough quantities to meet demand, **prices rise**.

However, at some point, **supply surpasses** demand.

Supply is increased (producers make more) to satisfy demand.

At this point, **prices begin to fall**…

… until the **market settles** at a price that balances supply and demand.

Prices come from supply and demand.

in short-term markets (such as those for perishable goods), as opposed to long-term ones (such as for gold). He applied mathematics to economic theories and produced the "Marshallian Cross:" a graph showing supply and demand as crossing lines. The point at which they intersect is the "equilibrium" price, which perfectly balances the needs of supply (the producer) and demand (the consumer).

The law of supply
The amount of products a firm chooses to produce is determined by the price at which it can sell them. If the assorted costs of production (labor, materials, machines, and premises) amount to more than the market is willing to pay for the product, production will be seen as unprofitable and be reduced or stopped. If, on the other hand, the market price for the item is substantially more than the costs of production, the company will seek to expand production to make as much profit as possible. The theory assumes that the firm has

no influence over the market price and must accept what the market offers.

For example if the costs of producing a computer amount to $200, production will be unprofitable if the market price of the computer drops under $200. Conversely, if the market price of the computer is $1,000, the firm producing it will seek to produce as many as possible to maximize profits. The law of supply can be visualized using a supply curve

(see opposite), where every point of the curve provides the answer to how many units a firm will be willing to sell at a particular price.

Furthermore, there must be a distinction between fixed and variable costs. The above example assumes that production can be increased with the unit cost of production remaining stable. However, this is not the case. If the computer factory can produce only 100 machines per day, yet there is demand for 110, the producer » must judge whether it makes sense to open a completely new factory, with the vast additional costs this incurs, or whether it makes more sense to sell the computers at a slightly higher price to reduce demand to only 100 per day.

The nature of demand

The law of demand sees matters from the viewpoint of the consumer rather than the producer. When the price of a good increases, demand inevitably falls (except for essential goods such as medicines). This is because some consumers will no longer be able to afford the item, or because they decide that they can gain more enjoyment by spending the money elsewhere.

Using the same example as previously, if the computer costs only $50, the volume of sales will be high since most people will be able to afford one. On the other hand if it costs $10,000, the demand will be very low, since only the very wealthy will be able to afford them. As prices increase, demand falls.

There is a limit to how low prices can fall to stimulate demand. If the price of the computer falls to

When the demand price is equal to the supply price, the amount produced has no tendency either to be increased or to be diminished; it is in equilibrium.
Alfred Marshall

below $5, everyone will be able to afford to buy one, but nobody needs more than two or three computers. Consumers realize that their money is better spent on something else, and demand flattens out.

Price is not the only factor that affects demand. Consumer tastes and attitudes are also a major factor. If a product becomes more fashionable, the whole demand curve shifts to the right; consumers demand more of the product at each price. Given the static position of the supply curve, this drives up the price. Because consumer tastes can be manipulated through techniques such as advertising, producers can influence the shape and position of the demand curve.

Finding an equilibrium

While consumers will always seek to pay the lowest price they can, producers will look to sell at the highest price they can. When prices are too high, consumers lose interest and move away from the product. Conversely, if prices are too low, it no longer makes financial sense for the producer to continue to make the product. A happy medium must be reached—an equilibrium price acceptable to both consumer and producer. This price is found at the point where the supply curve intersects the demand curve, producing a price at which consumers are happy to pay and producers are happy to sell.

Many factors complicate these relatively simple laws. The position and size of the market are crucial in price determination, as is time. The price at which producers are happy to sell is not just influenced by the costs of production.

For instance, consider a market stall selling fresh produce. The farmer arrives having already paid for the costs of production, buying the seeds, the labor involved in planting and harvesting the crop, and his transport to the market. He knows that to make a profit, he must sell each apple for $1.20.

Fruit sellers may have to throw away any unsold apples at the end of the day. The urgency to sell in time is a major factor in determining the price at which to sell perishable goods.

Producers of goods such as Coca-Cola may influence demand through advertising that promotes the product and the brand. As demand rises, the price of the product may also rise.

Therefore, at the start of the day, he decides to market his apples at $1.20. If his sales are going well, he may feel he can make more money and raise his price to $1.25. This may cause a slowdown in sales, but if he manages to sell his entire stock, he will be happy. However, if the end of the day is nearing and he finds that he still has quite a few apples left, he might decide to drop his price to $1.15 to avoid being left

The price of any commodity rises or falls by the proportion of the number of buyers and sellers… [this rule] holds universally in all things that are to be bought and sold.
John Locke

with an excess of apples that are likely to rot before his next chance to sell them.

In this example the costs of production are fixed, and the urgency of selling the crop is the pressing factor. This is useful in illustrating the differences between short- and long-term markets. The farmer will decide how many apples to plant for his next harvest, based on his sales this time, and in this way the market should eventually arrive at equilibrium.

The farmer's market is also limited by distance. There is only a certain radius within which it makes economic sense to sell his products. For instance the cost involved in shipping his apples overseas would make his prices uncompetitive with domestic producers. This means that, to some extent, the farmer is at liberty to set his prices slightly higher because his customers cannot travel to seek alternatives.

The opposite scenario to the fruit farmer is the market for a global commodity such as gold. In this long-term market the holder

of the gold is under no time pressure to sell. He can be confident that it will maintain its value. The larger the market and the more widespread the knowledge of the market, the more likely it is that the commodity has found its equilibrium price. This makes any small change in market price significant, and any change will spark a flurry of buying and selling.

Although these examples introduce further complexity into the market, they hold true to the basic rule that suppliers will only sell at a price they find acceptable, while buyers will only buy at a price they find reasonable.

The examples all relate to a market in which physical goods are traded, but supply and demand is relevant throughout economic reasoning. The model is applicable to the labor market, for instance. Here the individual is the supplier, selling his or her labor, and employers are the consumers, looking to buy labor as cheaply as possible. Money markets are also analyzed as a supply and demand system, with the interest rate acting as the price.

Economists call Marshall's work "partial equilibrium" analysis because it shows how a single market reaches equilibrium or balance through the forces of supply and demand. However, an economy is made up of many different interacting markets. The question of how all these can come together in a state of "general equilibrium" is a complex problem that was analyzed by Léon Walras (p.120) in the 19th century. ∎

YOU ENJOY THE LAST CHOCOLATE LESS THAN THE FIRST
UTILITY AND SATISFACTION

IN CONTEXT

FOCUS
Theories of value

KEY THINKER
William Jevons (1835–82)

BEFORE
1871 Austrian economist Carl Menger is credited with the theory of diminishing marginal utility in his book *Principles of Economics*.

AFTER
1890 British economist Alfred Marshall creates the demand curve using marginal utilities in his *Principles of Economics*.

1944 US economists John von Neumann and Oskar Morgenstern extend utility theory to situations with uncertain outcomes.

1953 In *The Behavior of Rational Man at Risk*, French economist Maurice Allais demonstrates how people behave differently from the way utility theory predicts.

Demand is **inversely related** to price: it increases when the price falls.

↓

This means that consumers will only buy more of a good **if the price falls** because…

↓

… each extra unit consumed gives **less pleasure** than the previous one; for example…

↓

… **you enjoy the last chocolate less than the first.**

A ristotle was the first person to observe that too much of a useful thing would be no use. The idea that the more we consume of a product, the smaller the increases in satisfaction we receive has become enshrined in economic theory as the law of diminishing marginal utility (DMU). Marginal refers to changes on the "border," such as eating one more chocolate. Utility is the "pleasure or pain" in the decision to consume. In his *Theory of Political Economy* (1871), British economist William Jevons showed that utility could be measured in a way that relates to the quantity of the commodity available.

Demand curves
The concept of DMU became more important as economists struggled to understand what determines the price of commodities. If everyone generally agrees that each extra chocolate adds less utility, then it makes sense that we will only demand extra chocolates if the price falls, because additional chocolates will give less pleasure— so we will only buy them if they cost less. The resulting demand is negatively related to price, and this,

See also: The paradox of value 63 ▪ The labor theory of value 106–07 ▪ Supply and demand 108–13 ▪ Risk and uncertainty 162–63

along with supply, helps to determine the equilibrium or "natural" price of a chocolate.

There are many notable exceptions to the law of DMU, such as finding the last piece of a puzzle, which is very satisfying. Addictive goods, such as drugs or alcohol, also seem to be exceptions—the more they are consumed the more they are enjoyed. The principle also makes certain assumptions, such as "consumption should be continuous." Eating a whole box of chocolates at one time, for instance, is more likely to demonstrate the principle of DMU than eating them spaced out over a day.

Positive contributions

DMU has important applications, not least in justifying a more equal distribution of income to create greater welfare for society. If the government was to take $1 from a very wealthy person and give it to a very poor person, the total utility of society should increase.

Utility theory has been extended to situations in which individuals have to make decisions in the face of uncertainty and risk. In this case they make decisions on the basis of their preferences over goods and their assessments of the probability of different outcomes. In the 1950s the US mathematician Leonard J Savage showed how different people make different choices—decisions are affected not only by the different levels of utility people attach to commodities, but also by their comfort with risk: risk-averse people make choices that minimize the level of risk they face. ■

William Jevons

Born in Liverpool, England, in 1835, William Jevons was the son of an iron merchant. He developed an interest in economics from his father, who wrote about legal and economic matters. In 1855, his father's firm collapsed, and money worries forced William to cut short his study of natural sciences at University College London (UCL) and work in Australia as an analyst. Five years later he returned to UCL and completed his studies.

In 1863, Jevons became a tutor in Manchester, where he met and married Harriet Taylor. The family moved to London in 1876, when Jevons took a professorship at UCL. Despite struggling with ill-health, he was a prolific and important writer in the fields of economics and logic. He is famous for creating a logic piano, an early mechanical computer that could analyze the truthfulness of an argument. He accidentally drowned in 1882, aged only 47.

Key works

1865 *The Coal Question*
1871 *The Theory of Political Economy*
1874 *Principles of Science*

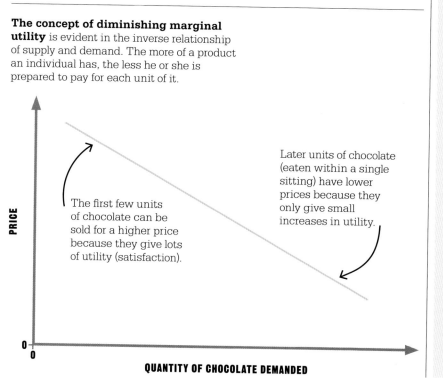

The concept of diminishing marginal utility is evident in the inverse relationship of supply and demand. The more of a product an individual has, the less he or she is prepared to pay for each unit of it.

PRICE

The first few units of chocolate can be sold for a higher price because they give lots of utility (satisfaction).

Later units of chocolate (eaten within a single sitting) have lower prices because they only give small increases in utility.

QUANTITY OF CHOCOLATE DEMANDED

WHEN THE PRICE GOES UP, SOME PEOPLE BUY MORE
SPENDING PARADOXES

IN CONTEXT

FOCUS
Decision making

KEY THINKER
Robert Giffen (1837–1910)

BEFORE
1871 Austrian economist Carl Menger demonstrates how the demand for commodities is determined by their marginal utility.

AFTER
1909 British economist Francis Edgeworth doubts the existence of Giffen goods in *Free Trade in Being*.

1947 US economist George Stigler dismisses Marshall's examples of Giffen goods in *Notes on the History of the Giffen Paradox*.

2007 US academics Robert Jensen and Nolan Miller revive the argument in *Giffen Behavior: Theory and Evidence*, which reports the existence of a Giffen good in poor, urban areas of China.

I n 1895, British economist Alfred Marshall (p.110) demonstrated how supply and demand create the price of goods. After he explained the general rules, such as the greater the demand, the smaller the price, he went on to show how there can be an interesting exception. Marshall suggested that a price rise could, in some circumstances, create a surprising increase in demand. He attributed the discovery of this exception to a well-known Scottish economist and statistician of the time, Sir Robert Giffen. Today, commodities for which demand rises as their prices rise are known as Giffen goods.

The original Giffen good was bread, the most important staple of the poorest section of the British population in the 19th century. The poorest of the working classes spent a large part of their income on bread, a food that was necessary for life but was seen as inferior to the perceived luxury of meat. Marshall said that as the price of bread rose, the poorest people had to spend more of their income on bread to get enough calories to

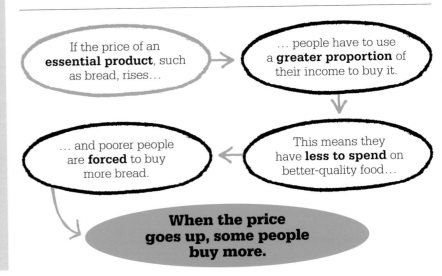

If the price of an **essential product**, such as bread, rises… → … people have to use a **greater proportion** of their income to buy it.

↓

… and poorer people are **forced** to buy more bread. ← This means they have **less to spend** on better-quality food…

When the price goes up, some people buy more.

See also: Supply and demand 108–13 ▪ Elasticity of demand 124–25 ▪ Conspicuous consumption 136

survive—they had to buy bread instead of meat. As a result, if the price of bread increased, so did demand.

Inferior and poor

Giffen goods rely on a number of assumptions. First, the commodity has to be an inferior good, that is, a good that people choose to buy less of as their income rises because there are better alternatives—in this case meat in preference to bread. Second, the consumer must spend a large portion of their income on this product, hence the fact that the example refers to the poorest section of society. Finally, there must be no alternatives to the product. In the case of bread, there is no cheaper alternative staple.

Given these assumptions, an increase in the price of bread creates two effects. It causes people to buy less bread because the satisfaction it creates per pound of spending falls compared to other goods. This substitution effect would cause bread to follow the general rule of higher price causing lower demand. However, as the price of bread rises, it also reduces the power to spend on other things, and because bread is an inferior good, this lower income will make the demand for bread rise. What makes the Giffen good so special is that because the poor spend so much of their income on bread, the income effect is so large that it outweighs the substitution effect, and so when the price goes up, some people buy more. Another example of a Giffen good is that of potatoes during the Irish Potato Famine of 1842–53, where rising prices allegedly caused an increase in the demand for potatoes.

Elusive evidence

Marshall came under attack from Francis Edgeworth (1845–1926), another British economist, for postulating the existence of a good that contradicts a basic rule of demand, without any hard evidence. In theory, Giffen goods are consistent with consumers' behavior—the interaction of income and substitution effects—that

A girl buys rice in Bangladesh, where the government subsidized the price of staples in 2011 in a drive to improve food security for the poor.

underlies demand curves. But if Giffen goods exist at all, they are rare: evidence comes from special contexts, and some of the most famous cases are dubious. Yet economists continue to search for them. In a 2007 study Harvard economists Robert Jensen and Nolan Miller presented evidence of Giffen behavior in the demand for rice among poor families in China. ▪

A new Rolls Royce limousine goes on show in Shaanxi Province, China. Economists believe that luxury cars are desirable for their high price.

Veblen goods

Veblen goods are named after Thorstein Veblen, a US economist who formulated the theory of "conspicuous consumption" (p.136). They are strange because demand for them increases as their price rises. Unlike Giffen goods, however, which must be inferior, these goods must signal high status.

A willingness to pay higher prices is to advertise wealth rather than to acquire better quality. A true Veblen good, therefore, should not be noticeably higher quality than the lower-priced equivalents. If the price falls so much that it is no longer high enough to exclude the less well off, the rich will stop buying it.

There is much evidence of this behavior in the markets for luxury cars, champagne, watches, and certain clothing labels. A reduction in prices might see a temporary increase in sales for the seller, but then sales will begin to fall.

A SYSTEM
OF FREE MARKETS
IS STABLE

ECONOMIC EQUILIBRIUM

IN CONTEXT

FOCUS
Markets and firms

KEY THINKER
Léon Walras (1834–1910)

BEFORE
1851 Francis Edgeworth publishes a mathematical assessment of economics in *Mathematical Psychics*.

AFTER
1906 Vilfredo Pareto develops a new theory of equilibrium that takes account of the compatibility of individual incentives and constraints.

1930s John Hicks, Oskar Lange, Maurice Allais, Paul A. Samuelson, and others continue to develop the theory of general equilibrium.

1954 Kenneth Arrow and Gérard Debreu provide a mathematical proof of general equilibrium.

There has long been something appealing for economists about the idea that the economy may behave with the same mathematical predictability of scientific laws such as Newton's laws of motion. Newton's laws reduce the whole complex, teeming, physical universe to three simple, reliable mathematical relationships. Is it possible to find similar relationships in the complex, changing world of markets?

In 1851, a British professor named Francis Edgeworth published *Mathematical Psychics*, an early mathematical work on economics. He realized that economics deals with relationships between variables, which means that it can be translated into equations. Edgeworth thought about economic benefits in utilitarian terms. In other words believing that outcomes could be measured in terms of units of happiness, or pleasure.

Other economists were also intrigued by the idea of a mathematical approach. In Germany the economist Johann von Thünen developed equations

Léon Walras argued that the sum of all the excess demand in an economy equals zero. In an economy with just apples and cherries, excess demand for apples means excess supply of cherries.

for a fair working wage and the most profitable use of land. In France Léon Walras, an academic who would later be described as "the greatest of all economists," was trying to discover a complete mathematical, scientific framework for the entire discipline. Walras was ardent in his conviction that it was possible to discover economic laws that would make economics a "pure moral science" (describing human behavior) that went hand in hand with the "pure natural science" of Newton. His

Léon Walras

Marie Esprit Léon Walras was born in Normandy, France, in 1834. As a young man he was captivated by bohemian Paris, but his father persuaded him that one of the romantic tasks of the future was to make economics a science. Walras was convinced—though he maintained his bohemian life until, destitute, he went to Lausanne as economics professor in 1870. It was there he developed his theory of general equilibrium.

Walras believed that the organization of society was a matter of "art" outside the scientific realm of economics.

He had a strong sense of social justice and campaigned for land nationalization as a prelude to equal land distribution. In 1892, he retired to the town of Clarens overlooking Lake Geneva, where he fished and thought about economics until he died in 1910.

Key works

1874–77 *Elements of Pure Economics*
1896 *Studies in Social Economics*
1898 *Studies in Applied Economics*

See also: The circular flow of the economy 40–45 ▪ Free market economics 54–61 ▪ Supply and demand 108–13 ▪ Efficiency and fairness 130–31 ▪ Markets and social outcomes 210–13 ▪ Complexity and chaos 278–79

general equilibrium theory was devised to explain the production, consumption, and prices across an entire economy.

Supply and demand

Walras began by focusing on how exchanges worked—how the prices of goods, the quantity of goods, and the demand for goods interact. In other words he was trying to pin down just how supply and demand tally. He believed that the value of something for sale depends essentially on its *rareté*—which means "rarity," but was used by Walras to express just how intensely something is needed. In this respect Walras differed from many of his contemporaries, including Edgeworth and William Stanley Jevons (p.115), who believed that utility—either as pleasure or usefulness—is the key to value.

Walras began to construct mathematical models to describe the relationship between supply and demand. These revealed that as price escalates, demand falls and supply climbs. Where demand and supply match, the market is in a state of equilibrium, or balance. This reflected the same kind of simple balancing forces that were evident in Newton's laws of motion.

General equilibrium

To illustrate this equilibrium, imagine that today the current market price of mobile phones is $20. In a local market store owners have 100 phones for which they want $20. If 100 buyers visit the market, each willing to pay $20, the market for cheap mobiles is in equilibrium because the supply »

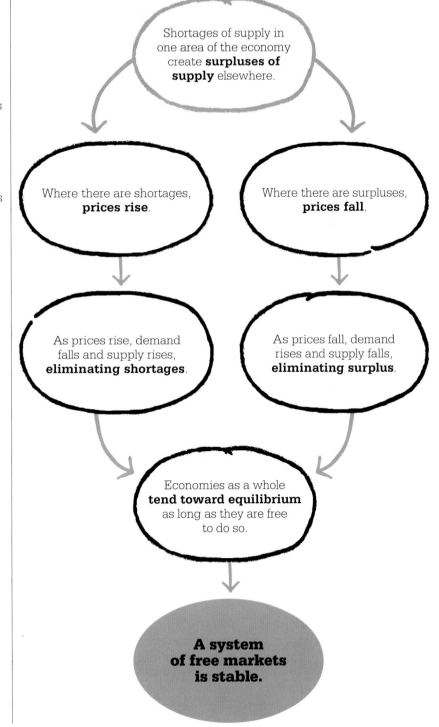

Shortages of supply in one area of the economy create **surpluses of supply** elsewhere.

Where there are shortages, **prices rise**.

Where there are surpluses, **prices fall**.

As prices rise, demand falls and supply rises, **eliminating shortages**.

As prices fall, demand rises and supply falls, **eliminating surplus**.

Economies as a whole **tend toward equilibrium** as long as they are free to do so.

A system of free markets is stable.

An auctioneer takes bids at a cattle auction. Walras imagined an auctioneer who provides perfect information for the market. He announces prices, and a sale only takes place at the point of equilibrium.

and demand are perfectly balanced with no shortages or surpluses. Walras went on to apply the idea of equilibrium to the whole economy in order to create a theory of general equilibrium. This was based on the assumption that when goods are in surplus in one area, the price must be too high. Prices are judged "too high" by comparison, so if one market's prices are "too high," there must be another where prices are "too low," causing a surplus in the higher-priced market.

Walras created a mathematical model for the whole economy, including goods such as chairs and wheat and factors of production such as capital and labor. Everything was interlinked and dependent on everything else. He insisted that interdependency is key; price changes do not take place in a vacuum—they only occur because of a change in supply or demand. Moreover, when prices change, everything

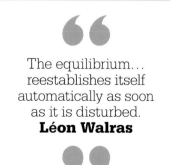

> The equilibrium... reestablishes itself automatically as soon as it is disturbed.
> **Léon Walras**

else also changes. One small change in one part of the economy can ripple through the entire economy. For example, suppose that a war breaks out in a major oil-producing country. Prices of oil across the world will rise, which will have far-reaching effects on governments, firms, and individuals—from increased prices at gas stations and increased heating costs at home, to being forced to cancel a now-expensive vacation or business trip.

Toward equilibrium

Walras succeeded in reducing his mathematical model of an economy to a few equations containing prices and quantities. He drew two conclusions from his work. The first was that a state of general equilibrium is theoretically possible. The second was that wherever an economy started, a free market could move it toward general equilibrium. So a system of free markets could be inherently stable.

Walras showed how this might happen through an idea he called *tâtonnement* (groping), in which an economy "gropes" its

way up to an equilibrium just as a climber gropes his way up a mountain. He thought about this by imagining a theoretical "auctioneer" to whom buyers and sellers submit information about how much they would buy or sell goods at different prices. The auctioneer then announces the prices at which supply equals demand in every market, and only then does buying and selling begin.

Flaws in the model

Walras was quick to point out that this was simply a mathematical model, designed to help economists. It was not intended to be taken to be a description of the real world. His work was largely ignored by his contemporaries, many of whom believed that real-world interactions are too complex and chaotic for a true state of equilibrium to develop.

On a technical level Walras's complex equations were too difficult for many economists to master, which was another reason why he was ignored, although his student Vilfredo Pareto (p.131) later developed his work in new directions. In the 1930s, two

> There was... a set of prices, one for each commodity, which would equate supply and demand for all commodities.
> **Kenneth Arrow**

decades after Walras's death, his equations came under the scrutiny of the brilliant Hungarian-born American mathematician, John von Neumann. Von Neumann exposed a flaw in Walras's equations, showing that some of their solutions produced a negative price—which meant sellers would be paying buyers.

However, Walras's ideas have been rescued by the work of US economists Kenneth Arrow and Lionel W. McKenzie and French economist Gérard Debreu (p.211) who, in the 1950s, developed a sleeker model (pp.210–13). Using rigorous mathematics, Arrow and Debreu derived conditions under which Walras's general economic equilibrium would hold.

They found that when people's decisions about buying and selling are "rational"—in the sense that they are consistent—then it is possible for all the markets in an economy to be in equilibrium. A requirement for consistency is the "transitivity" of people's preferences: if you prefer apples over oranges, and oranges over grapes, then you must prefer apples over grapes.

Computable economies

Improvements to computers in the 1980s allowed economists to calculate the effects of interactions between multiple markets in actual economies. These computable general equilibrium (CGE) models applied Walras's idea of interdependence to particular situations to analyze the impact of changing prices and government policies.

The attraction of CGE is that it can be used by large organizations—such as governments, the World Bank, and the International Monetary Fund—to make quick and powerful calculations showing the state of the whole economy as well as seeing the effects of changing different parameters.

Today, analysis of partial equilibrium—considering the forces that bring supply and demand into balance in a single market—is the first thing that an economics student learns. Walras's insights about general equilibrium also continue to generate work at the cutting edge of economic theory. For most economists equilibrium and the existence of forces that return an economy to this state remain fundamental principles. These ideas are perhaps the essence of mainstream economic analysis. ∎

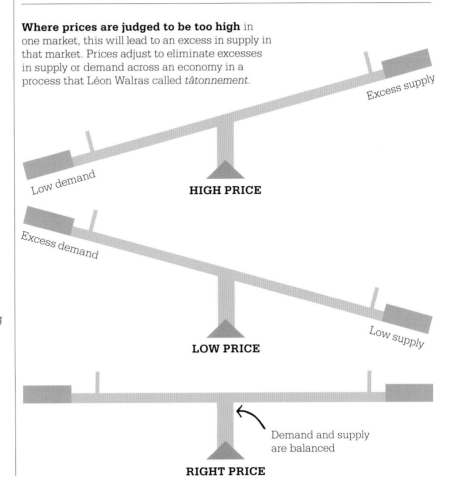

Where prices are judged to be too high in one market, this will lead to an excess in supply in that market. Prices adjust to eliminate excesses in supply or demand across an economy in a process that Léon Walras called *tâtonnement*.

Excess supply — Low demand — **HIGH PRICE**

Excess demand — Low supply — **LOW PRICE**

Demand and supply are balanced — **RIGHT PRICE**

IF YOU GET A PAY RAISE, BUY CAVIAR NOT BREAD
ELASTICITY OF DEMAND

The "elasticity" of demand is its responsiveness to changes in another factor, such as price. British economist Alfred Marshall (p.110) is generally credited as the first economist to define the concept in 1890, but the German statistician Ernst Engel published a paper five years earlier, showing how changes in income alter the level of demand. The origins of the concept may be disputed, but its importance is not. Elasticity of demand quickly became one of the most widely used tools of economic analysis.

Marshall had been one of the first to formalize the idea that demand fell as prices rose. It took only a small step from this to see how the demand for different products (such as bread and caviar) varied by differing amounts when the price of those products changed. Marshall saw that when prices changed for necessities such as bread, demand changed very little. Bread is very unresponsive to changes in price because it has few substitutes. On the other hand demand for luxuries might be much more responsive to price—such a product is said to be "price-elastic." Marshall recognized that among

Designer clothes are luxury goods that take up a greater proportion of income as a person's income rises. Necessities such as bread will take a declining proportion of income.

people on average incomes, demand for a luxury such as caviar is much more sensitive to price change than it is among the super-rich, who can afford as much as they like.

Engel's law

Ernst Engel argued that as people grow richer, they increase spending on food by less than their increase in income. Demand for food is "income-inelastic"—an idea that became known as Engel's law.

See also: Utility and satisfaction 114–15 ▪ Spending paradoxes 116–17 ▪
Supply and demand 108–13 ▪ The competitive market 126–29

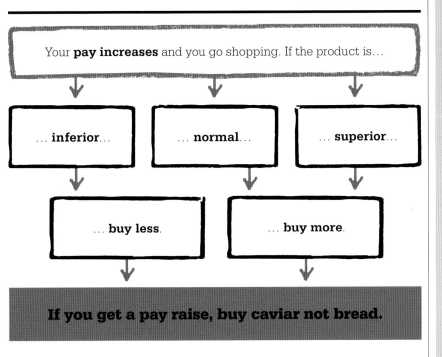

Your **pay increases** and you go shopping. If the product is…

… **inferior**… … **normal**… … **superior**…

… **buy less**. … **buy more**.

If you get a pay raise, buy caviar not bread.

Ernst Engel

Born in Dresden, Germany, in 1821, Ernst Engel studied mining at the École Des Mines in Paris, France, where he came under the influence of Frédéric Le Play, a pioneer in the study of family budgets. On his return to Germany Engel became the director of the statistical bureaus of Saxony and then Prussia, where he formulated the law that was to bear his name.

In 1881, Engel wrote an article attacking Chancellor Otto von Bismarck's agricultural protectionism and was promptly "retired" on health grounds. Engel was part of the German historical school of economics. A prolific writer, he believed in reforming policy to improve the lives of the working classes. Perhaps his greatest legacy was his influence in the creation of institutions for statistical analysis in many European countries. Engel died near Dresden in 1896, aged 76.

Key works

1857 *Production and Consumption in Saxony*
1883 *The Worth of People*
1895 *The Cost of Living for Belgian Workers*

Engel studied the budgets of 199 households in Belgium and showed that while demand for basic necessities such as food grew less quickly as income rose, demand for luxuries—such as vacations—grew at least as quickly as the increase in income. Economists have identified two types of products

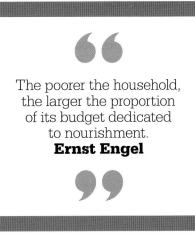

The poorer the household, the larger the proportion of its budget dedicated to nourishment.
Ernst Engel

or goods. The first—normal goods—are those where demand rises in line with income. Luxuries are a special type of normal good, known as a superior good, where demand rises proportionately more than the rise in income. The second type of goods—inferior goods—see demand fall as income rises.

Some groups of goods, such as food, contain both luxuries and necessities (such as caviar and bread). This means that it may be misleading to judge the impact of increasing income on food as a group. A further complication is that a product is not always normal or inferior—this may change at different levels of income. Given extra income, very poor people might buy more bread, those on high incomes might buy more caviar, but the super-rich might choose to give up caviar and dine on edible gold flakes instead. ▪

COMPANIES ARE PRICE TAKERS NOT PRICE MAKERS

THE COMPETITIVE MARKET

IN CONTEXT

FOCUS
Markets and firms

KEY THINKER
Alfred Marshall (1842–1924)

BEFORE
1844 Jules Dupuit, a French engineer, originates the idea of consumer surplus—a measurement of welfare that can be used to assess the impact of competition.

1861 John Elliott Cairnes clarifies the logic of J. S. Mill's and David Ricardo's theories of competition.

AFTER
1921 Frank Knight develops the notion of perfect competition.

1948 Friedrich Hayek's *Individualism and Economic Order* attacks Marshall's view of perfect competition.

In the late 18th century Adam Smith (p.61) wrote about the impact of competition on firms' abilities to set prices and make profits above a "natural" level. However, there was no formal analysis of the situation until British economist Alfred Marshall (p.110) published *Economic Principles* in 1890. The ideas in Marshall's model remain a key part of mainstream economic theory, although the theory has been criticized as not representing the true nature of competition.

Perfect competition
The model that Marshall developed to explain why firms were unable to set their own prices has become known as "perfect competition."

See also: Monopolies 92–97 ▪ Supply and demand 108–13 ▪ Economic liberalism 172–77 ▪ Price discrimination 180–81 ▪ Markets and social outcomes 210–13

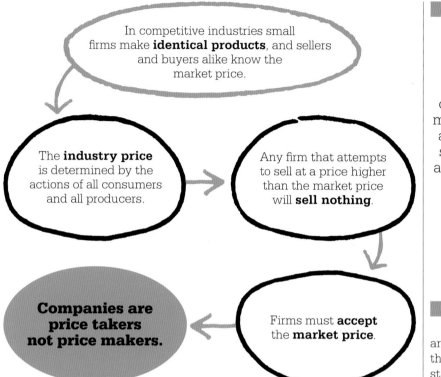

In competitive industries small firms make **identical products**, and sellers and buyers alike know the market price.

The **industry price** is determined by the actions of all consumers and all producers.

Any firm that attempts to sell at a price higher than the market price will **sell nothing**.

Firms must **accept** the **market price**.

Companies are price takers not price makers.

A perfect market is a district… in which there are many buyers and many sellers all so keenly on the alert and so well acquainted with one another's affairs that the price of a commodity is always practically the same for the whole of the district.
Alfred Marshall

In fact, Marshall himself preferred the terms "free competition" and "perfect markets."

The model is based on a set of assumptions, derived from the ideas of the classical economists, about conditions in the market and the behavior of firms.

The first assumption is that there is such a large number of firms selling the product to such a large number of customers that each of the firms and customers individually represents a negligible part of the market.

The second assumption is that every firm is trying to sell an identical product. Third, the model assumes that all the firms are free to enter or leave the industry at will, and they are able to move or acquire the factors of production they need to produce goods with perfect ease.

Competition in action

The market for foreign currency meets the conditions of perfect competition, and it is a useful example for exploring its operations. Globally, there are so many firms selling foreign currency that they each make up a tiny fraction of the market for euros, for example. They sell to millions of buyers who all need to buy currency, and each buyer (a single tourist, for example) also makes up an insignificant part of the market.

Second, the euro or dollar that the tourist buys from each company is exactly the same, so the buyers are indifferent about which firms they buy from. Third, anyone can start buying and selling foreign currency without any legal, social, or technological barriers being placed in their way—entry to the market is easy.

In a perfect market there is perfect information—all the participants know exactly what the "going price" is. Those buying and selling foreign exchange know how much is being paid for a currency at all times. In addition each firm knows everything about the other firm's costs of production. This transparency implies that no consumer can be fooled into paying a higher price, and that firms know the best and cheapest way to supply the product. Finally, self-interested firms aim to maximize profits. Workers will look for the highest-paid work, and capitalist investors will look for markets with the highest profits. »

The assumptions of Marshall's model create certain consequences for firms in perfectly competitive industries. One of the most important of these is that firms have no power over the price that they can charge. This is because there are so many firms selling an identical product that if any one firm attempts to sell at a price higher than its competitors, it will sell nothing. This is virtually guaranteed because the consumer has perfect knowledge about the prices being asked by all firms. In this way the market price is determined by the collective interaction of all the firms and consumers, and each firm has to accept that one particular price is the price at which they can sell the product. They have to "take" the price, not make it.

Competitive selling

The standard representation of Marshall's perfectly competitive industry (see below) demonstrates this idea. For instance, at any moment in time there will be a world price of wheat—such as $350 per ton—which is determined by the industry. At this industry price (shown as a dotted line in the graph), each farm can sell as much as it likes, but it will sell nothing at any price higher than this (because buyers can go elsewhere). Farms can choose to sell at a lower price than other farms if they desire, but this would be of no advantage to them—a lower price will not attract extra demand, because in perfect competition each farm is a tiny part of the total world supply (in wheat, this is around 700 million tons). By lowering the price, the farm would merely lower its profits. The farm has only to decide what output it needs to produce to maximize profits. In the case demonstrated by the graph, it is 3,000 tons, which the farmer knows can be sold for $350 per ton.

In this example, the farm is selling wheat for much more than the cost of producing it. By selling 3,000 tons at $350 per ton, the farm's revenue is $1.05 million; its costs, however, are $450,000 ($150 × 3,000 tons). The farm's profit is

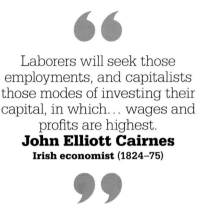

revenue minus cost—in this case, $600,000. This is an example of what classical economists such as David Ricardo (p.84) describe as "the market price moving away from the natural price." However, in a perfectly competitive market these high profits cannot be sustained in the long term.

Short-term profits

Classical economists such as Smith and Ricardo were well aware of the consequences—in competitive markets—of a price being well above that required to cover costs. The high level of profits would act as an incentive for new firms to enter the industry. The lack of barriers to entry in a perfect market allows any firm to enter the market easily. In our example it is easy to imagine farmers switching out of barley production and into wheat production if wheat is more profitable to produce. The impact of the new entrants would be to increase total supply, and through competitive pressure drive the price downward, so that in a short time firms would only be able to make a "normal" level of profit. This would be when the price just

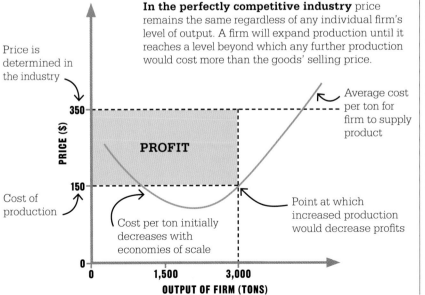

In the perfectly competitive industry price remains the same regardless of any individual firm's level of output. A firm will expand production until it reaches a level beyond which any further production would cost more than the goods' selling price.

Price is determined in the industry

Cost of production

PRICE ($)

350

150

0

PROFIT

Average cost per ton for firm to supply product

Point at which increased production would decrease profits

Cost per ton initially decreases with economies of scale

0   1,500   3,000

OUTPUT OF FIRM (TONS)

covered the costs of production—the excess profits (shown on the graph in blue) would vanish.

When the assumptions that underlie perfect competition are violated, firms can make large profits in the long run. For instance, if there are any barriers to entering an industry—such as technological or legal barriers—excess profits do not get competed away. The most extreme form of this is that of a monopoly. To maximize profits, a monopolist charges a higher price and produces less than would be the case in a perfectly competitive market. This is why economists believe that perfectly competitive markets are more socially beneficial than monopolized ones. Under conditions of lower output produced by a monopoly, consumers could gain from extra units of production. But in perfectly competitive markets, these extra units are produced as more firms enter the market—prices drop as high profits are competed away.

Impossibility of perfection

There are a number of controversies around Marshall's model of perfect competition. First, there are few—if any—real industries that come close to the assumptions required for the model to be useful. In fact, both currency markets and agriculture are unlikely to be good examples of the theory of perfect competition because of the existence of large firms that can influence price, and because governments can and do manipulate these markets. The defenders of perfect competition argue that the model represents a theoretical, ideal form of market structure that is useful for understanding how firms behave, even if there are no industries that actually meet its requirements.

A more fundamental criticism is that perfect competition as described by Marshall has lost its real meaning; in fact, there is no "competition" in the model. Firms are seen as making identical products, responding passively to prices, and accepting that they will end up making normal profits. This is a long way from the situation suggested by Smith, where firms desperately try to make different, higher-quality products than their competitors, which they seek to sell at higher prices, while also intermittently

Traders determine prices of commodities such as wheat through competing with each other. In competitive markets no single trader has the power to influence the price.

introducing new technologies to reduce their costs and consistently raise profits.

Attacks on perfect competition around this point continued through the 20th century. The Austrian-born British economist Friedrich Hayek (p.177) argued that competition is a dynamic discovery process in which entrepreneurs seek new profit opportunities in a world of constant change—it is not simply the sterile copying of prices suggested by Marshall's model. ∎

Marshall on risk, uncertainty, and profit

In 1921, US economist Frank Knight (p.163) published *Risk, Uncertainty, and Profit*, which analyzed the effects of uncertainty on Marshall's model of perfect competition. Knight defined risk as a measurable uncertainty, such as the chance of a champagne bottle exploding. The proportion of bottles that burst is practically constant, and the producer can therefore add it to costs or insure against it. For this reason risk does not disrupt the competitive equilibrium; entrepreneurs do not earn profits as a reward for taking predictable risks. On the other hand real uncertainty is immeasurable—it comes principally from not being able to see into the future. For Knight, entrepreneurs accept the responsibility of working with an uncertain future and take decisions on this basis. The amount that entrepreneurs will earn is unknown because the future is unknown.

MAKE ONE PERSON BETTER OFF WITHOUT HURTING THE OTHERS
EFFICIENCY AND FAIRNESS

IN CONTEXT

FOCUS
Welfare economics

KEY THINKER
Vilfredo Pareto (1848–1923)

BEFORE
1776 Adam Smith's *The Wealth of Nations* relates self-interest to social welfare.

1871 British economist William Jevons says that value depends entirely on utility.

1874 French economist Léon Walras uses equations to determine the overall equilibrium of an economy.

AFTER
1930–50 John Hicks, Paul Samuelson, and others use Pareto optimality as the basis of modern welfare economics.

1954 US economist Kenneth Arrow and French economist Gérard Debreu use mathematics to show a connection between free markets and Pareto optimality.

In the 19th century a group of British philosophers known as the utilitarians introduced the idea that the happiness of individuals can be measured and added up, or aggregated. Italian economist Vilfredo Pareto disagreed. In his *Manual of Political Economy*, he introduced a weaker definition of social welfare that has come to dominate modern economics. His argument is based on a ranking of relative happiness known as "ordinal utility," rather than an absolute measurement of happiness ("cardinal utility").

Pareto said that individuals know their own preferences and will do what suits them best. If everyone follows their own tastes,

A government wants to **improve the welfare** of its people…

… but **individual welfare** is unmeasurable in absolute (not relative) terms.

A reasonable aim would be to reach a state of **Pareto efficiency**…

… where **each individual trades** to improve their own welfare…

… **until they reach a compromise, or equilibrium, where you can't make one person better off without hurting the others.**

See also: Free market economics 54–61 ▪ Economic equilibrium 118–23 ▪ Markets and social outcomes 210–13

constrained as they are by the obstacles they face, society will soon reach a point where no one can be made better off without hurting someone else. This state is known as Pareto optimality, or Pareto efficiency.

Pareto efficiency

Suppose a couple named Jane and John both like rice. If we have a sack of rice, any division of it between them—even one where one person gets all the rice—would be optimal, because only taking rice *away* from a person is said to hurt them. In this way Pareto efficiency is different from fairness.

In most situations there are many goods and tastes. For instance, if John likes rice but not chicken, and Jane likes chicken but not rice, an allocation in which John had everything would be Pareto inefficient: a transfer of chicken from John to Jane would help Jane without hurting John. Often preferences aren't so clear cut: both might like chicken and rice but to different degrees. In that case Jane and John can exchange just small amounts of chicken and rice until an optimal allocation emerges.

We can all agree

Using Pareto efficiency reduces the need to judge between conflicting interests. Avoiding such judgments is the hallmark of positive economics (describing how things are), as opposed to normative economics (prescribing how they should be). Pareto argued that free markets are efficient in his sense of the term. This formalized Adam Smith's idea that self-interest and free market competition operate for the common good (pp.54–61). ▪

Vilfredo Pareto

Born in France in 1848, Vilfredo Pareto was the son of an Italian marquis and a French mother. The family moved to Italy when he was four, and Pareto was schooled in Florence, then in Turin, where he acquired a PhD in engineering. While working as a civil engineer, he became interested in economics and free trade. In 1893, he was recommended by his friend, the Italian economist Maffeo Pantaleoni, to succeed Léon Walras (p.120) to the chair of political economy at the University of Lausanne in Switzerland. He took up the post at the age of 45, and it was there that he made his major contributions to the field, including his theories on income distribution.

Pareto continued to teach until 1911. His works were prolific, covering sociology, philosophy, and mathematics as well economics. He died in Geneva in 1923.

Key works

1897 *Course of Political Economy*
1906 *Manual of Political Economy*
1911 *Mathematical Economics*

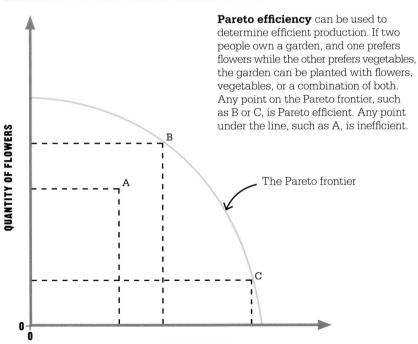

Pareto efficiency can be used to determine efficient production. If two people own a garden, and one prefers flowers while the other prefers vegetables, the garden can be planted with flowers, vegetables, or a combination of both. Any point on the Pareto frontier, such as B or C, is Pareto efficient. Any point under the line, such as A, is inefficient.

The Pareto frontier

QUANTITY OF FLOWERS

QUANTITY OF VEGETABLES

THE BIGGER THE FACTORY, THE LOWER THE COST
ECONOMIES OF SCALE

IN CONTEXT

FOCUS
Markets and firms

KEY THINKER
Alfred Marshall (1842–1924)

BEFORE
1776 Adam Smith explains how large firms can lower unit costs through labor division.

1848 John Stuart Mill suggests that only large firms can adapt successfully to certain business changes, and that this can lead to the creation of natural monopolies.

AFTER
1949 South African economist Petrus Johannes Verdoorn shows that increasing growth creates increasing productivity through economies of scale.

1977 Alfred Chandler publishes *The Visible Hand: the Managerial Revolution in American Business*, which describes the rise of giant corporations and mass production.

From the beginning of the Industrial Revolution, when manufacturing shifted from small-scale outfits to large factories, it became apparent that bigger firms could produce at a lower cost. As a firm grows and produces more, it uses more machinery, labor, and raw materials, so a bigger factory has higher total costs. But it can also produce more for a lower unit cost. This fall in average costs is known as economies of scale.

In 1890, British economist Alfred Marshall (p.110) explored

this effect in *Principles of Economics*. He pointed out that when firms increase their output, all they can do in the short run is alter the number of workers to increase production—nothing else. As extra workers add less to output than the workers before them, costs per unit rise. Yet in the long run, if a firm is able to double the size of its factory, workforce, and machines, it will be able to take advantage of the specialization of labor, and costs will fall.

In the 1960s, US economist Alfred Chandler (1918–2007), showed how the growth of large corporations caused a new Industrial Revolution at the start of the 20th century. Large enterprises came to dominate industries, producing more goods at lower cost and driving competitors out of business. These large firms often enjoyed a "natural monopoly." ∎

Alfred Chandler described the development of large US corporations, such as those in the auto industry, into vast production-line industries.

See also: Diminishing returns 62 ▪ The division of labor 66–67 ▪ Monopolies 92–97 ▪ The competitive market 126–29

THE COST OF GOING TO THE MOVIES IS THE FUN YOU'D HAVE HAD AT THE ICE RINK
OPPORTUNITY COST

IN CONTEXT

FOCUS
Theories of value

KEY THINKER
Friedrich von Wieser
(1851–1926)

BEFORE
1817 David Ricardo argues that the value of a commodity is determined by the amount of labor hours used to produce it.

AFTER
1920 Alfred Marshall argues in *Principles of Economics* that both supply and demand have a role in determining price.

1949 Ludwig von Mises explains in *Human Action* how prices convey important information in markets.

1960 Italian economist Piero Sraffa questions the opportunity cost measure of value in *Production of Commodities by Means of Commodities*.

Economists at the end of the 1800s were still wrestling with what determined the value of a product. By 1914, Austrian economist Friedrich von Wieser was convinced that the value of something was determined by what had to be given up in order to get it. In a world where people have infinite wants and yet have only a fixed amount of resources to meet those wants, he argued that scarcity would create the need for choices. He called this concept "opportunity cost" in *Foundations of Social Economy* (1914). In 1935, British economist Lionel Robbins argued that a tragedy of human life is that the consequence of choosing to do one thing is that something else has to be given up.

True cost
This means that the cost of going to the movies, for example, is not really the cost of admission to the cinema but also the enjoyment you give up from your next best choice of activity. So although there is a monetary consequence of choosing

Economics brings into view that conflict of choice which is one of the permanent characteristics of human existence.
Lionel Robbins

one course of action, opportunity cost means more. You can't watch a movie and ice skate at the same time. Sometimes there is what can be called an opportunity cost even if there is no monetary cost. Weiser thought that ultimately the price of a product was determined by how much it was desired, and this is measured by what people were willing to give up to get it, rather than how much it cost to produce. ∎

See also: Economic man 52–53 ∎ The labor theory of value 106–07 ∎ Utility and satisfaction 114–15

WORKERS MUST IMPROVE THEIR LOT TOGETHER
COLLECTIVE BARGAINING

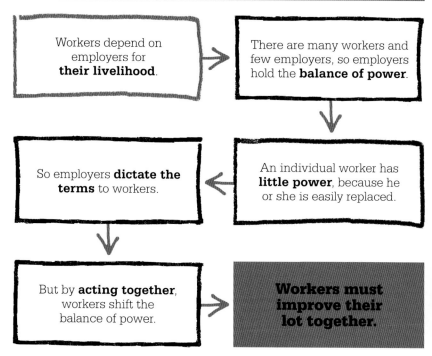

Workers depend on employers for **their livelihood**.

There are many workers and few employers, so employers hold the **balance of power**.

So employers **dictate the terms** to workers.

An individual worker has **little power**, because he or she is easily replaced.

But by **acting together**, workers shift the balance of power.

Workers must improve their lot together.

The term "collective bargaining" was coined by British socialist reformer Beatrice Webb in 1891 to describe the process by which workers organize into unions, which negotiate pay and conditions with employers on the workers' behalf. Webb and her husband, Sidney, campaigned against poverty, and their books brought about change at government level. In 1894, they published *History of Trade Unionism*, documenting the rise of the unions during the Industrial Revolution in Britain, when large numbers of workers were thrown together in the new factories. Conditions were harsh, job security almost non-existent, and wages

See also: Marxist economics 100–05 ▪ The labor theory of value 106–07 ▪ Depressions and unemployment 154–61 ▪ The social market economy 222–23 ▪ Sticky wages 303

> If a group of workmen concert together, and send representatives to conduct the bargaining on behalf of the whole body, the position is at once changed.
> **Beatrice Webb**
> **Sidney Webb**

often close to the breadline. The Combination Acts of 1799 and 1800 outlawed trade unions, and any worker who combined with another to gain a wage increase or a decrease in hours was sentenced to three months in jail. After the acts were repealed in 1824, trade unions formed rapidly, especially in the textile industry. A series of strikes led to a new law, limiting union rights to meetings for collective bargaining purposes.

As union membership in Europe increased throughout the 19th century, a struggle developed between those who saw unions as following in the tradition of crafts guilds, negotiating for better working conditions for their members, and those who saw unions as the vanguard of a revolution, fighting for a better world for all working people.

A continuing struggle

Collective bargaining was widely adopted because it works for employers as well as workers. It dramatically simplifies the process of agreeing to conditions because one agreement can often be applied industrywide.

However, since the 1980s trade unions and the power of collective bargaining have shrunk dramatically. US economist Milton Friedman (p.199) has argued that unionization gives higher wages for union members at the expense

Public sector workers demonstrate in Madrid, Spain, in 2010 to protest against job cuts. Today, trade unions are stronger in the public sector than the private sector in most countries.

of jobs and depresses wages in industries that are not unionized. Perhaps for this reason or more political ones, governments have often sought to curtail union power by outlawing sympathetic strikes.

The globalization of production has also isolated groups of workers within countries. The terms under which people work on a global product are often locally determined between workers and the company, rather than set industrywide across the whole country. ▪

Beatrice Webb

Born in Gloucestershire, UK, in 1858, Beatrice Webb was the child of a radical member of parliament. She grew up with a keen interest in social questions and became fascinated in the structural problems underlying poverty. In 1891, she met her lifelong partner, Sidney Webb, and the pair became central to the British Labour movement. They formulated the idea of "the national minimum"—a minimum level of wages and quality of life below which a worker could not be allowed to fall. They also founded the London School of Economics and the magazine *The New Statesman*. The Webbs helped to shape the trade union movement. They created a blueprint for the UK's National Health Service and welfare systems around the world. Beatrice Webb died in 1943.

Key works

1894 *History of Trade Unionism* (with Sidney Webb)
1919 *The Wages of Men and Women*
1923 *The Decay of Capitalist Civilization*

PEOPLE CONSUME TO BE NOTICED
CONSPICUOUS CONSUMPTION

IN CONTEXT

FOCUS
Society and the economy

KEY THINKER
Thorstein Veblen
(1857–1929)

BEFORE
1848 British philosopher
John Stuart Mill's theory of
political economy assumes
that utility (satisfaction) lies
at the heart of economics.

1890 British economist
Alfred Marshall moves the
focus of economics away from
markets and towards the
study of behavior.

AFTER
1940 Hungarian economist
Karl Polanyi argues that
economic behavior is rooted
in society and culture.

2010 US economist Nathan
Pettit says that "conspicuous
consumption" and the
resulting debt played a key
role in crippling global
financial markets in 2008.

The US economist Thorstein Veblen was the first to note that economic behavior is driven by psychological factors, such as fear and status-seeking, as much as by rational self-interest. Having grown up in a Norwegian farming community in Minnesota, Veblen was an outsider who observed the extremely rich and self-satisfied Americans of the 1890s. In 1899, he published his devastating critique, *The Theory of the Leisure Classes*, which argued that the defining qualities of New York high-society were like those of primitive tribal chieftains—a surfeit of leisure and money. The rich did not buy things because they needed them but to display their wealth and status. Veblen was the first to describe this as "conspicuous consumption."

Consumption trap

Today, "Veblen goods" (p.117) are luxury items such as Porsche cars and Rolex watches. A person's satisfaction increases the more of them they have and the less of them that other people have. Veblen believed that rich societies can suffer from a "relative consumption trap" in which production is squandered on these types of goods. As more people consume them, there may be no gains in overall well-being. Some economists have argued that wasteful consumption, fueled by credit card usage, contributed to the global financial crisis of 2008. ∎

US oil tycoon John D. Rockefeller (left), pictured here with his son, was the first person to be worth more than $1 billion. Rockefeller was part of the New York society Veblen criticized.

See also: Economic man 52–53 ▪ Spending paradoxes 116–17 ▪ Economics and tradition 166–67 ▪ Behavioral economics 266–69

MAKE THE POLLUTER PAY
EXTERNAL COSTS

IN CONTEXT

FOCUS
Economic policy

KEY THINKER
Arthur Pigou (1877–1959)

BEFORE
16th century London
households are forced to pay
for sewage cesspits in their
own houses, rather than throw
sewage into the streets.

AFTER
1952 British economist
James Meade tells a fable
of beekeepers who received
no benefit from their bees
pollinating nearby orchards, so
stopped raising enough bees.

1959 British economist Ronald
Coase argues that the way to
cope with external costs is to
focus on property rights so
that pollution is owned and
its costs negotiated.

1973 James Cheung shows
the fable of the bees to be
false since apple-growers
and beekeepers do negotiate.

If a supermarket threw old
boxes into a nearby garden to
save money on waste disposal,
they would clearly be responsible
for clearing it up. However, when
the damage is less obvious but has
a cost to society—such as air
pollution from a factory—can the
market system devise a solution?

Taxing polluters
In the 1950s economists began to
refer to such costs as externalities
because these costs aren't reflected
in market prices and affect third
parties. This is a market failure:
because the factory doesn't have to
face the true social costs of its
actions, it will create too much
pollution relative to what would be
socially efficient. British economist
Arthur Pigou argued that the way
to deal with this was to tax the
polluter. This "Pigouvian tax," as
it came to be called, was intended
to ensure that the full costs
of pollution were factored into the
polluter's decisions so a business
would only pollute if buyers were
prepared to pay for the damage.

Governments now use this idea in
policies such as carbon taxes to
reduce carbon emissions. As well
as being economically efficient,
many believe that it is morally right
to make the polluter pay, and shift
the responsibility for the problem
to business. However, imposing
a Pigouvian tax is not simple. As
Pigou himself pointed out, correctly
estimating the true cost of pollution
is not a trivial matter. ■

In general, industrialists
are interested, not in
the social, but only in the
private, net product
of their operations.
Arthur Pigou

See also: The tax burden 64–65 ▪ Markets and social outcomes 210–13 ▪
The theory of the second best 220–21 ▪ Economics and the environment 306–09

PROTESTANTISM HAS MADE US RICH

RELIGION AND THE ECONOMY

IN CONTEXT

FOCUS
Society and the economy

KEY THINKER
Max Weber (1864–1920)

BEFORE
1517 Martin Luther publishes
The Ninety-Five Theses,
starting the religious conflict
that leads to the Reformation.

1688 The Glorious Revolution
ends any chance of Catholicism
returning to Britain and paves
the way for the world's first
Industrial Revolution.

AFTER
1993 Swedish social scientist
Kurt Samuelsson argues that
Puritan leaders did not truly
endorse capitalistic behavior.

2009 Harvard economist
Davide Cantoni publishes
*The Case of Protestantism
in 16th Century Germany*, in
which he claims to find "no
effects of Protestantism on
economic growth."

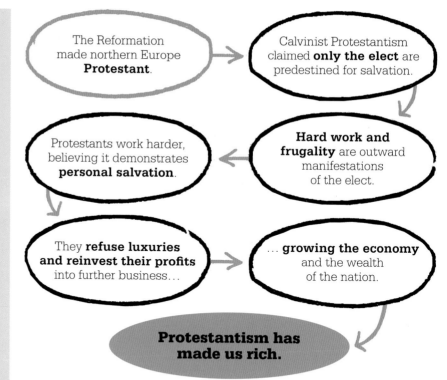

The Reformation made northern Europe **Protestant**.

Calvinist Protestantism claimed **only the elect** are predestined for salvation.

Protestants work harder, believing it demonstrates **personal salvation**.

Hard work and frugality are outward manifestations of the elect.

They **refuse luxuries and reinvest their profits** into further business…

… **growing the economy** and the wealth of the nation.

Protestantism has made us rich.

The German sociologist Max Weber was interested in the contrasting levels of economic success in various countries during the 16th to 19th centuries. In *The Protestant Ethic and the Spirit of Capitalism*, he argued that northern Europe and the US had fared better than the Catholic societies of South America and the Mediterranean because of Protestant beliefs in predestination, vocation, and the work ethic.

For Catholics divine reckoning is a future event: one must live a decent life and perform good deeds

See also: Economic man 52–53 ▪ Economics and tradition 166–67 ▪ Institutions in economics 206–07 ▪ Market information and incentives 208–09 ▪ Social capital 280

The village blacksmith held an important place in the community, according to Max Weber, because he dealt frequently with many people in the course of his God-given vocation.

in order to be saved. But Protestant teachings, especially those stemming from Calvinist Protestantism, claimed that there was a pre-selected "elect" destined to be saved, who would live a virtuous life as a consequence of being part of the elect. Their actions in this physical life would not lead to their salvation, but merely show that

they were already destined for heaven. The Bible encourages hard work and frugality, so Protestants aimed to embody these qualities and demonstrate that they were among the saved, while everyone else faced damnation. Forbidden to buy luxuries, they reinvested their profits back into their business.

God-given vocations

Catholicism held that the only God-given vocation was priesthood, but Protestants thought that people could be called to any of the secular crafts and trades. The belief that they were serving God encouraged them to work with religious fervor, leading them to produce more goods and make more money.

Weber believed that the Protestant faith led inevitably to a capitalist economic society because it gave believers the chance to view the pursuit of profit as evidence of devotion, rather than of morally suspect motives such as greed and ambition. The idea of predestination also meant that believers need not worry about

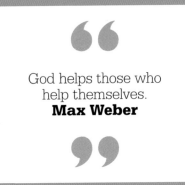

> God helps those who help themselves.
> **Max Weber**

social inequalities and poverty, because material wealth was a sign of spiritual wealth.

Weber's argument can be challenged, however. The leading European power in the 16th and 17th centuries, and the first global superpower, was the thoroughly Catholic Spanish Empire. Other conflicting cases can also be found in the rise of Asian countries that have never been Protestant, or even Christian. Japan is the third largest economy in the world, and China is growing fast. ∎

Max Weber

Karl Emil Maximilian Weber was one of the founding fathers of modern social science as well as an economist. He was born in 1864 in Erfurt, Germany, and was brought up in a prosperous, cosmopolitan, and intellectual family. His father was an outgoing civil servant, while his mother was a strict Calvinist Protestant.

Weber studied law at the universities of Heidelberg and Berlin, then held professorships in economics at various German universities until his father's death in 1897 left him too depressed to teach. After volunteering for

service in World War I he changed his political views and became a prominent critic of the Kaiser. Weber commanded widespread respect in the political establishment and after the war helped write the Weimar Republic's constitution. He resumed teaching, but in 1920 died of Spanish flu.

Key works

1904–05 *The Protestant Ethic and the Spirit of Capitalism*
1919 *Politics as a Vocation*
1923 *General Economic History*

THE POOR ARE UNLUCKY, NOT BAD
THE POVERTY PROBLEM

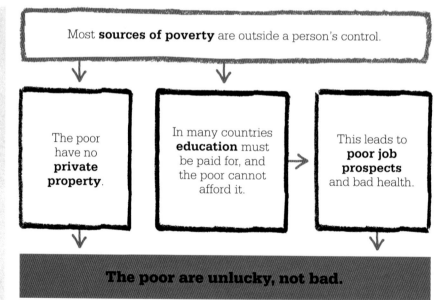

Most **sources of poverty** are outside a person's control.

The poor have no **private property**.

In many countries **education** must be paid for, and the poor cannot afford it.

This leads to **poor job prospects** and bad health.

The poor are unlucky, not bad.

In high-income countries governments often account for 30–50 percent of spending in the economy. About half of this consists of "social transfers," or welfare spending. In historical terms such high social spending is a comparatively new development, dating from the 1930s and 40s.

Welfare spending has a long history. In the 16th century England's Poor Law assumed there were three types of poor people: the deserving poor (the old, the young, and the sick), the deserving unemployed (those willing to work but unable to find employment), and the undeserving poor (beggars). The first two groups were given food and money donated by local people, but the third group were treated as criminals. With industrialization the view of the poor changed, and by the 18th century many people thought that the poor had only themselves to blame. British

See also: Demographics and economics 68–69 ▪ Development economics 188–93 ▪ Entitlement theory 256–57

economists David Ricardo (p.84) and Thomas Malthus (p.69) asked for the Poor Laws to be abolished, claiming handouts weakened the incentive to work.

This view became widely held, but there was an alternative view given by British philosopher John Stuart Mill (p.95) in 1848. Mill argued that economics is concerned only with production— the distribution of wealth is society's choice. In his work on politics he usually argued in favor of limiting the role of government, but in this case he said the state should step in to help those unable to help themselves and provide citizens with the education they needed to earn a living.

As the right to vote broadened in European countries during the 19th and 20th centuries, it was accompanied by greater demands for social spending and the redistribution of wealth. Elaborate public health and education systems developed with those for welfare benefits.

These unsanitary living conditions of the poor in London, as depicted by Gustave Doré in 1872, afflicted most of the cities of Europe. Adults, children, and vermin fought for precious space.

21st-century poverty

After 1800, a great divergence of wealth developed between Europe and North America, and the rest of the world. Poverty has been a persistent problem in South Asia and Sub-Saharan Africa. Economists have emphasized the role of health, education, and transportation, as well as direct support to the poor in reducing poverty.

Indian economist Amartya Sen (p.257) argued that poverty is about limitations in "capabilities and functionings"—the things people can succeed in doing or being— not the goods or services they have access to. This idea is reflected in continuing questions about whether the poverty line is absolute (meeting basic requirements) or relative (such as a percentage of the average income). ▪

Development goals

In September 2000, 189 world leaders from the United Nations signed eight Millennium Development Goals to be met by 2015. The goals are: end poverty and hunger, universal education, gender equality, child health, maternal health, combat diseases (HIV/AIDS, TB, and malaria), environmental sustainability, and global partnership. One target was to halve the number of people in extreme poverty by 2015.

According to the World Bank, the percentage of people in developing countries who earn less than $1 a day fell from 30.8 percent in 1990 to 14 percent in 2008, after adjustments were made for the different prices of goods in the different countries. This was largely thanks to progress in East Asia. However, $1 is a desperate level. The average "poverty line" used by developing countries is $2 a day. In 2008, 2.5 billion people in developing countries (43 percent) had incomes below this line.

A man begs in Fortaleza, Brazil. According to the United Nations, today's poor face "dehumanizing conditions." The UN is committed to halving world poverty by 2015.

SOCIALISM
IS THE ABOLITION OF
RATIONAL ECONOMY

CENTRAL PLANNING

IN CONTEXT

FOCUS
Economic systems

KEY THINKER
Ludwig von Mises
(1881–1973)

BEFORE
1867 Karl Marx sees scientific socialism as organized like an immense factory.

1908 Italian economist Enrico Barone argues that efficiency can be achieved in a socialist state.

AFTER
1929 US economist Fred Taylor says that mathematical trial and error can achieve equilibrium under socialism.

1934–35 Economists Lionel Robbins and Friedrich Hayek emphasize the practical problems with socialism— such as the scale of computation required and the absence of risk taking.

Modern production is **complex and varied**.

Only **prices and profits** can efficiently guide investment.

Under socialism the **state owns** the means of production.

Without private ownership and rivalry there is **little information or incentive** for efficient production.

Socialism is the abolition of rational economy.

T he German philosopher Karl Marx described socialist economic organization in his great work *Capital* in 1867 (pp.100–05). A socialist economy, he argued, required state ownership of the means of production (such as factories). Competition was wasteful. Marx proposed running society as if it were one enormous factory and believed that capitalism would lead inevitably to revolution.

Economists took Marx's ideas seriously. When Italian economist Vilfredo Pareto (p.131) used mathematics to demonstrate how free market competition produces efficient outcomes, he also suggested that these could be achieved by a central planner under socialism. His compatriot, the economist Enrico Barone, took this notion further in *The Ministry of Production in a Collectivist State* (1908). Just a few years later, Europe was engulfed by World War I, which many saw as a catastrophic failure of the old order. The Russian Revolution of 1917 provided an example of a socialist takeover of the economy, and the war's defeated powers—Germany, Austria, and Hungary—saw socialist parties take power.

Free market economists seemed unable to offer theoretical counter-arguments to socialism. But then in 1920, Austrian economist Ludwig von Mises raised a fundamental objection, claiming that planning under socialism was impossible.

Calculating with money
Von Mises' 1920 article *Economic Calculation in the Socialist Commonwealth* carried a simple challenge. He said that production

in the modern economy is so complex that the information provided by market prices—which is generated through the rivalry of many producers focused on making profits—is essential to planning. We need prices and profits to establish where demand lies and guide investment. His ideas started a debate between capitalism and socialism, called the "socialist calculation" or "systems debate."

Imagine planning a railway between two cities. Which route should it take, and should it even be built at all? These decisions require a comparison of benefits and costs. The benefits are savings in the transport expenses of many different users. The costs include labor hours, iron, coal, machinery, and so on. It is essential to use a common unit to make this calculation: money, the value of which is based on market prices. Yet, under socialism, genuine money prices for these items no

> In the socialist commonwealth, every economic change becomes an undertaking whose success can be neither appraised in advance nor later retrospectively determined. There is only groping in the dark.
> **Ludwig von Mises**

longer exist—the state has to make them up. Von Mises said that this was not as much of a problem for consumer goods. It is not difficult to decide, based on consumer tastes, whether to devote land to producing 1,000 gallons of wine or 500 gallons of oil. Nor is it a problem for simple production, as in a family firm. One person can easily make a mental calculation as to whether to spend the day building a bench, making a pot, picking fruit, or building a wall. However, complex production requires formal economic calculation. Without such help, von Mises claimed, the human mind "would simply stand perplexed before the problems of management and location."

Market prices

In addition to using money prices as a common unit with which to evaluate projects, economic calculation under capitalism has two other advantages. First, market

Boris Kustodiev's *The Bolshevik* reflected the idealistic policies of the Russian Revolution. Within four years they had floundered and were replaced by the New Economic Policy.

prices automatically reflect the valuations of everyone involved in trade. Second, market prices reflect production techniques that are both technologically and economically feasible. Rivalry among producers means only the most profitable production techniques are selected.

Von Mises argued that genuine market prices rely on the existence of money, which must be used at all stages—for buying and selling the goods involved in production, and for buying and selling them in consumption. Money is used in a more limited way in the socialist system: for paying wages and buying consumer goods. But money is no longer needed at the state-owned production end of the economy, just as it is not needed »

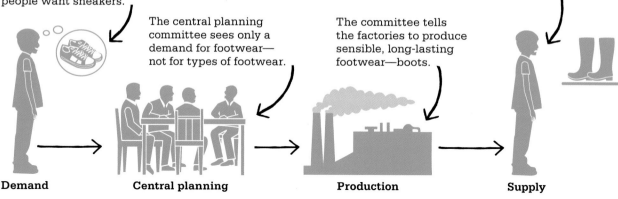

There is demand for different types of footwear in the economy —for example, some people want sneakers.

Planned economies lack basic market information about demand, so a central planning committee has to guess the type and level of demand for any item. Their ideas about what people want or need are unlikely to be accurate.

Everyone ends up with boots, even if some people wanted sneakers.

The central planning committee sees only a demand for footwear— not for types of footwear.

The committee tells the factories to produce sensible, long-lasting footwear—boots.

Demand   **Central planning**   **Production**   **Supply**

for the internal workings of a factory. Von Mises considered alternatives to money, such as Marx's idea of valuing products by the number of hours of labor that have gone into making them. But such a measure ignores the relative scarcity of different materials, the different qualities of the labor, or the actual (as opposed to labor) time that the production process takes. Only market prices take all these factors into account.

Changing prices
Von Mises, and his followers in the Austrian School of economists, did not believe that societies reach equilibrium, where they "naturally" hover around a certain level, or state of balance. He argued that economies are in constant disequilibrium; they are always changing, and participants are surrounded by uncertainty. Furthermore, a central planner cannot simply adopt the prices that previously prevailed under a market system. If central planning relies on prices from a different system, how could socialism possibly supersede the market economy?

Von Mises's challenge sparked several responses. Some economists claimed that a central planner could equate supply and demand through trial and error, similar to the process that Léon Walras (p.120) had suggested for establishing equilibrium in a market economy. However, this mathematical approach was really no different from the arguments of Barone, and any discussion of mathematical equilibrium was considered unrealistic by the Austrian School.

Von Mises's supporters, Lionel Robbins and Friedrich Hayek (p.177), added that such computation was not practical. Moreover, the socialist system could not replicate the risk taking in the face of uncertainty undertaken by entrepreneurs in the market system. In 1936, economists Oskar Lange and Abba Lerner proposed a system of "market socialism" whereby many separate firms are owned by the state and seek to maximize profits, given prices set by the state. Hayek, the Austrian School's new champion, led the response to market socialism (pp.172–77), arguing that only the free market could provide the necessary incentives and information.

Socialism in action
For some of its life the Soviet Union operated a form of market socialism. At first it appeared to do well, but the economic system suffered from persistent problems. There were periodic attempts at reform, shifting targets from output to sales, and trying to give more discretion to state firms. But state firms often hid resources from central planners, met targets through shortcuts that did not meet customer needs, and neglected tasks outside their plans. There was considerable waste, and output fell well short of targets. When the system collapsed, the Austrian School's concerns about incentives and information seemed to have been justified by events.

Von Mises was equally critical of any form of government intervention in the market economy. He claimed that intervention produces adverse side effects that lead to further intervention until, step-by-step, society is led into full-blooded socialism. In the market economy firms make profits by serving consumers, and in his opinion— and that of the Austrian School— there should be no restrictions on such a worthwhile activity. The Austrian School does not accept the concept of market failure, or at least sees it as trumped by government failure. It believes monopoly is caused by governments rather than by private enterprise. Externalities (outcomes that are not reflected in market prices) such as pollution are taken into consideration by consumers or solved by voluntary associations or the responses of people whose property rights are affected by the externality.

For the Austrian School one of the worst forms of government intervention is interference in the money supply. They claim that when governments inflate the supply of money (by printing more money, for example) it leads to interest rates that are too low, which in turn result in bad investments. The only thing to do when a bubble bursts is to accept the commercial failures and ensuing depression. They recommend abolishing central banks and basing money on a real commodity standard, such as gold. The Austrian School are firm believers in laissez-faire (hands-off) government.

In 1900, there were five leading schools of economics. Marxism, the German Historical School (which was also critical of the market system), and three versions of the mainstream free market approach: the British School (led by Alfred Marshall), the Lausanne School (centered on general equilibrium through mathematical equations), and the Austrian School, led by Carl Menger (p.335). The British and Lausanne schools became mainstream economics, but the Austrian School trod an uncompromising path. Only recently, following the 2008 financial crisis and the retreat of socialism, has it begun to grow in popularity. ∎

Socialist economies saw themselves as vast production lines, assembling everything the economy needed. During World War II this command style of production line worked relatively efficiently.

Ludwig von Mises

The leader of the Austrian School, Ludwig von Mises was the son of a railway engineer. He was born in Lemberg, Austria–Hungary, in 1881 and studied at the University of Vienna, where he regularly attended the seminars of the economist Eugen von Böhm-Bawerk. From 1909–34, von Mises worked at the Vienna Chamber of Commerce, serving as principal economic adviser to the Austrian government. At the same time he also taught economic theory at the university, where he attracted a dedicated following but never became professor. In 1934, concerned by Nazi influence in Austria, he took a professorship at the University of Geneva. In August, 1940, shortly after the German invasion of France, he emigrated to New York and taught economic theory at New York University from 1948–67. He died in 1973.

Key works

1912 *The Theory of Money and Credit*
1922 *Socialism: An Economic and Sociological Analysis*
1949 *Human Action: A Treatise on Economics*

CAPITALISM DESTROYS THE OLD AND CREATES THE NEW
CREATIVE DESTRUCTION

IN CONTEXT

FOCUS
Economic systems

KEY THINKER
Joseph Schumpeter
(1883–1950)

BEFORE
1867 Karl Marx states that capitalism moves forward by crisis, repeatedly destroying a whole range of productive forces.

1913 German economist Werner Sombart argues that destruction opens the way for creation, just as a shortage of wood led to the use of coal.

AFTER
1995 US economist Clayton M. Christensen distinguishes between disruptive and sustaining innovation.

2001 US economists Richard Foster and Sarah Kaplan argue that even the most exceptional corporations cannot beat the capital markets indefinitely.

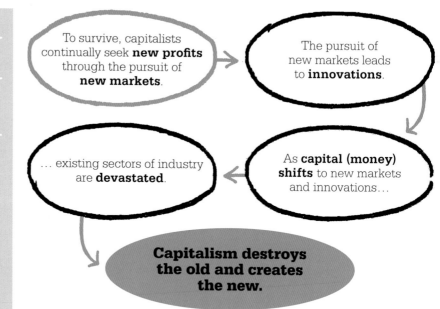

To survive, capitalists continually seek **new profits** through the pursuit of **new markets**.

The pursuit of new markets leads to **innovations**.

As **capital (money) shifts** to new markets and innovations…

… existing sectors of industry are **devastated**.

Capitalism destroys the old and creates the new.

When a recession bites and companies and jobs start to disappear, there is often a demand for government intervention to counteract these effects. The Austrian economist Joseph Schumpeter, writing in the depths of the Great Depression in the 1930s, disagreed. He insisted that recessions are how capitalism moves forward, weeding out the inefficient and making way for new growth in a process originally described by Karl Marx (p.105) as "creative destruction."

Schumpeter believed that entrepreneurs are at the heart of capitalist progress. Where Adam Smith (p.61) saw profit arising from the earnings of capital, and Marx from the exploitation of labor, Schumpeter said that profit comes from innovation—which does not derive from capital or labor. He saw

See also: Free market economics 54–61 ▪ Boom and bust 78–79 ▪
Marxist economics 100–05 ▪ Technological leaps 313

the entrepreneur as a new class of
person, an "upstart" outside the
capital-owning or working class
who innovates, creating new
products and forms of production in
uncertain conditions.

The entrepreneur's creative
response to economic change
makes him or her stand out from
the owners of existing firms, who
only make "adaptive responses" to
minor economic change. Forced to
borrow to bring their innovations
to market, entrepreneurs take risks
and inevitably meet with resistance.
They disturb the old system and
open up new opportunities for
profit. For Schumpeter innovation
creates new markets far more
effectively than Smith's "invisible
hand" or free-market competition.

Breaking through
Schumpeter argued that, although
a new market may grow after an
innovation, others soon imitate
and begin to eat into the profits
of the original innovator. In time
the market begins to stagnate.
Recessions are a vital way of
moving things forward again,
clearing away the dead wood, even
if the process is painful. In recent
years business strategists such

Apple's iPhone was introduced by
visionary entrepreneur Steve Jobs.
It was an industry "game changer,"
forcing competitors to come up with
products that could rival it.

> New products and new
> methods compete with the
> old… not on equal terms but at
> a decisive advantage that may
> mean death to the latter.
> **Joseph Schumpeter**

as US economist Clayton M.
Christensen have distinguished
between two types of innovations.
"Sustaining" innovations maintain
an ongoing system and are often
technological improvements.
On the other hand "disruptive"
innovations upset the market and
really get things moving, changing
the market through product
innovation. For example, although
Apple did not invent the technology
of the digital music player, it
combined a high-design product
(iPod) with a music download
program (iTunes) to provide a
new way of accessing music.

Marx believed that creative
destruction gave capitalism huge
energy but also explosive crises
that would destroy it. Schumpeter
agreed but argued that it would
destroy itself due to its success,
not failure. He saw monopolies as
the engine of innovation but said
these were doomed to grow into
over-large corporations, whose
bureaucracy would eventually
stifle the entrepreneurial spirit
that had given them life. ▪

Joseph Schumpeter

Born in 1883 in Moravia,
then part of the Austro-
Hungarian Empire, Joseph
Schumpeter was the son of
a German factory owner. His
father died when he was four,
and Schumpeter moved with
his mother to Vienna. There
she married an aristocratic
Viennese general who helped
launch the brilliant young
economist on a whirlwind
career that saw him become
a professor of economics,
the Austrian Minister for
Finance, and President
of the Biedermann Bank.

After the bank collapsed
in 1924 and Austria and
Germany succumbed to
nazism, Schumpeter moved
to the US. He became a
lecturer at Harvard, where
he acquired a small cult
following. Schumpeter died
in 1950 at the age of 66.

Key works

1911 *The Theory of Economic
Development*
1939 *Business Cycles*
1942 *Capitalism, Socialism
and Democracy*
1954 *History of Economic
Analysis*

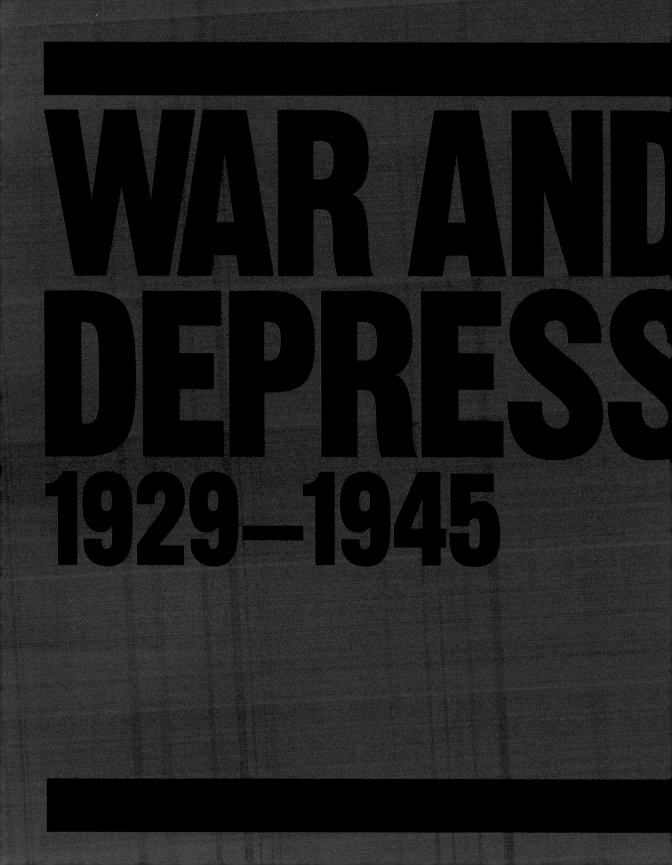

WAR AND DEPRESS

1929–1945

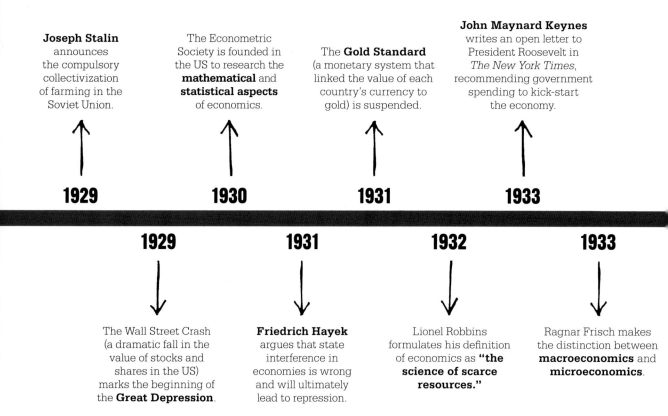

Joseph Stalin announces the compulsory collectivization of farming in the Soviet Union.

The Econometric Society is founded in the US to research the **mathematical** and **statistical aspects** of economics.

The **Gold Standard** (a monetary system that linked the value of each country's currency to gold) is suspended.

John Maynard Keynes writes an open letter to President Roosevelt in *The New York Times*, recommending government spending to kick-start the economy.

1929   **1930**   **1931**   **1933**

1929   **1931**   **1932**   **1933**

The Wall Street Crash (a dramatic fall in the value of stocks and shares in the US) marks the beginning of the **Great Depression**.

Friedrich Hayek argues that state interference in economies is wrong and will ultimately lead to repression.

Lionel Robbins formulates his definition of economics as **"the science of scarce resources."**

Ragnar Frisch makes the distinction between **macroeconomics** and **microeconomics**.

I n the years following World War I confidence in traditional economic thinking was put to the test by events in Europe and North America. Social and political unrest had led to a communist revolution in Russia while hyperinflation had made the German economy collapse.

During the 1920s the US enjoyed such prosperity that in 1928 President Herbert Hoover said, "We in America are nearer to the final triumph over poverty than ever before in the history of any land." One year later the Wall Street Crash took place: shares collapsed and thousands of firms folded. By 1932, more than 13 million Americans were unemployed. The US recalled the huge loans they had previously made to Europe, and European banks collapsed. For

much of the decade, many countries worldwide were in a severe depression. It was during this period that the British economist Lionel Robbins formulated his often-quoted definition of economics as "the science of scarce resources."

A new approach

Trust in the free market's ability to provide stability and growth was shaken, and economists looked for new strategies to tackle economic ills, particularly unemployment. Some began to examine the institutional problems of developed capitalist economies. US economists Adolf Berle and Gardiner Means, for example, showed how managers were running corporations for their own benefit rather than for the firm's. The most pressing need was to find a means of stimulating the

economy, for which a completely new approach was needed. The answer came from British economist John Maynard Keynes (p.161), who recognized the failings of a totally free market—one that is untouched by any form of intervention. Where previous generations had trusted the market's own workings to right the system's shortcomings, Keynes advocated state intervention, and specifically government spending, to boost demand and lift economies out of depression.

At first his ideas were met with skepticism, but they later gained support. His model envisioned the economy as a machine that could be regulated by governments through adjusting variables such as the money supply and public spending. In 1933, Keynes's arguments provided a rationale for

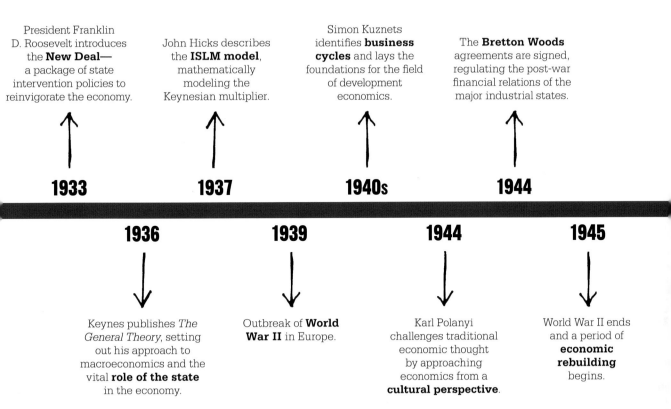

President Franklin
D. Roosevelt introduces
the **New Deal—**
a package of state
intervention policies to
reinvigorate the economy.

John Hicks describes
the **ISLM model**,
mathematically
modeling the
Keynesian multiplier.

Simon Kuznets
identifies **business
cycles** and lays the
foundations for the field
of development
economics.

The **Bretton Woods**
agreements are signed,
regulating the post-war
financial relations of the
major industrial states.

1933　　　**1937**　　　**1940s**　　　**1944**

1936　　　**1939**　　　**1944**　　　**1945**

Keynes publishes *The
General Theory*, setting
out his approach to
macroeconomics and the
vital **role of the state**
in the economy.

Outbreak of **World
War II** in Europe.

Karl Polanyi
challenges traditional
economic thought
by approaching
economics from a
cultural perspective.

World War II ends
and a period of
**economic
rebuilding**
begins.

President Franklin D. Roosevelt to
kick-start the US economy with the
stimulus policies known as the
New Deal. Government money was
used to fund huge infrastructure
projects, and all banks were placed
under federal control. The New Deal
formed the basis for economic
policy in America and Europe
following World War II.

Norwegian economist Ragnar
Frisch (p.336) drew attention to the
two different ways in which an
economy could be studied—in part
(microeconomics) or as a whole
system (macroeconomics). The new
field of econometrics (mathematical
analysis of economic data) emerged
as a useful tool in economic
planning and forecasting. Modern
macroeconomics took its approach
from Keynes, and his approach was
widely admired. However, despite

the Keynesian solution to the
depression of the 1930s, the idea of
state intervention was still seen by
many economists as unhealthy
interference with the market
economy. Some Americans saw it
as alien to the "American way,"
while European economists
associated it with socialism.
Keynes himself saw it as part of a
British Liberal tradition, in which
the hard facts of economics are
tempered by social considerations.

Global differences
Economics developed certain
national characteristics, with
different schools of thought
developing along broadly cultural
lines. In Austria a radical school
of thought evolved that supported
an absolutely free market, based
largely on the work of Friedrich

Hayek (p.177). His stance was
as much anti-communist as it was
pro-capitalist. He argued that the
freedom and democracy of the West
was bound up with its free market
economies, while the tyranny of
communist regimes, with their
planned, centralized economies,
removed this freedom. Others took
this view further, arguing that
competitive markets are essential
to growth, as evidenced by the
higher standards of living in
Western capitalist countries.

The migration of many German
and Austrian thinkers to Britain and
the US during the 1930s led these
ideas to become widespread. Later
on, as faith in Keynesian economics
began to wane, a new generation of
economists reintroduced the idea
that markets should be left to their
own devices. ■

UNEMPLOYMENT IS NOT A CHOICE

DEPRESSIONS AND UNEMPLOYMENT

In 1936, John Maynard Keynes published his groundbreaking work *The General Theory of Employment, Interest, and Prices*, often referred to simply as *The General Theory*. The book was important because it forced people to consider the workings of the economy from a completely different perspective. It made Keynes one of the world's most famous economists.

Ever since the Scottish economist Adam Smith (p.61) had published *The Wealth of Nations* in 1776, outlining what came to be known as classical economics, the economy had been viewed as a perfectly balanced collection of individual markets and decision makers. The consensus among economists was that the economy would spontaneously and naturally achieve a state of equilibrium with all those who wanted to work finding employment.

Keynes was to turn much of the basic cause-and-effect of the classical model on its head. He also argued that the macroeconomy (the total economy) behaved quite differently from the microeconomy (a section of the economy). Originally tutored in the classical school, Keynes claimed that he struggled to escape from its habitual modes of thought. His success in doing so, however, led to a radical economic approach that suggested an entirely different set of causes for unemployment and equally different solutions.

This Edgar Degas painting of 1875 shows absinthe drinkers idling in a café. Until Keynes's ideas were published in 1936, alcohol abuse and other vices were seen as causes of worklessness.

Classical economics states that **unemployment is always a choice**—there are jobs if people are prepared to work for lower wages.

But wages change slowly, so during recessions, as prices fall, the value of wages rise—and firms **demand less labor**.

As demand in the economy slumps, workers are **trapped in unemployment**, and firms are trapped in underproduction.

Unemployment is not a choice.

Anxious crowds gather on Wall Street on October 29, 1929, the day the stock market crashed. Half the value of US shares was wiped out in a day, starting the Great Depression.

For a century prior to the publication of *The General Theory*, poverty, rather than unemployment, was the enduring problem. Until the 1880s countries such as Britain and the US, which were undergoing rapid growth as a result of the Industrial Revolution, enjoyed general advances in living standards, but pockets of grinding poverty remained.

The idle poor

Economists had long seen poverty as the greatest social policy issue, but by the end of the 19th century the unemployment of workers began to cause increasing concern. At first it was thought the problem was caused by illness or some defect in the character of the worker, such as idleness, vice, a lack of enterprise, or a lack of a work ethic. This meant that unemployment was seen as a problem for individuals who were for some reason unable to work, rather than a problem for society in general. It was certainly not seen as an issue that public policy needed to concern itself with.

In 1909, British social campaigner Beatrice Webb (p.135) produced *The Minority Report of the Royal Commission on the Poor Laws*. This was the first document to lay out the concept and policies of a welfare state, and it claimed that "the duty of so organizing the national labor market as to prevent or minimize unemployment should be placed upon a Minister." The term "involuntary unemployment" came into use for the first time. With this came the idea that unemployment is caused not by the shortcomings of individuals, but by surrounding economic conditions outside of their control.

Involuntary unemployment

By 1913, the concept of involuntary unemployment was understood as defined by the British economist Arthur Pigou (p.336): it was a situation where workers in an industry were willing to provide more labor at the current wage level than was being demanded. Even today this definition would be regarded as a good representation of the involuntary nature of unemployment, in that it suggests that the workers have been left with no choice about whether they work or not. At this time the classical view of unemployment still dominated. This held that unemployment was largely voluntary, that it existed because workers chose not to work at the going wage rate or would rather be involved in some "non-market activity," such as child care. Those holding this view insisted that any involuntary unemployment would be dealt with by automatic and self-correcting mechanisms of the free market.

Under the classical view involuntary unemployment could not persist for long: the play of markets would always quickly return the economy to full employment. There is evidence »

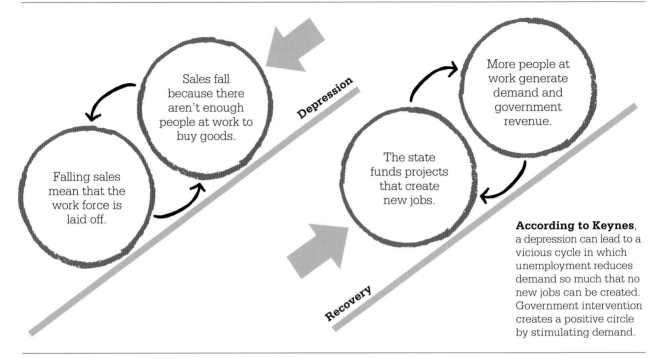

Sales fall because there aren't enough people at work to buy goods.

Falling sales mean that the work force is laid off.

Depression

More people at work generate demand and government revenue.

The state funds projects that create new jobs.

Recovery

According to Keynes, a depression can lead to a vicious cycle in which unemployment reduces demand so much that no new jobs can be created. Government intervention creates a positive circle by stimulating demand.

to suggest that Keynes originally had some sympathy with this view. In *A Treatise on Money* (1930), he wrote that firms have three choices when prices fall faster than costs: to put up with the losses, close the business, or embark on a struggle with the employees to reduce their earnings per unit of output. Only the last of these, Keynes said, was capable of restoring real equilibrium from the national point of view.

However, after the 1929 stock market crash in the US and the Great Depression that swept across the world in its aftermath, Keynes changed his mind. The financial collapse of Wall Street trapped the economies of the world in a cycle of falling production—it fell by 40 percent in the US. By 1931, US national income had fallen from a pre-crash level of $87 billion to $42 billion; by 1933, 14 million Americans were unemployed. Their gaunt figures haunted the landscape, and the rapid fall in

living standards is evident in the images of poverty and desperation from that era. Witnessing this devastation inspired Keynes to write *The General Theory*.

The Great Depression
Keynes took the world of the Great Depression as his starting point. The normal workings of the market seemed unable to create the pressure necessary to correct the

> 66
> The difficulty lies not in the new ideas but in escaping from the old ones.
> **John Maynard Keynes**
> 99

problem of high, persistent, involuntary unemployment in the economy. In general, the number of people at work is determined by the level of real wages—the level of wages relative to the prices of goods and services being offered. In times of recession prices of goods tend to fall faster than levels of wages because demand for goods lowers and prices fall, while workers resist cuts in their wage packets. This causes the real wage to rise. At this higher level of real wages the number of people willing to work will increase, and the number of workers demanded by firms will fall because they are more expensive. The result is unemployment.

Sticky wages
One way to eliminate unemployment would be for the excess labor (the people not working) to create pressure on money wages to fall by being willing to work for less than the

Men seek work in a Chicago job agency in 1931. By 1933, more than 10 million Americans had lost their jobs. The state responded with a stimulus package named The New Deal.

going wage. Classical economists believed that markets were flexible enough to adjust and bring down real wages. But Keynes suggested that money wages might be "sticky" (p.303) and would not adjust: involuntary unemployment would persist. Keynes argued that workers were unable to price themselves back into work by accepting lower wages. He pointed out that after a collapse in demand, such as that seen in the Great Depression, firms might be willing to employ more workers at lower real wages, but in reality they cannot. This is because the demand for output is constrained

The unemployment rate in several countries between 1919 and 1939 is shown here. Most economies recovered in the 1920s only to suffer soaring unemployment with the onset of the Great Depression in 1930.

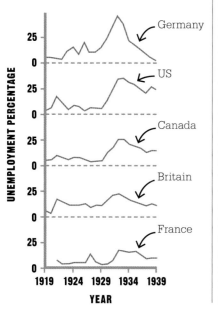

by a lack of demand in the whole economy for the goods they make. Workers want to supply more, and firms want to make more because otherwise factories and machinery lie idle. A lack of demand has trapped workers and firms into a vicious cycle of unemployment and underproduction.

The government's role

Keynes saw that the solution to the problem of involuntary unemployment lay outside of the control of both the workers and the firms. He claimed that the answer was for governments to spend more in the economy so that the overall demand for products would rise. This would encourage firms to take on more workers, and as prices rose, real wages would fall, returning the economy to full employment. To Keynes it did not matter how the state spent more. He famously said that "the treasury could fill old bottles with banknotes and bury them… and leave it to private enterprise on well tried principles

of laissez-faire to dig the notes up again." As long as the government injected demand into the economy, the whole system would start to recover.

Real wages

The General Theory is not easy to understand—even Keynes said he found it "complex, ill-organized, and sometimes obscure"—and there is still considerable debate about exactly what Keynes meant, particularly by the difference between involuntary and voluntary unemployment. One explanation for high unemployment being involuntary is based on the idea that a firm's demand for labor is determined by the real wage that firms have to pay. Workers and firms can only negotiate what the money wage is for that job or that industry—they have no control over the price level in the wider, general economy. In fact lower wages will generally reduce both the cost of production and therefore the prices of goods as well, meaning the real wage » will not fall by the level required to remove the unemployment. In this way the unemployment is involuntary because workers are powerless to do anything about it. There is a commonly held view that trade unions can resist the adjustment of wages to the level required for full employment through the process of collective action, so that those who are unemployed are prevented from getting work. Keynes placed this type of unemployment in the voluntary category, arguing that workers as a whole are agreeing openly, or tacitly, not to work for less than the current wage. Keynes' reasoning was different from that of later economics, which became dominated by mathematical modeling. Much of macroeconomics in the post-war period was about clarifying what

Keynes said and framing it in terms of more formal models and equations. British economist John Hicks (p.165) formulated Keynesian ideas in terms of a financial model known as the ISLM model. After the war this became the standard macroeconomic model, and it is still one of the first things taught to economics students.

New interpretations
Modern considerations of Keynes' work suggest that what workers are most concerned with is their wage relative to other workers. Workers have an idea of their position in a theoretical "league table" of pay and will fiercely fight any wage reductions that would push them further down the table. It is interesting to note that a general increase in the price level through inflation, which would

also cause a reduction in real wages, is resisted less strongly because it affects all workers equally.

Economic theories known as efficiency wages models (p.302) ask why firms don't cut wages to increase profits and suggest that firms are reluctant to do so because a wage cut would demotivate the existing workers, who would see their relative position in the league table undermined. The net effect of cutting wages would in fact be a loss in profits because the benefit of lower wages is more than offset by the reduction in productivity that results from low morale or skilled workers leaving. In this way workers cannot choose to price themselves into work. Related "New Keynesian" models of wage determination provide other explanations for rigid wages (p.303).

If by a regularization of national demand we prevent… the involuntary idleness of unemployed men, we make a real addition to the national product.
**Sidney Webb
Beatrice Webb**

President Franklin D. Roosevelt invested in vast new infrastructure projects, such as the Hoover Dam on the Colorado River. Even so, the government was not pursuing Keynesian policies.

Is an accountant driving a taxi an out-of-work accountant or an in-work taxi driver? Keynesians might say that he is involuntarily unemployed. New classical economists say he has got a job.

Classical resurgence

Keynesianism became discredited in the 1970s as European economies ran into trouble. Classical ideas about unemployment were revived by the so-called "new classical" school of economists, who once again denied the possibility of persistent involuntary unemployment. The US economist Robert Lucas (1937–) was one of the leaders of the assault on Keynesianism. When he was asked how he would describe an accountant who was driving a taxi because he could not find a job as an accountant, Lucas replied, "I would describe him as a taxi driver, if what he is doing is driving a taxi." For the modern classicists the market always clears, and workers always have a choice whether to work or not.

Efficiency wage theorists might agree that all workers who want jobs in a recession might be able to get one, but they think that some workers—like the accountant—are underutilized and are not maximizing their value to the economy. As a taxi

The sooner involuntary unemployment is disposed with, the better.
Robert Lucas

driver, the man is still an involuntarily unemployed accountant. When demand in the economy returns to a normal level, he will return to his most productive and efficient occupation: accountancy. Fundamental difference in views about the ability of markets to adjust lie at the heart of the debate between Keynesians and the classical economists.

Classical reality

Keynes would probably have agreed with the American Nobel Prize-winning economist Joseph Stiglitz (p.338), who said that during the Great Depression in the US one quarter of the unemployed workforce of Chicago might be said to have chosen to be unemployed because they could have migrated west to California to pick fruit on farms, along with the millions of others who did so. He said that nonetheless, this still represents a massive failure of the market, and if classical theory suggests that there is nothing more to be done than commiserate with the unemployed on their bad luck, we would be better off not consulting the theory at all. ∎

John Maynard Keynes

Born in 1883, the year that Karl Marx died, John Maynard Keynes was an unlikely savior of the working class. Raised in Cambridge, England, by academic parents, he lived a life of privilege. He won a scholarship to Cambridge University, where he studied mathematics, then spent time working in the India Office of the British government and published his first book: *Indian Currency and Finance*.

Keynes was an advisor at both the Paris Peace Conference after World War I and at the Bretton Woods Conference in 1944. He always did several things at once (while writing *The General Theory,* he built a theater), and he counted leading writers and artists among his friends. Keynes made his fortune on the stock market and used much of it to support his artist friends. He died of heart problems in 1946.

Key works

1919 *The Economic Consequences of the Peace*
1930 *A Treatise on Money*
1936 *The General Theory of Employment, Interest, and Money*

SOME PEOPLE LOVE RISK, OTHERS AVOID IT
RISK AND UNCERTAINTY

IN CONTEXT

FOCUS
Decision making

KEY THINKER
Frank Knight (1885–1972)

BEFORE
1738 Dutch-Swiss
mathematician Daniel
Bernoulli formulates a theory
of risk aversion and utility.

AFTER
1953 French economist
Maurice Allais discovers a
paradox in decision making
that contradicts expected
utility theory.

1962 US economist Daniel
Ellsberg shows how people's
decisions in conditions of
uncertainty are not based
purely on probability.

1979 Israeli psychologists
Daniel Kahneman and
Amos Tversky question
the rationality of economic
decisions in their prospect
theory, based on real-life
experiments.

Less risky investments tend to have **lower returns**.

Riskier investments tend to have **higher returns**.

Risk-averse investors are prepared to accept a lower payoff in order to get a guaranteed return.

Risk-loving investors are prepared to accept more risk in order to get a higher return.

Some people love risk, others avoid it.

There is an element of risk in any business venture or investment in a market economy. Before deciding on a course of action, an individual has to consider the possible outcomes and weigh their potential returns against their probability, that is, calculate the "expected utility." If there is a safe alternative, this one is generally preferred to the riskier option, unless the expected return on the riskier option is considerably more attractive. The greater the risk, the higher the profit has to be to attract investors.

The similarity to weighing the odds in gambling is clear, and early studies of risk were made by 18th-century mathematicians, who

See also: Economic man 52–53 ▪ Irrational decision making 194–95 ▪ Paradoxes in decision making 248–49 ▪ Financial engineering 262–65 ▪ Behavioral economics 266–69

> Profit arises out of the inherent, absolute unpredictability of things.
> **Frank Knight**

analyzed the probabilities in gambling games. In the 1920s US economist Frank Knight became one of the first economists to analyze the relationship between risk and profit in a free market economy. He also made a distinction between risk and uncertainty. Risk, by his definition, occurs when the outcome of a course of action is not known, but where it is possible to determine the probability of various possible outcomes. This allows a mathematical assessment of the level of risk, which can then be insured against. Also, the expected utility can then be compared realistically with alternatives.

For Knight "uncertainty" describes a situation where the probability of outcomes is not known so the various possible outcomes cannot be compared in terms of expected utility. This means that the risk cannot be measured mathematically. Knight argues that when firms are prepared to accept this uninsurable uncertainty, and their risk-taking pays off, it produces profits—even when the economy is in a state of long-term equilibrium.

Investors and entrepreneurs often operate under conditions of risk and uncertainty, recognizing the potential for high returns. On occasions this "who dares, wins" attitude can become extreme, as in the cases of bond traders and bankers who have made headlines for losing or gaining vast fortunes. Most people, such as ordinary savers who place their life savings in a fixed-interest saving account, prefer to play it safe, forgoing profits in return for a risk-free investment. There is essentially a spectrum of risk preferences, ranging from the risk-loving to the risk-averse, just as there is a range of levels of risk. The attraction of a higher return can begin to tempt even the risk-averse to take on some level of risk.

Levels of risk

Risk applies to all kinds of economic activities, including investing money in stocks and shares, making unsecured rather than secured loans, and selling goods in a completely new market. Our personal economic decisions are also framed in terms of risk: whether we work for an employer or start up our own business, and how we invest our personal savings. Insurance markets exist because we are risk averse. Insurers and actuaries, credit-rating agencies, and market research can help us assess the level of risk and whether the returns make it worth taking, but some unfathomable degree of uncertainty will always remain. ▪

Traders in a futures market in São Paulo, Brazil, are effectively betting on the future movements of commodity prices. Even a small price change can result in enormous profits or losses.

Frank Knight

One of the foremost economists of his generation, Frank Knight was born in Illinois in 1885. He studied philosophy at Cornell, switching to economics after a year. His PhD dissertation formed the basis of his best-known work, *Risk, Uncertainty and Profit*.

Knight was the first Professor of Economics at the University of Iowa, and then moved to Chicago University in 1927, where he remained for the rest of his life.

He was an early member of the Chicago School of economists. His students included future Nobel prize winners Milton Friedman, James Buchanan, and George Stigler, who described Knight as having "unceasing intellectual curiosity."

Key works

1921 *Risk, Uncertainty and Profit*
1935 *The Ethics of Competition*
1947 *Freedom and Reform: Essays in Economics and Social Philosophy*

GOVERNMENT SPENDING BOOSTS THE ECONOMY BY MORE THAN WHAT IS SPENT
THE KEYNESIAN MULTIPLIER

IN CONTEXT

FOCUS
The macroeconomy

KEY THINKER
John Maynard Keynes
(1883–1946)

BEFORE
1931 British economist Richard Kahn sets out an explicit theory to explain the multiplying effects of government spending suggested by John Maynard Keynes.

AFTER
1971 Polish economist Michal Kalecki further develops the notion of the multiplier.

1974 US economist Robert Barro revives the idea of "Ricardian equivalence" (that people alter their behavior to adjust to government budget shifts). This implies there are no multiplier effects from government spending.

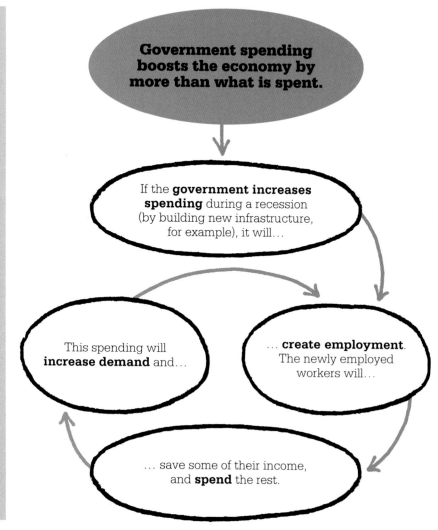

Government spending boosts the economy by more than what is spent.

If the **government increases spending** during a recession (by building new infrastructure, for example), it will…

… **create employment.** The newly employed workers will…

… save some of their income, and **spend** the rest.

This spending will **increase demand** and…

See also: The circular flow of the economy 40–45 ■ Gluts in markets 74–75 ■ Borrowing and debt 76–77 ■ Depressions and unemployment 154–61

Macroeconomics seeks to explain the working of entire economies. In 1758, the French economist François Quesnay (p.45) demonstrated how large amounts of spending by those at the top of the economic tree— the landlords—was multiplied as others received money from them and re-spent it.

In the 20th century British economist John Maynard Keynes looked specifically at why prices and labor do not revert to equilibrium, or natural levels, during depressions. Classical economics—the standard school of thought from the 18th to the 20th centuries—says that this should naturally occur through the normal working of the free market. Keynes concluded that the fastest way to help an economy recover was to boost demand through an increase in short-term government spending.

A key idea here was that of the multiplier, discussed by Keynes and others, notably Richard Kahn, and then developed mathematically by John Hicks. This says that if a government invests in large projects (such as road building) during a recession, employment will rise by more than the number of workers employed directly. National income will be boosted by more than the amount of government spending.

This is because workers on the government projects will spend a portion of their income on things made by other people around them, and this spending creates further employment. These newly employed workers will also spend some of their income, creating yet more employment. This process will continue, but the effect will lessen on each round of spending, since each time some of the extra

Vast infrastructure projects, such as the Three Gorges Dam, China, can create thousands of jobs. The new workers' wages then pour back into the economy, creating a second round of spending.

income will be saved or spent on goods from abroad. A standard estimate is that every $1 of government spending might create an increase in income of $1.40 through these secondary effects.

In 1936, British economist John Hicks devised a mathematical model based on the Keynesian multiplier, known as the ISLM model (Investment, Savings, the demand for Liquidity, and the Money supply). It could be used to predict how changes in government spending or taxation would impact on the level of employment through the multiplier. During the post-war period it became the standard tool for explaining the working of the economy.

Some economists have attacked the principle of the Keynesian multiplier, claiming that governments would finance spending through taxation or debt. Tax would take money out of the economy and create the opposite effect to that desired, while debt would cause inflation, lessening the purchasing power of those vital wages. ■

John Hicks

The son of a journalist, John Hicks was born in Warwick, England, in 1904. He received a private-school education and a degree in philosophy, politics, and economics from Oxford University, all funded by mathematical scholarships. In 1923, he began lecturing at the London School of Economics alongside Friedrich Hayek and Ursula Webb, an eminent British economist who became his wife in 1935. Hicks later taught at the universities of Cambridge, Manchester, and Oxford. Humanitarianism lay at the heart of all his work, and he and his wife traveled widely after World War II, advising many newly independent countries on their financial structures. Hicks was awarded the Nobel Prize in 1972. He died in 1989.

Key works

1937 *Mr. Keynes and the Classics*
1939 *Value and Capital*
1965 *Capital and Growth*

> ❝
> Besides the primary employment created by the initial public works expenditures, there would be additional indirect employment.
> **Don Patinkin**
> US economist (1922–95)
> ❞

ECONOMIES ARE EMBEDDED IN CULTURE

ECONOMICS AND TRADITION

conomists believe that people are rational, in that they will take the action that promises the highest economic return, whether this is choosing a car or a president. The Austrian-born economist Karl Polanyi turned this idea on its head. He said that the important thing about people is that they are social beings submerged in a "soup" of culture and tradition. It is this soup that is the nourisher of economic life, he claimed, not the profit motives of calculating individuals.

Island economics

In *The Great Transformation* (1944), Polanyi wrote about the Trobriand Islands, off Papua New Guinea, whose tribal economy was driven by non-economic behavior in

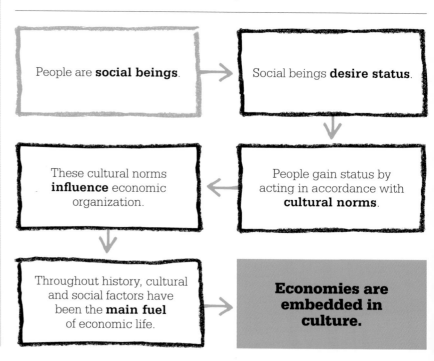

People are **social beings**. → Social beings **desire status**.

↓

People gain status by acting in accordance with **cultural norms**.

←

These cultural norms **influence** economic organization.

↓

Throughout history, cultural and social factors have been the **main fuel** of economic life. → **Economies are embedded in culture.**

See also: Economic man 52–53 ▪ Religion and the economy 138–39 ▪ Institutions in economics 206–07 ▪ Social capital 280

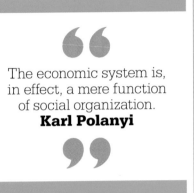

> The economic system is, in effect, a mere function of social organization.
> **Karl Polanyi**

striking ways. Trade, even today, happens through gifts, not by haggling. Islanders make dangerous voyages to neighboring tribes to give presents of red-shell necklaces and white armbands, and the practice is regulated by customs and magical rites known as *kula*. The gifts are not kept, but passed on. By showing generosity, the islanders enhance their social standing. The drive for status, not profit, is the motor of trade.

Tribal economies are, of course, different from those of today's industrialized countries. Polanyi argued that as European nations developed, custom and tradition were supplanted by the anonymity of the market. Even so, the soup of culture and social ties still sustains advanced economies.

The Israeli economic historian Avner Offer (1944–) has documented the role of non-market precepts in modern economic life, including those of gift giving and favors. Like the islanders, modern societies practice wealth redistribution—otherwise it would not be possible to build roads or raise armies. Home-based economic activities such as cooking, cleaning, and child care—in both traditional

and modern economies—are done for their usefulness rather than for profit. Offer estimates that in late-20th-century Britain, this type of non-market production amounts to 30 percent of national income.

Individualistic economies

Polanyi believed that economies come from the "substantive" features of societies—their special histories and quirks of culture. For the economic purist all this is irrelevant, obscuring what really propels economies: the signals that prices send to rational individuals in whom the thirst for gain trumps religion or culture, even in the most traditional communities. These two positions can only be resolved if it is possible to reduce the social norms that govern whole societies to the actions of self-interested individuals. Polanyi rejected this. He believed that modern markets and social structures are in conflict, and that where markets expand, social upheaval inevitably follows. ∎

Trobriand islanders follow unusual customs of gift exchange. Red-shell necklaces are carried clockwise around the islands by sea; white arm bands are circulated counter-clockwise.

Karl Polanyi

Born in Vienna to Jewish parents in 1886, Karl Polanyi was brought up in Budapest, Hungary, where he studied law. As a student he mixed with radicals such as the Marxist philosopher Georg Lukács and the sociologist Karl Mannheim. During World War I he served in the Austro-Hungarian army, then moved to Vienna, working as a journalist. He married a young revolutionary, Ilona Duczynska, and the two of them fled to Britain in 1933 to escape the rise of nazism.

In London Polanyi worked as a journalist and taught working people whose poor living conditions left a lasting impact on him. From 1940 until his retirement he lectured in the US but had to live in Canada and commute because his wife's involvement in the Hungarian Revolution banned her from entering the country. He died in 1964.

Key works

1944 *The Great Transformation*
1957 *Trade and Markets in the Early Empires* (with C. Arnsberg and H. Pearson)
1966 *Dahomey and the Slave Trade* (with A. Rotstein)

MANAGERS GO FOR PERKS, NOT THEIR COMPANY'S PROFITS
CORPORATE GOVERNANCE

IN CONTEXT

FOCUS
Markets and firms

KEY THINKERS
Adolf Berle (1895–1971)
Gardiner Means (1896–1988)

BEFORE
1602 The Dutch East India Company is the first joint-stock company to issue shares and begins trading on the Amsterdam Stock Exchange.

1929 The Dow Jones loses 50 percent of its value in one day, Black Thursday, kick-starting the Great Depression.

AFTER
1983 US economists Eugene Fama and Michael Jensen publish *The Separation of Ownership and Control*, viewing the company as a series of contracts.

2002 The Sarbanes-Oxley Act becomes law in the US, laying down stricter standards for US boardrooms.

Most people assume that the basic principle of a free market economy is that companies are run by management in the best interests of the shareholders. According to the US economists Adolf Berle and Gardiner Means, this view is entirely wrong. Their 1932 book, *The Modern Corporation and Private Property*, shined a light on corporate governance and showed how the balance of power had swung from the owners of a company toward the management.

The failure of corporate governance became a big issue in 2008 when many felt that the pay of top executives rose out of proportion to their company's results and falling share prices.

Berle and Means claimed that the dominance of management began during the Industrial Revolution with the emergence of the factory system. An increasing number of workers came together under one roof, where they handed their labor over to management in exchange for a wage. Modern corporations bring together the wealth of innumerable individuals (the shareholders). They hand control of it to a small management group, this time in return for a dividend. Both result in a powerful management answerable to no one.

Apathetic shareholders
Berle and Means identified modern shareholders as passive owners. These owners surrender their wealth to the governance of the company and no longer make decisions about how to "look after" their investments—they have passed that responsibility, and that power, to management. The apathy of small-time shareholders results in them either merely maintaining the status quo or failing to exercise their voting options. This may be beyond their grasp in any case— if they really wished to change things, they would have to hold a

See also: Public companies 38 ▪ Free market economics 54–61 ▪
The competitive market 126–29 ▪ Institutions in economics 206–07

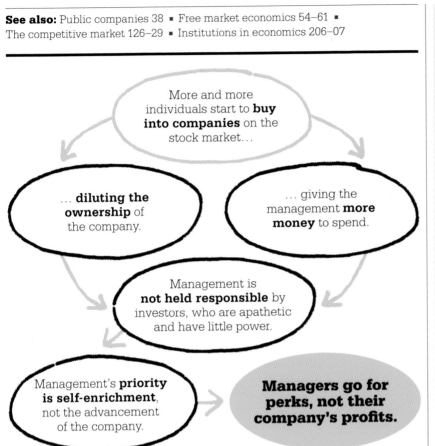

> More and more individuals start to **buy into companies** on the stock market…
>
> … **diluting the ownership** of the company.
>
> … giving the management **more money** to spend.
>
> Management is **not held responsible** by investors, who are apathetic and have little power.
>
> Management's **priority is self-enrichment**, not the advancement of the company.
>
> **Managers go for perks, not their company's profits.**

larger shareholding or galvanize a sufficient number of shareholders to force through a change. As a result, the owners of companies have a smaller and smaller influence in the running of their companies. This is not a problem when management interests coincide with those of the shareholders. However, if we assume that management are acting in a self-interested way and seeking their own personal profit, their interests will be very different from those of the owners.

Berle and Means argued for a change in corporate law that would return power to shareholders over the corporations. They insisted that shareholders should be given rights to hire and fire management and to hold regular general meetings. When their book was first published, US corporate law did not generally include such measures, and Berle and Means were instrumental in the founding of the modern corporate legal system.

Corporate failures

Today, the failure of corporate governance is the focus of popular discontent with capitalism. Since taxpayers have become majority owners in some large corporations, corporate leadership is in the spotlight, revealing the self-interest of some chief executives who are awarded ever increasing pay and bonuses. Many feel that shareholders remain powerless in the face of the corporate machine. ▪

Executive pay

Berle and Means warned of the dangers of self-interested executives in 1932, but some people argue that the problem has become worse in the US and Europe in the last 20 years. Shareholders vote to choose the board of directors, but executive pay is set by a remuneration committee composed of other high-earners. They keep pay high to enforce a "market rate," and they can then look forward to receiving a large pay raise due to "market forces." Shareholders have the power to dismiss the board, but this would not be well received by the markets—which, in turn, could cause share prices to fall.

The problem is worsened by the fact that many shares are held by hedge funds (speculative investment firms) with no long-term interest in the company. Fund managers aim to receive large pay increases in line with chief executive officers (CEOs), so it is not in their interest to vote against high remuneration packages.

Today, a merry-go-round of remuneration committee members sets corporate pay. Legislation that would allow shareholders a voice in these committees seems likely.

THE ECONOMY IS A PREDICTABLE MACHINE
TESTING ECONOMIC THEORIES

IN CONTEXT

FOCUS
Economic methods

KEY THINKER
Ragnar Frisch (1895–1973)

BEFORE
1696 English economist Gregory King publishes *Natural and Political Observations*, containing the first quantitative (measurable) analysis of economics.

1914 US economist Henry Moore publishes *Economic Cycles: Their Law and Cause*, laying the foundations for statistical economics, the forerunner of econometrics.

AFTER
1940 Austrian economist Ludwig von Mises argues that empirical methods cannot be applied to social sciences.

2003 British economist Clive Granger wins the Nobel Prize for his analyses of the relationship between economic variables over time.

In the 1930s Norwegian economist Ragnar Frisch developed a new discipline that he called "econometrics." His aim was to develop methods to explain and predict the movements of the economy. Econometrics is the application of mathematical testing methods to economic theories, providing a statistical basis on which to prove or disprove a theory. Economic beliefs, such as "a better education leads to a higher salary," may be correct, but can only be proven through an equation that takes data on educational attainment levels and compares it with salary levels. Econometrics also enables economists to analyze past market trends and predict future performance by extracting patterns from economic data.

Intermediate between mathematics, statistics, and economics we find a new discipline which… may be called econometrics.
Ragnar Frisch

Statistical pitfalls
Although econometrics is an important tool of empirical explanation, there are pitfalls. For instance, past market trends are no real guarantee of future market performance. It is also difficult to take all variables into account. In the education example educational attainment is not the only factor that affects the wage—other, unmeasurable skills might also play a role. These kinds of problems can weaken the validity of the results of economic models. It is also important not to confuse statistical significance with economic significance. ∎

See also: Measuring wealth 36–37 ▪ Inflation and unemployment 202–03 ▪ Financial engineering 262–65 ▪ Complexity and chaos 278–79

ECONOMICS IS THE SCIENCE OF SCARCE RESOURCES
DEFINITIONS OF ECONOMICS

I n 1932, the British economist Lionel Robbins provoked controversy by publishing his *Essay on the Nature and Significance of Economic Science*, which contained a new definition of economics. Robbins defined it as the science of human actions in the face of limited resources with multiple uses. He based his definition on the fact that human needs are infinite, yet there are only a finite amount of resources.

As one need is fulfilled, another one takes its place. However, there are only limited resources (land, labor, entrepreneurship, and capital) available to fulfill these desires. Scarcity means that every desire can never be satisfied.

Needs versus resources
The tension between unlimited needs and limited resources is the basis of economics. Every resource has an alternative use—for example, if a field is used for grazing livestock, it cannot produce a crop at the same time. This means that we have to decide the best way of using resources. Robbins believed that this is the key problem facing every society—deciding which goods to produce, and in what quantity, in order to best satisfy consumers. It is the very scarcity of resources that gives them their value.

Today, Robbins's definition is widely accepted, but some argue that economics should be seen in broader terms—as an investigation of how societies generate more resources over time. ∎

Lionel Robbins's definition focuses on the fact that scarcity forces an economic choice—such as whether to use a field to feed cattle or grow wheat.

See also: Demographics and economics 68–69 ∎ Opportunity cost 133 ∎ Markets and social outcomes 210–13 ∎ Shortages in planned economies 232–33

WE WISH TO PRESERVE

A FREE

SOCIETY

ECONOMIC LIBERALISM

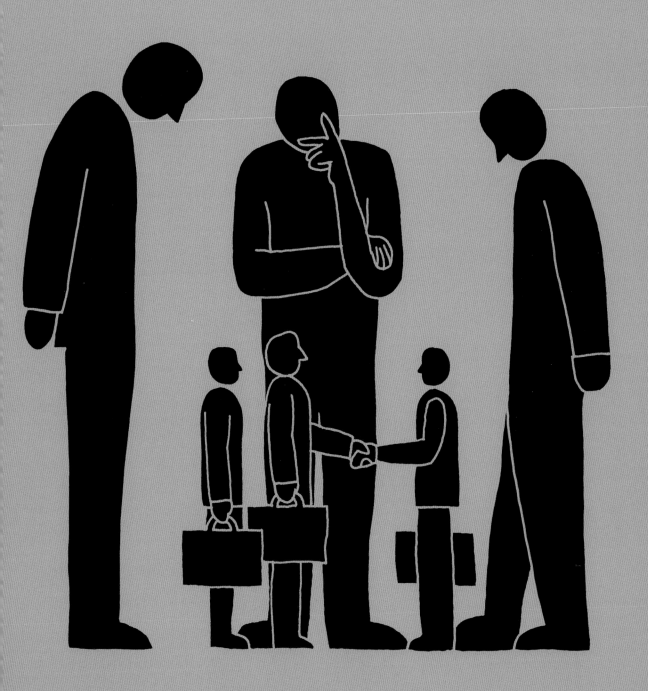

IN CONTEXT

FOCUS
Society and the economy

KEY THINKER
Friedrich Hayek (1899–1992)

BEFORE
1908 Italian economist Enrico Barone shows how a central government planner can replace the free market if it can calculate prices.

1920 Ludwig von Mises refutes Barone's argument.

1936–37 Oskar Lange argues against von Mises's position.

AFTER
1970s Hayek's arguments for free markets gain ground.

1991 US historian Francis Fukuyama says free market capitalism has defeated all possible alternatives.

Late 2000s Criticisms of government bank bailouts prompt a revival of interest in Hayek's ideas.

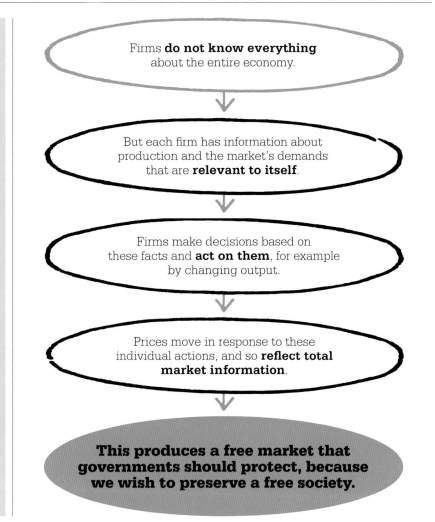

Firms **do not know everything** about the entire economy.

But each firm has information about production and the market's demands that are **relevant to itself**.

Firms make decisions based on these facts and **act on them**, for example by changing output.

Prices move in response to these individual actions, and so **reflect total market information**.

This produces a free market that governments should protect, because we wish to preserve a free society.

Mainstream economics has always had its critics. Its focus on mathematical formulas and its sometimes sweeping assumptions have led economists to challenge both its methods and its lack of empirical evidence. Many of these critics have been from the political Left, who see the mainstream as providing a glossy support for an unjust free market.

One minority tradition, the Austrian School, has argued quite differently. Vociferous defenders of the free market, but critical of the mainstream, they have carved out a unique place within the discipline. Most prominent of these radicals was an Austrian-British economist, Friedrich Hayek. Hayek vies with John Maynard Keynes (p.161) for the title of the 20th century's most influential economist, and he made a range of contributions to political and economic thought. These covered economics, law, political theory, and neuroscience. His writings maintained a closely argued, consistent set of principles, which he saw as being in the tradition of classical liberalism: support for free markets, support

for private property, and deep pessimism about the ability of governments to shape society.

Creating dictatorships

The argument for which Hayek is best remembered appeared in 1944 in *The Road to Serfdom*. At the time there was a growing enthusiasm for government intervention and central planning. Hayek argued that all attempts to impose a collective order on society are doomed to failure. He said they would lead, inexorably, to the totalitarianism of fascism or Stalinist communism. Since all planning necessarily acts against the "spontaneous order" of the market, it can only occur with a degree of force, or coercion. The more that a government draws up plans and imposes them, the more coercion is needed. As governments are poorly informed about the detailed workings of the market, planning is bound to steadily fail in its aims, while becoming increasingly coercive to compensate for those failings. At that point a society would lurch toward a totalitarian state, in which all freedom was extinguished, however moderate the planners' initial goals.

Economists of the Left had argued that a centrally planned economy was not only possible, but more efficient than a free market. Their first significant opponent, in 1920, was another member of the Austrian School, Ludwig von Mises (p.147). He argued that socialism—here defined as central planning—is not economically viable. It offers no rational means of pricing commodities since it relies on the *diktat* (unquestionable command) of one central planner or committee to perform the allocation decisions that in a free market are undertaken by many hundreds of thousands of individuals. The amount of information needed to assess the scarcities and surpluses of a market and set prices correctly is so huge that the attempt is doomed to failure. Socialism, wrote von Mises, is the "abolition of the rational

The totalitarian state of North Korea suffers regular shortages and famine. Economists of the Austrian School claim that this is the inevitable result of central planning that ignores markets.

economy." Only a free market with private property can provide the basis for the decentralized pricing decisions a complex economy requires.

Socialism defended
Polish economist Oskar Lange, however, disagreed with von Mises. He famously responded to von Mises' claims in a 1936 article, *On the Economic Theory of Socialism*, using a development of general equilibrium theory. This theory, which was not perfected until after World War II, is a mathematical representation of a market economy stripped to its bare essentials. All imperfections in markets have been removed, and all participants in the market are fully informed and concerned only with their self-interest. On this basis, Lange said, a central planning board could fix the initial set of prices for the economy, and then allow all those in society to trade freely, adjusting their demand and supply

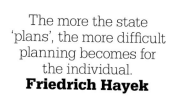

> The more the state 'plans', the more difficult planning becomes for the individual.
> **Friedrich Hayek**

around the prices given. The planning board could then adjust prices according to demand and supply. The outcome, he argued, would be efficient. A planner could also reduce income inequalities and constrain the market's tendency to short-term thinking.

Lange had taken the usual assumptions of microeconomics (that supply and demand »

determine price), and turned them on their head. His work later formed the basis for welfare economics, which looks at how free markets can achieve socially desirable aims.

The Austrian School

However, Hayek and his colleagues offered quite a different version of the free market's virtues. They did not assume that markets lack imperfections or that individuals are completely informed. To the contrary, they argued, it is because individuals and firms are poorly informed and society imperfect that the market mechanism is the best way to distribute goods. This view became an important tenet of the Austrian School of thought.

In a situation of continual ignorance, Hayek argued, the market is the best available means not to provide information, but to acquire it. Each individual and every firm knows their own situation best:

they have goods and services people demand, they can plan for the future, and they see the prices that are relevant to them. Information is specific and dispersed among all those in society. Prices move in response to actions by individuals and firms, and so come to reflect the entire amount of information available to society as a whole.

Hayek maintains that this "spontaneous order" is the best available means to organize a complex modern economy, given that knowledge about society can never be perfect. Attempts to impose collective restraints on this order represent a reversion to primitive, instinctual orders of society—and the free market must be defended against this.

Collective tyranny

The idea of spontaneous order came to dominate Hayek's thinking, and his writing turned

increasingly to political questions. These were discussed most fully in *The Constitution of Liberty* (1960), which argues that government should act only to preserve the spontaneous workings of the market, in as far as this is possible. Private property and contracts are legally sacrosanct, and a free society must observe rules that bind all parties—including the state itself. Beyond this, the state can, if the need arises, act against those collectivist forces threatening to undermine the rule of law. Hayek was broadly in favor of democracy, but critical of its inclination in some cases toward a "democratic tyranny of the collective."

Birth of neoliberalism

Following World War II the necessary rebuilding of countries led to a Keynesian consensus, which proposed increased government intervention in the economy.

The free flow of information between individual sellers and vendors (left) results in the correct pricing of goods, according to Hayek. Centrally planned economies, on the other hand, impose the view of one person or committee (right), curtailing individual freedom to communicate and firms' ability to trade.

Auctions are free markets where prices arise from the direct and rapid exchange of localized information between buyers and sellers.

At the same time Hayek and others in the Austrian School formed the Mont Perelin Society, which acted as a guiding influence on the free market think tanks that arose during the breakdown of the Keynesian consensus in the 1970s. A similar new approach to economic policy sprang up in South America, but it was its adoption by the governments of Ronald Reagan in the US and Margaret Thatcher in the UK that made it globally significant. This was neoliberalism, and it followed closely the ideas of the once-maligned Austrian School.

Nationalized industries were privatized, and governments rolled back their intervention in the workings of the market. The Soviet Union collapsed, giving further impetus to the apparent triumph of Hayekian themes in politics. Across the world even those parties once most adamantly opposed to free markets came to believe that there was no viable alternative, including Britain's Labour Party—who had been the direct target of Hayek's *Road to Serfdom*.

Mainstream economists strongly influenced by free market thinking, such as Milton Friedman, have risen to influence. By 2000, a "new consensus" prevailed in macroeconomics that emphasized the limited role of the state.

New relevance

Despite the apparent triumph of Austrian themes in economics and Hayek's 1974 Nobel Prize, the distinctive methods and theory of the Austrian School remained largely confined to the fringes. However, the collapse of the global financial system in 2007–08 and the subsequent bank bailouts have provoked a renewed interest in its doctrines. Austrian School economists have been prominent in attacking bank bailouts, claiming that they represent an unwarranted interference in the market. The Free Banking School, which calls for an end to the government monopoly of the money supply, takes its cue from a 1976 Hayek paper, *Denationalization of Money*, and its ideas have gained ground. Keynesian programs of increased government spending have been similarly criticized. With mainstream economics in a continuing state of turmoil, the Austrian School is set to achieve fresh influence. ∎

Friedrich Hayek

Friedrich August von Hayek was born in Vienna, Austria, to a family of intellectuals. By the age of 23, he had received doctorates in law and politics in addition to spending a year in the Italian army during World War I. Initially drawn to socialism, he attended Ludwig von Mises' seminars while in Vienna, and with von Mises' support founded the Austrian Institute of Business Cycle Research. In 1923, he traveled to New York for a year, and the accuracy of US newspaper accounts of the war compared to those in Austria led to his deep distrust of governments.

In 1931, he moved to London to teach at the London School of Economics and became embroiled in a very public, two-year argument with John Maynard Keynes. Hayek became a British citizen in 1938, but in 1950 left London for the University of Chicago. He died aged 93 in Freiburg, Germany, in 1992.

Key works

1944 *The Road to Serfdom*
1948 *Individualism and Economic Order*
1988 *The Fatal Conceit*

INDUSTRIALIZATION CREATES SUSTAINED GROWTH

THE EMERGENCE OF MODERN ECONOMIES

IN CONTEXT

FOCUS
Growth and development

KEY THINKER
Simon Kuznets (1901–85)

BEFORE
1750s French economist François Quesnay states that wealth comes from agriculture, not from industry.

1940 British-Australian economist Colin Clark argues that economic growth involves a shift from agriculture to manufacturing and to services.

AFTER
1967 US economist Edward Denison highlights the important contribution of technological change and productivity growth to economic growth.

1975 US economists Hollis Chenery and Moshe Syrquin find evidence that as agriculture declines, economies grow, and then industry and services increase.

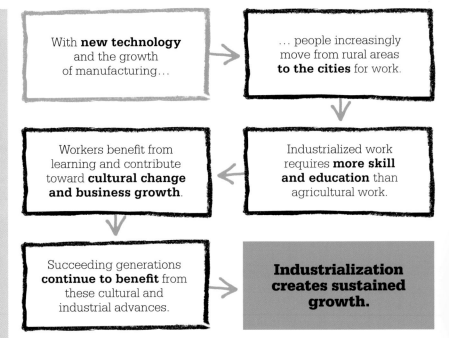

With **new technology** and the growth of manufacturing…

… people increasingly move from rural areas **to the cities** for work.

Industrialized work requires **more skill and education** than agricultural work.

Workers benefit from learning and contribute toward **cultural change and business growth**.

Succeeding generations **continue to benefit** from these cultural and industrial advances.

Industrialization creates sustained growth.

The Russian-born economist Simon Kuznets described the emergence of the modern economy as a controlled revolution—in which the factory replaces the farm. The resulting higher living standards require economic and social changes that run deeper than might at first be suggested by a simple, numerical rate of growth. Kuznets called this process "modern economic growth," and showed how success in achieving this is what sets rich countries apart from the rest.

The key characteristic of Kuznets' growth theory is that income per person grows rapidly, even in the face of an expanding population: there are more people and they are richer. This expansion is driven by the spread of factories and machines.

See also: Agriculture in the economy 39 ▪ Demographics and economics 68–69 ▪ Economies of scale 132 ▪ Market integration 226–31 ▪ Technological leaps 313

With an increase in capital to sustain industrial growth, workers are redeployed out of small family enterprises into impersonal firms and factories. Yet new technologies and large-scale production methods cannot be exploited if people are illiterate, superstitious, or tied to the village. For Kuznets this growth causes profound social changes, with an increase in urbanization and a weakening of religion.

Industrial Revolution

Britain was the first country to achieve modern economic growth. The Industrial Revolution of the 18th century put Britain on the path to becoming an advanced industrialized nation. Steam power and inventions reshaped production. Workers left the fields and entered the factories. Cities grew. New means of transport and communication technologies allowed British firms to penetrate the global economy. Its own economy did not transform overnight, but the changes—technological, social, and institutional—kept going. They led to unprecedented

improvements in the living standards of a growing population.

The spread of true modern economic growth has been limited. Among the rich nations, including the US, Australia, and Japan, the process continues today. After a first wave of industrialization these economies have typically evolved

The steam hammer, invented in 1837, was one of the machine tools that increased the pace of industrialization, allowing machines to build machines.

away from heavy industry and toward the service sector, which will inevitably involve further kinds of social change. ∎

Simon Kuznets

Simon Kuznets was born in Pinsk, in present-day Belarus, in 1901. His involvement with economics began early—he became head of a Ukrainian statistical office while still only a student. After the Russian Revolution Kuznets' family left for Turkey, then the US; he followed them in 1922.

Kuznets enrolled at Columbia University in New York, earning a PhD in 1926. He then worked at the National Bureau of Economic Research, where he developed the modern system of national income accounting used to this day by governments worldwide. In 1947,

Kuznets helped set up the International Association for Research in Income and Wealth, advising many governments. He taught widely, and in 1971 won the Nobel Prize for his analysis of Modern Economic Growth. He died in 1985, aged 84.

Key works

1941 *National Income and Its Composition, 1919–1938*
1942 *Uses of National Income in Peace and War*
1967 *Population and Economic Growth*

DIFFERENT PRICES TO DIFFERENT PEOPLE
PRICE DISCRIMINATION

In the 1840s the French engineer and economist Jules Dupuit suggested that tolls should be set for the bridges and roads he was building. He proposed to charge people according to how much each was willing to pay. Dupuit was the first economist to consider setting different prices for different people for the same service. This is known as price discrimination. It can usually only happen where there is some degree of monopoly power, which allows firms to charge different prices.

In 1920, three different "degrees" of price discrimination were identified by the British economist

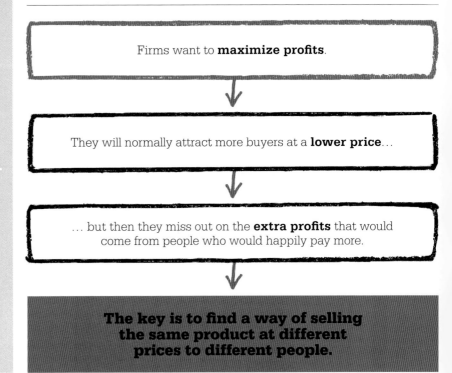

Firms want to **maximize profits**.

They will normally attract more buyers at a **lower price**...

... but then they miss out on the **extra profits** that would come from people who would happily pay more.

The key is to find a way of selling the same product at different prices to different people.

See also: Markets and morality 22–23 ▪ Effects of limited competition 90–91 ▪ Monopolies 92–97 ▪ The competitive market 126–29 ▪ Efficient markets 272

Arthur Pigou (p.336). First degree discrimination is the model that Dupuit used: a firm charges each individual the maximum he or she is willing to pay. In practice this is rare because it requires the seller to know every individual's valuation of the good.

Second degree discrimination involves reducing the price for each additional unit that is bought. This option is often used in supermarket deals, in offers such as "buy one bottle of soda and get the second for half price."

Third degree discrimination, which is probably the most common form, involves identifying customers by their differing characteristics. Movie theaters, for example, offers cheaper tickets for children and senior citizens.

Discriminatory effects

In her 1933 book *The Economics of Imperfect Competition*, the British economist Joan Robinson looked at the results of price discrimination on society. Most customers instinctively think that price discrimination in all three forms is unfair. If each bottle of soda costs

Students have low incomes, so high prices effectively bar them from doing or buying certain things. Student discount rates bring activities and goods within an affordable range.

Price discrimination is the act of selling the same article produced under single control at a different price to the different buyers.
Joan Robinson

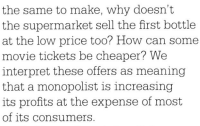

the same to make, why doesn't the supermarket sell the first bottle at the low price too? How can some movie tickets be cheaper? We interpret these offers as meaning that a monopolist is increasing its profits at the expense of most of its consumers.

Robinson found that if the monopolist produces the same output but charges higher prices to certain people, then consumers do lose out. However, sometimes price discrimination can allow people to do things they could not otherwise afford. When rail companies price discriminate, for instance, commuters in peak times are charged higher prices, but in off-peak periods it makes sense for the firm to set much lower prices, because they need to encourage people to take a train. So even though some consumers pay more, a larger number may find themselves able to travel at the lower price. In this way it is possible for consumers in total to benefit when firms set different prices to different people. ▪

Joan Robinson

Born in 1903 into a wealthy English family, Joan Violet Robinson (née Maurice) is considered to be the greatest female economist of the 20th century. She was educated at St Paul's Girls' School, London, and studied economics at Cambridge University. She married young and then traveled to India for two years before returning to Cambridge to teach. Here, she became part of a team around John Maynard Keynes that included economist Richard Kahn, with whom she formed a lifelong intellectual partnership. Robinson enjoyed traveling, and lectured abroad widely until her 70s—she was familiar to students in North and South America, Australia, Africa, and most of Europe. An original thinker who was unafraid of controversy, she is said to be the best economist never to win the Nobel Prize. She died at the age of 80.

Key works

1933 *The Economics of Imperfect Competition*
1937 *Essays on the Theory of Unemployment*
1956 *The Accumulation of Capital*

POST-W
ECONOM
1945–1970

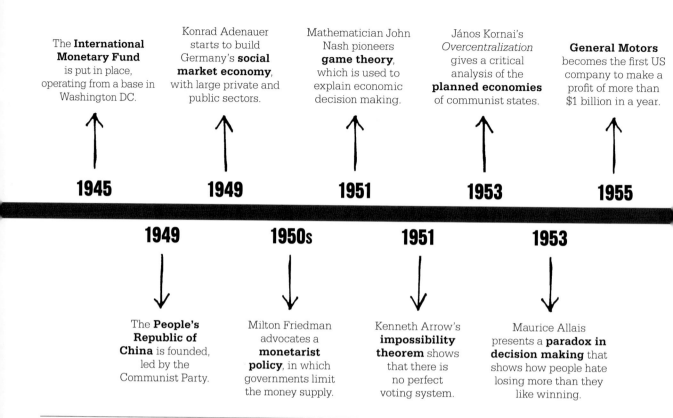

The **International Monetary Fund** is put in place, operating from a base in Washington DC.

Konrad Adenauer starts to build Germany's **social market economy**, with large private and public sectors.

Mathematician John Nash pioneers **game theory**, which is used to explain economic decision making.

János Kornai's *Overcentralization* gives a critical analysis of the **planned economies** of communist states.

General Motors becomes the first US company to make a profit of more than $1 billion in a year.

1945　　**1949**　　**1951**　　**1953**　　**1955**

1949　　**1950s**　　**1951**　　**1953**

The **People's Republic of China** is founded, led by the Communist Party.

Milton Friedman advocates a **monetarist policy**, in which governments limit the money supply.

Kenneth Arrow's **impossibility theorem** shows that there is no perfect voting system.

Maurice Allais presents a **paradox in decision making** that shows how people hate losing more than they like winning.

The years immediately following World War II were, inevitably, a time for rebuilding economies. Even before the end of the war, politicians and economists had started planning for peace. They were working to avoid the problems that had followed World War I and to establish a peaceful world of international economic cooperation.

The League of Nations, an international organization set up to maintain peace, had collapsed at the beginning of the war, and in 1945, it was replaced by the more robust United Nations (U.N.). One of the U.N.'s first tasks was to vote on proposals drawn up by delegates to the U.N. Monetary and Financial Conference, now better known by its location—Bretton Woods, in New Hampshire. Here, delegates from the Soviet Union, the UK, and the US agreed on the founding of major new institutions, such as the International Monetary Fund (IMF), the International Bank for Reconstruction and Development (IBRD), and the General Agreement on Tariffs and Trade (GATT).

Post-war Keynesianism
The British delegate at Bretton Woods was John Maynard Keynes (p.161), whose 1919 book, *The Economic Consequences of the Peace*, had warned what might happen after World War I as a result of economic policy. Keynes's work had inspired President Franklin D. Roosevelt to lift the US out of the Great Depression of the 1930s by the state spending package of the New Deal. It was not surprising that his ideas were equally influential after World War II. In the US Keynesian policies were enthusiastically advocated by economists such as Canadian-American John Kenneth Galbraith and quickly adopted by the liberal democratic government. In Britain the incoming Labor government brought in measures that set up a welfare state. The rebuilding of the economies of Japan and Germany was to mark a turning point in their histories. Germany, in particular, experienced an "economic miracle," the *Wirtschaftswunder*, under Chancellor Konrad Adenauer. The success of their social market economy, tempering free market economics with government intervention, became the model for many Western European economies in the second half of the 20th century. However, other

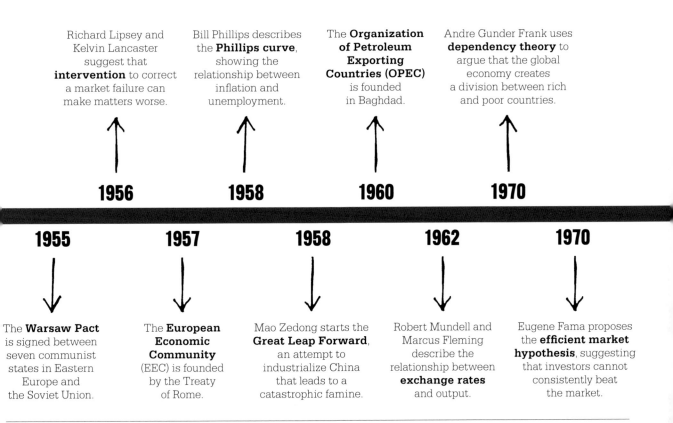

Richard Lipsey and Kelvin Lancaster suggest that **intervention** to correct a market failure can make matters worse.

Bill Phillips describes the **Phillips curve**, showing the relationship between inflation and unemployment.

The **Organization of Petroleum Exporting Countries (OPEC)** is founded in Baghdad.

Andre Gunder Frank uses **dependency theory** to argue that the global economy creates a division between rich and poor countries.

1956   **1958**   **1960**   **1970**

1955   **1957**   **1958**   **1962**   **1970**

The **Warsaw Pact** is signed between seven communist states in Eastern Europe and the Soviet Union.

The **European Economic Community** (EEC) is founded by the Treaty of Rome.

Mao Zedong starts the **Great Leap Forward**, an attempt to industrialize China that leads to a catastrophic famine.

Robert Mundell and Marcus Fleming describe the relationship between **exchange rates** and output.

Eugene Fama proposes the **efficient market hypothesis**, suggesting that investors cannot consistently beat the market.

countries were not moving along the same lines. Much of Asia was under communist rule, and the Iron Curtain now separated Europe into East and West. This was the era of the Cold War between the Soviet bloc and the West. The spread of communist regimes prompted a reaction among many economists in the West, especially those with experience of their tyranny.

Free market revival
Influenced by Austrians such as Ludwig von Mises (p.147) and Friedrich Hayek (p.177), the US's Chicago School of economists took a conservative stance against the prevailing mood of Keynesianism. They advocated a move back to a free market system with less government interference. The roots of this idea lay in the neoclassical

economics of the turn of the 20th century, which focused its analysis on supply and demand. Economists of the Chicago School turned to science for inspiration. Kenneth Arrow (p.209) used mathematics to prove the stability and efficiency of markets, and Bill Phillips (p.203) used ideas from physics to describe the trade-off between inflation and unemployment. Some Western economists, such as Maurice Allais (p.195), introduced ideas from psychology in the 1950s and 60s. This inspired new models of decision making that challenged the belief in "rational economic man" first described by Adam Smith.

Huge advances in communication technologies made the world seem a smaller place during the post-war decades, and economists became more aware than ever before of the

international nature of economics. Although the US and Europe still dominated economic thinking outside the communist states, more notice was being taken of the developing countries, not just as a source of raw materials but as economies in their own right.

Globalization continued apace, and economists began to examine the reasons for the gap between rich and poor countries, and how this could be narrowed. Ideas for development moved from capital investment to debt relief, but it became clear that the problems were more complex, involving politics, culture, and economics. At the same time economists began increasingly to suggest that perhaps economic prosperity was not the only—or even the best—way to measure a country's well-being. ∎

IN THE WAKE OF WAR AND DEPRESSION, NATIONS MUST COOPERATE

INTERNATIONAL TRADE AND BRETTON WOODS

The gold standard was a monetary system that backed paper money with gold, thereby guaranteeing its value. It came into effect in Britain in 1821 and was adopted internationally in 1871.

The system provided a stable anchor for the international monetary system by fixing the exchange rates of various currencies relative to the price of gold. It also acted as a mechanism for making gold transfers between countries to reflect new balances of trade and capital flows. However, World War I placed exceptional demands on government financing, and the system began to break down.

Some countries suspended their gold standard membership to allow substantial borrowing and expenditure, often financed simply by printing money. The war's end did not see a smooth return to the status quo—countries such as Germany had exhausted their gold reserves and could not return to membership, while other nations reentered the standard at wildly variable rates.

Abandoning gold

During the Great Depression of the 1930s nations left the gold standard in droves as they tried to expand their economies by devaluing their currencies to promote exports. At the same time international trade, which had been fairly unrestricted before the war, became subject to an increasing range of restrictions, as countries tried to maintain their position in a shrunken world market. These policies helped to prolong the Depression since each new restriction or devaluation further reduced the world market.

Dresden was among countless cities in Europe and Asia destroyed during World War II. The International Bank for Reconstruction and Development was set up to fund reconstruction.

See also: Comparative advantage 80–85 ▪ Depressions and unemployment
154–61 ▪ Market integration 226–31 ▪ International debt relief 314–15

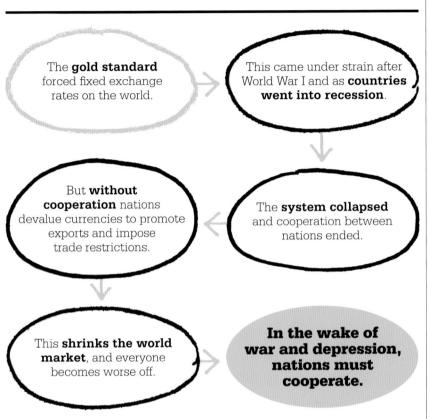

The **gold standard** forced fixed exchange rates on the world.

This came under strain after World War I and as **countries went into recession**.

But **without cooperation** nations devalue currencies to promote exports and impose trade restrictions.

The **system collapsed** and cooperation between nations ended.

This **shrinks the world market**, and everyone becomes worse off.

In the wake of war and depression, nations must cooperate.

After World War II, the Allied powers turned to the question of post-war economic reconstruction. A conference was held in June, 1944, at Bretton Woods, New Hampshire, where delegates agreed to a US plan to peg currencies against the dollar. The dollar, in turn, was to be maintained by the US government at a fixed rate of exchange with the price of gold.

This system was overseen by a new International Monetary Fund (IMF), which would be responsible for providing emergency funding, while the International Bank for Reconstruction and Development (now part of the World Bank group) was established to provide funding for development projects. In 1947, a General Agreement on Tariffs and Trade (GATT) aimed to rebuild international trade. Together these new organizations sought to renew economic cooperation among nations, the lack of which had been so costly between the wars.

This system held for nearly 30 years of exceptional economic growth, but it was structurally flawed. Continuous US trade deficits (where imports exceed exports) helped keep the system working, but dollars flooded abroad until the stockpiles exceeded US gold reserves, pushing the price of gold in dollars above the fixed price of gold. As US government expenditure increased, the strain worsened. In 1971, President Nixon suspended the dollar–gold link, ending the Bretton Woods system. ▪

The International Monetary Fund

Created by the Bretton Woods agreement, the International Monetary Fund (IMF) is today one of the world's most controversial international bodies. It was established initially as an emergency fund for countries experiencing financial difficulties arising from balance of payments deficits, debt crises, or often both. More than 180 member countries contribute toward a central fund, depending on the size of their economy, and they can apply for cheap loans from that fund. When the Bretton Woods fixed-exchange system was abandoned in 1971, the IMF's role changed. It began to impose strict conditions on its loans. Since the late 1970s these were heavily influenced by neoliberal ideas (pp.172–77), which advocated privatization and cutting government spending. Economists have criticized the IMF for making crises worse, such as the East Asian crisis of the late 1990s.

Traders watch as the crisis caused by the collapse of the Thai baht spreads across Asia in 1997. The Thais had given in to pressure from the IMF to float the baht.

ALL POOR COUNTRIES NEED IS A BIG PUSH

DEVELOPMENT ECONOMICS

IN CONTEXT

FOCUS
Growth and development

KEY THINKERS
Paul Rosenstein-Rodan
(1902–85)
Walt Rostow (1916–2003)

BEFORE
1837 German economist
Friedrich List argues the use
of import protection to help
establish domestic industry.

AFTER
1953 Estonian economist
Ragnar Nurkse proposes the
policy of balanced growth for
developing countries.

1957 Austrian-Hungarian
economist Peter Bauer
criticizes the idea of the big
push and the orthodoxy of
state planning.

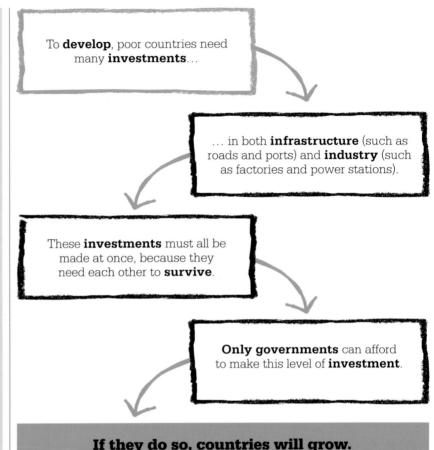

To **develop**, poor countries need many **investments**…

… in both **infrastructure** (such as roads and ports) and **industry** (such as factories and power stations).

These **investments** must all be made at once, because they need each other to **survive**.

Only governments can afford to make this level of **investment**.

If they do so, countries will grow. All poor countries need is a big push.

One of the central questions for economists is "how did poor nations become rich?" After World War II this question reemerged with new force. The crumbling of colonial empires had spawned young, independent nations whose living standards were falling farther and farther behind those of their former masters. Many of them were experiencing rapid population growth and needed a corresponding growth in the goods and services they produced in order to improve living standards.

Europe had quickly recovered from the war, aided by the Marshall Plan—a huge infusion of funds from the US government that funded the rebuilding of infrastructure and industries. The Polish economist Paul Rosenstein-Rodan argued that to make economic progress, the newly independent countries of the 1950s and 60s needed a "big push" in investment, just as Europe had received from the Marshall Plan.

Another related idea was that countries pass through a series of stages, taking them from traditional societies to mass consumer-based economies. Walt Rostow, the US economist who put forward this theory, said that for traditional nations to develop, massive capital investments would be required: it is the big push that triggers a take-off into self-sustained growth. This eventually transforms poor countries into mature economies with high living standards for the majority of the population. The question of how the investments needed for a big push might be made became the central question of the new field of development economics.

Building simultaneously
Rosenstein-Rodan argued that in less-developed countries the market fails to funnel resources efficiently into beneficial investments that generate growth. This is because big projects such as roads, ports,

and factories are complementary: the existence of one makes the others more economically viable. This can lead to a logical dilemma: the first investment might only be profitable once a second has been made, but the second investment is only viewed as profitable if the first has been made. For instance, a factory needs a power station nearby to be economically viable, but the power station is only profitable if there is a factory to buy its power. Two outcomes are possible: one in which there is no factory and no power station, another in which there are both.

The same kind of argument applies to more complex mixes of production. Imagine that a huge shoe factory is built in an underdeveloped economy. It makes $15 million worth of shoes, and the sales revenues go into wages and profits. However, this factory is only viable if all the incomes it generates (for its workers) are spent on shoes, while in fact people spend their money on a range of goods. Suppose people spend 60 percent of their incomes on bread, 20 percent on clothes, 10 percent on paraffin, and 10 percent on shoes. If factories making bread, clothes, paraffin, and shoes were built in exactly this ratio, the incomes generated from these enterprises would be spent on each industry's products in the same proportion. Only when these industries exist together, in the right proportions, do they become viable.

Essential linkages

The German economist Albert Hirschman used the term "linkage" to describe the interconnections between industries. For instance, a paint plant helps the development of a car industry by increasing the supply of paint. Hirschman called this a "forward linkage." The expansion of the paint industry also increases demand for the chemicals used to make paint, and so increases the profitability of chemicals factories. This is known

> Most industries catering for mass consumption are complementary in the sense that they provide a market for, and thus support, each other.
> **Ragnar Nurkse**
> **Estonian economist (1907–59)**

as a "backward linkage." In practice, industries have multiple forward and backward linkages to other industries, creating a complex web of interactions, which can lead to the economic viability of an entire diversified production base.

The big push involves countries going from having nothing to having everything. From having »

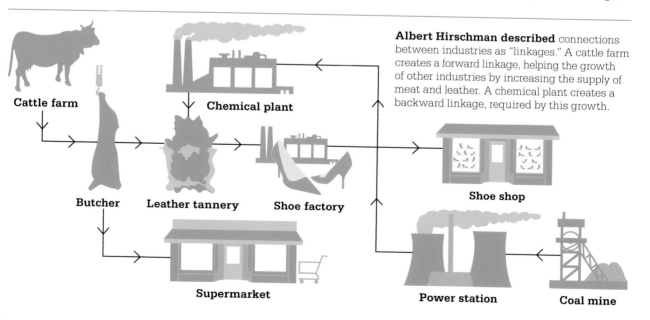

Albert Hirschman described connections between industries as "linkages." A cattle farm creates a forward linkage, helping the growth of other industries by increasing the supply of meat and leather. A chemical plant creates a backward linkage, required by this growth.

Cattle farm

Chemical plant

Butcher

Leather tannery

Shoe factory

Shoe shop

Supermarket

Power station

Coal mine

A large nut-shelling factory built with Indian investment employs workers to shell nuts in Tanzania. Other industries sprang up to service the factory, aiding the country's general development.

no power station and no factory, developing economies suddenly need to have both. Starting from a position where they have no industrial sectors, they must establish all of them at once. But because each investment requires others, it is difficult for individual entrepreneurs to lead the push. For this reason Rosenstein-Rodan and others like him argued that the big push has to come from the state, not from private markets.

In line with this thinking post-war governments across the developing world became involved in large investment programs, undertaking industrial and infrastructure projects as part of national development plans. Less-developed nations were viewed as having dual economies, consisting of traditional agricultural sectors (containing a lot of unproductive labor) alongside modern sectors made up of new industries. The idea was that the big push would siphon off excess labor from the rural areas and deposit it in the new industrial enterprises. This way of thinking provided the rationale for large infusions of foreign aid, intended as the fuel for the investment drive.

State-directed investment has led to beneficial industrialization in some places. Some Southeast Asian countries saw industrial expansion and fast income growth; their successful tying together of an activist state and big business became known as the Developmental State model. However, the conditions in which the Marshall Plan was enacted in 1948 were different from those in the newly independent nations of the 1950s; many attempts at a big push ran into trouble.

Inefficient investment

At early stages the investments needed for economic development may seem obvious. Even so, coordinating an investment drive across many industries is a huge task. Governments can only create viable industries if they know the correct balance of production—the right share of shoes, clothes, and bread—which is implied by the composition of consumer demand. It is only possible to exploit the interactions between different kinds of production when there is detailed knowledge of the forward and backward linkages between industries. Not all governments have the expertise, information, or political clout to do this successfully.

What many countries ended up with was bloated, inefficient, state-owned industries that failed to trigger take-off into sustained growth. Industrialization was frequently attempted behind trade tariffs—foreign goods were shut out of the domestic market in the hope that this would give fledgling industries a chance to develop. The state's protection of firms from foreign competition generated "rent-seeking"—wasteful lobbying of the government by commercial interest groups seeking to preserve their privileges. Often this led to cozy relationships between governments and politically connected industrialists, which hampered competition and innovation.

During the 1970s, the big push came under intellectual attack by by economists who believed that developing economies were not fundamentally different from developed ones. They said economically rational behavior and the power of price signals were as valid in poor as in rich countries. Investment was important, but it needed to be correctly distributed around the economy. Markets, not governments, were the best arbiter of where to invest.

This new wave of thinking held that developing economies were hampered not by the inherent inefficiency of their markets, but by the wrong policies. Too much state involvement had undermined the price mechanism (where prices are set by supply and demand), and had disrupted its ability to allocate resources efficiently. Good policy involved "getting prices right" and allowing the market mechanism to operate freely so that resources would be put to the best use.

> ❝
> Complementarity of different industries provides the most important set of arguments in favor of a large-scale planned industrialization.
> **Paul Rosenstein-Rodan**
> ❞

The way forward was to roll back the boundaries of the state, remove rent-seeking, and let the price mechanism take over.

In the 1980s this revision in thinking led to the rise of free market development policy. The World Bank and the International Monetary Fund (IMF) introduced "structural adjustment programs" to inject market principles into African economies. The so-called "shock therapy," used in Eastern Europe by these institutions after the fall of communism, was aimed at rapidly establishing market systems. However, these free market experiments eventually came under attack for making poverty worse while also failing to build dynamic, diversified economies.

Market-friendly policies

Today, disillusionment with structural adjustment has led to a new consensus, fusing the insights of the early development thinkers

Singapore became a modern nation-state in 1965. Government policies attracted foreign investment and the state thrived on its export industries, such as refined petroleum.

with a more sanguine view of markets. Markets are now seen as vital in poor countries for creating incentives for mobilizing resources in a profitable way. At the same time economists such as American Joseph Stiglitz have pointed to market failures at the small-business level that commonly restrain developing countries. For instance, profitable investments can't be made when small firms can't get loans. The state may have a role to play in correcting these failures, and in this way help the price mechanism to function more smoothly. This consensus, sometimes called the market-friendly approach, sees the state and markets as complementary.

However, at the start of the 21st century, there was a resurgence of more explicit big push ideas. In 2000, the United Nations drew up development targets for 2015, which included universal primary education, the eradication of hunger, and the reduction of child mortality rates. This involves promises by donor countries to keep up aid flows and requires large, coordinated investments across a range of sectors and infrastructure projects. ∎

Post-war development in Latin America

After World War II many Latin American governments intervened in their economies to promote industrialization across a broad range of sectors. They restricted imports and set up new industries to produce the same goods, imposing tariffs and exchange controls to stifle foreign competition.

Governments also invested directly in the infrastructure that industry needed, helped by foreign aid and technical assistance. This process was known as Import Substitution Industrialization, and it was most successful in countries that had internal markets that were large enough to allow heavy industry to sit alongside consumer-oriented enterprises in a viable way, such as Brazil and Venezuela.

Critics argue that Latin American countries should have focused on strengthening the sectors in which they had a comparative advantage, encouraging firms to become internationally competitive and to export their products.

Bolivia's oil industry enjoyed record investments from its government in 2011. Privatized in the 1990s, the industry was renationalized in 2006.

PEOPLE ARE INFLUENCED BY IRRELEVANT ALTERNATIVES
IRRATIONAL DECISION MAKING

IN CONTEXT

FOCUS
Decision making

KEY THINKER
Maurice Allais (1911–2010)

BEFORE
1944 John von Neumann and Oskar Morgenstern publish *A Theory of Games and Co-operative Behavior*, laying the foundations for expected utility theory.

1954 US mathematician L. J. Savage shows how people calculate the probabilities of uncertain events.

AFTER
1979 Daniel Kahnemann and Amos Tversky explain some discrepancies between psychological experiments and the claims of economic theory.

From 1980s Behavioral economics is established, integrating psychology with the mathematical techniques of economics.

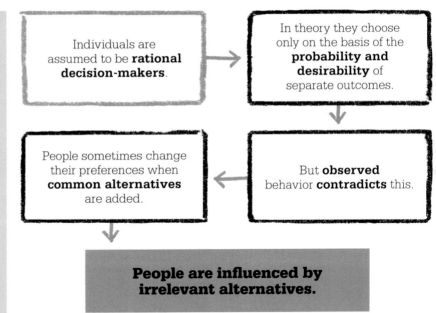

Individuals are assumed to be **rational decision-makers**.

In theory they choose only on the basis of the **probability and desirability** of separate outcomes.

But **observed** behavior **contradicts** this.

People sometimes change their preferences when **common alternatives** are added.

People are influenced by irrelevant alternatives.

In 1944, the Hungarian-born mathematician John von Neumann and the German-born economist Oskar Morgenstern developed expected utility theory to describe how people make decisions under conditions of uncertainty. "Utility" is a measure of satisfaction, and economists use units of utility to talk about the amount of satisfaction gained from various outcomes. The theory assumes that people are rational when faced with choices in which there are no guaranteed outcomes: they weigh the utility gained from each possible outcome by the probability that it will occur, then choose the option that promises the greatest utility. The model uses a mathematical approach to decision making, and has been used to analyze all sorts of economic behavior in situations of uncertainty.

See also: Economic man 52–53 ▪ Risk and uncertainty 162–63 ▪ Paradoxes in decision making 248–49 ▪ Behavioral economics 266–69

Maurice Allais challenged this theory from what he referred to as the American School of economics.

He pointed out that expected utility theory is based on an assumption, known as the independence axiom, that says people will dispassionately look at the likelihood of outcomes and the utility they will gain from each one. In particular, they will view each choice independently, ignoring any factors that are common to each option. Allais said that this was rarely, if ever, true. His contention became known as the Allais paradox.

Irrational choice

We cannot directly see people's thought processes when they choose, but we can observe the choices they make and see if these are consistent with rationality and the independence axiom. Imagine that you are given a choice between an apple and an orange, and you choose the apple. Now imagine that you are offered the choice of an apple, an orange, and a peach. The independence axiom assumes that you might choose the apple again, or the peach, but you would not choose the orange— because the addition of the peach cannot change your preference for apples over oranges.

The violations of independence that Allais detected, however, take place in situations of uncertainty. Suppose you had a choice between two "lotteries," each of which has several possible outcomes with particular probabilities. The first lottery gives you a 50 percent chance of an apple and a 50 percent chance of a peach. The second lottery gives you a 50 percent chance of an orange and a 50 percent chance of a peach. Because you prefer apples to oranges, you should choose the first lottery: under the independence axiom, the addition to each lottery of a peach—making the peach equally probable as an outcome in both choices—should make no difference to the choice of apple over orange. But in practice, very often it does.

In experiments using more complex forms of this kind of choice, people frequently violate

> Whatever their attraction might be, none of the fundamental postulates forumulated by the American School can withstand analysis.
> **Maurice Allais**

the independence axiom. This conflicts with the standard economic idea that humans always act rationally. For some reason the presence of other choices in a set of options seems to matter to people— it makes a difference. The discovery of these kinds of behaviors has spawned the new field of behavioral economics (pp.266–69), which attempts to devise more psychologically realistic models of decision making. ▪

Maurice Allais

Maurice Allais was born in Paris, France, in 1911. His father died during World War I, and this affected Allais deeply. He excelled at school and studied mathematics at the elite École Polytechnique, graduating first in his class in 1933. He then served in the military before working first as an engineer, then as departmental manager for the École Nationale Supérieure des Mines. During this time he also published his first pieces on economics. In 1948, the École Nationale allowed him to focus entirely on teaching and writing, and he became their professor of economic analysis. A polymath, Allais also made contributions to physics. In 1978, he was the first economist to be awarded a gold medal by France's National Centre of Scientific Research, and in 1988, he won the Nobel Prize for economics. He died in 2010.

Key works

1943 *In Search of an Economic Discipline*
1947 *Economy and Interest*
1953 *The Behavior of Rational Man Confronting Risk*

GOVERNMENTS SHOULD DO NOTHING BUT CONTROL THE MONEY SUPPLY

MONETARIST POLICY

IN CONTEXT

FOCUS
Economic policy

KEY THINKER
Milton Friedman
(1912–2006)

BEFORE
1911 Irving Fisher formalizes the quantity theory of money, which proposes that prices are directly related to the size of the money supply.

1936 John Maynard Keynes questions the effectiveness of policies to control the money supply.

AFTER
1970s Robert Lucas develops models that assume "rational expectations."

1970s–80s Many countries adopt formal monetary growth targets, by which governments attempt to control growth in the size of the money supply in order to keep down inflation.

The Great Depression saw millions of Americans migrate west in search of work on farms. Milton Friedman blamed the slump on the Federal Reserve's reduction in the money supply.

W riting in the 1930s, John Maynard Keynes (p.161) argued that policies aimed at controlling the money supply were often ineffective. He believed that altering interest rates or the money supply did not affect the economy in a predictable way. Instead, governments could better use fiscal policy—changing the mix of government spending and taxation—to protect against unemployment or inflation. By 1945, his views were widely accepted.

From the 1950s, however, US economist Milton Friedman began to challenge Keynes with the idea that "money matters." Friedman believed that money affects output in the short run and prices only in the long run. He argued that monetary policy has a valuable role to play in managing the economy: an idea now known as monetarism.

In 1963, Friedman published *A Monetary History of the United States, 1867–1960* with his colleague Anna Schwartz. They tracked the role of money in business cycles, finding that fluctuations in monetary growth preceded fluctuations in output growth. In particular they attributed the Great Depression of 1929–33 to the incompetence of the Federal Reserve, the central bank of the US, allowing or causing the quantity of money to fall by more than one third.

Theory of consumption

Keynes's case for government spending in a slump was based partly on his ideas about consumption. He argued that as people's income rises, their consumption also goes up, but not by as much. In a slump people hoard money, which prolongs the slump. State spending in such a

See also: The Keynesian multiplier 164–65 ▪ Inflation and unemployment 202–03 ▪ Saving to spend 204–05 ▪ Rational expectations 244–47

situation increases incomes and has a large, predictable effect on consumption, restoring the economy to full employment.

In 1957, Friedman published *A Theory of the Consumption Function*, an important work that began to challenge the Keynesian orthodoxy. Friedman argued that people distinguish between "permanent income"—their stable long-term earnings, which they feel confident to consume—and "transitory income", which is less permanent, can be positive or negative, and which does not affect their consumption. Those with high incomes will have high transitory »

A man papers his wall with money during the German hyperinflation of 1923. Friedman thought that state intervention to reduce unemployment inevitably led to high inflation.

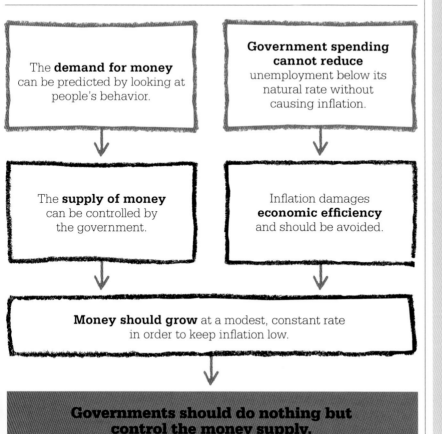

The **demand for money** can be predicted by looking at people's behavior.

Government spending cannot reduce unemployment below its natural rate without causing inflation.

The **supply of money** can be controlled by the government.

Inflation damages **economic efficiency** and should be avoided.

Money should grow at a modest, constant rate in order to keep inflation low.

Governments should do nothing but control the money supply.

Milton Friedman

Born in Brooklyn, New York, in 1912, Milton Friedman was the son of Hungarian immigrants. He was taught by the US's top economists—at Rutgers, New Jersey, for his bachelor's degree; Chicago for his master's; and Columbia, New York, for his PhD. At Chicago he met economics student Rose Director. They married in 1938, and collaborated throughout their careers. From 1935 to 1946, he worked as a statistician and economist in New York and Washington. From 1946 to 1976, he taught at the University of Chicago. It was there that he became well-known. His fame increased with the 1980 TV series and book *Free to Choose*. He was an advisor to Presidents Richard Nixon and Ronald Reagan. He died in 2006.

Key works

1957 *A Theory of the Consumption Function*
1963 *A Monetary History of the United States, 1867–1960* (with Anna Schwartz)
1967 *The Role of Monetary Policy* Presidential address to the American Economic Association

Inflation is taxation
without legislation.
Milton Friedman

income and consume only a small share of their total income; those with the lowest incomes will have negative transitory income and will consume more than their income. But if you add all their incomes together, the positive and negative transitory incomes largely cancel each other out. Friedman's theory seemed to fit the evidence well. In a cross-section of the population, consumption did not rise much with income. But, measured over time and looking at the total population (so that transitory income effects cancelled out), consumption did rise with income. Friedman concluded that Keynes's model of consumption was wrong. State spending would be treated as transitory income and would simply "crowd out" private spending. Continuing slumps caused by inadequate consumption would not happen.

Quantity theory of money
Friedman aimed to show that monetary policy works: a change to the amount of money in the economy has a predictable effect on total incomes. Keynes had suggested that this relationship was unstable because people held money for different reasons; some of these reasons were what he

called "speculative" and hard to pin down. To help prove the quantity theory right, Friedman needed to show that the demand for money is stable. He had to come up with a testable theory about the demand for money.

In 1956, Friedman published *The Quantity Theory of Money: A Restatement*. He treated money as a good, a "temporary abode of purchasing power." The market demand for a good depends on people's overall budget and its relative price against other competing goods, as well as buyers' tastes. Friedman thought that the demand for money would be influenced by various factors. First, it would increase with the general level of prices, since money is wanted for its purchasing power over real goods. It would also be influenced by people's "real" wealth or their permanent income, and the returns on money, bonds, equities, and durable goods. Finally, demand for money would be influenced by "tastes," which in this context means factors such as economic uncertainty, which leads people to want to hold money.

Given a well-defined level of demand for money, an extra supply of money would not be required by consumers: they would already be holding the money that they needed. They would therefore spend any extra cash. Prices do not adjust instantly in the short run, so this would lead to higher output. But in the long run, prices would adjust, and the only effect of the extra money would be higher prices. Friedman's approach can therefore be seen as a revival of the quantity theory of money, a formula that states MV = PT, where "M" is the money supply and "V" represents how quickly money circulates. "P" is the price level,

and by multiplying this by "T," the number of transactions, we arrive at the total value of transactions. Roughly, this equation says that if V and T are constant then a higher money supply means a higher price level. In the long run money has no "real" effects on the economy.

Natural unemployment
The word "monetarism" was first used in 1968, the year that Friedman presented a new account of the Phillips Curve (p.203). This showed the supposedly stable relationship between inflation and unemployment, which allowed governments to choose between less inflation with more unemployment, or more inflation with less unemployment. Friedman denied that such a trade-off exists, except in the very short run. He said there is a single "natural rate" of unemployment, which consists of unemployed workers temporarily in the process of looking for jobs. In practice the economy is at full

Between 1975 and 1999, the US government set yearly targets for growth in the money supply. However, it regularly grew by more than the upper limit of the government target.

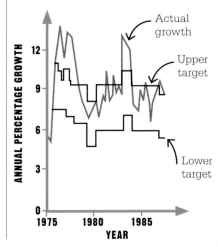

In 1973, Chile became the first country to implement monetarist policies. Under dictator Augusto Pinochet, a radical program of cuts and privatizations was carried out.

employment when unemployment is at this natural rate. If governments spend money to reduce unemployment below the natural rate, pushing up inflation, wage earners will further inflate their wage demands. Two things can then happen. Unemployment can return to the natural rate, at the new, higher inflation rate. Or the government tries to maintain the lower unemployment level, but at the cost of a spiral of accelerating inflation.

The conclusion was clear: it is futile for governments to try to stabilize employment through fiscal policy. Increasing the money supply likewise only leads to higher prices. In the long run the Phillips Curve is a straight vertical line at the natural rate of unemployment.

The time lag between monetary changes and output changes is often only a few quarters. Price movements can take between one to two years or more to come through. These lags are considerably variable. For this reason Friedman advised governments against trying to use monetary policy to actively manipulate markets because it is easy to misread what is happening in the economy. They should follow a simple rule: ensure that money, however it is defined, increases by a constant amount—2–5 percent (depending on the definition of money chosen) annually.

The new classical macroeconomics school, led by US economists Robert Lucas and Thomas Sargent, put forward a revised version of this argument based on rational expectations of future economic policy. Friedman's model treated expectations as if they only adapted to past mistakes. Lucas and Sargent argued that people's expectations are forward-focused. People can see what governments might plan, so any government attempt to reduce unemployment below the natural rate will lead immediately to higher inflation. In other words the Phillips Curve is vertical in the short run as well—governments don't ever have the power to reduce unemployment.

Monetarism in practice

It did not take long for Friedman's warnings to be proven correct. In the 1970s the supposed Phillips Curve trade-off fell apart when both inflation and unemployment increased together—a phenomenon known as stagflation. Governments started to introduce targets for growth in the money supply into their planning. Germany, Japan, the US, the UK, and Switzerland adopted monetary targeting in the 1970s. However, it proved hard to control monetary growth. One problem was which form of money to target. Most central banks targeted a broad version of money, which included bank time deposits (deposits that cannot be withdrawn for a fixed period of time). However, this proved hard to control.

Attention then focused on the narrow monetary base, namely notes, coins, and reserves held at the central bank. This was easier to control but did not seem to enjoy a stable relationship with so-called broad money.

Monetarist experiments were largely unsuccessful, but the impact of monetarism was significant. It grew from a policy prescription about the money supply to a program aimed at reducing government involvement in all aspects of the economy. Few today would disagree that "money matters." Monetary policy receives as much attention as fiscal policy and is usually aimed at controlling inflation. But the purest form of monetarism and its policy implications rely on controversial assumptions: that there is a predictable demand for money and that the money supply can easily be controlled by the authorities. In the 1990s countries moved away from monetary targeting. Many began to use the exchange rate to control inflation or to tie interest rate policy directly to inflation trends. ■

US president Ronald Reagan and UK prime minister Margaret Thatcher were close conservative allies. Both pursued strict monetarist policies in their early years in office.

THE MORE PEOPLE AT WORK, THE HIGHER THEIR BILLS
INFLATION AND UNEMPLOYMENT

For 30 years after World War II the world's more developed economies enjoyed their longest ever period of growth. Unemployment was low, incomes rose, and economists thought they had overcome the crises of the 1930s.

This confidence stemmed from a belief in the power of government intervention to manage the economy, which was powerfully summarized in the Phillips Curve. In 1958, New Zealander Bill Phillips published *The Relationship Between*

Unemployment and the Rate of Change of Money Wages, showing a link between wage inflation and unemployment in the UK from 1861–1957. Years of high inflation were years of low unemployment, and vice versa.

Inflation or employment?
Later work showed similar, stable relationships for other developed countries. Governments realized that there was a trade-off between inflation and unemployment. They

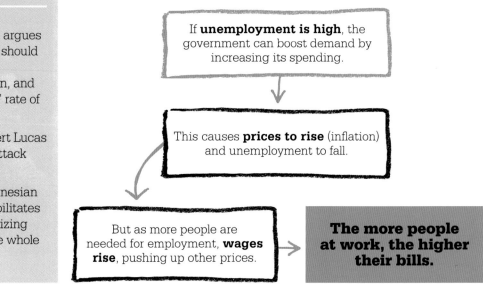

If **unemployment is high**, the government can boost demand by increasing its spending.

This causes **prices to rise** (inflation) and unemployment to fall.

But as more people are needed for employment, **wages rise**, pushing up other prices.

The more people at work, the higher their bills.

See also: Depressions and unemployment 154–61 ▪ The Keynesian multiplier 164–65 ▪ Monetarist policy 196–201 ▪ Rational expectations 244–47 ▪ Sticky wages 303

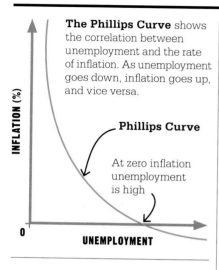

The Phillips Curve shows the correlation between unemployment and the rate of inflation. As unemployment goes down, inflation goes up, and vice versa.

Phillips Curve

At zero inflation unemployment is high

could pick their preferred point along the Phillips Curve, choosing either low unemployment and high inflation, or low inflation and high unemployment, and adjust their policies to suit. By increasing or reducing their spending, and tightening or slackening monetary policy (the money supply and interest rates), they could regulate aggregate demand (total spending) to fix the economy on the curve. The economy was treated like a giant machine. All major questions about the macroeconomy—the country's whole economic system—could seemingly be reduced to technical fixes rather than battles over ideology.

The curve fit well with the Keynesian macroeconomics (pp.154–61) that was prevalent at the time. When unemployment was high, it was assumed that the dip in labor and product markets would drag wages and prices downward. Inflation would be low. When employment was high, additional demand in the economy—perhaps from government spending—did not increase output and employment,

but pulled prices and wages upward. Inflation would rise. However, by the 1970s this stable relationship appeared to have collapsed. Unemployment and inflation rose together in a condition known as "stagflation." US economist Milton Friedman (p.199) explained it in a way that came to dominate macroeconomic theory. He said that as well as showing a relationship between actual prices and unemployment, the Phillips Curve needed to take account of expectations of inflation. People realized that when the government increased spending to boost the economy (and raise employment), inflation would surely follow. Consequently, any increase in government spending during periods of high unemployment was taken as a sign of impending inflation, and workers asked for wage increases before prices actually rose. In the long run, said Friedman, there is no trade-off between unemployment and inflation. The economy is fixed at a "natural rate" of unemployment.

Government attempts to stabilize the economy had merely pushed up expectations of future inflation, and actual inflation had risen as a result.

Friedman's challenge cleared the way for an assault on Keynesian macroeconomics, and governments turned to ways of improving the supply of capital and labor, rather than focusing their efforts on regulating demand. ▪

By 1931, unemployment in the US had reached nearly 23 percent, with a corresponding fall in prices. The government launched a program of public works to create jobs.

Bill Phillips

Born in New Zealand in 1914, Alban William Phillips moved to Australia in his early twenties, working for a time as a crocodile hunter. He traveled to China in 1937, fled when the Japanese invaded, and arrived in the UK in 1938 to study engineering. At the outbreak of World War II Phillips joined the RAF. Captured by the Japanese in 1942, he spent the rest of the war in a prison camp. In 1947, he took up sociology and enrolled

at the London School of Economics, but switched to economics at the post-graduate level. He became a professor there in 1958. In 1967, he moved to Australia to teach but had a stroke two years later and retired to New Zealand.

Key works

1958 *The Relationship Between Unemployment and the Rate of Change of Money Wages*
1962 *Employment, Inflation, and Growth: An Inaugural Lecture*

PEOPLE SMOOTH CONSUMPTION OVER THEIR LIFE SPANS
SAVING TO SPEND

IN CONTEXT

FOCUS
Decision making

KEY THINKER
Franco Modigliani
(1918–2003)

BEFORE
1936 John Maynard Keynes publishes *The General Theory of Employment, Interest and Money*, proposing a simple mathematical function to describe consumption.

1938 Keynesian economist Alvin Hansen predicts long-term stagnation in the US economy.

AFTER
1978 US economist Robert Hall estimates a function to describe US consumption, potentially confirming a version of Friedman's theory.

1982 US economists Robert Hall and Frederick Mishkin propose that households follow a "rule of thumb" when planning their consumption.

Households devote a **varying proportion** of their **current income** to consumption.

⬇

This is because individuals are **rational, look to the future**, and **dislike shocks**.

⬇

They consume based on their **expectations** of **lifetime income**, not on current income.

⬇

They **save when young**, and use up their **savings** when old.

⬇

People smooth consumption over their life spans.

I n 1936, John Maynard Keynes's *The General Theory of Employment, Interest, and Money* put the issue of consumption center stage: if total demand in the economy is critical to making it run smoothly, the groups who make up that demand matter a great deal. Public spending came under government control. Investment by firms was related to the interest rate. But consumption by households presented more of a challenge.

Keynes (p.161) claimed that households consume a fraction of their income and save the rest, with richer households saving more. The proportion all households spend determines the size of the "multiplier" (pp.164–65)— the amount that government spending increases when put into practice. It creates jobs and income, which is multiplied by the spending of those who received the extra jobs and income—and in this way they impact on the general economy. For Keynesian economists this multiplier effect lies behind the way the economy moves between boom and recession over time. For this reason getting an accurate picture of consumption is critical.

See also: Economic man 52–53 ∎ Borrowing and debt 76–77 ∎ The Keynesian multiplier 164–65 ∎ Rational expectations 244–47

Keynes's theory makes three empirical predictions. First, richer households will save more than poorer ones. Second, over time, as the economy grows, the amount people spend will rise less quickly than income, since households will be growing richer and so spending proportionately less of their income. Third, following on from this, richer economies will become increasingly "lethargic:" when consumption falls in ratio to income, it reduces the multiplier and the economy begins to stagnate.

Lifetime savings

However, the theory's predictions did not match well with reality. The ratio between household consumption and income over the long run turned out to be stable across a wide range of countries, rather than decreasing with growth. It fluctuated over short periods of time but did not move consistently in any particular direction. After World War II economists predicted stagnation, but economies everywhere boomed.

Retirement is only enjoyable when we have funds to replace our income. Franco Modigliani said that our awareness of this makes us save over time to allow for constant consumption.

> 66
> Successive generations
> seem to be less and
> less thrifty.
> **Franco Modigliani**
> 99

Two solutions to the mystery gained acceptance. Both proposed that rational individuals do not consume blindly out of their current income, but look to the future and develop expectations about how much they need to save. In 1954, Italian economist Franco Modigliani suggested this relates to stages in life. When people are economically active, they save toward old age. When they are older, they use up their savings. They try to keep consumption constant, smoothing its path over time. This is known as the life-cycle hypothesis.

Three years later US economist Milton Friedman (p.199) proposed the related theory that people smooth their consumption over time around their "permanent income"— an expectation of future earnings, based mostly on current wealth. Any extra income is "transitory" and will be saved. This is known as the permanent income hypothesis.

More recent developments in consumption theories have suggested that in fact consumers tend to use "rules of thumb" and other forms of "non-rational" behavior when making decisions about how much to spend or save. ∎

Franco Modigliani

Franco Modigliani was born in Rome, Italy, in 1918. He initially studied law at the University of Rome, but switched to economics. In 1938, Mussolini passed a series of anti-Semitic laws, and Modigliani—a fervent antifascist—left for Paris and then New York with his wife, the antifascist activist Serena Calabi. He supported his growing family by bookselling while studying. He took a series of teaching posts before becoming a professor of economics at the Massachusetts Institute of Technology (MIT). In 1985, he won the Nobel Prize for his pioneering analyses of savings and financial markets. After his death in 2003, the economist Paul Samuelson said that he had been the "greatest living macroeconomist."

Key works

1954 *Utility Analysis and the Consumption Function* (with Richard Brumberg)
1958 *The Cost of Capital, Corporation Finance and the Theory of Investment* (with Merton Miller)
1966 *The Life Cycle Hypothesis of Saving*

INSTITUTIONS MATTER

INSTITUTIONS IN ECONOMICS

IN CONTEXT

FOCUS
Society and the economy

KEY THINKER
Douglass North (1920–)

BEFORE
1904 US economist Thorstein Veblen argues for the primacy of institutions in explanations of economic performance.

1934 US economist John Commons states that economies are complex webs of institutions and divergent interests.

AFTER
1993 US economist Avner Greif uses game theory to analyze the historical development of institutions that allowed trade to develop.

2001 Turkish-US economist Daron Acemoğlu explains institutional differences between countries in terms of their colonial origins.

Standard economics assumes the existence of markets. It also assumes that governments have the policy levers necessary to encourage markets towards beneficial kinds of trade, investment, and innovation. However, institutional economists go deeper—they search for the origin of markets, their involvement with the state, and the political and social conditions that help economic activity.

US economist Douglass North defined institutions as the "humanly devised constraints that shape human interaction." These constraints are the "rules of the game," and appear in both formal and informal guises.

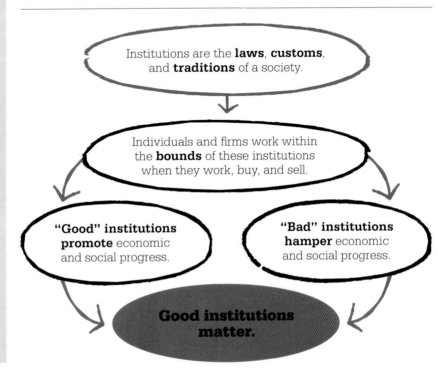

Institutions are the **laws**, **customs**, and **traditions** of a society.

↓

Individuals and firms work within the **bounds** of these institutions when they work, buy, and sell.

"Good" institutions promote economic and social progress.

"Bad" institutions hamper economic and social progress.

Good institutions matter.

See also: Property rights 20–21 ▪ Public companies 38 ▪ Economics and tradition 166–67 ▪ Social capital 280 ▪ Resisting economic change 328–29

Formal constraints are the rules that are rooted in the law and politics of each country, while informal constraints are a society's social codes, customs, and traditions. Combined, these make up North's institutions, and they set the broad rules of the game within which humans interact as workers, consumers, and investors.

Markets and property

Property rights—of physical and intellectual property—are an institution essential for economic growth. North investigated the emergence of property rights in England, claiming that they began in 1688, the year in which the Crown was made subservient to Parliament. Before then, the monarch would commonly expropriate resources, riding roughshod over private property rights. North found that after the power of the Crown was restricted, exchange became less costly and incentives improved. His view has been challenged, but the approach remains influential.

North's example reveals a tension that lies at the heart of institutional economics. The state guarantees order, which gives it the

The German Bundestag (parliament) was a new institution set up after 1945. Its role was important in shaping post-war Germany's law and economy.

power to activate property rights, because they cannot survive under anarchy. However, it is this very power that also allows the state to use resources for its own benefit.

The Turkish-American economist Daron Acemoğlu (1967–) showed that this tension is rooted in societies' colonial origins. In regions such as Africa where infectious diseases threatened, colonists did not stay long. Institutions were set up with the purpose of extracting natural resources quickly for a state's self-enrichment, not to foster economic growth. In the more congenial North American colonies, however, settlers established institutions that promoted long-term growth.

Institutions determine the success or failure of economies—they create the essential structure. Economists have yet to identify clearly the institutional mutation that triggers economic progress. Reform to institutions is difficult, with the past always leaving traces in the present. ▪

> Institutions provide the incentive structure of an economy.
> **Douglass North**

Douglass North

Douglass North was born in Cambridge, Massachusetts. As a student at the University of California in Berkeley, he refused to serve in World War II, and after graduating joined the US merchant marines to avoid fighting. During his three-year service he read many economics books, and found it hard to choose between studying photography (a lifelong hobby) and economics on his return to the US. Economics won out, and he received a PhD from Berkeley in 1952. He began teaching at the University of Washington, where he helped to found the new field of cliometrics (the economic and statistical analysis of history).

North taught at the University of Washington until 1983, but in 1966 he spent a year in Geneva studying European economic history, awakening his interest in the role of institutions. He was awarded the Nobel Prize for economics in 1993.

Key works

1981 *Structure and Change in Economic History*
1990 *Institutions*

PEOPLE WILL AVOID WORK IF THEY CAN
MARKET INFORMATION AND INCENTIVES

IN CONTEXT

FOCUS
Decision making

KEY THINKER
Kenneth Arrow (1921–)

BEFORE
From 1600 "Moral hazard" is used to describe situations where individuals may not be honest.

1920s–30s US economist Frank Knight and British economist John Maynard Keynes grapple with the problem of uncertainty in economics.

AFTER
1970 US economist George Akerlof publishes *The Market for Lemons*, looking at the problem of limited information about a good's quality.

2009 Mervyn King, governor of the Bank of England, describes government bailouts of the banking system as "the biggest moral hazard in history."

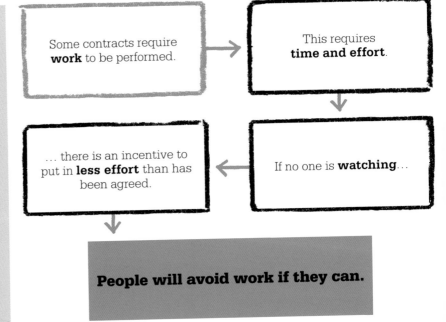

Some contracts require **work** to be performed.

This requires **time and effort**.

… there is an incentive to put in **less effort** than has been agreed.

If no one is **watching**…

People will avoid work if they can.

The standard model of economic behavior, first set out by Adam Smith (p.61) in the 18th century, assumes that all the participants in markets are rational and well-informed. However, this is not always the case.

US economist Kenneth Arrow was among the first to analyze the problem of less-than-complete information in markets. He pointed out that, while two sides can agree to write a contract, there is no guarantee that either will fulfill it. Where one party cannot observe the behavior of the other, there may be an incentive for the less-observed party not to deliver on all clauses of the contract, unknown to the other. There is an imbalance of information because actions are hidden.

See also: Provision of public goods and services 46–47 ▪ Economic man 52–53 ▪ Markets and social outcomes 210–13 ▪ Game theory 234–41 ▪ Market uncertainty 274–75 ▪ Incentives and wages 302

Travel insurance may encourage vacationers to try out more hazardous activities. As a result insurance firms raise the price of coverage.

Moral hazard

This situation is known as "moral hazard." In the insurance market, for instance, an insurance policy may act as an incentive for the person insured to take more risks because he or she knows that the insurer will cover the cost of any damages. The result is that insurers offer less insurance coverage, since they are fearful of encouraging excessive risk-taking and ultimately bearing excessive costs. This means there will be a market failure: those obtaining insurance will pay too much, and many people could find themselves excluded from the insurance market altogether. Arrow suggested that, in these circumstances, there is a case for government intervention to correct the market failure.

Moral hazard can emerge in any situation where one person (the "principal") is trying to get another (the "agent") to behave in a certain way. If the behavior desired by the principal takes effort by the agent, and if the principal cannot observe the agent's actions, the agent has motive and opportunity to avoid work. Insurance contracts are between firms and their customers, but the problem can emerge even within one firm: employees may shirk their duties when an employer isn't watching over them. These principal–agent problems often come about with long-term contracts for complex tasks. In such circumstances every requirement cannot be stipulated in advance, and moral hazard can emerge in unforeseen ways. Principal–agent problems have led to the development of a large literature on the management of complex tasks, dealing with the best way to word the contracts.

Too big to fail?

Moral hazard has more recently become a critical issue in political arguments following the 2008 financial crisis. When banks are described as "too big to fail," a version of moral hazard may be at work. Major banks know their failure could cause a recession, so they may believe that they will be supported by governments no matter what. Economists have suggested that this leads banks to take on excessively risky investments. The euro crisis of 2012 is also thought to be an example of moral hazard at play: countries such as Greece were suspected of having run economies on the grounds that the country was "too big to fail." ▪

Kenneth Arrow

A native New Yorker, American Kenneth Arrow was born in 1921. He was educated entirely in New York, graduating in social science from City College before going on to receive an MA in mathematics from Columbia University. He switched to economics, but after the outbreak of World War II he was sent to join the US Army Air Corps as a weather officer, researching the use of wind.

After the war Arrow married Selma Schweitzer, with whom he had two sons. He began lecturing at Columbia in 1948, then had professorships in economics at Stanford and Harvard. In 1979 he returned to Stanford, until his retirement in 1991. He is best known for his work on general equilibrium and social choice, and won the Nobel Prize in 1972 for his pioneering contributions to economics.

Key works

1951 *Social Choice and Individual Values*
1971 *Essays in the Theory of Risk-bearing*
1971 *General Competitive Analysis* (with Frank Hahn)

THEORIES ABOUT MARKET EFFICIENCY REQUIRE MANY ASSUMPTIONS

MARKETS AND SOCIAL OUTCOMES

IN CONTEXT

FOCUS
Welfare economics

KEY THINKER
Gérard Debreu (1921–2004)

BEFORE
1874 French economist Léon Walras shows that a competitive, decentralized economy can achieve a stable equilibrium.

1942 Polish economist Oscar Lange provides an early proof of the efficiency of markets.

AFTER
1967 US economist Herbert Scarf demonstrates a method for applying real-world economic data to general equilibrium models.

1990s New models of the macroeconomy integrate general equilibrium analysis with real-world economic data over time.

By the 1860s and 70s mainstream economics had developed a distinctive set of claims about the world, offering mathematical models that allowed economists to assess individual behavior in certain market conditions. These models were taken from the rapidly developing mathematics that described the natural world. This development, sometimes called a "marginalist revolution," involved a claim that value is determined by people's preferences and resources rather than by a more objective or absolute standard, and it allowed pressing theoretical questions to be posed in new ways. Did Adam

See also: Free market economics 54–61 ▪ Economic equilibrium 118–23 ▪ Efficiency and fairness 130–31 ▪ The theory of the second best 220–21

Market prices reflect demands for and supplies of each commodity.

So in theory prices **completely reflect** both consumers' preferences and the limits to an economy's resources.

But this only happens if you **make assumptions** that rarely occur in the real world.

This implies that markets lead to an **"efficient" economic outcome**.

Theories about market efficiency require many assumptions

Gérard Debreu

Born in Calais, France, in 1921, Gérard Debreu was educated at the École Normale Supérieure in Paris during the German occupation. After a period of service in the French army, Debreu returned to his studies of mathematics and developed an interest in economic problems. In 1949, a fellowship allowed him to visit some of the top universities in the US, Sweden, and Norway, bringing him up to date with economic developments that were then unknown in France. In the US he became part of the highly influential Cowles Commission, which had been convened in the 1930s to pursue the mathematical treatment of economic issues. He worked at the US universities of Stanford and Berkeley, teaching economics and mathematics. In 1983, he was awarded the Nobel Prize. He died in 2004.

Key works

1954 *Existence of an equilibrium for a competitive economy* (with K. Arrow)
1959 *Theory of Value: An Axiomatic Analysis of Economic Equilibrium*

Smith's "invisible hand" of the market really guide self-interested individuals to the best available outcomes? Were markets more, or less, efficient than other ways of guiding society? Could completely free markets even exist?

Stable markets
French economist Léon Walras (p.120) was one of the pioneers of this revolution in theory. He attempted to show that markets, left to their own devices, can achieve a stable outcome for the whole of society, perfectly balancing the demands of consumers and firms with the supply of goods and services. »

Governments redistribute wealth by taxing goods such as gasoline. Under certain assumptions, it can be shown that the free market adjusts to achieve efficient use of goods despite taxes.

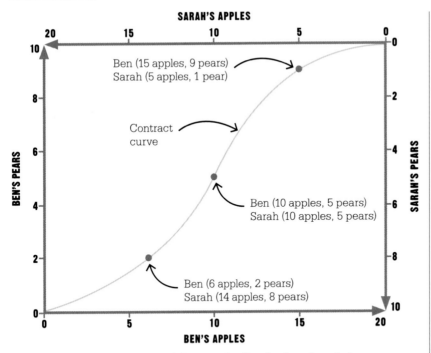

SARAH'S APPLES

BEN'S PEARS

SARAH'S PEARS

BEN'S APPLES

Ben (15 apples, 9 pears)
Sarah (5 apples, 1 pear)

Contract curve

Ben (10 apples, 5 pears)
Sarah (10 apples, 5 pears)

Ben (6 apples, 2 pears)
Sarah (14 apples, 8 pears)

An Edgeworth box is a way of showing the distribution of goods in an economy. In this example the economy contains two people—Ben and Sarah —and two goods—20 apples and 10 pears. Each point in the box represents a possible distribution of apples and pears between Ben and Sarah. The yellow line is the contract curve, which represents the possible allocation of goods that could be reached by Ben and Sarah after trading with each other. Trading to points on this curve leads to Pareto efficiency.

It was known that a single market could achieve this balance, or equilibrium, but it was not clear that a whole set of markets could do the same thing.

The problem of "general equilibrium" was rigorously solved in 1954 by French mathematician Gérard Debreu and US economist Kenneth Arrow (p.209). Applying advanced mathematics, they showed that under certain circumstances a set of markets could achieve an overall equilibrium. In a sense Arrow and Debreu had reworked Adam Smith's argument that free markets would lead to social order. But Smith made a stronger claim than the purely factual one that markets tend toward a point of

stability. He also said that this equilibrium was desirable because it entailed a free society.

Pareto-efficient outcomes
Modern economists measure desirability using a concept known as "Pareto efficiency" (pp.130–31). In a Pareto-efficient situation it is impossible to make one person better off without making another person worse off. An improvement takes place in an economy if goods change hands in such a way that at least one person's welfare increases and no one else's falls. Arrow and Debreu connected market equilibrium with Pareto efficiency. In doing so they rigorously probed Smith's ultimate contention that market outcomes are good. They

did this by proving two theorems, known as the "fundamental theorems of welfare economics."

The first welfare theorem holds that any pure free market economy in equilibrium is necessarily "Pareto efficient"—that it leads to a distribution of resources in which it is impossible to make someone better off without making someone else worse off. Individuals begin with an "endowment" of goods. They trade with each other and reach an equilibrium, which the theorem holds will be efficient.

Pareto efficiency is a weak ethical criterion. A situation in which one rich person has all of a desired good and eveyone else has none of it would be Pareto efficient because it would be impossible to remove some of the good from the rich person without making him worse off. So this first welfare theorem says that markets are efficient but says nothing about the critical issue of distribution.

The second welfare theorem deals with this problem. In an economy there are typically many Pareto-efficient allocations of resources. Some will be fairly equal distributions, some highly unequal.

> How this coordination [of supply and demand] takes place has been a central preoccupation of economic theory since Adam Smith.
> **Kenneth Arrow**

> An allocation of resources could be efficient in a Pareto sense and yet yield enormous riches to some and dire poverty to others.
> **Kenneth Arrow**

The theorem says that any of these Pareto-efficient distributions can be achieved using free markets—a concept represented by economists as a "contract curve." However, to achieve a particular one of these allocations, an initial redistribution of individual endowments needs to be made. Then trading can begin, and the particular Pareto-efficient allocation of resources occurs.

The practical implication here is that a government can redistribute resources—through the levying of taxes—and can then depend upon the free market to ensure the eventual allocation is efficient. Equity (fairness) and efficiency go hand in hand.

Real-world limits
Arrow and Debreu's results depend on stringent assumptions: when these don't hold, efficiency may be compromised, a situation that economists call "market failure." For the theorems to hold, individuals have to behave according to economic rationality. They need to respond perfectly to market signals, something that is clearly not the case in reality. The behavior of firms has to be competitive, while in practice the world is full of monopolies.

In addition, welfare theorems don't hold when there are economies of scale, such as in situations in which there are large firms with high set-up costs—for example, in the case of many public utilities companies. A further important condition for the efficiency of equilibrium is that there should be no "externalities." These are costs and benefits that do not register in market prices. For example the noise from a motorcycle workshop might hurt the productivity of a firm of accountants next door, but the workshop owners do not take this broader cost into account because it doesn't affect their private costs. Externalities hamper efficiency. Also, if individuals don't have full information about prices and about the characteristics of the goods they are buying, then markets are likely to fail.

What the theorems tell us
It is tempting to ask what is the point of this model if its assumptions are so removed from reality as to be inapplicable to any situation, but theoretical models aren't intended to be faithful descriptions of reality: if they were, Arrow and Debreu's model would be useless. Instead, their theorems answer a central question: under what conditions do markets bring efficiency? The stringency of these conditions, then, tells us by how much and in what ways real economies stray from the benchmark of full efficiency. Arrow and Debreu's conditions point to what we might do to move closer to efficiency. For instance, we might try to price pollution to deal with externalities, to break up monopolies to make markets more competitive, or to create institutions to help inform consumers about the goods that they buy.

The work of Arrow and Debreu formed the foundation of much of our post-war economics. Attempts were made to refine their findings and to investigate the efficiency of economies under different assumptions. Large macroeconomic models, both theoretical and empirical, were built using Arrow and Debreu's general equilibrium approach. Some have criticized the equilibrium approach for failing to take into account the chaotic, truly unpredictable nature of real-world economies. These voices have become louder recently with the failure of these kinds of models to predict the 2008 financial crash. ■

Equilibrium models failed to predict the crisis of 2008, which began when Lehman Brothers Bank collapsed and fired all its staff. This led to criticisms of the models' basic assumptions.

THERE IS NO PERFECT VOTING SYSTEM

SOCIAL CHOICE THEORY

IN CONTEXT

FOCUS
Welfare economics

KEY THINKER
Kenneth Arrow (1921–)

BEFORE
1770 French mathematician Jean-Charles de Borda devises a preferential voting system.

1780s English philosopher and social reformer Jeremy Bentham proposes a system of utilitarianism—aiming for the greatest happiness of the greatest number.

1785 Nicolas de Condorcet publishes *Essay on the Application of Analysis to the Probability of Majority Decisions*, in which he sets out the original voting paradox.

AFTER
1998 Indian economist Amartya Sen is awarded the Nobel Prize for his work on welfare economics and social choice theory.

At a first glance, the mathematics of voting may seem to have little to do with economics. However, in the area of welfare economics, and in social choice theory in particular, it plays a crucial role. Social choice theory was developed by US economist Kenneth Arrow in the 1950s. He saw that in order to evaluate the economic well-being of a society, the values of its individual members have to be taken into account. In the interests of making collective decisions that determine the welfare and social state of a society, there must be a system for individuals to express their preferences, and for these to be combined. The collective

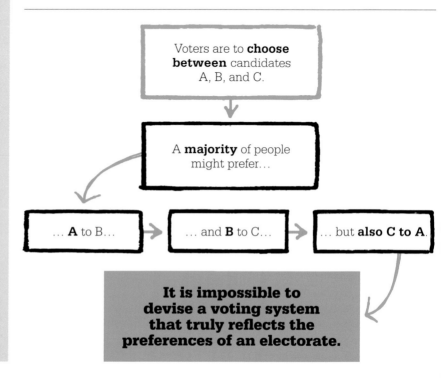

Voters are to **choose between** candidates A, B, and C.

A **majority** of people might prefer…

… **A** to B… → … and **B** to C… → … but **also C to A**.

It is impossible to devise a voting system that truly reflects the preferences of an electorate.

See also: Efficiency and fairness 130–31 ▪ Markets and social outcomes 210–13 ▪ The social market economy 222–23

> In a capitalist democracy there are essentially two methods by which social choices can be made: voting… and the market mechanism.
> **Kenneth Arrow**

decision-making process is dependent on a fair and efficient system of voting. However, in *Social Choice and Individual Values* (1951), Arrow demonstrated that there is a paradox at work.

Voting paradox

The so-called voting paradox was first described almost 200 years earlier by the French political thinker and mathematician Nicolas de Condorcet (1743–94). He found that it is possible for a majority of voters to prefer A over B, and B over C, and yet at the same time express a preference for C over A. For example, if one-third of voters rank the choices A-B-C, another third B-C-A, and the remaining third C-A-B, then a majority clearly favor A over B, and B over C. Intuitively, we would expect that C is at the bottom of the list of options. But a majority also prefer C over A. Making a fair collective decision in such cases is clearly problematic.

Arrow showed that a voting system that truly reflects the preferences of the electorate is not just problematic, but impossible. He proposed a set of fairness criteria that need to be satisfied by an ideal voting system. He then demonstrated that it was not possible for any one system to satisfy all these conditions. In fact, when a majority of reasonable assumptions are met, there is a counterintuitive outcome. One of the criteria for fairness was that there should be no "dictator"—

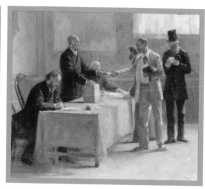

The right to vote at the ballot box, shown here in 19th-century France, is entrenched in Western civilization and almost universal, but the truly perfect voting system is elusive.

no individual who determines the collective decision. Yet paradoxically, when all the other conditions are adhered to, just such a dictator emerges.

The well-being of many

Arrow's paradox (also known as the general possibility theorem) is a cornerstone of modern social choice theory, and Arrow's fairness criteria have formed the basis for devising fair methods of voting that take into account the preferences of individuals.

Social choice theory has now become a major field of study in welfare economics, evaluating the effects of economic policies. This field, which began as the development of abstract theorems, has been applied to concrete economic situations in which governments and planners have to continuously weigh the well-being of many. Much of this has profound implications for the fundamental economic problems of the allocation of resources and the distribution of wealth. ▪

What are social welfare functions?

There are various methods of assessing the well-being of a society. The 19th-century utilitarians thought that peoples' individual levels of utility, or happiness, could be added up, rather like incomes, to measure overall welfare. Later economists developed "social welfare functions" in an attempt to do the same, but these didn't necessarily involve the measurement of utility. Kenneth Arrow and others formulated these functions as a means of turning individual preferences into rankings of possible social states (their economic position in society). There is an ethical dimension to social welfare thinking. A simple form of utilitarianism emphasizes the maximization of total happiness less its distribution. Another, proposed by US philosopher John Rawls (1921–2002), maximizes the well-being of the least well-off person in society.

THE AIM IS TO MAXIMIZE HAPPINESS, NOT INCOME

THE ECONOMICS OF HAPPINESS

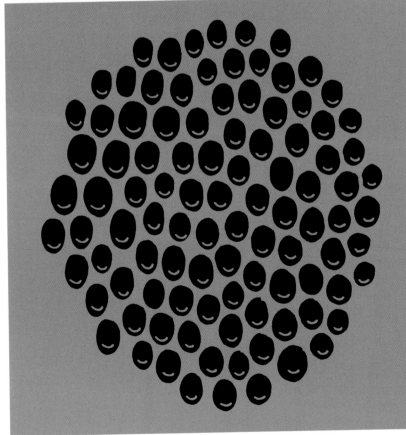

IN CONTEXT

FOCUS
Society and the economy

KEY THINKER
Richard Easterlin (1926–)

BEFORE
1861 John Stuart Mill argues that a moral act is one that maximizes overall happiness.

1932 Simon Kuznets publishes the first national income accounts for the US based purely on conventional economic variables.

AFTER
1997 British economist Andrew Oswald argues that joblessness is the main reason for unhappiness.

2005 British economist Richard Layard publishes *Happiness: Lessons from a New Science*, revisiting the debate about the link between happiness and income.

The first modern national accounts for a country were created for the US in the 1930s by Russian-American economist Simon Kuznets. His pioneering work later led to the creation of national accounts in the UK, Germany, and other developed countries. These accounts involved summing up all the transactions made in an economy over a year to arrive at a figure for its national income, which became known as a country's gross domestic product (GDP). Early economists, such as the Frenchman François Quesnay, had attempted to derive similar measures, but their efforts had foundered due to the apparent

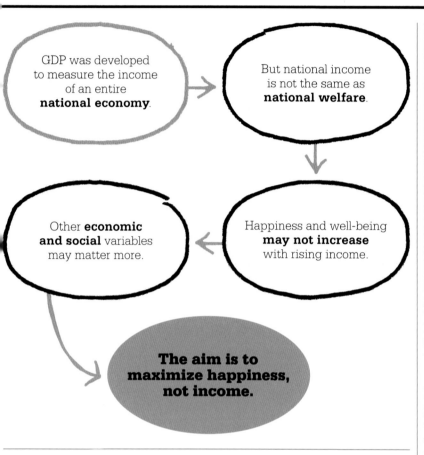

GDP was developed to measure the income of an entire **national economy**.

But national income is not the same as **national welfare**.

Happiness and well-being **may not increase** with rising income.

Other **economic and social** variables may matter more.

The aim is to maximize happiness, not income.

Envy is one cause of unhappiness. Whether or not your neighbors have more than you can be a more important factor to your well-being than how much you have yourself.

size of the task. It became possible only through developments in statistics, survey techniques, and studies of the whole economy.

Crunch number

From their first appearance, GDP figures presented an almost irresistible lure for politicians, journalists, and economists. In a simple form they appear to present a figure that sums up all the most important facts about an economy. Rising GDP means more jobs and higher wages, while falling GDP means unemployment and uncertainty. After World War II debates over economic policy very rapidly turned into little more than a series of arguments over how best to increase GDP. Different policies were pursued, but they all had the same aim.

However, this overlooked some important questions. GDP is only a number, and perhaps not the most important one. There is no necessary connection between GDP and real social welfare, as Kuznets himself once pointed out in a US Congressional hearing. Rising GDP can be distributed very unevenly, so a few people have a great deal of money while many others have very little. Other factors that make people happy, such as familial or friendly relationships, simply do not register on its scale.

Nonetheless, GDP became the paramount statistic in economics and was taken to show that a country was doing well. It was widely believed, if never quite demonstrated, that even where GDP did not perfectly match welfare, both welfare and GDP would move in the same direction.

A direct challenge to the concept of GDP and national income was provided in 1974 by US economist Richard Easterlin. He looked at surveys of people's reported happiness in 19 countries for the previous three decades and suggested that the link between GDP and welfare was not as robust as people thought. Easterlin found that reported happiness increased with income, much as expected. But for those earning above subsistence levels, the variation in reported happiness across »

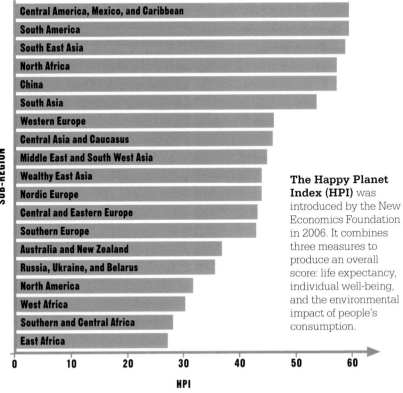

SUB-REGION (y-axis)

- Central America, Mexico, and Caribbean
- South America
- South East Asia
- North Africa
- China
- South Asia
- Western Europe
- Central Asia and Caucasus
- Middle East and South West Asia
- Wealthy East Asia
- Nordic Europe
- Central and Eastern Europe
- Southern Europe
- Australia and New Zealand
- Russia, Ukraine, and Belarus
- North America
- West Africa
- Southern and Central Africa
- East Africa

HPI (x-axis): 0 10 20 30 40 50 60

The Happy Planet Index (HPI) was introduced by the New Economics Foundation in 2006. It combines three measures to produce an overall score: life expectancy, individual well-being, and the environmental impact of people's consumption.

different countries did not vary greatly, despite large differences in national income. People in rich countries were not necessarily the happiest.

Over time, the picture seemed even more peculiar. In the US there were continual, comparatively rapid increases in GDP over the period since 1946, but the levels of happiness reported in surveys did not appear to follow suit—in fact, it declined over the 1960s. Money, it seemed, really did not buy you happiness.

The results of Easterlin's surveys became known as the Easterlin paradox. They sparked fresh research into the relationship between economics and well-being that had otherwise been dormant since the late 19th century. Researchers tried to assess the ways in which decisions by individuals, firms, and government can impact how people feel about themselves and society.

One explanation was offered by the concept of the "hedonic treadmill," first proposed in 1971 by US psychologists Phillip Brickman and Donald Campbell. They suggested that people adapt very rapidly to their current levels of well-being, maintaining this level regardless of events, good or bad. When income rises, they rapidly adapt to the new level of material security, treating it as normal and so being no happier than they were previously. An extreme version of this theory would imply that, beyond subsistence incomes, nearly all economic development is irrelevant for welfare, because people's happiness is determined by something altogether different, such as character or friendships. Alternatively, researchers have put forward the importance of status and comparisons with others. For example, if no one in a society has a car, not having a car makes little difference. But as soon as some people obtain cars, others without

A spring festival in Bhutan is celebrated with dancing. In 1972, the king decreed that his government would pursue policies that maximized "Gross National Happiness."

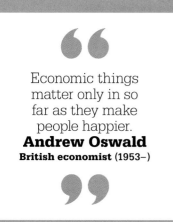

> Economic things matter only in so far as they make people happier.
>
> **Andrew Oswald**
> British economist (1953–)

a car might experience this as a loss of status. "Keeping up with the Joneses" means that as economies grow, the new wealth has limited positive impact on reported happiness. Everyone ends up in a rat race, frantically trying to out-consume everyone else. The more unequal the society, the worse this becomes.

Challenging the paradox
As interest in the Easterlin paradox grew during the 2000s, the paradox began to be challenged. Using data from a broader set of countries, US economists Betsey Stevenson and Justin Wolfers suggested in 2008 that happiness does increase with income across different countries, and that rising income also leads to greater well-being.

In general, researchers have discovered that while higher incomes do not translate easily into increased levels of happiness, losing incomes has a seriously detrimental effect on well-being. Redundancy and unemployment hit well-being particularly hard, as do serious illness and new disabilities.

In other words there is some relationship between GDP and national income, but it is not a simple one. As better data has become available, the notion of happiness and well-being as a possible target for government policy has gained ground. In turn, this has led to the slow displacement of GDP as the critical economic variable of interest. The argument is simple: if widely-reported economic variables do not capture important aspects of economic and social life, focusing on those variables could lead to bad policymaking. If policies were based on "happiness indicators"

The people of the Bahamas score very highly in the Satisfaction with Life Index, which was devised by British psychologist Adrian White to measure feelings of well-being.

rather than GDP alone, new priorities would emerge. These might include measures to encourage a better work–life balance. Unemployment might be considered more costly, and greater measures taken to alleviate it. Broader measures of well-being are already in use, particularly in discussions about developing countries: for instance, the human development index combines income with life expectancy and education. It has been argued that a narrow focus on GDP growth helped to obscure the problems created by the buildup of debt prior to the financial crash of 2008. Had broader indicators been available, more attuned to perceptions of well-being and closer to people's real interests, the single indicator of rising GDP alone would not have been cause for celebration. ∎

Measuring happiness

In 2007, French President Nicolas Sarkozy asked economists Joseph Stiglitz, Amartya Sen, and Jean-Paul Fitoussi to investigate the measurement of social and economic progress, and to look at how broader measures of welfare might be introduced. Their report, published in 2009, argued that it is necessary to shift the focus of economic policymaking from measures of economic production (such as GDP), to measures of well-being and sustainability. In particular, their report highlighted the fact that the gap between common economic indicators and reported well-being appears to be widening.

An alternative system of measurement would, of necessity, use a range of different indicators such as health and the environmental impact of lifestyles, rather than attempt to summarize everything through just a single number.

POLICIES TO CORRECT MARKETS CAN MAKE THINGS WORSE
THE THEORY OF THE SECOND BEST

IN CONTEXT

FOCUS
Economic policy

KEY THINKERS
Kelvin Lancaster (1924–99)
Richard Lipsey (1928–)

BEFORE
1776 Adam Smith claims the "invisible hand" of the self-regulating market is superior to government intervention.

1932 British economist Arthur Pigou advocates the use of taxes to correct market failures.

1954 In *Existence of an Equilibrium for a Competitive Economy*, Gérard Debreu and Kenneth Arrow demonstrate that an entirely free market economy can maximize the welfare of its participants.

AFTER
From 1970s Welfare economics is developed through the work of economists Joseph Stiglitz, Amartya Sen, and others.

In theory, a free market is the **most efficient** economy possible.

⬇

But real economies **contain many distortions** that are inefficient and may cause harm.

⬇

Distortions may be **linked**, and it may not be possible for a government to remove some of them.

⬇

Attempts at removal may **worsen the effects** of other distortions, so governments should act with caution.

⬇

Policies to correct markets can make things worse.

Standard economic theory holds that where markets are available for all goods and services, and everybody using those markets is well-informed, the economy will be efficient. It is not possible to change the distribution of resources to make one person better off without making another person worse off, so society's welfare is as good as it can be in a free market. The best available policy, according to the free-marketeers, is for government to remove imperfections in markets, bringing them as close as possible to the ideal.

Working with imperfection

There are, however, strict conditions before efficient policies can be achieved. In 1956, Australian economist Kelvin Lancaster and his Canadian colleague Richard Lipsey demonstrated that in some circumstances, policies aimed at improving market efficiency may make it worse overall. In a paper entitled *The General Theory of Second Best*, they looked at cases where a market imperfection was permanent—and where there was no way for a government to correct

See also: Free market economics 54–61 ▪ Economic equilibrium 118–23 ▪
External costs 137

or remove it. There was no "first best" solution. In such cases government intervention elsewhere in the economy might worsen the effects of existing imperfections, pulling the market still further away from the ideal. Lancaster's and Lipsey's insight was that where an imperfection in one market cannot be removed, all the other markets will work around it. They will achieve a relatively efficient distribution of resources, given the existing imperfection.

The least bad

Lancaster and Lipsey then went further: the best available policy option, when one distortion can be corrected but others cannot, may turn out to be the opposite of that demanded by theory. For instance, it might be better for government to distort a market further, if it wants to improve welfare overall. Ideal policies, then, cannot be guided by abstract principles alone. They have to be based on a thorough understanding of how markets operate together.

One classic example is that of a monopolist who pollutes a river during production. The pollution is both costly for society and an inevitable result of production. It cannot be removed from the process and is a permanent market imperfection. But the monopoly can be removed.

Standard economic theory would tell the government to break up the monopoly and introduce more competition to the markets. This would drag the economy closer to the efficient ideal. But competing producers would produce more than a single producer, and also worsen the pollution. The result for society's welfare as a whole is uncertain. People might gain from increased output and lower costs, but they would lose out from more pollution. The "second best" solution might be to leave the monopoly in place.

The theory of the second best remains critical to economic policy, recommending that governments act with caution rather than attempting to achieve an ideal. ∎

Richard Lipsey

A Canadian economist born in 1928, Richard Lipsey is best known for the theory of the second best, formulated with Kelvin Lancaster. He is emeritus professor at Simon Fraser University, Canada, having taught in the US and the UK. In 1968, his defense of the Phillips Curve (p.203) against the criticism of Milton Friedman (p.199) formed one of the great debates in economics. Lipsey is the author of a standard textbook in economic theory, *Positive Economics*, and recently has helped develop evolutionary economics, co-authoring an influential book on the processes of historical change.

Key works

1956 *The General Theory of the Second Best* (with Kelvin Lancaster)
2006 *Economic Transformations: General-Purpose Technologies and Long-Term Economic Growth* (with K. Carlaw, C. Bekar)

Choosing the least bad solution
(1) A monopolist is causing pollution. Both the monopoly and the pollution are imperfections in the market.

(2) A government could remove the monopoly and replace it with competing firms. However, as a result of more firms competing, the pollution could get much worse.

MAKE MARKETS FAIR

THE SOCIAL MARKET ECONOMY

IN CONTEXT

FOCUS
Society and the economy

KEY THINKERS
Walter Eucken (1891–1950)
Wilhelm Röpke (1899–1966)
Alfred Müller-Armack
(1901–78)

BEFORE
1848 Karl Marx and
Friedrich Engels publish
the *Communist Manifesto*.

1948 German economists
Walter Eucken and Franz
Böhm establish the journal
ORDO, which gives its name
to ordoliberalism, a movement
that advocates the social
market economic model.

AFTER
1978 Chinese Premier
Deng Xiaoping introduces
capitalist elements into the
Chinese economy.

1980s Milton Friedman's
monetarist arguments against
government intervention are
adopted by the US and UK.

I n the aftermath of World
War II West Germany had
to rebuild its economy and
political system from scratch.
Chancellor Konrad Adenauer
carried out this task in 1949,
following the Allied occupation.

The model he chose had its roots in
the ideas of Franz Böhm and Walter
Eucken of the Freiburg school of
the 1930s, which resurfaced in the
1940s as "ordoliberalism." Its chief
advocates were Wilhelm Röpke
and Alfred Müller-Armack.

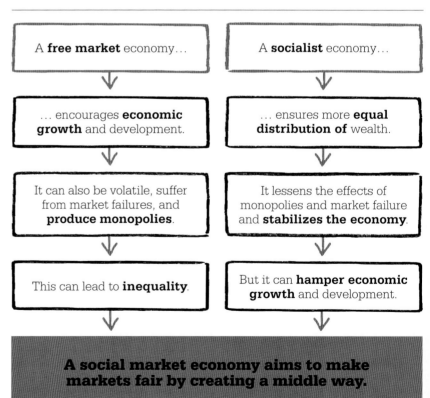

A **free market** economy…

… encourages **economic growth** and development.

It can also be volatile, suffer from market failures, and **produce monopolies**.

This can lead to **inequality**.

A **socialist** economy…

… ensures more **equal distribution of** wealth.

It lessens the effects of monopolies and market failure and **stabilizes the economy**.

But it can **hamper economic growth** and development.

A social market economy aims to make markets fair by creating a middle way.

See also: Markets and morality 22–23 ■ Free market economics 54–61 ■ Marxist economics 100–05 ■ Collective bargaining 134–35 ■ The Keynesian multiplier 164–65

East and West Germany reunified in 1990, a year after the fall of the Berlin Wall (right). East Germany abandoned its centrally planned economy to merge with West Germany's social market.

These economists aimed to achieve what Müller-Armack called a social market economy: not just a "mixed economy," with government providing a bare minimum of necessary public goods, but a middle way between free market capitalism and socialism that aimed for the best of both worlds. Industry remained in private ownership and was free to compete, but government provided a range of public goods and services, including a social security system with universal health care, pensions, unemployment benefits, and measures to outlaw monopolies and cartels (agreements between firms). The theory was that this would allow the economic growth of free markets but at the same time produce low inflation, low unemployment, and a more equitable distribution of wealth.

Economic miracle

The mixture of free markets with elements of socialism worked dramatically well. Germany experienced a *Wirtschaftswunder* ("economic miracle") in the 1950s that transformed it from post-war devastation into a major developed nation. Similar social market economies developed elsewhere, notably in Scandinavia and Austria. As Europe made moves toward economic union, the social market economy was extolled as the model for the European Economic Community in the 1950s. Many countries in Europe thrived under some form of social market economy, but by the 1980s some—most notably Britain—were attracted by the ideas of Milton Friedman (p.199), who advocated "smaller" government. British prime minister Margaret Thatcher criticized the European model for its state intervention and high taxes, which she believed hampered competition.

With the collapse of communism in the Eastern Bloc the planned economies of Eastern Europe were replaced by various versions of the mixed economy. At the same time some of the remaining communist countries made moves to introduce reform. In China, for example, Premier Deng Xiaoping adopted elements of free market economics to operate within the centralized economy, in what he described as a "socialist market economy with Chinese characteristics." His aim was to promote economic growth and become competitive on the world stage. Today, China's economy is still a long way from the European social market model, but it has made significant moves toward becoming a mixed economy. ■

The Nordic model

While the German social market is associated with right of center politics, the economies of Scandinavia developed along similar lines but were politically left of center, with more focus on making the markets fair. The so-called Nordic model is characterized by generous welfare systems and a commitment to fair distribution of wealth, achieved through high taxes and public spending. These countries have enjoyed high living standards and strong economic growth, helped by having small populations with strong manufacturing industries and, in the case of Norway, oil.

Today, there is pressure to reduce the role of the state in order to remain internationally competitive. However, change is gradual: governments are mindful that deregulation in Iceland in the 1990s led to economic growth followed by a financial crisis.

OVER TIME, ALL COUNTRIES WILL BE RICH

ECONOMIC GROWTH THEORIES

IN CONTEXT

FOCUS
Growth and development

KEY THINKER
Robert Solow (1924–)

BEFORE
1776 Adam Smith poses the question of what makes economies prosper in *The Wealth of Nations*.

1930s and 1940s Economists Roy Harrod of the UK and Russian-American Evsey Domar devise a growth model containing Keynesian (government interventionist) assumptions.

AFTER
1980s US economists Paul Romer and Robert Lucas introduce Endogenous Growth Theory, suggesting that growth is primarily the result of internal factors.

1988 US economist Brad DeLong finds little evidence for the basic convergence prediction of the Solow model.

I n the 1950s US economist Robert Solow devised a model of economic growth that predicted an equalization of living standards across the globe. His assumption was that capital has diminishing returns: extra investments add less and less to output. Because poor countries have little capital, extra capital would add a lot to output, and these returns pull in investment. Countries are assumed to have access to the same technology; by using it, poor countries use the additional capital to increase output. The effect is larger than would be the case in a richer

Capital in developed countries is subject to diminishing returns— **extra investment results in less and less** output.

But poor countries have had so little capital invested that investors can still make **high returns** on their investments.

Poor countries can use this **new capital with new technologies** to provide very rapid growth.

Poor countries **grow faster** than rich ones, and their living standards catch up.

Over time, all countries will be rich.

See also: Diminishing returns 62 ▪ Demographics and economics 68–69 ▪ The emergence of modern economies 178–79 ▪ Development economics 188–93 ▪ Technological leaps 313 ▪ Inequality and growth 326–27

Cyclists in Beijing, China, eye a Ferrari parked in the cycling lane. China and India have joined the club of converging ("catch-up") countries.

country. The upshot is that growth is higher in poor countries, and their living standards catch up with those of rich countries in an effect economists call convergence.

Since the 1950s a few Asian countries have caught up with the West, but many African countries have fallen farther behind. Solow's assumptions aren't always satisfied. Technology is not universal: even when knowledge is accessible there may be barriers to using it. Capital doesn't always flow to poor countries; for example, weak property rights and political instability can put investors off. Finally, the endogenous growth theory, developed in the mid-1980s, goes beyond Solow's model by more realistically analyzing the effects of technological change. In this theory new techniques developed by one firm can benefit other firms. This can lead to increasing returns on investment. So, rather than convergence, the result may be divergence between countries.

Living standards

Convergence can be measured using factors other than income. Health and literacy are related to income but imperfectly so: some poor countries have relatively healthy and educated populations. Life expectancies can increase dramatically through simple medical interventions such as immunization. So, in non-income aspects of living standards, poor countries have had more success in catching up.

Despite this, many economists remain focused on explaining income differences. Attention has shifted away from a concern with capital and technology toward the institutional prerequisites needed for developing countries to converge with richer ones. ▪

Robert Solow

Robert Solow was born in New York in 1924. His experience of the Great Depression made him want to understand how economies grow and how living standards can be improved. He entered Harvard University in 1940 but left to join the US Army in 1942, serving in World War II. After returning, he was mentored by the economist Wassily Leontief, and his PhD thesis won Harvard's Wells Prize—$500 and a book publication. Solow thought he could do better than his thesis, so he never published it or cashed his check. In the 1950s he took a position at the Massachusetts Institute of Technology (MIT), where he published his ideas outlining a new model of economic growth. This research inspired new fields in the study of economic growth and earned him the 1987 Nobel Prize.

Key works

1956 *A Contribution to the Theory of Economic Growth*
1957 *Technical Change and the Aggregate Production Function*
1960 *Investment and Technical Progress*

GLOBALIZATION IS NOT INEVITABLE

MARKET INTEGRATION

IN CONTEXT

FOCUS
Global economy

KEY THINKER
Dani Rodrik (1957–)

BEFORE
1664 English economist Thomas Mun says that growth requires reductions in imports.

1817 British economist David Ricardo says that international trade makes countries richer.

1950 Raúl Prebisch and Hans Singer argue that developing countries lose out from globalization because of unequal terms of trade.

AFTER
2002 Joseph Stiglitz criticizes globalization as promoted by the World Bank and the IMF.

2005 World Bank economist David Dollar argues that globalization has reduced poverty in poor countries.

lobalization is a term that means different things to politicians, business people, and social scientists. To an economist it means the integration of markets. Economists have long thought this a good thing.

In the 18th century Adam Smith (p.61) attacked the old mercantilist ideas of protectionism, which aimed to restrict the inflow of foreign goods. He argued that international trade would expand the size of markets and allow countries to become more efficient by specializing in certain products. Often, market integration is seen as inevitable because it rides on the back of a wave of new technology—such as smarter phones, faster planes, and an expanding internet. But globalization is also affected by choices made by nations—sometimes conscious, sometimes accidental. Although technological change tends to bring nations together, policy choices can push them apart.

Modern globalization is not unprecedented. Globalization has waxed and waned over time as nations have made different policy choices. Sometimes these choices have added to the effect of technological progress on the integration of markets; sometimes, they have hindered it.

Market integration is the fusing of many markets into one. In one market a commodity has a single price: the price of carrots would be the same in east Paris and west Paris if these areas were part of the same market. If the price of carrots

Christopher Columbus stumbled across the Americas on an expedition intended to find a new trade route to China. Such efforts to globalize trade have taken place for centuries.

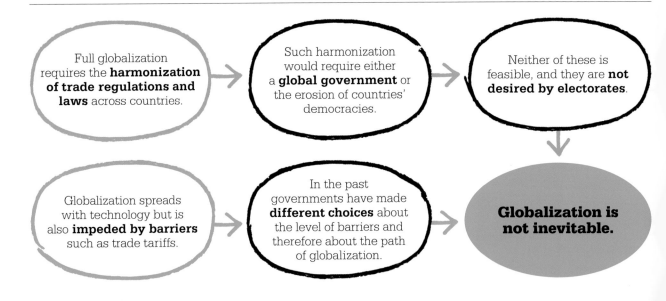

Full globalization requires the **harmonization of trade regulations and laws** across countries.

→

Such harmonization would require either a **global government** or the erosion of countries' democracies.

→

Neither of these is feasible, and they are **not desired by electorates**.

↓

Globalization spreads with technology but is also **impeded by barriers** such as trade tariffs.

→

In the past governments have made **different choices** about the level of barriers and therefore about the path of globalization.

→

Globalization is not inevitable.

in west Paris was higher, sellers of carrots would move from the east to the west and prices would equalize. The price of carrots in Paris and in Lisbon might be different, though, and high transport costs and other kinds of expenses might mean that it would be uneconomical for Portuguese sellers to move their stocks to France if prices were higher there. In distinct markets the price of the same good can be different for long periods of time.

Global market integration means that price differences between countries are eliminated as all markets become one. One way to track the progress of globalization is to look at trends in how prices converge (become similar) across countries. When the costs of trading across borders fall, there is more potential for firms to take advantage of price differences, for Portuguese carrot sellers to enter the French market, for example. Trading costs fall when new forms of transport are invented, or when existing ones become faster and cheaper. Also, some costs are man-made: states erect barriers to trade, such as tariffs and quotas on imports. When these are reduced, the cost of international trading falls.

The rise of global trade

Long-distance trade has existed for centuries, at least since the trade missions of the Phoenicians in the first millennium BCE. Such trade was driven by growing populations and incomes, which created a demand for new products. But the underlying barriers to trade that divided up markets, such as transport costs, did not change that much. Globalization only really took off in the 1820s, when price differences started to close up. This was caused by a transport revolution—the advent of steamships and railroads, the invention of refrigeration, and the opening of the Suez Canal, which slashed the journey time between Europe and Asia. By the eve of World War I the global economy was highly integrated, even by late 20th-century standards, with unprecedented flows of capital, goods, and labor across borders.

From the 19th century onward, technological change helped to integrate markets. It is this that makes globalization seem irreversible—once technology such as steam-powered transport is invented, it is not then uninvented but tends to become economically viable in more countries. Much of this development is outside the direct control of governments. However, at a stroke, governments

> … 'deep' economic integration is unattainable in a context where nation states and democratic politics still exert considerable force.
> **Dani Rodrik**

can put up tariffs and other types of barriers to trade that choke off imports and stymie trade.

The most dramatic policy-related reversal of globalization in modern times occured during the Great Depression of the 1930s. As countries headed into recession, governments imposed tariffs. These were intended to switch the demand of their consumers toward domestically produced goods. In 1930, the US enacted the »

By the mid-19th century Britain had new technology such as these mechanized looms in cotton mills, which allowed it to export and compete in multiple markets around the world.

Improvements in transport have been a major driver in globalization. In Shanghai, China, the US has invested in a gigantic "mega-port" that will make shipping safer.

Smoot–Hawley tariff, which raised tariffs on imported goods to record levels. These tariffs reduced demand for foreign goods. Foreign countries retaliated by imposing their own tariffs. The result was a collapse in world trade that worsened the effects of the Depression. It took decades to rebuild the world economy.

Integration

By the end of the 20th century globalization across most markets had returned to the levels seen just before World War I. Today, markets are more integrated than ever as transportation costs have continued to fall and most tariffs have been scrapped altogether.

One vision of the future of globalization involves the elimination of other kinds of barriers to trade caused by institutional differences between countries. Markets are embedded in institutions—in property rights, legal systems, and regulatory regimes. Differences in institutions between countries create trading costs in the same way that tariffs or distance do. For example, there may be different laws in Kenya and China about what happens when a buyer fails to pay. This might make it hard for a Chinese exporter to recover what it is owed in the event of a dispute, which could make the firm reluctant to enter the Kenyan market. Despite the removal of tariffs the world is far from being a single market. Borders still matter because of these kinds of institutional incompatibilities. Complete integration requires the ironing out of legal and regulatory differences to create a single institutional space.

Some economists argue that this process is underway and inevitable, and that global markets drive the harmonization of institutions across countries. Consider a multinational firm choosing a country in which to locate its factory. In order to attract the firm's investment, a government might cut business tax rates and loosen regulatory requirements. Other competing countries follow suit. The resulting lower tax revenues make countries less able to finance welfare states and educational programs. All policy decisions become oriented toward maximizing integration with global markets. No goods or services would be provided that are incompatible with this.

Globalization v. democracy

The Turkish economist Dani Rodrik (1957–) has criticized this vision of "deep integration," arguing that it is undesirable and far from inevitable, and that in reality considerable institutional diversity persists between countries. Rodrik's starting point is that choices about the direction of globalization are subject to a political "trilemma." People want

Liberalizing the money markets

The liberalization of capital (money) markets, where funds for investment can be borrowed, has been an important contributor to the pace of globalization. Since the 1970s there has been a trend towards a freer flow of capital across borders. Current economic theory suggests that this should aid development. Developing countries have limited domestic savings with which to invest in growth, and liberalization allows them to tap into a global pool of funds. A global capital market also allows investors greater scope to manage and spread their risks.

However, some say that a freer flow of capital has raised the risk of financial instability. The East Asian crisis of the late 1990s came in the wake of this kind of liberalization. Without a strong financial system and a robust regulatory environment capital market globalization can sow the seeds of instability in economies rather than growth.

The East Asian crisis began when the Thai government attempted to float the baht on the international markets, ending its link to the dollar.

> The 19th century contained a very big globalization bang.
> **Jeffrey G. Williamson**
> **K. H. O'Rourke**

Nations may want democracy, independence, and deep global economic integration. Yet at any one time, only two out of three may be compatible with each other. In the diagram each side of the triangle represents a possible combination.

Democracy

Deep economic integration

Independent nation-state

market integration because of the prosperity that it can bring. People want democracy, and they want independent, sovereign nation-states. Rodrik argues that the three of these are incompatible. Only two are possible at any one time. How the trilemma is resolved implies different forms of globalization.

The trilemma comes from the fact that the deep, or more complete, integration of markets requires the removal of institutional variations between countries. But electorates in different countries want different types of institutions. Compared to US voters, those in European countries tend to favor large welfare states. So a single global institutional framework in which nation-states still existed would mean ignoring the preferences of electorates in some countries. This would conflict with democracy, and governments would be placed in what US journalist Thomas Friedman (1953–) has called a "golden straitjacket." On the other hand a global institutional framework in which democracy reigned would require "global federalism"—a single worldwide electorate and the dissolution of nation-states.

Today, we are far from either the golden straitjacket or global federalism. Nation-states are strong, and persistent institutional diversity across countries suggests that the varied preferences of different populations are still important. Since World War II Rodrik's trilemma has been resolved by sacrificing deep integration. Markets have been brought together as much as possible given nations' varied institutions. Rodrik calls this the "Bretton Woods compromise," referring to the global institutions that were established after the war (pp.186–87)—the General Agreement on Tariffs and Trade (GATT), the World Bank, and the International Monetary Fund (IMF). These organizations aimed at preventing a repeat of the catastrophic backlash seen in the 1930s through a form of managed integration, in which nation-states were free to pursue their own domestic policies and develop along varied institutional paths.

The liberalization era since the 1980s saw an undermining of the Bretton Woods compromise, with the policy agenda being increasingly driven by the aim of deep integration. Rodrik argues that institutional diversity should be preserved over deep integration. European electorates' desire for welfare states and public health systems is not just about economics, but also their view of justice. Institutional diversity reflects these different values. More practically, there is more than one institutional route to a healthy economy. The requirements for growth in today's developing countries may be different from those for developed nations. Imposing a global institutional blueprint runs the risk of placing countries in a straitjacket that suffocates their own economic development. Globalization may have limits, and it may be that the complete fusion of economies is neither feasible nor—ultimately—desirable. ∎

SOCIALISM LEADS TO EMPTY SHOPS

SHORTAGES IN PLANNED ECONOMIES

IN CONTEXT

FOCUS
Economic systems

KEY THINKER
János Kornai (1928–)

BEFORE
1870 Economists William Jevons, Alfred Marshall, and Léon Walras focus on optimizing efficiency within budget constraints.

AFTER
1954 Gérard Debreu and Kenneth Arrow identify the conditions under which demand equals supply in all the markets of a competitive economy.

1991 The Soviet Union collapses and central planning ends.

1999 Economists Philippe Aghion, Patrick Bolton, and Steven Fries publish *The Optimal Design of Bank-Bailouts*, arguing that banks face a soft budget constraint.

In competitive markets firms' **revenues must be higher than their costs**, or they will go bankrupt.

↓

In planned economies, if firms do not cover their costs, the state steps in to **protect them** from bankruptcy.

↓

This means that costs (materials and labor) do not have to be closely matched to **output or demand**.

↓

Socialism leads to empty shops.

After an initial dramatic rush of growth after World War II the centrally planned economies of Eastern Europe faced increasingly obvious problems. They could mobilize resources on a large scale for well-defined tasks, such as producing military armaments, but seemed to have difficulty meeting more complex demands. Shortages abounded, as—despite planning—goods and services were not delivered on time, in the required quantity, or at an appropriate quality. The gap between the East and the West yawned wider.

Soft budget constraints

In response, a number of regimes attempted to introduce reforms to the planning system. Hungary went further than most, introducing elements of market competition from the 1960s onward. In theory, this was supposed to introduce the benefits of the market, provoking innovation and expanding choice, while retaining the ability of the plan to deliver broad social goods like full employment. In practice, after some initial successes the system continued to produce shortages and inefficiency.

Attempting to understand the problem, Hungarian economist János Kornai hit on the concept of the "soft budget constraint." In competitive markets, firms' decisions are normally subject to "hard" budget constraints: their revenues must at least cover their costs, or they will face financial losses. This disciplines firms to economize on inputs and sell output in a way that maximizes profits. Kornai noticed that in planned economies such as Hungary's, firms were not subject to this discipline: they faced soft, not hard, budget constraints. The state cushioned firms from the threat of bankruptcy—firms that produced essential goods would never be forced to close. Even after some market reforms were implemented, the state continued to bail out failing firms. In addition, firms could use political bargaining to get away with underpaying for supplies, or avoiding taxation.

Soft budget constraints mean that firms do not have to cover costs with revenues. They tend to demand excessive amounts of inputs relative to production levels. This leads to excess demands for particular inputs, and then shortages arising from inefficiency. Shortages eventually trickle down to consumers, who find shop shelves bare. Kornai argued that shortages would mean that consumers would be subject to "forced substitution," the necessity of having to purchase the next best available good, given a shortage.

Bailouts

Inefficiencies such as these added up to serious weaknesses in planned economies. Guaranteed bailouts and a lack of budgetary discipline meant firms had little incentive to supply goods and services efficiently.

Kornai describes soft budget constraints as a "syndrome" of central planning that cannot be cured, because only a complete systemic change would bring a solution. The problem is not confined to socialist countries—Kornai has argued that major banks

Shortages were a feature of life in centrally planned economies. If a line began forming, shoppers would often join it, because it meant that some essential good was briefly available.

in the West face soft budget constraints, since they expect to be bailed out by their governments, leading to inefficiently high levels of risk-taking in the banking system. On the other hand introducing hard budget constraints into every state or local-authority decision—such as sending an insolvent family to jail—might be seen as unjust. In practice, even the most free market economies contain a mix of hard and soft budget constraints. ▪

János Kornai

János Kornai is a Hungarian economist best known for his work on the planned economy. He experienced the horrors of fascism firsthand—his father died in Auschwitz—and this drove him to communism. He studied philosophy in Budapest, but changed to economics after reading Marx's *Capital*. In 1947, Kornai began working on the Communist Party newspaper, but he broke with the Party in the early 1950s, shaken by the regime's torture of an innocent friend. His critical articles resulted in his dismissal from the paper in 1955. Refused permission to leave Hungary, he worked at the Hungarian Academy of Sciences until 1985, when he took up a post at Harvard. Kornai returned to Hungary in 2001. He has criticized neoclassical economics for preferring abstract theorizing to addressing and answering the "big questions."

Key works

1959 *Overcentralization in Economic Administration*
1971 *Anti-equilibrium*
1992 *The Socialist System*

WHAT DOES THE OTHER MAN THINK I AM GOING TO DO?

GAME THEORY

IN CONTEXT

FOCUS
Decision making

KEY THINKER
John Nash (1928–)

BEFORE
1928 US mathematician John
von Neumann formulates the
"minimax rule" that says the
best strategy is to minimize
the maximum loss on any turn.

AFTER
1960 US economist Thomas
Schelling publishes *The
Strategy of Conflict*, which
develops strategies in the
context of the Cold War.

1965 German economist
Reinhard Selten analyzes
games with many rounds.

1967 US economist John
Harsanyi shows how games
can be analyzed even if there
is uncertainty about what
sort of opponent you are
playing against.

Considering how another person might react when you do something involves making strategic calculations. Successfully negotiating your way through social and economic interactions is a bit like a game of chess, where players must choose a move on the basis of what the other player's countermove might be. Up to the 1940s economics had largely avoided this issue. Economists assumed that every buyer and seller in the market was very small compared to the total size of the market so nobody had

Our everyday interactions involve strategic decisions that are similar to a game of chess, where players choose their moves on the basis of how they think their opponent will respond.

any choice about the price they paid for a good or the wage they sold their labor for. Individual choices had no effects on others, it was reasoned, so they could safely be ignored. But as early as 1838, French economist Antoine Augustin Cournot (p.91) had looked at how much two firms would produce on the basis of

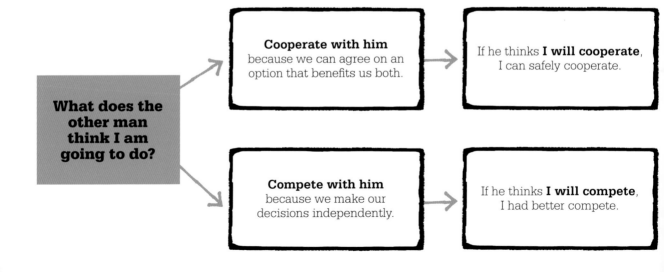

What does the other man think I am going to do?

Cooperate with him
because we can agree on an option that benefits us both.

If he thinks **I will cooperate**, I can safely cooperate.

Compete with him
because we make our decisions independently.

If he thinks **I will compete**, I had better compete.

what they thought the other firm was going to do, but this was an isolated case of analyzing strategic interactions.

In 1944, US mathematicians John von Neumann and Oskar Morgenstern published the groundbreaking work, *Theory of Games and Economic Behavior.* They suggested that many parts of the economic system were dominated by a small number of participants, such as large firms, trade unions, or the government. In such a situation economic behavior needed to be explained with reference to strategic interactions. By analyzing simple two-person games that are "zero-sum" (one person wins and the other loses), they hoped to create general rules about strategic behavior between people in every situation. This became known as game theory.

Von Neumann and Morgenstern looked at cooperative games in which players were given a number of possible actions, each with its own particular result, or payoff. The players were given the opportunity to discuss the situation and come to an agreed plan of action. A real example of such a game was provided by US mathematician Merrill Flood, who allowed his three teenagers to bid for the right for one of them to work as a babysitter for a maximum payment of $4. They were allowed to discuss the problem and form a coalition, but if they were unable to agree between themselves then the lowest bidder would win. To Flood, there were easy solutions to the problem, such as settling by lot or splitting the proceeds

equally. However, his children were unable to find a solution and eventually one of them bid 90 cents to do the work.

Nash equilibrium
In the early 1950s a brilliant young US mathematician named John Nash extended this work to look at what happens when players make independent decisions in non-cooperative situations— where there is no opportunity for communication or collaboration. Cooperation is a possible outcome but only if each player sees

cooperation as maximizing their own individual chances of success. Nash identified the state of equilibrium in such games where neither player wants to change their behavior. Players are choosing their best strategy on the basis that their opponents are also selecting their best strategies. Nash identified the state in such games where neither player wants to change their behavior as "each player's strategy is optimal against those of the others." This is now known as the Nash equilibrium. »

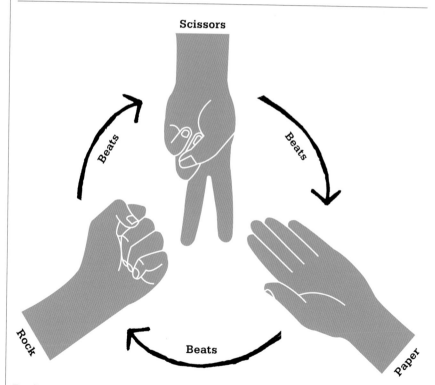

Rock-paper-scissors is an example of a simple zero-sum game in which if one player wins, then the other loses. The game is played by two players. Each player must make one of three shapes with their hand at the same time. The shape one player makes will either match, beat, or lose to their opponent's shape: rock beats scissors, scissors beats paper, and paper beats rock. Game theorists analyze games such as this to discover general rules of human behavior.

The prisoner's dilemma is an example of a non-cooperative game in which neither party can communicate with the other. The "Nash equilibrium" of the game is for both players to betray.

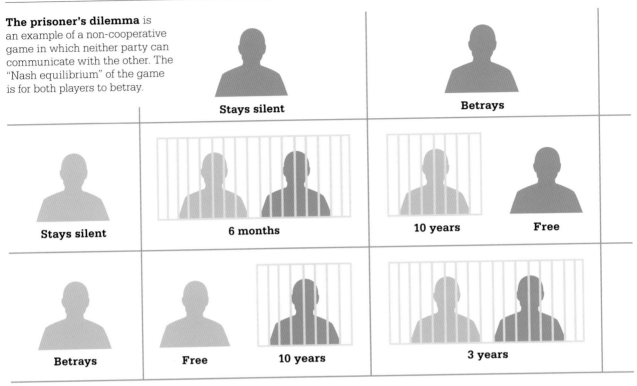

	Stays silent	Betrays
Stays silent	6 months	10 years / Free
Betrays	Free / 10 years	3 years

There was an incredible blooming of game theory after World War II, much of it at the think tank RAND (the name comes from Research ANd Development). Set up by the US government in 1946, RAND was charged with putting science at the service of national security. They employed mathematicians, economists, and other scientists

> Game theory is rational behavior in social situations.
> **John Harsanyi**
> US economist (1920–2000)

to research areas such as game theory, which was seen to be particularly relevant to the politics of the Cold War.

In 1950, the game theorists at RAND devised two examples of non-cooperative games. The first was published under the name "So Long Sucker." This game was specifically designed to be as psychologically cruel as possible. It forced players into coalitions, but ultimately to win you had to double-cross your partner. It is said that after trials of the game, husbands and wives often went home in separate taxis.

The prisoner's dilemma
Perhaps the most famous example of a non-cooperative game is the prisoner's dilemma. It was created in 1950 by Melvin Dresher and Merrill Flood and builds on Nash's work. The dilemma involves two

captured criminals who are kept separate during interrogation and offered the following choices: They are told that if they both testify against each other, they will each get a medium jail sentence that will be painful but bearable. If neither will testify against the other, then they will both receive a short sentence that they will cope with easily. However, if one agrees to testify and the other does not, then the man who testifies will go free, and the man who stayed silent will receive a long sentence that will ruin his life.

The dilemma for each prisoner is this: to betray or not to betray. If he betrays his partner, he will go free or end up with a medium sentence. If he trusts his partner not to betray him, he could end up with a short sentence or a very long time in prison. To avoid the possibility of the "sucker's payoff"—ending up with a long sentence—the Nash equilibrium is always to betray. What is interesting is that the "dominant" (best) strategy of mutual betrayal does not maximize welfare for the group. If they had both refused to betray, their total jail time would have been minimized.

Dresher and Flood tested the prisoner's dilemma on two of their colleagues to see whether Nash's prediction would be true. They made a game where each player could choose to trust or betray the other player. The payoffs were designed so that there was a sucker's payoff, but also an option for a cooperative trade that would benefit both players, a solution that reflected von Neumann and Morgenstern's earlier work involving cooperative games. The experiment was run over 100 rounds. This iterative version of the game gave players the chance to punish or reward the previous behavior of their partner. The results showed that the Nash equilibrium of

Expensive technology, such as the Stealth Bomber, was developed during the Cold War. To avoid the "sucker's payoff," game theory suggested that both sides should spend this money.

> **"**
> Each player's strategy is optimal against those of the others.
> **John Nash**
> **"**

betrayal was only chosen 14 times against 68 times for the cooperative solution. Dresher and Flood concluded that real people learn quickly to choose a strategy that maximizes their benefit. Nash argued that the experiment was flawed because it allowed for too much interaction, and that the only true equilibrium point was betrayal.

Peace–war game
The iterative version of the prisoner's dilemma came to be known as the peace–war game. It was used to explain the best strategy in the Cold War with the Soviet Union. As new technologies such as intercontinental ballistic weapons were developed, each side had to decide whether to invest enormous sums of money to acquire these weapons. The new technology might lead to the ability to win a war relatively painlessly if the other side didn't develop the new weapon. The consequence of not developing »

John Nash

Born in 1928 into a middle-class American family, John Nash was labeled as backward at school due to his poor social skills. However, his parents recognized his outstanding academic ability. In 1948, he won a scholarship to Princeton University. His former tutor wrote a one-line letter of recommendation: "This man is a genius." At Princeton Nash avoided lectures, preferring to develop ideas from scratch. It was there that he developed the ideas on game theory that were to earn him his Nobel Prize. In the 1950s he worked at the RAND Corporation and MIT (Massachusetts Institute of Technology), but by now his mental state was worsening. In 1961, his wife committed him for treatment for his schizophrenia. Nash battled with the condition for the next 25 years but never stopped hoping that he would be able to add something else of value to the study of mathematics.

Key works

1950 *Equilibrium Points in N-person Games*
1950 *The Bargaining Problem*
1952 *Real Algebraic Manifolds*

it was either a huge savings of money if the other side didn't develop it either, or the sucker's payoff of a total defeat if they did.

The importance of Nash's work in a wider context was to show that there could be an equilibrium between independent self-interested individuals that would create stability and order. In fact it was argued that the equilibrium achieved by individuals trying to maximize their own payoffs produced safer and more stable outcomes in non-cooperative situations than when the players tried to accommodate each other.

Nash shared the 1994 Nobel Prize for economics with two other economists who helped to develop game theory. Hungarian-born economist John Harsanyi showed that games in which the players did not have complete information about the motives or payoffs of the other players could still be analyzed. Since most real life strategic decisions are made in the fog of uncertainty, this was an important breakthrough. A real life example might be when financial markets cannot be sure of the central bank's attitude toward inflation and unemployment, and therefore cannot know whether it will increase interest rates to reduce inflation or reduce rates to increase employment. Since the profits of firms in the financial markets are determined by the rate of interest that the central bank will set in the future, firms need to be able to assess the risk of lending more or less money. Harsanyi showed that even if the markets cannot tell which target the central bank is more concerned with, game theory can identify the Nash equilibrium, which is the solution to the problem.

The centipede game

Another economist responsible for advancing game theory was the German Reinhard Selten, who introduced the concept of sub-game perfection in games that are multi-staged. The idea is that there should be an equilibrium at each stage or "sub-game" of the overall game. This can have major implications. An example of such a game is the centipede game, where a number of players pass a sum of

> You know what you are thinking, but you do not know why you are thinking it.
> **Reinhard Selten**

money between them, and each time they do so the pile of money is increased by 20 percent. There are two ways for the game to end: the money is passed between them for 100 rounds (hence the name centipede), and then the total pot of money is shared, or at some stage one player decides to keep the pile of money that he or she has been given. Each player's choice is to cooperate by passing the money on or defect and keep the money. In the last round the player does best by defecting and taking it all.

When haggling with a buyer, a seller may start with a price many times what he is happy to accept, but in doing so risks losing the sale.

Getting to the truth

In 1960, Russian-born economist Leonid Hurwicz began to study the mechanisms by which markets work. In classical theory it is assumed that goods will be traded efficiently: at a fair price and to the people who want them most. In the real world markets do not work like this. For instance Hurwicz recognized that both the buyer and seller of a secondhand car have an incentive to lie about how much each values it.

Even if both parties revealed how much they were willing to buy or sell for and agreed to split the difference in the price, it is unlikely that this mechanism would create an optimal outcome. Sellers will naturally claim to want a much higher price than they actually require, while buyers will offer much less than they are willing to pay. In such circumstances they will fail to come to an agreement even though they both want to make a deal. Hurwicz concluded that if the participants could be persuaded to reveal the truth, then the benefits to both parties would be maximized.

In cooperative games players have the chance to form alliances. In many of these games, such as a tug of war, the only chance an individual has of winning is to cooperate with others.

This implies that in the second-to-last round defection is also a better choice—anticipating the future defection of your rival. By continuing this logic backward, it seems that defection dominates in every round so that the sub-game perfect choice is to defect on the first round. This result appears paradoxical, however, given that the sum of money in the first round is very small and hardly worth defecting over.

This idea has been applied to the situation where there is a large chain store with outlets all over the country, and a rival is preparing to enter the market in one or more locations. The chain store could threaten to cut prices in the location that the new firm is thinking of entering. This threat would appear to be both credible and worthwhile since it would not cost the chain store too much profit and would deter the firm from trying to enter in that area.

When I used to theorize about a nuclear standoff, I didn't really have to understand what was happening inside the Soviet Union.
Thomas Schelling

The optimal strategy in terms of Nash equilibrium appears to be for the chain store to fight a price war, and for the new firm not to try to enter the market. However, according to Selten, if the existing firm were forced to cut prices every time a new firm tried to enter one of its markets, the cumulative losses would be too great. Thus, by looking forward and reasoning backward, the threat of a price war is irrational. Selten concludes that the new firm's entry without a price war is sub-game perfect.

Bounded rationality

These paradoxes come from the assumption that individuals playing games are fully rational. Selten proposed a more realistic theory of decision making. Although people do sometimes make decisions through rational calculation, often they do so on the basis of past experience and rules of thumb. People may not always use rational calculation. Instead, they may be what game theorists call "boundedly rational:" able to

choose the more intuitively appealing solutions to games that may not be sub-game perfect.

Game theory is not without its critics, who say that it tells great stories but fails the main test of any scientific theory: it can make no useful predictions about what will happen. A game might have many equilibriums. An industry resulting in a cartel might be as rational a result as one that descends into a price war. Further, people don't make decisions based on "If I do this and they do this and I do that and they do that" ad infinitum.

The US economist Thomas Schelling has addressed this issue by studying the idea that the triggers for behavior are not simply based on mathematical probabilities. In the "coordination game," where both players are rewarded if they think of the same playing card, what card in the pack would you select if you wanted to try to match with someone else? Would you pick the ace of spades? ∎

RICH COUNTRIES IMPOVERISH THE POOR
DEPENDENCY THEORY

IN CONTEXT

FOCUS
Growth and development

KEY THINKER
Andre Gunder Frank
(1929–2005)

BEFORE
1841 German economist Friedrich List argues against free trade and for protectionism in domestic markets.

1949–50 Hans Singer and Raúl Prebisch claim that the terms of trade between poor and rich countries deteriorate over time.

AFTER
1974–2011 US sociologist Immanuel Wallerstein develops Frank's development theories to devise world-systems theory. This uses a historical framework to explain the changes that were involved in the rise of the Western world.

Poor countries are told that their economies will grow if they **open their borders** to international trade.

Rich countries are in a dominant position, so they **exploit the poor countries** through unequal trading terms.

This exploitation causes the economies of poor countries to **stagnate or shrink**…

… while rich countries **become richer**.

Rich countries impoverish the poor.

Rich countries claim that they do not set out to keep poor countries poor—rather that relationships between them should help both parties. However, in the 1960s German economist Andre Gunder Frank claimed that the development policies of the Western world, along with free trade and investment, perpetuate the global divide. They preserve the dominance of the rich world and keep poor countries poor. Frank called this "dependency theory."

Unbalanced trading
Rich Western countries were never junior trading partners to a bloc of powerful and economically advanced countries, as poor countries are today. For this reason some economists have pointed out that policies that helped the advanced countries develop may not benefit today's poor countries.

The liberalization of international trade is often extolled by economists as a guaranteed way of helping underdeveloped economies. However, Frank's dependency theory claims that such policies often lead to situations where rich countries take advantage of poorer ones. Underdeveloped countries

See also: Protectionism and trade 34–35 ▪ Comparative advantage 80–85 ▪ Development economics 188–93 ▪ Economic growth theories 224–25 ▪ Market integration 226–31 ▪ Asian Tiger economies 282–87 ▪ International debt relief 314–15

Many Nigerian oil workers work for foreign firms. These firms have poured investment into Nigeria but may benefit disproportionately from low local wages and valuable raw materials.

When richer countries bring industry and investment to poorer countries, they claim that they will help grow the poor countries' economies. The dependency theorists claim that in reality local resources are often exploited, workers are poorly paid, and the profits are distributed to foreign shareholders rather than being reinvested into the local economy.

An alternative route

To avoid the kinds of dangers outlined by the dependency theorists, some poor countries have taken a different route. Far from opening themselves up to world trade, globalization, and foreign investment, they have decided to do the opposite and insulate themselves. Some argue that the rise of the Asian Tigers—Hong Kong, Singapore, Taiwan, and South

> Underdevelopment is not due to the survival of archaic institutions and… capital shortage… it is generated by… the development of capitalism itself.
> **Andre Gunder Frank**

Korea—and the extraordinary economic growth of China expose flaws in the dependency view. Here were a group of developing economies for whom international trade was an engine of rapid growth and industrialization. Most recently, dependency theory has found echoes in the anti-globalization movements, which continue to question the classical approach. ▪

produce raw materials, which are bought by richer countries, who then produce manufactured goods that are sold internally or between developed countries. This leads to an unbalanced trading system where the majority of the poor countries' trade is with richer, developed countries, while the richer countries' trade is mainly internal or with other developed nations. Only a small proportion is with the developing countries. As a result poorer countries find themselves in a weak bargaining position—they are trading with larger, richer powers—and they are denied the favorable trading terms they need to progress.

It is argued that these forces lead to a separation of the global economy into a "core" of rich countries to which wealth flows from a "periphery" of marginalized poor countries. The economies of poor countries also tend to be organized in such a way that they discourage investment, which is a key driver of growth in the economy of any country.

Unequal export: raw and manufactured goods

In 1949 and 1950, economists Hans Singer of Germany and Raúl Prebisch of Argentina independently published papers illustrating the disadvantage faced by developing countries when trading with the developed world. They observed that the terms of trade (the amount of imports a nation can buy with a given amount of exports) is worse for countries whose primary export is a raw material or commodity than for countries whose main export is manufactured goods. This can be explained by the fact that, as incomes rise, demand for food and commodities tend to remain steady.

On the other hand higher incomes provoke stronger demand for manufactured and luxury goods. This leads to price rises and results in the poorer country being able to afford fewer imported manufactured goods in return for the money it receives from exports.

YOU CAN'T FOOL THE PEOPLE

RATIONAL EXPECTATIONS

IN CONTEXT

FOCUS
The macroeconomy

KEY THINKERS
John Muth (1930–2005)
Robert Lucas (1937–)

BEFORE
1939 British economist
John Hicks analyzes the
way that expectations of
the future change.

1956 US economist
Philip Cagan uses
"adaptive expectations"
to explain forecasts based
on the past.

AFTER
1985 US economist Gregory
Mankiw contributes to the
emergence of the "New
Keynesian" economics,
which uses new models that
incorporate people's rational
expectations of the future into
their calculations.

The rise of government
intervention and spending
after World War II provided
an important new way for
economists to think about the
whole economy. In particular
they believed that the government
could boost the economy by using
monetary and fiscal (tax and
spend) policies to achieve
permanently higher output
and lower unemployment.

Early criticisms of these
Keynesian models involved a
closer examination of the idea of
"expectations." Expectations
matter because what people think
will happen in the future affects
their behavior in the present.

See also: Economic man 52–53 ▪ Borrowing and debt 76–77 ▪ The Keynesian multiplier 164–65 ▪ Monetarist policy 196–201 ▪ Behavioral economics 266–69 ▪ Efficient markets 272 ▪ Independent central banks 276–77

People are rational and make predictions using all the information available to them.

They form **rational expectations** about the future.

They will **anticipate the effects** of government attempts to boost the economy...

... and **adjust their behavior**, rendering the government policy ineffective.

You can't fool the people.

A father passes on his knowledge of car maintenance to his son. The son will make future economic decisions, such as which car to buy, based partly on this knowledge.

However, this only works in the short term: once people's expectations catch up, they realize that their real wages have not risen, and the economy reverts to its original lower level of employment.

Rational expectations

This way of modeling expectations was simple but flawed. If people only looked at the past when making their forecasts about the future, they would be likely to get their forecasts persistently wrong. Unexpected shocks to the economy, pushing it away (even temporarily) from its previous path would be turned into permanent errors in forecasting. But if people made persistent forecasting errors, they would persistently lose out against the market—and this did not seem to be a realistic picture of people's behavior.

It was dissatisfaction with the theory of adaptive expectations that helped lead US economist John Muth toward a theory of "rational expectations" in 1961. At the heart of his theory is a very simple idea. If buyers in a »

Initially, expectations were taken to be "adaptive." This assumes that people form expectations of the future based solely on what happened before—if Event A led to Event B, it will do so again. In each case individuals adjust for the gap between what they expected to happen and the actual outcome.

The need to allow for expectations within economic theory was acknowledged to weaken the outcome of Keynesian policies (pp.154–61), where governments increase spending to raise demand. These policies assume that if people's wages are increased as a result of a government boost to the economy, an increase in their real economic activity will occur—they will supply more work. In reality the increased demand also leads prices to rise, so in real terms, their wages have not. People are temporarily fooled into thinking that their increased money wages reflect a raise in real wages because they take a while to realize that prices have also risen—their expectations about future price increases adjust slowly. In this way it is possible for a government to increase economic output through monetary or fiscal policy by (in effect) fooling people.

A farmer in Australia inspects his crop. Farmers do not decide what to plant based solely on the past. They also weigh factors such as the weather and levels of demand.

market are rational, they do not simply guess at future prices by looking at previous ones. Instead, they will attempt to forecast future prices based on the information available and—critically—using a correct model of the economy. They will make educated predictions rather than blindly following past behavior. They will do this because if they do not form their expectations rationally, they will be punished by the market and lose money.

We use rational expectations all the time. Farmers, for instance, make decisions about what to plant based on past prices, current conditions, and future probabilities. They do not assume that if they grow the same amount of the same commodity they did five years earlier, it will achieve the same market price now—and neither do the commodity dealers trading in agricultural goods. Punishment from the market forces people to behave rationally and, over time, their expectations can be assumed to be as good as the best available economic model. The theory of rational expectations is deceptively

simple but has startling consequences. Under adaptive expectations government intervention might work temporarily because it could take people by surprise. They would not anticipate future government policies and so an unexpected expansion of spending would act like a positive "shock" in the economy, with short-term real effects. Even these temporary effects are impossible under the theory of rational expectations since people's forecasts for price increases adjust immediately.

Anticipating events
In 1975, two US economists, Thomas Sargent and Neil Wallace, claimed that if expectations are rational, not only would individuals begin to expect government intervention, but they would adjust their behavior in such a way that policy would be rendered ineffective. Assuming rational expectations, people would know that the government had an incentive to generate shocks, such as trying to keep down unemployment. They

It is rather surprising that expectations have not previously been regarded as rational dynamic models, since rationality is assumed in all other aspects of entrepreneurial behavior.
John Muth

would adjust their expectations accordingly. For example, individuals would understand that when a government attempts to use monetary policy (such as cutting interest rates) to maintain employment, it leads to higher inflation. People therefore alter their expectations of wage and price increases accordingly. Instead of feeling wealthier, their expectation of inflation cancels out the effects of lower rates of interest looked for by the government. In this way monetary policy becomes completely ineffective because it will always be accounted for, and people's changed behavior will undo it.

Policy makers had previously believed that there was a trade-off between unemployment and inflation—that governments could boost the economy and achieve higher employment in the long run with higher inflation (pp.202–03). Under rational expectations, this trade-off dissolves. Unemployment is determined by the productive capacities of the economy: the productivity and technological capacities of its firms and the efficiency of its markets. Policy makers cannot boost the economy beyond this level of employment.

The Lucas critique
US economist Robert Lucas pointed out that if individuals' expectations do adjust with policy, this means that the whole structure of the economy—the sets of relationships between different households, firms, and the government—alters with changes in policy. As a result the effects of policy are not always those that are intended.

This became known as the "Lucas critique," and it was powerful enough to convince most economists that attempts to model the whole economy through its structural relationships, as Keynesian models do, are flawed. Modeling should instead focus on people's deeper underlying preferences, and the resources and technologies that direct individual behavior. Lucas suggested a "new classical" approach to macroeconomics, offering a partial return to the pre-Keynesian world. Later "real business cycle" models claimed that changes in employment are driven by changes in "real" labor factors, such as productivity increases or changes in people's preferences for leisure over work. The critical feature of both real business cycles and new classical models is that they model the macroeconomy on the result of individuals' rational behavior.

Although people do not have entirely rational expectations in reality, the assumption that they do helps economists to build workable models that are useful guides to the

functioning of the economy. Rational expectations have come under criticism by behavioral economists who work on more psychologically realistic models. ∎

> ❝
> The benefits of inflation derive from the use of expansionary policy to trick economic agents into behaving in socially preferable ways even though their behavior is not in their own interest.
> ❞
> **Robert Hall**
> US economist (1943–)

Traders in financial markets form rational expectations based partly on the actions of their colleagues at work. Failure to read the signs will lead to punishment by the market.

John Muth

US economist John Muth was born in 1930. He studied industrial engineering at Washington University in St. Louis, then mathematical economics at Carnegie Mellon (then called Carnegie Tech) in Pittsburgh. Carnegie had an extraordinary faculty in the 1950s, when Muth studied for his PhD there—it included future Nobel laureates Franco Modigliani, John Nash, Herb Simon, and later Robert Lucas.

Muth's first paper on rational expectations was published in 1961 and was little noticed at the time. A shy, modest man, Muth was unable to find a publisher for a later art in the subject and so moved to work in other fields, p ng seminal work in the fie operations managem and artificial intelligence. Other economics researchers such as Lucas and Simon furthered Muth's work on rational expectations and won major awards for their contributions, but Muth remained unacknowledged by the wider world. He went on to teach at Michigan State and Indiana, both universities that lacked status but allowed him to satisfy his broad intellectual curiosity. He is considered to be the father of the "rational expectations revolution." Muth died in 2005.

Key works

1960 *Optimal Properties of Exponentially Weighted Forecasts*
1961 *Rational Expectations and the Theory of Price Movements*
1966 *Forecasting Models*

PEOPLE DON'T CARE ABOUT PROBABILITY WHEN THEY CHOOSE
PARADOXES IN DECISION MAKING

By the 1960s mainstream economics had settled on a set of principles for understanding people's decision making. Human beings are rational, calculating individuals. When confronted with different options and an uncertain future, they assign a probability to each possible future outcome and make their choice accordingly. They seek to boost their "expected utility" (the amount of satisfaction they expect) based on their beliefs about the probability of different future outcomes, opting for the choice with the highest expected utility.

But this set of ideas was challenged by results suggesting that, even under experimental conditions, humans do not behave according to the theory. One of the most important of these challenges was posed in the Ellsberg paradox, popularized by US economist Daniel Ellsberg in 1961, but

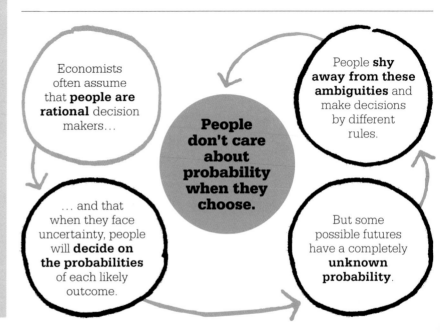

Economists often assume that **people are rational** decision makers…

… and that when they face uncertainty, people will **decide on the probabilities** of each likely outcome.

People don't care about probability when they choose.

People **shy away from these ambiguities** and make decisions by different rules.

But some possible futures have a completely **unknown probability**.

See also: Economic man 52–53 ▪ Economic bubbles 98–99 ▪ Risk and uncertainty 162–63 ▪
Irrational decision making 194–95 ▪ Behavioral economics 266–69

A probability experiment offered a choice of bets. Players were told there were 30 red balls in an urn, together with 60 balls that were an unspecified mixture of black and yellow. Drawing a red ball would win $100; a black would win $100. Most players opted for a bet on the red.

A further choice offered $100 if a red or yellow ball was drawn, or $100 if a black or yellow was drawn. This time, most players opted for black or yellow. In each case, players showed a preference for known odds over unknown odds.

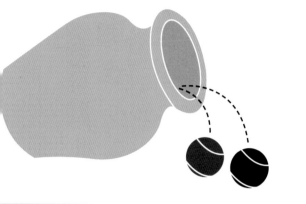
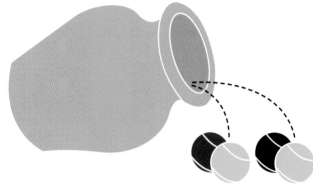

drawing on an idea originally described by John Maynard Keynes (p.161) in the 1930s.

Aversion to ambiguity

Ellsberg described a thought experiment in which a cash prize was offered if a ball of a particular color was drawn from an imaginary urn (see above). The bets made by the experiment's participants demonstrated that people tend to make a reasoned choice when given some information from which the degree of probability, and therefore risk, can be assessed. However, their behavior changes if a future outcome seems ambiguous, and this is the paradox that departs from expected utility theory. People prefer to know more about the uncertainties they face, rather than less. In the words of former US Defense Secretary Donald Rumsfeld (1932–), people prefer the "known unknowns" to the "unknown unknowns." The outcome of the experiment has been reproduced in several real

experiments since Ellsberg published his paper. It has become known as "ambiguity aversion," and sometimes "Knightian uncertainty" after the US economist Frank Knight (p.163). In seeking to know more about "unknown unknowns," people may act inconsistently with previous, more logical choices, and put questions of probability aside when making their choice.

Know the unknowns

Ellsberg's paradox has proved controversial. Some economists claim that it can safely be contained within conventional theory, and that experimental conditions do not properly reproduce people's behavior when faced with real-life ambiguity. However, the financial crisis of 2008 has provoked fresh interest in the problem of ambiguity. People want to know more about the unknown, unquantifiable risks that expected utility theory cannot account for. ▪

Daniel Ellsberg

Born in 1931, Daniel Ellsberg studied economics at Harvard University, and joined the US Marine Corps in 1954. In 1959, he became an analyst for the White House. He received his PhD in 1962, in which he first presented his paradox. Ellsberg, then working with top security clearance, became disillusioned with the Vietnam War. In 1971, he leaked top secret reports detailing the Pentagon's belief that the war could not be won, before handing himself over to the authorities. His trial collapsed when it was revealed that White House agents had used illegal wiretaps of his house.

Key works

1961 *Risk, Ambiguity, and the Savage Axioms*
2001 *Risk, Ambiguity, and Decision*

SIMILAR ECONOMIES CAN BENEFIT FROM A SINGLE CURRENCY

EXCHANGE RATES AND CURRENCIES

IN CONTEXT

FOCUS
Global economy

KEY THINKER
Robert Mundell (1932–)

BEFORE
1953 Milton Friedman argues that freely floating exchange rates would enable market forces to resolve problems with balance of payments (the difference between the value of exports and imports).

AFTER
1963 US economist Ronald McKinnon shows that small economies would benefit from a currency union since they can mitigate shocks better than large economies.

1996 US economists Jeffrey Frankel and Andrew Rose argue that the criteria for a currency area are themselves affected by prior economic development.

By the early 1960s the institutions of the post-war economies were well established. Toward the end of World War II the Bretton Woods system (pp.186–87) was set up to regulate the financial relations between the big industrial states, basing Western capitalism on a system of fixed exchange rates that controlled the flows of capital and money worldwide. International trade had recovered after the slump of the interwar years, and economic growth was rapid.

However, there were glitches in this system. First there were problems with balance of payments —the difference between what a country pays for imports and what it earns from exports. Balance of payments crises occurred because countries could not easily adjust their exchange rates within the international system. Coupled with tight labor markets and inflexible domestic prices, the previously automatic, market-led mechanisms that allowed countries to adjust to external economic shocks did not function very well. The result was a series of crises that arose when countries were unable to pay for

imports by using the proceeds of their exports. Alongside this, a series of moves toward the integration of European economies began to float the possibility of a currency union between European countries. This started with the Treaty of Paris in 1951, which established common trading areas for coal and steel. In 1961, Canadian economist Robert Mundell was the first to attempt an analysis of what he called an "optimal currency area."

Currency areas

Mundell sought to answer what might at first seem an odd question: over what geographical area should one type of currency be used? At the time this issue had barely been posed. It had simply been taken for granted that national economies used their own national currencies. The idea that this might not be the best arrangement had not really occurred to anyone. Mundell realized that while history had provided nations with their own currencies, this did not mean it had provided them with the best possible currency arrangements. There were clearly costs involved in

Different regions specialize in producing different goods. → Specialization leads to **trade between regions**. → But trading in **multiple currencies** creates additional costs. ↓ These costs can be eliminated if the regions are in **similar phases** of growth and slump because… ← … there is **no need for exchange rates** tailored to local conditions. ← **Similar economies can benefit from a single currency.**

See also: Boom and bust 78–79 ▪ Comparative advantage 80–85 ▪ International trade and Bretton Woods 186–87 ▪
Market integration 226–31 ▪ Speculation and currency devaluation 288–93

A small region that crosses national borders may benefit from a single currency. An area may import electricity from a power station across the border without the costs of exchange rates.

using many different currencies, since these had to be exchanged if trade was to take place. At one extreme, having a different currency for every zip code in a city would be very inefficient. On the other hand one currency for the entire world would be an undesirable straitjacket on so many diverse economies. Mundell asked what was the most efficient point between these two extremes.

First of all it is important to understand why countries need different currencies. A country with its own currency can make decisions about its money supply and interest rates, and can therefore set its monetary policy tailored to its own domestic economic conditions. Also, when the exchange rates of its currency are not fixed, the exchange rate with its trading partners can adjust

It hardly appears within the realm of political feasibility that national currencies would ever be abandoned in favor of any other arrangement...
Robert Mundell

to offset trade imbalances. Suppose a country specializing in agriculture is trading with a manufacturing economy. A sudden increase in productivity in the manufacturing economy might cause an excess demand for agricultural products and an excess supply of manufactured goods. The manufacturing economy slips into a balance of payments deficit, importing more (by value) than it exports. The deficit causes the manufacturing country's currency to depreciate, making its exports cheaper, and therefore boosting them and restoring equilibrium.

But suppose instead that the manufacturing economy and the agricultural economy shared a currency. In this case the type of adjustment described above would not be possible, and it might be that separate currencies would be more beneficial. It might also be the case that a single economic area—such as that constituted by the

manfacturing economy—is in fact made up of several nation-states. It would therefore be efficient for them to share a currency.

Business cycles
Later thinking on the subject helped clarify the conditions under which a currency area would be most economically viable. For a region to be best suited to a single currency, it would need flexible markets for capital and labor, allowing both to move freely in response to market demands. Prices and wages would, as a result, need to be flexible, adjusting to demand and supply changes and signaling to mobile capital and labor where they should move. The different parts of the region would also need to share broadly similar business cycles, allowing the shared central bank for the single currency to act appropriately for the whole region. There would also need to be mechanisms for »

Crowds gather in Frankfurt, Germany, for the launch of the euro, the single currency of the eurozone, on January 1, 1999. For a while the euro traded alongside national currencies.

dealing with situations when business cycles weren't completely synchronized across the region. The most obvious of these would be fiscal transfers—taking taxes from one area enjoying growth and redistributing to another in recession. This last condition, and the failure to implement it, was to have grave consequences for Europe.

Introducing the euro

The idea of a single currency for Europe began taking shape in 1979, when the European monetary system (EMS) was formed to stabilize exchange rates. Finally, in 1999, the eurozone (the area of the single currency) was established with 11 member states of the European Union (EU). While EU states traded heavily with each other and their institutions had removed restrictions on the movement of labor, capital, and goods, it was deemed necessary to implement further constraints on euro membership to ensure that the currency could function effectively.

The "convergence criteria," enshrined in the 1992 Maastricht Treaty, were drawn up to make sure that all those countries wishing to join the euro would share similar economies and be at similar stages in their business cycles (growth or recession). The previous exchange rate mechanism (ERM) had already attempted to fix national currencies against each other within the EU. The euro went a step further, removing all national currencies and, in effect, permanently fixing exchange rates. Important new rules on government debt were introduced. Under the stability and growth pact of 1997, no country was to have a national debt of more than 60 percent of its gross domestic product (GDP) and the

Robert Mundell

Born in Kingston, Canada, in 1932, Robert Mundell studied at the University of British Columbia in Vancouver before moving to the University of Washington in Seattle. He earned his PhD at the Massachusetts Institute of Technology in 1956. He was professor of economics at the University of Chicago from 1966–74, when he moved to Columbia University in New York.

Apart from his academic work, Mundell has acted as adviser to the governments of Canada and the US, and to organizations including the United Nations and the International Monetary Fund. Alongside his work on optimal currency areas, Mundell developed one of the first models to show how macroeconomic (whole economy) policy interacts with foreign trade and exchange rates. He was awarded the Nobel Prize in economics in 1999 in recognition of his work on macroeconomics.

Key works

1968 *International Economics*
1968 *Man and Economics*
1971 *Monetary Theory*

> ... countries with tight international trade ties and positively correlated business cycles are more likely to join, and gain from [European Monetary Union]...
> **Jeffrey Frankel**
> **Andrew Rose**

annual deficit was not to exceed 3 percent of GDP. A new European Central Bank would act for the euro area, replacing the national central banks and setting monetary policy across all the member states.

Fatal flaw

However, the provisions for the euro did not contain a mechanism for risk-sharing—crucially, they did not include a means for fiscal (tax revenue) transfers across European countries. The reason for this was simple, and political. Despite the long establishment of some transfer mechanisms, such as the Common Agricultural Policy, there was no desire in any EU country to lose its ability to set its own taxes and spending levels. Fiscal transfers across the continent would have required a strong, central authority, able to take taxes from surplus

The eurozone was established in 1999 as the monetary union of the 11 European Union states shown here. By 2012, there were 17 eurozone members, with eight more scheduled to join.

regions and redistribute to those in deficit—for example, to tax Germany and spend in Greece. But the political will to perform this was lacking. Instead, Europe's leaders hoped that the stability and growth pact would provide enough of a bind on government activities that an explicit fiscal transfer mechanism would not be needed.

Eurozone crisis

For nearly a decade after its launch the euro functioned well. European trade increased by up to 15 percent by some estimates. Capital and labor markets became more flexible. Growth, particularly in the poorer countries of Ireland and southern Europe was impressive. But underneath this picture were profound problems. Differences in labor costs helped exacerbate trade imbalances between different countries. The euro area as a whole was broadly in balance with the rest of the world, exporting roughly as much as it imported. But within the euro area, huge differences appeared. Northern Europe had

growing trade surpluses that were matched by rising deficits in the south. Without the mechanisms to provide for fiscal transfers between surplus and deficit countries, these deficits were (in effect) funded by the creation of rising debts in the south. When the financial crisis broke in 2008, the unbalanced system was pushed over the edge.

The euro crisis has raised questions about whether Europe is an optimal currency area. Some countries have seemed ill-matched in trading terms, and the absence of a fiscal transfer mechanism has meant that these imbalances could not be overcome. The stability and growth pact was not robust enough to force distinct national economies to converge.

Euro member countries face difficult choices. If a mechanism to undertake fiscal transfers can be constructed, euro countries may be able to overcome their own unevenness. If the political consensus for such a mechanism can't be reached, the existence of the euro may be threatened. ■

FAMINE CAN HAPPEN IN GOOD HARVESTS

ENTITLEMENT THEORY

IN CONTEXT

FOCUS
Growth and development

KEY THINKER
Amartya Sen (1933–)

BEFORE
1798 Thomas Malthus concludes that an increasing population will lead to famine and death in *An Essay on the Principle of Population*.

1960s The commonly held view is that famine is due to a decline in food availability.

AFTER
2001 British economist Stephen Devereux argues that entitlement theory misses the political causes of famine.

2009 Norwegian academic Dan Banik publishes *Starvation and India's Democracy*, showing how starvation and undernutrition can still occur despite a functioning democracy.

Families **exchange their labor for money**, with which they buy food to survive.

↓

If there is a **change in the price** of their labor or food…

↓

… and wages become too low to buy the minimum amount of food a family needs…

↓

… the family will **starve**, even if plenty of food is being produced.

↓

Famine can happen in good harvests.

Indian economist Amartya Sen grew up during the Great Bengal famine of 1943. He was only nine years old when a man arrived in his school who hadn't eaten in 40 days. Prior to this meeting, Sen had been unaware of the suffering that was taking place in his region. None of his family, nor his friends' families, were affected. Even at this young age, Sen was shocked at the class-based nature of the suffering. Almost 40 years later, the memory of the Bengal famine drove Sen to research and write about the subject in *Poverty and Famines: An Essay on Entitlement and Deprivation* in 1981. Sen concluded that, contrary to popular belief, famine is not caused primarily by a shortage of food. Bad harvests, droughts, or reductions of food imports are often contributing factors, but a more important factor is the way the food is distributed.

Entitlement

An absolute scarcity of food is very rare; it is far more common for food supplies to be unavailable to those who need them the most. Sen termed the bundles of goods and services that individuals have

See also: Markets and morality 22–23 ▪ Demographics and economics 68–69 ▪ Supply and demand 108–13 ▪ The poverty problem 140–41 ▪ Development economics 188–93

Famines such as the Congo famine of 2008 were caused by economic failure, according to Amartya Sen. He claimed that famine has never been known to occur in a functioning democracy.

access to as their "entitlements." Famines are an example of an entitlement failure, and entitlements depend on more than just the amount of food produced. In a modern, exchange-based economy most people do not produce their own food; they exchange a commodity (their labor) in return for another commodity (money), which is then exchanged again for food. Whether a family has enough food to live on depends on what it can sell or exchange in comparison to the price of food. A famine occurs when families' entitlements (the goods they have access to, not the amount generally available) fall below the minimum amount needed to survive. This may happen if the price of food rises or wages fall.

Sen analyzed the Bengal famine of 1943 and more recent famines in Africa and Asia to collect empirical evidence to support his theory. In Bengal he discovered that the total food production, although lower than the year before the famine began, was still higher than in previous, famine-free years. He concluded that the principal cause of the famine was the inability of farm laborers' wages to keep pace with the inflation-fueled rising price of food in Calcutta (now Kolkata). India, then under British rule, was going through a boom as the British government pumped in money as part of its war effort. This resulted in laborers suffering a reduction in their ability to buy food, and so they starved.

Sen argued that democratic countries in particular should be able to prevent the worst famines. His groundbreaking approach led to an overturning of beliefs and approaches to famine. ▪

Amartya Sen

Amartya Sen was born in Santiniketan, West Bengal, India, in 1933. His father was a professor of chemistry, but Sen chose economics, graduating from the University of Calcutta (now Kolkata) in 1953. In the same year he attained a second degree from Cambridge University, UK. At 23, Sen became the youngest ever Head of Economics at Jadavpur University, Calcutta. A prize fellowship enabled him to diversify his studies into philosophy. Sen has taught at universities in Kolkata and Delhi in India; MIT, Stanford, Berkeley, and Cornell in the US; and Oxford and Cambridge in the UK. In 1988, he received the Nobel Prize for economics. He moved to Harvard University in 2004, where he is professor of economics and philosophy. Sen has married twice and has four children.

Key works

1970 *Collective Choice and Social Welfare*
1981 *Poverty and Famines: An Essay on Entitlement and Deprivation*
1999 *Development as Freedom*

CONTEMPORARY ECONOMY
1970–PRESENT

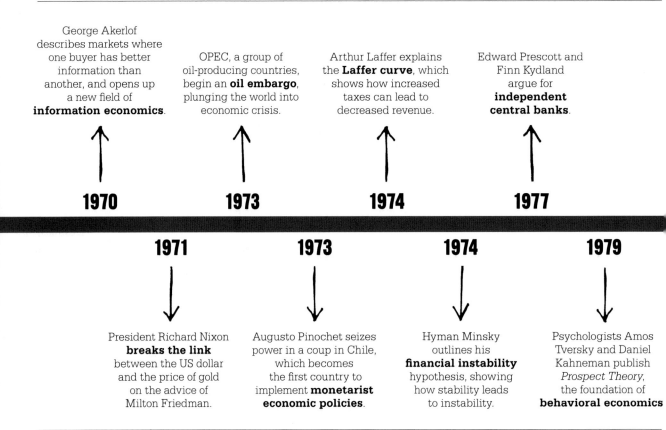

George Akerlof describes markets where one buyer has better information than another, and opens up a new field of **information economics**.

OPEC, a group of oil-producing countries, begin an **oil embargo**, plunging the world into economic crisis.

Arthur Laffer explains the **Laffer curve**, which shows how increased taxes can lead to decreased revenue.

Edward Prescott and Finn Kydland argue for **independent central banks**.

1970   **1973**   **1974**   **1977**

1971   **1973**   **1974**   **1979**

President Richard Nixon **breaks the link** between the US dollar and the price of gold on the advice of Milton Friedman.

Augusto Pinochet seizes power in a coup in Chile, which becomes the first country to implement **monetarist economic policies**.

Hyman Minsky outlines his **financial instability** hypothesis, showing how stability leads to instability.

Psychologists Amos Tversky and Daniel Kahneman publish *Prospect Theory*, the foundation of **behavioral economics**

I n the 25 years following World War II Keynesian policies, which advocated an active state intervention in the economy, made the Western world prosperous. In the words of British Prime Minister Harold Macmillan, people had "never had it so good." However, in the early 1970s an oil crisis triggered an economic downturn. Unemployment and inflation both rose rapidly. The Keynesian model no longer seemed to be working.

For some years conservative economists had been arguing for a return to more free market policies, and now their arguments were being taken more seriously. US economist Milton Friedman (p.199), was now the foremost economist of the Chicago School, which opposed Keynesian ideas. He suggested that

rather than tackling unemployment, inflation should be the focus of economic policy, and the only role of the state should be in controlling the money supply and allowing markets to work—a doctrine known as monetarism.

Rise of the Right
As faith in Keynesian policies waned, the right-wing parties of Ronald Reagan and Margaret Thatcher, both staunch believers in Friedman's monetarist economics, took power in the US and Britain. The policies they introduced in the 1980s marked a return to the old beliefs in the stability, efficiency, and growth of markets if left to their own devices.

The social policies of so-called Reaganomics and Thatcherism were influenced by the Austrian-

born economist Friedrich Hayek (p.177), who put the individual, not the state, at the heart of economic thinking, and by economists who saw tax cuts as a means of increasing tax revenue.

Liberalization became the new watchword. Deregulation of financial institutions not only made it easier for firms to borrow, but also allowed lenders to indulge in the new forms of financial engineering that promised high returns with zero risk. Throughout the 1980s the economic mood was changing worldwide. Reforms in the Soviet Union were to lead to the eventual breakup of the Soviet bloc, reinforcing conservative economists' views that socialist policies did not work. Mainland Europe, however, resisted the American swing from Keynes

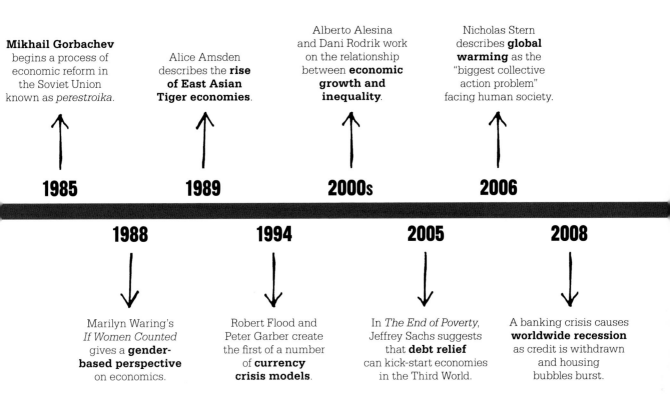

Mikhail Gorbachev begins a process of economic reform in the Soviet Union known as *perestroika*.

Alice Amsden describes the **rise of East Asian Tiger economies**.

Alberto Alesina and Dani Rodrik work on the relationship between **economic growth and inequality**.

Nicholas Stern describes **global warming** as the "biggest collective action problem" facing human society.

1985   **1989**   **2000s**   **2006**

1988   **1994**   **2005**   **2008**

Marilyn Waring's *If Women Counted* gives a **gender-based perspective** on economics.

Robert Flood and Peter Garber create the first of a number of **currency crisis models**.

In *The End of Poverty*, Jeffrey Sachs suggests that **debt relief** can kick-start economies in the Third World.

A banking crisis causes **worldwide recession** as credit is withdrawn and housing bubbles burst.

to Friedman and only gradually adopted more free market economic policies.

Rethinking free markets

Although monetarism and the liberalization of markets may have helped to make markets more efficient through the 1980s and 90s, some economists were uneasy about the sustainability of these policies. As early as 1974, US economist Hyman Minsky (p.301) had warned of the inherent instability of financial institutions. An acceleration of the "boom and bust" cycles seemed to confirm his hypothesis. Deregulation encouraged risky borrowing, which led to the collapse of firms and banks. Other economists challenged the efficiency and rationality of the market, arguing

that the "scientific" models of the economy were based on the wrong sciences: new ideas in mathematics and physics, such as complexity theory and chaos theory, were perhaps better analogies, and behavioral psychology could better explain the actions of "economic man" than economists' standard notion of rationality.

Meanwhile, younger economies were developing, especially in Asia, where reforms were transforming the Chinese and Indian economies. A new economic bloc emerged to rival the West, in the form of the BRIC nations (Brazil, Russia, India, and China). The prosperity of these new economic powers stimulated a renewed interest in so-called development economics since other countries remained locked in poverty by crippling debt and

political instability. At the same time the technology that had brought economic prosperity now posed an economic threat in the form of global warming and climate change, which needed to be dealt with at an international level.

In the first decade of the 21st century a succession of financial crises rocked the Western economies, and it seemed that free market policies had failed. Once again, economics became concerned with the inequalities and social consequences of free markets. A few economists even wondered whether the failure of free markets was heralding the collapse of capitalism that Karl Marx (p.105) had predicted. Not for the first time, the world seemed to be on the verge of profound economic change. ■

IT IS POSSIBLE TO INVEST WITHOUT RISK

FINANCIAL ENGINEERING

IN CONTEXT

FOCUS
Banking and finance

KEY THINKERS
Fischer Black (1938–95)
Myron Scholes (1941–)

BEFORE
1900 French mathematician
Louis Bachelier demonstrates
that stock prices follow a
consistent but random process.

1952 US economist Harry
Markowitz proposes a method
to build optimal portfolios
based on diversifying risk.

1960s Capital Asset Pricing
Model (CAPM) is developed to
determine the correct rate of
return for a financial asset.

AFTER
1990s Value-at-Risk (VaR) is
developed to measure the risk
of loss on a portfolio.

Late 2000s Global financial
markets collapse.

During the 1960s the
institutional foundations
of the post-war world were
steadily eroded. The Bretton Woods
system (pp.186–87) of fixed exchange
rates, pegged against a US dollar
that was in turn locked into a fixed
price against gold, was starting to
buckle. The US was running
persistent trade deficits (where
imports outstrip exports), while
recurrent balance-of-payments
crises elsewhere provoked calls for
the introduction of freely floating
exchange rates. In 1971, President
Richard Nixon took definitive
action: he unilaterally canceled the
dollar to gold relationship, ending
the whole Bretton Woods system.

See also: Financial services 26–29 ▪ Public companies 38 ▪ Risk and uncertainty 162–63 ▪
Behavioral economics 266–69 ▪ Efficient markets 272 ▪ Financial crises 296–301

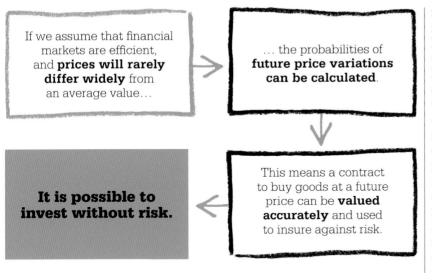

If we assume that financial markets are efficient, and **prices will rarely differ widely** from an average value…

… the probabilities of **future price variations can be calculated**.

This means a contract to buy goods at a future price can be **valued accurately** and used to insure against risk.

It is possible to invest without risk.

reduce risk and insure against the future. This is known as a "hedge." However, the derivative contract can work the other way around. Instead of providing insurance against the future, it can be used to gamble on the future. A forward contract locks in the delivery of goods for a certain price on a certain date. But if the immediate market price (the "spot price") on that date is less than the price in the forward contract, an easy profit could be made. Of course if the market price is more than the one specified, it results in a loss. Furthermore, as derivative contracts do not involve payment for actual assets or commodities, but only for the right to buy those products in the future, they allow people to deal in huge quantities. Derivatives give traders leverage—more "bang for their buck."

Letting go of the asset
Derivative contracts became standardized and could then be bought and sold on a market like any other commodity. The first »

At the same time domestic economies were experiencing steadily rising rates of inflation. Keynesianism (pp.154–61), the economic thinking that had dominated the post-war years, came under sustained intellectual attack. The financial markets, which had been tightly regulated since the 1930s, pushed for a removal of restrictions on their activities. These restrictions were finally lifted in 1972, when the Chicago Mercantile Exchange was allowed to write the first derivative contract on exchange rates.

Futures contracts
Derivatives have existed for centuries. A derivative is a contract written not directly for a commodity itself, but for some attribute associated with it. For instance, a typical early

derivative contract is a "forward," which specifies the price and future date for delivery of a commodity, such as coffee. The advantage of this arrangement is that it allows producers to lock their customers into a price in the future, regardless of how—in agricultural commodities —harvests and production actually turn out. The derivative aimed to

The price of rice may vary with changes in weather. A forward contract, where one party agrees to buy the rice at a certain price on a certain day, allows the grower to manage risk.

exchange to offer tradeable derivatives in agricultural products was the Chicago Board of Trade, in 1864. However, the possibility for speculation that all derivative contracts contain led to repeated bans on their use. "Cash-settled" contracts provoked particular concern. These were derivative contracts in which the delivery of the underlying asset did not have to take place on the specified day. Cash could be exchanged in its place. At this point all real connection between the underlying product and the derivative had been lost, and the possibilities for purely speculative behavior were immense.

Deregulation

Recognition of this speculative potential motivated governments to introduce strict regulations. From the 1930s onward, cash-settled derivatives in the US were classified as a form of gambling, rather than investment, and strictly

Option contracts are a type of derivative that give someone the option to buy or sell something, such as coffee, at a certain price on a certain date. The option need not be exercised.

controlled. Exchanges were not allowed to trade them. But with the collapse of the fixed exchange-rate system in 1971, a need rapidly emerged for hedging against potentially volatile floating exchange rates. Restrictions were lifted, and the market for derivatives quickly expanded.

This provided the background to a critical problem. There was no reliable means to accurately price derivatives since they were, by nature, highly complex contracts. Even a simple "option" (providing the right but not the commitment to trade an underlying asset at a certain point in the future) had a price that was determined by several variables, such as the current price of the underlying asset, the time to the option's deadline, and the expected price variation. The problem of providing a mathematical formula for this problem was finally solved in 1973 by US economists Myron Scholes and Fischer Black, and expanded upon by fellow American Robert C. Merton the same year.

These economists built on certain assumptions and insights about financial markets to simplify the problem. First, they made use of the "no arbitrage" rule. This means that prices in a properly functioning financial market reflect all the information available. An individual share price would tell you both the value of the company today, and what market traders expect of it in the future. It should be impossible to earn guaranteed profits by hedging against future risk because prices already

incorporate all the information you are basing your hedge on. The second assumption was that it is always possible to put together an option contract that mirrors a portfolio of assets. In other words every possible portfolio of assets that can be assembled can be perfectly hedged by options. All risk vanishes with this insurance.

Third, they assumed that although asset prices fluctuate randomly over time, they vary in a regular way, known as the "normal distribution." This implies that, in general, prices will not move very far over a short time period.

By using these assumptions, Black, Scholes, and Merton were able to provide a mathematically robust model for pricing a standard option contract on the basis of the underlying asset's price movements. Derivative contracts, once seen as unreliable instruments, could now be processed on a huge scale using computer technology. The path was cleared for a vast expansion of derivatives trading.

The option pricing model Black, Scholes, and Merton devised provided a whole new way to think about financial markets. It could even run in reverse. Existing option prices could be fed backward

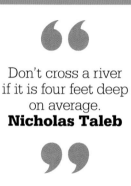

Don't cross a river if it is four feet deep on average.
Nicholas Taleb

In the years leading to the 2008 crash, banks assumed that investment risk followed a "normal distribution" pattern (the blue line), where there is a high probability of making a small gain, and a very low probability of making an extreme gain or loss. However, investment risk actually follows a different pattern (the dotted line), in which extreme events are far more common.

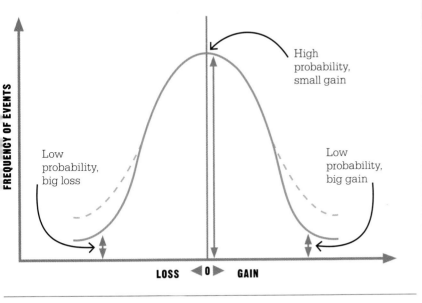

FREQUENCY OF EVENTS

High probability, small gain

Low probability, big loss

Low probability, big gain

LOSS ◀ 0 ▶ GAIN

into the pricing model to generate "implied volatilities." This created a new way to manage risk: instead of trading on the basis of prices or expected prices, portfolios of assets could be put together directly on the basis of their riskiness as implied by the market price. Risk itself, as described by the mathematical models, could be traded and managed.

The 2008 crash

The explosion in financial innovation, aided by sophisticated mathematics and ever-increasing computing power, helped drive the extraordinary expansion of the financial system over several decades. From negligible amounts in the 1970s the global market for derivatives grew on average by 24 percent a year, reaching a total of $596 trillion by 2008—about 20 times global GDP. Applications multiplied as firms found apparently

secure, profitable new ways to manage the risks associated with lending.

By September 2008, when the US investment bank Lehman Brothers filed for bankruptcy, it had become clear that this expansion had fatal weaknesses. Critical among these was the dependence on the assumption of a normal distribution: the idea that most prices cluster around an average, and extreme price movements are very rare. But this had been disputed as early as 1963, when French mathematician Benoît Mandelbrot suggested that extreme price movements were much more common than expected.

Post-crash, these models are being reexamined. Behavioral economists (pp.266–69) and econophysicists use models and statistical techniques drawn from physics to better understand financial markets and risk. ∎

Low risk, high rewards

US-Lebanese economist Nicholas Taleb claims that by underestimating the risk of extreme price movements, the apparently sophisticated financial models overexposed investors to the real risk. Collateralized debt obligations (CDOs) are a prime example. These are financial instruments that raise money by issuing their own bonds before investing that money in a mixture of assets such as loans. CDOs took on the risks of very low-quality (subprime) housing debts that had a high chance of defaulting, and mixed them with high-quality debt, such as US Treasury bills. They apparently offered low risk and high rewards. But this relied on an assumption that the combined risk of default followed a normal distribution pattern and was stable. As US subprime mortgages defaulted in increasing numbers, it became clear that this assumption did not hold, and the enormous CDO market imploded.

Black swans are rarely sighted but do exist. Nicholas Taleb refers to the highly unexpected, extreme movements of the market as "black swan events."

PEOPLE ARE NOT 100 PERCENT RATIONAL

BEHAVIORAL ECONOMICS

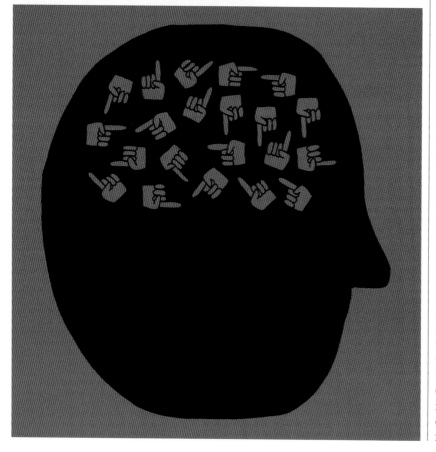

IN CONTEXT

FOCUS
Decision making

KEY THINKERS
Amos Tversky (1937–96)
Daniel Kahneman (1934–)

BEFORE
1940s US economist Herbert Simon argues that rational decision alone does not explain human decision making.

1953 French economist Maurice Allais criticizes expected utility theory, saying that real-life decisions are not always taken rationally.

AFTER
1990 Economists Andrei Shleifer and Lawrence Summers show that irrational decisions can affect prices.

2008 US psychologist and economist Dan Ariely publishes *Predictably Irrational*, showing irrationality has a pattern.

Until the 1980s standard economic theory was dominated by the idea of "rational economic man" (pp.52–53). Individuals were understood to be agents who look at all decisions rationally, weighing the costs and benefits to themselves and making a decision that will give them the best outcome. Economists thought that this was how people behaved in situations of both certainty and uncertainty, and they formalized the idea of rational decision making in expected utility theory (pp.162–63). In reality, however, people often make irrational decisions that don't give them the highest payoffs and may even hurt their own prospects.

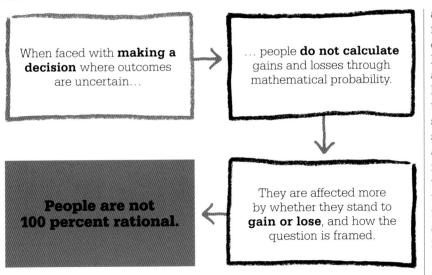

When faced with **making a decision** where outcomes are uncertain…

… people **do not calculate** gains and losses through mathematical probability.

They are affected more by whether they stand to **gain or lose**, and how the question is framed.

People are not 100 percent rational.

apply whether the individual was facing risks that involved gains or losses. However, Tversky and Kahneman found that individuals are risk-averse when facing gains but risk-loving when facing losses: the nature of individual preference seems to change. Their work showed that people are "loss averse," and so are willing to take risks to avoid losses, where they would not be willing to take risks to gain something. For example, the loss in utility from losing $10 appears to be greater than the gain in utility from gaining $10.

These quirks in behavior show that the way that choices are presented influences people's decisions, even if the ultimate outcomes are the same. For example, consider a situation where a disease is projected to kill 600 people. Two programs exist to counter the disease: A, which saves 200; and B, which offers a one-third chance that 600 people will be saved versus a two-thirds chance that no one will be saved. When the problem is explained to them in this way, the majority of people show themselves to be risk-averse—they opt for the »

Early studies of these quirks of behavior were made in 1979 by two Israeli-American psychologists, Amos Tversky and Daniel Kahneman. They looked at the psychology involved in decision making and backed up their hypotheses with empirical examples. Their key paper, *Prospect Theory: An Analysis of Decision under Risk*, outlined a theory that marked the start of a new branch of study known as behavioral economics. This aimed to make economists' theories about decision making more psychologically realistic.

Dealing with risk
Tversky and Kahneman found that people commonly violate economists' standard assumptions about behavior, particularly when consequences are uncertain. Far from acting with rational self-interest, people were found to be affected by the way a decision is presented and responded in ways that violate standard theory.

Economists had long understood that people are often "risk-averse." For example, if given a choice between definitely receiving $1,000 or having a 50 percent chance of receiving $2,500, people are more likely to choose the guaranteed $1,000—despite the fact that the average expectation of the second, uncertain, option is higher, at $1,250. The psychologists constructed the opposite situation, giving the same people the choice of either definitely losing $1,000, or having a 50 percent chance of no loss and a 50 percent chance of losing $2,500. In this situation, people who chose the safe option in the previous example now chose the riskier alternative of the gamble between no loss and a large loss. This is known as risk-seeking behavior.

The standard economic approach to decision making under uncertainty assumed that any one individual was risk-averse, risk-loving, or didn't mind either way. These risk preferences would

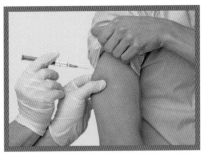

A government wishing to persuade people to be vaccinated should stress the increased probability of death if they are not vaccinated. People hate losing more than they love winning.

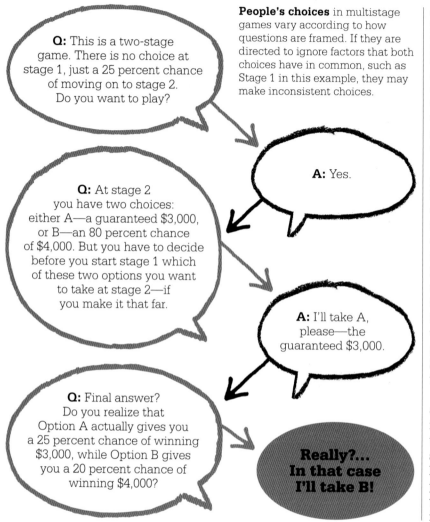

Q: This is a two-stage game. There is no choice at stage 1, just a 25 percent chance of moving on to stage 2. Do you want to play?

Q: At stage 2 you have two choices: either A—a guaranteed $3,000, or B—an 80 percent chance of $4,000. But you have to decide before you start stage 1 which of these two options you want to take at stage 2—if you make it that far.

Q: Final answer? Do you realize that Option A actually gives you a 25 percent chance of winning $3,000, while Option B gives you a 20 percent chance of winning $4,000?

A: Yes.

A: I'll take A, please—the guaranteed $3,000.

Really?... In that case I'll take B!

People's choices in multistage games vary according to how questions are framed. If they are directed to ignore factors that both choices have in common, such as Stage 1 in this example, they may make inconsistent choices.

certainty of saving 200 people. If the question is restated, however, with the choice being between program C, which guarantees the death of 400 people, or program D which offers a one-third chance that nobody will die versus a two-thirds chance that 600 people will die, most people will pick the risky program D.

The ultimate outcomes of the pairs of choices are the same: in both A and C we definitely end up with 400 dead, while with B and D, there is an expected outcome of 400 dead. Yet now people prefer the option that is more of a gamble. People are more willing to take risks to prevent lives being lost (a loss) than they are to save lives (a gain). We place more subjective value on losing something than gaining something—losing $10 feels worse, apparently, than gaining $10 feels good.

This tendency toward loss aversion means that, when choices for change are framed in such a way that the consequences are seen as negative, people are more likely to perceive the change as a problem. Knowing this can be used to influence people. For instance, if a government wants to encourage

Behavioral economics in action

The new field of behavioral economics has provided firms with new ways to drive their businesses. In 2006, a group of economists devised an experiment for a bank in South Africa that wanted to grant more loans. Traditional economists would have advised the bank to lower its interest rate to stimulate demand. Instead, the bank allowed the economists to experiment with various options to find out which

might be most profitable for the bank. They sent out 50,000 letters offering different interest rates—some high, some low. The letters also featured photos of employees, and a simple or complicated table showing the different chances of winning a prize if the letter was replied to.

By tracking which customers responded, it was possible to quantify the effect of psychological factors against the purely economic factor of

the interest rate. The experiment discovered that the interest rate was only the third most important factor in stimulating demand, and including a photo of a female employee in its marketing had an effect equal to dropping the interest rate by five points. This is a groundbreaking result: identifying psychological factors to stimulate demand can be a lot cheaper than lowering the interest rate.

people to adopt something, it is more likely to be successful if it emphasizes the positive gains involved in making that decision. If, on the other hand, it wants people to reject something, it should focus on what they stand to lose.

Processes and outcomes

Kahneman and Tversky also showed that the process by which decisions are made can affect choices even when the process doesn't affect the final payoffs.

For example, imagine a game of two stages in which a player is given a choice of two options at the second stage if they make it that far. However, they must make their choice before the first stage. An example of such a game is laid out on the opposite page.

In this two-stage game, most people choose the guaranteed $3,000 option. However, when the decision is shown as a straight choice between a lower chance of winning $4,000 or a higher chance of $3,000, most people choose the lower chance of winning more money. Why the change?

In the two-stage process people ignore the first stage because it is common to both outcomes. They see the options as a choice between a guaranteed win and merely the chance of a win, even though the probabilities are altered by the first stage. This contradicts standard economic rationality in which decisions are only influenced by final outcomes.

The end of rational man?

The key insights to this work—that we hate to lose more than we like to gain, and that we interpret losses and gains in terms of context—have helped illuminate why people make decisions that are not consistent with utility theory or

the idea of "rational economic man." The theory is a founding pillar of behavioral economics, and has also had wide-ranging influence on marketing and advertising. By understanding the way we make decisions, marketers are able to market their products much more effectively. A good example of this is in-store promotions, which offer "huge discounts" on items with initially inflated prices.

Prospect theory has implications for many kinds of common economic decisions.

> One may discover that the relative attractiveness of options varies when the same decision problem is framed in different ways.
> **Amos Tversky
> Daniel Kahneman**

A scalper sells a sports ticket for cash. The amount that seller and buyer value the ticket depends not just on its perceived utility, but also on factors such as the way the seller obtained it.

For example, the theory explains why people may travel to a different part of town in order to save $5 off a $15 DVD, but they are unlikely to make the same trip in order to save $5 off a $400 TV, even though their net wealth is impacted by the same amount in each case. Loss aversion also explains what is known as the endowment effect: people tend to place a higher value on an object when they own it—and do not want to lose it—than before they own it, when it is only a "potential gain."

Behavioral economics is vital to our understanding of the economy and has introduced psychological realism into modern economics. Prospect theory was the first to suggest that people are not simply 100 percent rational machines. The implications of this realization—for economic theories and government policies—are wide-ranging. For example, giving people a sense of ownership may affect how well they look after something. ∎

TAX CUTS CAN INCREASE THE TAX TAKE

TAXATION AND ECONOMIC INCENTIVES

IN CONTEXT

FOCUS
Economic policy

KEY THINKERS
Robert Mundell (1932–)
Arthur Laffer (1940–)

BEFORE
1776 Adam Smith suggests that moderate taxes might bring in more revenue than high ones.

1803 French economist Jean-Baptiste Say argues that supply creates its own demand.

AFTER
1981 US President Ronald Reagan cuts top-rate tax and capital gains tax.

2003 US President George W. Bush ignores criticism from leading economists and pursues a policy of tax cuts.

2012 In January the US government deficit hits an unprecedented $15 trillion.

Common sense tells us that if a government wants to raise more money to spend on public services, it must raise taxes, however unpopular that may be. Likewise, cutting taxes seems to imply cutting public services. However, some economists have suggested that this is not always the case, and that cutting taxes can result in governments collecting more, not less, money.

This is a key idea of 1980s "supply-side" economists. The supply side is the part of an economy that makes and sells things, as opposed to the demand side, which is the buying of goods.

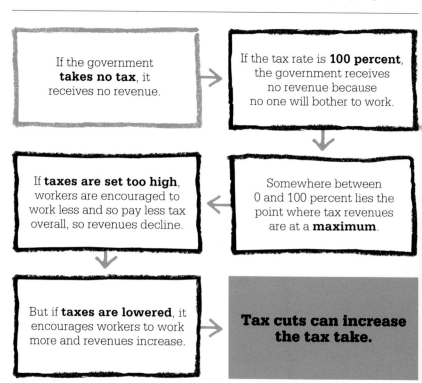

If the government **takes no tax**, it receives no revenue.

If the tax rate is **100 percent**, the government receives no revenue because no one will bother to work.

Somewhere between 0 and 100 percent lies the point where tax revenues are at a **maximum**.

If **taxes are set too high**, workers are encouraged to work less and so pay less tax overall, so revenues decline.

But if **taxes are lowered**, it encourages workers to work more and revenues increase.

Tax cuts can increase the tax take.

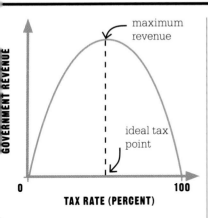

The Laffer curve displays the relationship between tax rates and government revenue. It shows that higher taxes do not always result in increased revenues.

Supply-side economists argue that the best way to make the economy grow is to improve conditions for the supply side, freeing companies from regulations, and cutting subsidies and high-rate taxes.

From tax to tax havens

The revenue argument for cutting taxes came from US economist Arthur Laffer. He said that if a government takes no tax, it will get no revenue. If it takes 100 percent tax, it will get no revenue either, since no one will work. But even below 100 percent, very high income tax rates discourage people from working. This reduction in hours worked outweighs the high tax rate, and the result is a fall in tax revenue. When top-rate taxes are very high, revenue can also be lost by the highest income earners leaving the country or putting their money in tax havens—countries charging little or no tax. Laffer drew a bell-shaped curve (left) to show that somewhere between the extremes of no tax and 100 percent tax, there is a point at which a government will maximize revenue.

The argument then is that from a starting point of high tax rates, tax cuts, along with other policies to strengthen the supply side, can enhance economic efficiency and generate more tax revenues. In the 1970s, when Laffer developed his theories, some countries taxed some people at 70 percent, and a few taxed the highest earners at 90 percent. Economists disagreed about where the peak on the Laffer

Many tax havens formed in the 1970s, when small islands and countries such as Monaco chose to impose low taxes—or none at all —in order to attract investment.

curve lies. Those on the political Right argued that the economy was at a point to the right of the peak of the curve, meaning that tax cuts would increase revenue. Those on the Left disagreed.

A win–win situation

For politicians on the Right, Laffer's theory was attractive. It meant that they could make themselves popular by cutting taxes, yet pledge to maintain public services, too. In 1981, President Ronald Reagan was able to cut top-rate taxes and still be a hero to many of the poorest US citizens. However, there is little evidence that the idea actually works. In the US and other countries tax rates are far below the level of the 1970s. However, the supposed tax revenue bonanza has not arrived. Instead, tax cuts have been funded largely by rising borrowing deficits. ▪

Supply-side economics

The theory of supply-side economics generated a considerable amount of controversy when it was developed in the 1970s. It emerged in response to the apparent failure of Keynesian policies of government intervention (pp.154–61) to deal with a flat economy combined with high inflation—a condition known as stagflation. The term was popularized by US journalist Jude Wanniski, but it was US economist Arthur Laffer's tax curve that caught economists' attention. The Laffer curve was developed under the guidance of Canadian economist Robert Mundell (p.254), who argued that if tax rates were cut, national output would increase, and tax revenues would rise. After a quick dip revenues did actually rise, but there has been huge debate ever since over whether he was proved right.

PRICES TELL YOU EVERYTHING
EFFICIENT MARKETS

A commonly held belief among investors is that they can "beat," or outperform, the stock market. The US economist Eugene Fama disagreed. His study, *Efficient Capital Markets* (1970), concluded that it is impossible to beat the market consistently. His theory is now known as the efficient market hypothesis.

Fama claimed that all investors have access to the same publicly available information as their rivals, so the prices of stocks fully reflect all the knowledge available. This is the "efficient market." No one can know what new information will be released, so it should be almost impossible for investors to make a profit without using information unavailable to the competition, or "insider trading," which is illegal.

However, problems with the hypothesis have been highlighted by behavioral economists. They point to the theory's failure to account for investor overconfidence and the "herd" instinct. These problems manifested themselves in

In an efficient market at any point in time the actual price of a security will be a good estimate of its intrinsic value.
Eugene Fama

the Dotcom bubble of the 1990s, where "irrational exuberance" was blamed for artificially inflating technology stock, and the more recent financial crisis of 2007–08.

After these crises many observers have declared the theory redundant; some have even blamed it for the crashes. Eugene Fama himself has conceded that uninformed investors can lead the market astray and result in prices becoming "somewhat irrational." ∎

See also: Economic bubbles 98–99 ▪ Testing economic theories 170 ▪ Financial engineering 262–65 ▪ Behavioral economics 266–69

OVER TIME, EVEN THE SELFISH COOPERATE WITH OTHERS
COMPETITION AND COOPERATION

In 1984, US economist Robert Axelrod wrote *The Evolution of Cooperation*. It was based on the results of a series of games, in which the strategies of game theory specialists were pitted against each other via computer programs to see which was most successful. The game they played was the prisoner's dilemma (p.238), a game involving two thieves captured by the police. Should each thief choose to confess, stay silent, or "sell out" the other thief? The game explores whether it is wiser to cooperate for mutual benefit or to act selfishly.

The best strategy
Axelrod discovered that cooperation can arise through self-interested actions. His series of games tested many strategies. The most successful strategy was simple tit-for-tat, where a player cooperates on the first move and then mirrors his or her opponent, so is never the first to "sell out." The most successful approaches were those that were "nice." Cooperation was found to produce mutually beneficial outcomes. But one must not be too nice—if someone is betrayed, it is essential to hit back in the next move. To maintain credibility, players must retaliate immediately if they are "sold out." This approach to the analysis of competition and cooperation has developed into a rich field that examines how social and even moral rules emerge. ∎

When President Bush and Russian President Putin signed the Treaty of Moscow in 2002, they cooperated to greatly reduce their nuclear arsenals, despite mutual distrust.

See also: Economic man 52–53 ▪ Effects of limited competition 90–91 ▪ Economics and tradition 166–67 ▪ Game theory 234–41

MOST CARS TRADED WILL BE LEMONS
MARKET UNCERTAINTY

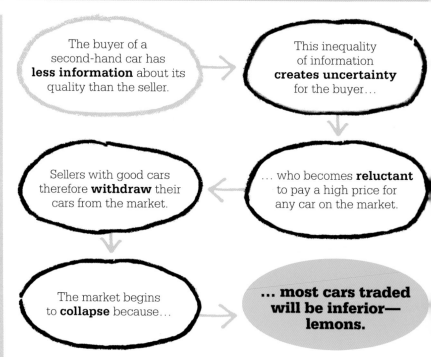

The buyer of a second-hand car has **less information** about its quality than the seller.

This inequality of information **creates uncertainty** for the buyer…

… who becomes **reluctant** to pay a high price for any car on the market.

Sellers with good cars therefore **withdraw** their cars from the market.

The market begins to **collapse** because…

… **most cars traded will be inferior— lemons.**

Until US economist George Akerlof started studying prices and markets in the 1960s, most economists believed that markets would allow everyone willing to sell goods at a certain price to make deals with anyone who wanted to buy goods at that price. Akerlof demonstrated that in many cases this is not true.

His key work, *The Market for Lemons* (1970), explains how uncertainty caused by limited information can cause markets to fail. Akerlof stated that buyers and sellers have different amounts of information, and these differences, or asymmetries, can have disastrous consequences for the workings of markets.

See also: Free market economics 54–61 ▪ Market information and incentives 208–09 ▪ Markets and social outcomes 210–13 ▪ Signaling and screening 281

Asymmetric information

The buyer of a second-hand car has less information about its quality than the seller who already owns the car. The seller will have been able to assess whether the car is worse than an average similar car—whether, it is a "lemon"—an item with defects. Any buyer that ends up with a lemon feels cheated. The existence of undetectable lemons in the market creates uncertainty in the mind of the buyer, which extends to concerns about the quality of all the second-hand cars on sale. This uncertainty causes the buyer to drop the price he is willing to offer for any car, and as a consequence prices drop across the market.

Akerlof's theory is a modern version of an idea first suggested by English financier Sir Thomas Gresham (1519–79). Gresham observed that when coins of higher and lower silver content were both in circulation, people would try to hold on to those of a higher silver content, meaning that "bad money drives good money out of circulation." In the same way sellers with better-than-average cars to sell will withdraw them from the market, because it is impossible for them to get a fair price from a buyer who is unable to tell whether that car is a lemon or not. This means that "most cars traded will be lemons." In theory this could lead to such low prices that the market would collapse, and trade would not occur at any price, even if there are traders willing to buy and sell.

Adverse selection

Another market in which lemons affect trade is the insurance market. In medical insurance, for instance, the buyers of policies know more about the state of their health than the sellers. So insurers often find themselves doing business with people they would rather avoid: the least healthy people. As insurance premiums rise for older age groups, a greater proportion of "lemons" buy

A car dealer can reduce a buyer's risk when selling a car by offering guarantees. In many cases markets adjust to account for asymmetric information.

policies, but firms are still unable to identify them accurately. This is known as "adverse selection," and the potential for adverse selection means that insurance companies end up with, on average, much greater risks than are covered by the premiums. This has resulted in the withdrawal of medical insurance policies for people over a certain age in some areas. ▪

George Akerlof

Born in Connecticut in 1940, George Akerlof grew up in an academic family. At school he became interested in the social sciences, including history and economics. His father's irregular employment patterns fostered his interest in Keynesian economics. Akerlof went on to study for an economics degree at Yale, then gained a PhD from MIT (Massachusetts Institute of Technology) in 1966. Shortly after joining Berkeley as an associate professor, Akerlof spent a year in India, where he explored the problems of unemployment. In 1978, he taught at the London School of Economics before returning to Berkeley as professor. He was awarded the Nobel Prize for Economics in 2001, alongside Michael Spence and Joseph Stiglitz.

Key works

1970 *The Market for Lemons*
1988 *Fairness and Unemployment* (with Janet Yellen)
2009 *Animal Spirits: How Human Psychology Drives the Economy* (with Robert J. Shiller)

THE GOVERNMENT'S PROMISES ARE INCREDIBLE
INDEPENDENT CENTRAL BANKS

IN CONTEXT

FOCUS
Economic policy

KEY THINKERS
Edward Prescott (1940–)
Finn Kydland (1943–)

BEFORE
1961 John Muth publishes *Rational Expectations and the Theory of Price Movements*.

1976 US economist Robert Lucas argues that it is naive to model government policy on solutions that have worked in the past.

AFTER
1983 US economists Robert Barro and David Gordon suggest that high inflation arises from discretionary government policy and propose central bank independence.

From 1980s Independent central banks are established in many countries worldwide and commit to simple policy rules.

If governments can act at their **discretion**, they can break their promises, therefore…

… the government's promises are not credible.

Rational individuals forecast this breaking of promises, and **change their own behavior** to suit.

This prevents **discretionary government policy** from working.

Governments should credibly commit to following **simple rules**, not use discretionary policy.

Following World War II, economics was dominated by Keynesian thinking (pp.154–61). This claimed that governments could maintain high employment through two types of discretionary policies, which are introduced to achieve specific goals through a particular set of actions. The two types of policy used for controlling employment were fiscal policy (government spending and taxation) and monetary policy (interest rates and the money supply).

In 1977, two economists—Finn Kydland of Norway and Edward Prescott of the US—published a paper entitled *Rules Rather than Discretion*, which argued that discretionary policy was in fact self-defeating. Their argument was based on the concept of rational expectations, which was developed by the US economist John Muth (p.247). Muth argued that since having incorrect beliefs about prices is costly, rational individuals seek to minimize their errors by planning ahead to avoid this.

Before this, macroeconomic models had operated on the assumption that individuals only look backward, naively expecting the future to look like the past. The

See also: Economic man 52–53 ▪ The Keynesian multiplier 164–65 ▪ Monetarist policy 196–201 ▪ Inflation and unemployment 202–03 ▪ Rational expectations 244–47

A government may try to deter the building of homes in a flood-prone area by not subsidizing flood insurance. But if it has bailed people out after a flood in the past, they will not be deterred.

new model predicted that if people collect information and are rational, they can—and will—anticipate government interventions. They then adapt their actions to the government policy they expect, and that policy is in turn rendered less potent. Discretionary policy can only work when individuals are taken by surprise, and it is hard to surprise rational individuals.

To see how this works, imagine a lenient teacher who is trying to make a lazy pupil do his homework. The teacher tells the student that if he doesn't hand his homework in, he will be punished. But the pupil knows that the teacher is lenient and does not like to punish. The pupil anticipates that if he doesn't hand in the work, he won't be punished. Knowing this, he does not do the homework. The teacher's aim of getting the pupil to hand in his homework is undermined by the pupil's rational behavior.

Kydland and Prescott said that government promises of low inflation face the same problem. The government does not like high unemployment. So it will boost the economy to keep unemployment low, but this will push up inflation. Like the teacher who threatens a punishment he will not inflict, the government has conflicting aims. Individuals know this and so do not believe the government's promise of low inflation. This undoes the aim of increasing demand to lead to higher employment, because people know

that higher wages will be offset by higher prices. Accounting for rational expectations, the effect of the boost is simply higher inflation.

An uncompromising rule

The solution for our teacher would be a compulsory school rule for punishing late homework so he would have to comply. In a similar way Kydland and Prescott proposed that instead of having a free reign to set economic policy, governments should commit to following clear rules. A more radical solution of the teacher's dilemma would be to delegate punishment-giving to a strict principal. In macroeconomic policy this kind of role can be taken by independent central banks, which place less weight on employment and more weight on low inflation than the government does. Their control of monetary policy allows the government to credibly commit to low inflation. The period of low inflation that arose in the 2000s is often attributed to the rise of independent central banks. ▪

Finn Kydland

Born on a farm in Gjesdal, Norway, in 1943, Finn Kydland was the oldest of six children. After high school he taught in a junior school for several years, where a fellow teacher suggested he study accountancy, which awakened his interest in business. He started an economics degree at the Norwegian School of Economic and Business Administration (NHH) in 1965. Kydland intended to become a business manager, but after graduation he became an assistant to economics professor Sten Thore, who moved to Carnegie Mellon University,

taking Kydland with him. Returning to NHH in 1973, Kydland published his key paper with Edward Prescott. In 1976, Kydland returned to the US, where he has taught ever since. In 2004, he was awarded the Nobel Prize for Economics.

Key works

1977 *Rules Rather than Discretion* (with E. Prescott)
1982 *Time to Build and Aggregate Fluctuations*
2002 *Argentina's Lost Decade* (with Carlos E. J. M. Zarazaga)

THE ECONOMY IS CHAOTIC EVEN WHEN INDIVIDUALS ARE NOT
COMPLEXITY AND CHAOS

No system yet discovered guarantees a good return in the stock market. One might have hoped that economics, with its theoretical models in which the economy always reverts to an equilibrium, would give us such a tool. Most economic theory is modeled on the laws of motion developed in the 1680s: every action leads to an outcome, and every event is linked in a causal chain backward and forward in time in what is called a "linear" process. Standard economics builds its large-scale predictions—the equilibrium that an economy will arrive at—from the combined effect of the behavior of rational individuals reacting to prices.

Looking for complexity

If the real world does indeed behave like this, why do we find it so hard to predict stock market crashes? Some economists feel the entire linear approach is obsolete. Austrian economist Friedrich Hayek (p.177) believed that economics is far too complex to model in the same way as physics. One response to such doubts is complexity theory, which emerged from the work on thermodynamics of Russian-Belgian chemist Ilya Prigogine (1917–2003). Unlike standard economics, this approach recognizes that predictable, regular actions by individuals do not necessarily lead to a stable, predictable economy.

In 1975, French economists Jean-Michel Grandmont and Alan Kirman argued that economies are "complex systems." In standard economic models of perfect competition individuals do not

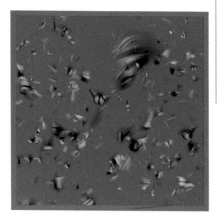

Tiny changes in initial conditions can cause large changes in outcomes. This is known as the "butterfly effect:" Edward Lorenz's suggestion that a butterfly flapping its wings in Brazil could lead to a cyclone in Texas.

See also: Economic man 52–53 ▪ Economic bubbles 98–99 ▪
Testing economic theories 170 ▪ Behavioral economics 266–69

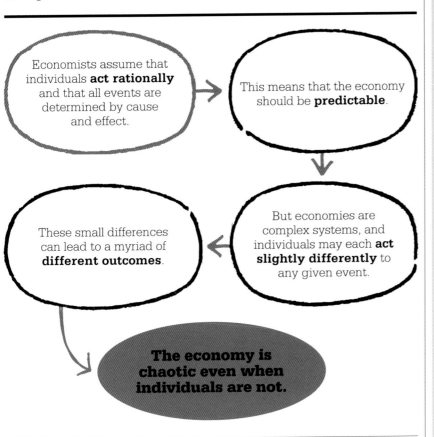

Economists assume that individuals **act rationally** and that all events are determined by cause and effect.

This means that the economy should be **predictable**.

These small differences can lead to a myriad of **different outcomes**.

But economies are complex systems, and individuals may each **act slightly differently** to any given event.

The economy is chaotic even when individuals are not.

Wild randomness

In the 1960s and 70s French-American mathematician Benoît Mandelbrot argued that economists are wrong to try to smooth out economic figures by looking for averages and ignoring extremes. He argued that it is the extremes that give the true picture.

Mandelbrot's criticism was aimed at those who model prices for shares and commodities on the assumption that one price leads directly to another and things average out in the long run. He believed that the mild elements of randomness built into these models are misleading. Models should be based on the assumption of "wild randomness"—the idea that individual freak occurrences matter as a change takes place. For Mandelbrot markets are far more volatile than economists suggest, and the mistake they continually make is to try to come up with laws that work in the same way as the laws of classical physics.

Small variations in velocity will shoot a pinball in totally different directions. Like a pinball player, economists cannot always predict which way stocks will go.

directly interact with each other; they just respond to prices, constantly changing their behavior and prices to achieve the best outcome. In a complex system such as an economy, individuals interact directly with each other using simple "rules of thumb" rather than rational calculations, a little like bees in a hive. This can lead to complex patterns of behavior in the economy as a whole.

Chaotic economies

Ideas related to Grandmont and Kirman's arguments are found in chaos theory, first developed in the 1950s by US mathematician and meteorologist Edward Lorenz.

Lorenz was trying to discover why the weather could not be predicted far into the future. His computer analyses revealed that minute changes in the atmosphere might multiply to produce dramatic changes in the weather.

To analyze chaotic movements, theorists have developed a form of "non-linear" mathematics. Much like the weather, they argue that a minute change in starting conditions can produce such a different outcome that the process appears chaotic, whether for stock market movements or economic growth. If they are right, then the predictable equilibriums that are the bedrock of most economic theories are very far off the mark. ▪

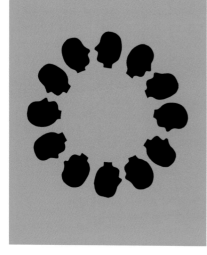

SOCIAL NETWORKS ARE A KIND OF CAPITAL
SOCIAL CAPITAL

IN CONTEXT

FOCUS
Society and the economy

KEY THINKER
Robert Putnam (1941–)

BEFORE
1916 The term "social capital" appears in an article by US educator Lyda J. Hanifan.

1988 US sociologist James Coleman describes social capital, applying it to the phenomenon of high school dropouts.

AFTER
1999 US political scientist Francis Fukuyama argues that social capital has not declined in developed countries such as the US.

2001 British Marxist economist Ben Fine criticizes the concept of social capital.

2003 British sociologist John Field says social capital theory means "relationships matter."

The word "capital" is most commonly used to refer to the machinery used in production: physical capital. A broader definition includes the skills of the labor force: human capital. The efficient use of physical and human capital has long been recognized as key to an economy, but in the 1990s US political scientist Robert Putnam suggested a less tangible form of capital, made up of social connections. He argued that social

A society of many virtuous but isolated individuals is not necessarily rich in social capital.
Robert Putnam

networks are also important to economic performance. Just as a screwdriver (physical capital) or a university education (human capital) can increase productivity, so do social contacts, because they affect the productivity of individuals and groups. The interactions between people at work, in their community, and in their leisure time, can be considered "social capital."

Social networks help individuals improve their skills, advance their careers, and increase overall productivity by encouraging cooperation and information sharing. Conversely, when these connections dwindle, economic performance suffers. Putnam pointed out that since the 1960s people in developed countries have become more isolated, living in urban areas with little sense of community. He argues that this has contributed to economic decline. While not all economists agree with his analysis, social capital is now generally accepted as a significant element of economic performance. ∎

See also: Protectionism and trade 34–35 ▪ Comparative advantage 80–85 ▪ Economies of scale 132 ▪ Market integration 226–31

EDUCATION IS ONLY A SIGNAL OF ABILITY
SIGNALING AND SCREENING

IN CONTEXT

FOCUS
Decision making

KEY THINKERS
Michael Spence (1943–)
Joseph Stiglitz (1943–)

BEFORE
1963 Kenneth Arrow addresses the problems of information economics, such as when one party to a transaction has better information than another.

1970 George Akerlof describes markets with information disparities in *The Market for Lemons*.

AFTER
1976 Michael Rothschild and Joseph Stiglitz pioneer "screening," by which an uninformed party can induce another to impart information.

2001 Michael Spence, George Akerlof, and Joseph Stiglitz win a Nobel Prize for their work in information economics.

A new field of economics was developed in the 1970s, when US economist George Akerlof published his insights on how disparities of access to information might be overcome (pp.274–75).

US economist Michael Spence said that, in practice, if Person 1 has more information than Person 2 in a transaction, Person 1 is likely to send a signal to allow Person 2 to make a more informed decision.

The example Spence gave was that of the job interview, where an employer has less information than the applicant about his or her potential productivity. The applicant provides a resume detailing educational achievements, which may have no relevance to the post applied for but do signal a willingness for hard work and application. In Spence's view higher education, unlike vocational training, mostly has a signaling function, and prospective "good" employees will invest in more education to signal their higher potential productivity.

The subject area of a student's degree and their knowledge of it are of secondary importance when applying for many jobs. Rather, their degree signals ability and a capacity for work.

The opposite of this process, for example where an employer uses the interview to elicit information, is known as screening. Someone buying a used car, or considering granting a loan, will use screening questions to glean information before deciding. Signaling and screening are used in all forms of business transactions. ∎

See also: Behavioral economics 266–69 ▪ Market uncertainty 274–75 ▪ Sticky wages 303 ▪ Searching and matching 304–05

THE EAST ASIAN STATE

GOVERNS

THE MARKET

ASIAN TIGER ECONOMIES

IN CONTEXT

FOCUS
Growth and development

KEY EVENT
Japanese investment
begins flowing into South
Korea's economy in 1965.

BEFORE
1841 German economist
Friedrich List argues that
protecting industry would
help economies to diversify.

1943 Polish economist Paul
Rosenstein-Rodan argues that
poor countries need a "big
push" to develop through
state investment.

AFTER
1992 US economist Alice
Amsden claims South Korea's
use of performance criteria
fostered industrial growth.

1994 US economist Paul
Krugman argues that the East
Asian takeoff was a result of
increases in physical capital
rather than true innovation.

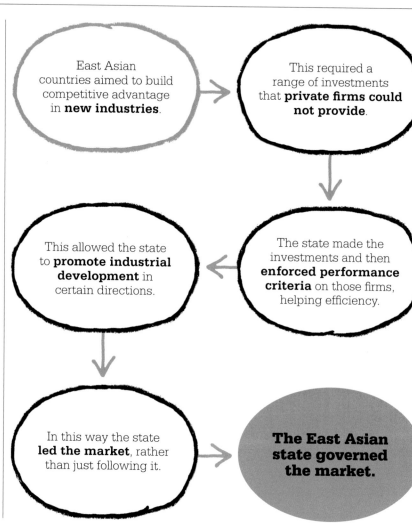

After World War II the economies of a cluster of East Asian nations grew dramatically. Led by a new set of actively interventionist governments, these countries were transformed from economic backwaters into dynamic industrial powers in just a few decades. The so-called Asian Tigers—South Korea, Hong Kong, Singapore, and Taiwan—were followed by Malaysia, Thailand, and Indonesia, and then by China. These countries achieved sustained growth in income per head faster than in any other region. GDP (gross domestic product, or total national income from goods and services) is often used to measure a nation's wealth. In 1950, South Korea's GDP-per-person (GDP divided by the size of the population) was half that of Brazil's; by 1990, it was double; by 2005, three times as high. This kind of growth resulted in a remarkable decline in poverty. By the late 20th century the original four Asian Tigers had living standards that rivaled those of Western Europe, a historically unprecedented change in fortunes that has been dubbed the "East Asian miracle."

The environment from which the Asian Tigers emerged was shaped by government intervention and dense links between the state and the economy, an economic model that came to be known as the "developmental state." After World War II there had been huge expectations of development in poorer nations, and the goal of rapid economic advancement became the driving force behind government economic policy. Powerful bureaucracies were involved in directing the economic activities of the private sector in ways that

See also: The emergence of modern economies 178–79 ▪ Development economics 188–93 ▪
Economic growth theories 224–25 ▪ Market integration 226–31 ▪ Trade and geography 312

South Korea's rapid development was initiated by Park Chung-hee, an army general, in 1961. He restored relations with Japan, Korea's former occupier, and attracted Japanese investment.

seemed to go far beyond anything attempted in Western Europe. However, their governments preserved private enterprise, and their new model had little in common with the state planning of the communist bloc. Asian Tiger states shaped development by steering investment toward strategic industries and promoting the technological upgrading of producers. This induced a shift of workers from agriculture to the expanding industrial sector. Large investments in education gave workers the skills needed for new industries, and industrial enterprises soon began to export their products, becoming the motors for sustained, trade-driven growth.

A new kind of state

This type of state had never been seen before. It challenged orthodox views about government's role in the economy. Standard economics

Now a major center of international finance, Hong Kong plays an important role in China's ongoing economic success while preserving its own system of government.

sees the state's job as correcting market failures—governments provide public goods, such as defense and street lighting, which private markets alone tend not to deliver. They ensure that institutions such as courts function properly so that contracts can be enforced and property rights protected, but beyond that their role is minimal. Once the basic prerequisites for market activity are in place, classical economics suggests that the state should withdraw and let the price mechanism do its work. It is thought that market-friendly institutions and a limited state were key to Britain's economic success during industrialization.

Some economists contend that this also occurred in successful East Asian economies: when these states fostered development, they did so by supporting markets, not by interfering with them. Their interventions helped to allocate resources and investment in ways that were in line with markets: in a sense the state "got prices right." To do this, governments cultivated

macroeconomic stability, vital for giving certainty to investors. They intervened to correct market failures through the provision of defense and schooling. They also built infrastructure such as ports and railways, whose high set-up costs deterred private firms. The East Asian developmental states were held to be successful because they followed the market.

Leading the market

The New Zealand economist Robert Wade argues that the East Asian development states both led and followed markets. They drove the expansion of favored industries by providing cheap credit and subsidies. By leading markets their chosen allocation of resources was markedly different from what it would have been, had it been dictated by markets alone.

US economist Alice Amsden has characterized this as the state deliberately "getting prices wrong" in order to build new types of competitive advantage. A crucial part of this was that the new »

The rapid rise of the Asian Tigers was based on exports. Large facilities to handle container ships, such as these in Singapore, were built by the state to promote growth.

"infant industries," pumped up with subsidies and trade protection, were eventually made to grow up. The state could enforce performance criteria on firms because it was able to withdraw preferential treatment as needed.

Robert Wade argues that the way these states chose to lead the markets explains the creation of comparative advantages in industries where none previously existed. Initially, the prices of goods from a new industry would normally be internationally uncompetitive. In addition, the production of a new product often requires the simultaneous setting up of other industries and infrastructure. The coordination of this process is difficult if left to private firms rather than the state.

Moreover, these protected, infant industries became competitive when they were given classical incentives to learn how to become more efficient. In order to achieve the economic education of new firms and the coordination of initial production, governments needed to act in violation of narrow market prices. This occurred in South

Korea's steel industry. In the 1960s the Korean government was advised by the World Bank not to enter the steel sector because it had no comparative advantage there—others could easily beat its prices. By the 1980s Posco, a large Korean firm, had become one of the world's most efficient steel producers.

Political interference

Attempts at interventionist policies in regions outside East Asia were unsuccessful, which tarnished the reputation of the developmental state. In Latin America and Africa the preferential treatment of firms and sectors generated poor incentives: firms were shielded from competition, but the state did not enforce performance criteria. Infant industries never grew into successful exporters.

In Latin America especially, preferential treatment became linked to politics with little economic payoff: some firms received subsidies and tariff protection but did not become more productive. Over time these firms became a drain on their governments' budgets, absorbing rather than

generating resources. "Getting prices wrong" did not help to build comparative advantages in new industries. It led instead to inefficient production and economic stagnation.

In East Asia successful states seemed better able to resist pressures from private interests. After setting up its new steel firm in the 1960s, the South Korean government ensured that the firm was meeting efficiency targets. If political interests had emerged that had prevented the state from disciplining the firm, the state would have become the servant of narrow interests, not of the overall economic efficiency of the economy. The state had to remain autonomous and resist pressures for favoritism from particular groups. At the same time the state provided firms with credit and technical assistance—to do this and to monitor firms' performance, it was necessary for the tentacles of the state to reach into the smallest cogs of the economy. The economic

> " The state… has set relative prices deliberately 'wrong' in order to create profitable investment opportunities.
> **Alice Amsden** "

bureaucracy needed to hold detailed information about all potential investments, and to maintain effective relationships with industrial managers.

US economist Peter Evans has called these markers of successful developmental states "embedded autonomy." Only when this is in place is there a chance for a state to "get prices wrong" without being co-opted by vested interests. Embedded autonomy is not easy to create, and its absence may be a factor behind the poor outcomes of state intervention in other developing regions.

The rise of China

With the East Asian financial crisis of the 1990s the developmental state model was again called into question. Many sensed that the institutions that had fostered rapid industrial growth after World War II had lost their potency by the late 20th century. On the other hand the spectacular rise of China has resurrected the idea of the developmental state, or at the very least of policies and institutions that produce rapid economic transformation while deviating from the prescriptions of standard, classical economics.

Like most Chinese cities, the eastern city of Hangzhou has seen rapid growth and a spreading urbanization as China has industrialized.

China began a series of reforms of its communist system in the late 1970s. It created its own brand of developmental state, which resembled the Asian Tigers, and had an authoritarian government that was responsible for promoting the private sector and exports. Agriculture was de-collectivized, and state-owned industries were given more autonomy and subjected to greater competition. These reforms helped unleash a vast expansion of private economic activity, without the introduction of Western-style property rights.

Alternative incentives emerged from China's unique institutions: for example, from the "Household Responsibility System," whereby local managers are held responsible for an enterprise's profits and losses, without the need for private property ownership. The results have been dramatic. While China remains poor relative to Western Europe, its rapid growth took 170 million people out of poverty during the 1990s, accounting for three-quarters of the poverty reduction in developing regions.

The histories of China and the Asian Tigers show that there is no unique path to development. The way that their states intervened in the economy was very different from anything that took place in Europe when it was developing. However, it seems that all development models, even successful ones, eventually run into constraints. The benefits of the development state petered out in the Asian Tigers in the 1990s— institutions that had worked in one decade began to fail in the next. One day the Chinese state, too, may lose its potency. It may have to reinvent itself if its spectacular rise is to continue. ∎

Industrial policy and incentives

The East Asian developmental states gave preferential treatment to firms in favored sectors while creating incentives for performance. They did this by requiring enterprises to meet performance criteria, partly through contests in which firms competed for prizes.

Typically, the criterion for winning was successful exports. The prize was credit lines or access to foreign exchange. In South Korea and Taiwan, for instance, firms had to show proof that they had won an export order. Only then did they receive their prize. South Korea launched competitions in which private firms bid for large projects in new industries such as shipbuilding. Successful firms received protection from the international market for a time. Performance criteria involved firms becoming internationally competitive by a certain deadline. Failing firms were punished.

The South Korean steel industry was a big success of the developmental state. By 2011, South Korea was the sixth largest steel producer in the world.

BELIEFS

CAN TRIGGER CURRENCY

CRISES

SPECULATION AND CURRENCY DEVALUATION

IN CONTEXT

FOCUS
Global economy

KEY THINKER
Paul Krugman (1953–)

BEFORE
1944 Greece experiences the largest currency crash in history.

1978 US economic historian Charles Kindleberger stresses the role of irrational behavior in crises.

AFTER
2009 US economists Carmen Reinhart and Kenneth Rogoff publish *This Time is Different: Eight Centuries of Financial Folly*, in which they draw similarities between crises over the centuries.

2010–12 Divergent national priorities, serious policy errors, and huge speculative pressures threaten the breakup of the euro.

A currency crisis is a large and sudden collapse in the value of one nation's currency relative to other currencies. For about 30 years after World War II the world's main currencies were governed by the Bretton Woods system (pp.186–87), which was based on fixed, but adjustable, exchange rates.

When this system ended in 1971, currency crises became more common. In general a currency crisis is triggered by people selling a country's currency in large amounts. This behavior seems to stem from the interaction of people's expectations and certain underlying economic weaknesses (known as "fundamentals")—in other words people's reactions to perceived problems. Economists have tried to model this interaction mathematically, but every time they think they have found a model that fits the data, a new type of crisis seems to emerge.

Currency crises in context

Like hurricanes, financial crises happen surprisingly often but are hard to predict. Centuries ago, when money was based on precious metals, a currency usually lost its value through currency debasement, which occurred when a ruler reduced the precious metal content of the coinage. After money began to be printed on paper by central banks, high inflation would cause a country's currency to collapse. This happened in Germany in 1923, where at one point prices were doubling every two days. However, a country does not need hyperinflation to have a currency crisis. For example during the Great Depression of 1929–33, prices of commodities such as minerals and food collapsed, and the currencies of Latin American countries, which were reliant on this export trade, fell with them.

Inconsistent policies

Writing in 1979, US economist Paul Krugman showed that for a currency crisis to happen, all that is needed is for a government to carry out policies that are inconsistent with the exchange rate.

Krugman's argument is the foundation for a first generation of currency crisis models. These models start by assuming that there is a fixed exchange rate between the home currency and an external currency, and that the home government is running a budget deficit (it is spending more than it is collecting in tax), which it is financing by printing money. By increasing the supply of the currency, this policy creates an inconsistency with the value of the currency set by the fixed exchange rate. Other things being equal, the policy will cause the "real" value of the home currency to fall.

Next, the models assume that the central bank sells its own reserves of foreign currency in order to support the currency. However,

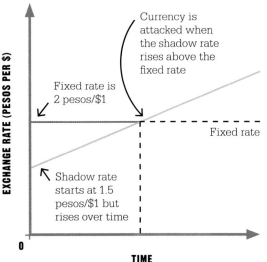

Currency is attacked when the shadow rate rises above the fixed rate

Fixed rate is 2 pesos/$1

Fixed rate

Shadow rate starts at 1.5 pesos/$1 but rises over time

EXCHANGE RATE (PESOS PER $)

TIME

In "first generation" crisis models, when one currency is fixed to another, its "real" value, or shadow rate, may fall below the value at which it is fixed. In this case this is the point at which the shadow exchange rate rises above 2 pesos/$1. When this happens, the currency is vulnerable to attack as speculators buy the country's foreign currency reserves in anticipation of a devaluation.

See also: Economic bubbles 98–99 ▪ Rational expectations 244–47 ▪ Exchange rates and currencies 250–55 ▪
Financial crises 296–301 ▪ Bank runs 316–21 ▪ Global savings imbalances 322–25

it is assumed that people can see that eventually the foreign currency reserves of the central bank will be exhausted. The exchange rate will then have to "float" (be traded freely) and decline. The model proposes that there is a "shadow exchange rate," which is what the exchange rate would be if the central bank were not defending the fixed exchange rate. People know what this shadow exchange rate is (and will be) at any given time by looking at the government deficit. The moment they see that it is better to sell the home currency at the fixed exchange rate than at the shadow exchange rate, they will launch a speculative attack and buy all the foreign currency reserves at the central bank. The home currency will then be forced to float, and the depreciating shadow exchange rate will become the actual exchange rate. The speculative attack occurs at the point where the steadily depreciating shadow exchange rate equals the fixed exchange rate.

This model seemed relevant to the currency crises in Latin America in the 1970s and 1980s, »

Women examine a new Zimbabwean dollar bank note in 2009. After a period of hyperinflation, the government revalued the currency by removing 12 zeroes from the old notes.

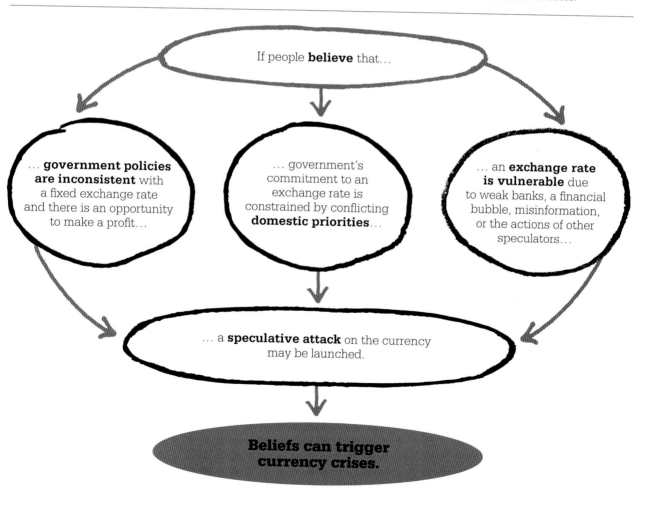

If people **believe** that…

… **government policies are inconsistent** with a fixed exchange rate and there is an opportunity to make a profit…

… government's commitment to an exchange rate is constrained by conflicting **domestic priorities**…

… an **exchange rate is vulnerable** due to weak banks, a financial bubble, misinformation, or the actions of other speculators…

… a **speculative attack** on the currency may be launched.

Beliefs can trigger currency crises.

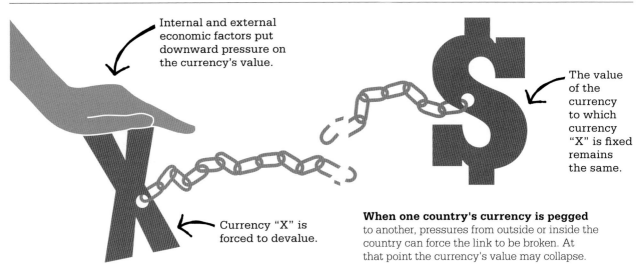

Internal and external economic factors put downward pressure on the currency's value.

The value of the currency to which currency "X" is fixed remains the same.

Currency "X" is forced to devalue.

When one country's currency is pegged to another, pressures from outside or inside the country can force the link to be broken. At that point the currency's value may collapse.

such as the crisis in Mexico in 1982. However, in 1992–93, a currency crisis erupted in the European Monetary System (EMS), which appeared to contradict this model. Under this system's Exchange Rate Mechanism (ERM), European countries effectively fixed, or pegged, their currencies to the German Deutsche Mark (DM). Several currencies came under pressure from speculators, notably the financier George Soros. It would be difficult to argue that countries such as the UK were running policies inconsistent with the targeted exchange rate. The UK had a very small budget deficit and had previously been running at a surplus, yet in 1992, the country was forced to withdraw from the ERM, to the great political embarrassment of Chancellor of the Exchequer (finance minister) Norman Lamont. A new model was needed to explain these events.

Self-fulfilling crises

In the first generation models, the government's policy is "fixed:" the authorities mechanically use up their foreign reserves to defend the currency. A second generation of

models allowed the government to have a choice. It may be committed to a fixed exchange rate, but this "rule" has an escape clause. If unemployment becomes very high, the government may abandon its commitment to the fixed exchange rate because the social costs of defending the currency (for instance through high interest rates) are too great. We can see these hard choices in the plight of Greece in 2012. However, without a speculative attack these extra social costs would not arise. These models imply that more than

The only absolutely sure-fire way not to have one's currency speculated against... is not to have an independent currency.
Paul Krugman

one outcome is possible, what economists call "multiple equilibriums." A speculative attack might occur if enough people believe that other people are going to attack the currency. They will then attack it, and a crisis will unfold. But if people don't hold these beliefs, the crisis may not happen. In these models crises are "self-fulfilling." At an extreme they suggest that a crisis could happen irrespective of the economic fundamentals of a country. These new models, based on the work of economists such as the American Maurice Obstfeld, seemed more realistic than the earlier ones since they allowed for governments' use of instruments, such as interest rates, to defend the currency, raising interest rates to prevent devaluation. They also seemed to dovetail with the experience of the ERM crisis, where government policies were constrained by high levels of unemployment.

Financial fragility

The East Asian crisis of 1997 (see opposite) seemed not to fit the first two types of model. Unemployment was not a concern, yet East Asian currencies came under sudden, massive speculative attack. In the second generation models the escape clause of devaluation was supposed to relieve the economy from social costs, but the sharp collapse of their currencies was followed by a severe—though short-lived—downturn. Financial fragility, caused by a banking boom and bust, played an important role. In light of this economists began to focus on the interaction of weaknesses in the economy and speculators' self-fulfilling expectations. This third generation model now took into account new kinds of financial fragilities, such as those that arise when firms and banks borrow in foreign currency and lend in local currency. Banks would be unable to pay their debts in the event of currency devaluation. These kinds of weaknesses could spark speculative attacks and crises.

As well as developing theories, economists have looked at the evidence for possible warning signs of currency crises. In a 1996 article Jeffrey Frankel and Andrew Rose reviewed currency crashes in 105 developing countries from 1971 to 1992. They found that devaluations occur when foreign capital inflows dry up, when the central bank's foreign currency reserves are low, when domestic credit growth is high, when major external (especially US dollar) interest rates rise, and when the real exchange rate (prices of traded goods from home relative to those abroad) is high, which means that a country's goods become uncompetitive in foreign markets. Economists argue that by monitoring such warning signs, crises may be predictable up to one or two years in advance.

Avoiding crises

Studies suggest that between 5 and 25 percent of recent history has been spent in one crisis or another. New crises will continue to surprise us, but there are signals —such as the real exchange rate, exports and the current account, and the amount of money in the economy relative to the central bank's international reserves— that may help to warn us when currency hurricanes are approaching. The experiences of the last few decades have exposed the financial roots of crises. Economists now talk of "twin crises"—vicious spirals of currency and banking crises. Rapid financial deregulation and liberalization of international capital markets are thought to have led to crises in countries with weak financial and regulatory institutions. As well as paying attention to the macroeconomic signs of future crises, governments also need to attend to these institutional vulnerabilities. ∎

The East Asian financial crisis

The 1997 East Asian crisis seemed to come from nowhere, overwhelming countries with strong growth records and government surpluses. Before the crisis most countries in the region had pegged their exchange rates to the US dollar. The first signs of trouble were businesses failing in Thailand and South Korea. On July 2, 1997, after months of battle to save its pegged rate, Thailand devalued. The Philippines was then forced to float on July 11, Malaysia on July 14, Indonesia on August 14. In less than a year the currencies of Indonesia, Thailand, South Korea, Malaysia, and the Philippines fell by between 40 and 85 percent. Only Hong Kong held out against the speculators.

The crisis has been blamed on a severe banking crisis. Borrowing was often short-term, and when foreign lenders withdrew their capital, contagion ensued, and currencies collapsed.

Icelanders take to the streets of Reykjavik to denounce the state's handling of the currency crisis in 2008, which saw the krona lose more than one third of its official value.

AUCTION WINNERS PAY OVER THE ODDS

THE WINNER'S CURSE

IN CONTEXT

FOCUS
Decision making

KEY THINKERS
William Vickrey (1914–96)
Paul Milgrom (1948–)
Roger Myerson (1951–)

BEFORE
1951 US mathematician
John Nash develops a concept
of equilibrium in games,
which becomes a tenet of
auction theory.

1961 Canadian economist
William Vickrey uses game
theory to analyze auctions.

AFTER
1971 It is shown that oil
companies bidding for drilling
leases may not be aware of the
"winner's curse."

1982 US economists Paul
Milgrom and Robert J. Weber
show that when bidders know
their competitors' valuations,
an "English auction" gives the
best price for the seller.

In an auction where the value
of the sale item is uncertain,
every bidder makes **his own
decision** on its value.

⬇

If they decide their
valuations privately,
there will be a range of
different valuations.

⬇

The true value of the item
will tend to be around the
midrange of the different
bidders' valuations.

⬇

The sale will go to the
bidder who **overestimates**
its value the most.

⬇

**Auction winners pay
over the odds.**

Auctions have been
around for a long time,
but economists have only
recently come to realize that they
are an ideal proving ground for the
competitive strategies of game
theory. Game theory came to
prominence in the 1950s when
mathematicians saw that simple
games could illuminate situations
in which people compete directly.
This idea proved hard to apply to
the real world. However, the strict
rules of an auction, with limited
participants and pokerlike buying
strategies, seemed much closer to
the theory.

Types of auction
The first person to apply game
theory to auctions was Canadian
economist William Vickrey in the
1960s. He compared the three most
common types of auctions. An
"English auction" is the method
used in British art houses, where
bidding goes up until only one
bidder is left. In a "Dutch auction,"
used in Dutch flower markets for
example, the price drops until it
reaches a price someone will pay.
In a "first-price auction" bidders
submit sealed bids, and the highest
bidder wins. Vickrey proposed a

See also: The competitive market 126–29 ▪ Risk and uncertainty 162–63 ▪ Social choice theory 214–15 ▪ Game theory 234–41

In an auction there is a danger that the winning bid will come from a bidder who has overvalued the item, a misfortune known as winner's curse.

fourth type of auction, similar to the first-price auction, but in which the winner pays as much as the second-highest bid.

Using mathematics, Vickrey proved that when bidders value items independently, all four types of auction yield the same revenue for the seller, a discovery known as "revenue equivalence theory."

Shaded bids

Vickrey showed that it is better for bidders to bid less than their valuations, a strategy auction theorists call "shading," otherwise they may end up paying over the odds. Shading gained special significance in the 1970s, when it seemed that oil companies bidding for offshore drilling rights often ended up paying far too much. Auction theorists discovered the

In Dutch auctions, as used in Holland's Aalsmeer flower market, the price starts high and then begins to drop. The first bidder to stop the price as it drops takes the flowers.

phenomenon of the "winner's curse:" an item goes to the bidder who overvalues it the most. Imagine that you submit a successful bid of $100 for a picture. You win because your bid is higher than all the others. Suppose the next highest bid had been $98. You could have bid lower—$98.01—and still been successful. In general the winning bidder pays "too much," in this case to the tune of $1.99.

Auction theory can be used to design auctions that maximize the seller's revenue and ensure that the good goes to the buyer who values it most. The success of the US government's spectrum auctions in the 1990s (see box, right) created a buzz about this new area of economics. For many it was proof that game theory was not just theory but really did apply in actual markets. Others insist that auctions are a special type of market, and that even they might not be fully explainable using game theory. What does seem true is that auctions have now expanded well beyond their traditional domains of government procurements and public bond sales. ▪

Selling the spectrum

Auction theory came into its own with a dramatic spate of government auctions in the US in the 1990s as industries were privatized. The biggest sell-off came when mobile phone companies prepared to pay huge sums for a share of the electromagnetic spectrum (the airwaves) on which to transmit. The US government wanted to maximize its return, but it also wanted to ensure that the sale went to the bidder who valued it most.

In 1993, the Federal Communications Commission (FCC) brought in auction theorists to design the auctions for the 2,500 so-called spectrum licenses. The telecom companies, meanwhile, hired auction theorists to design their bid strategies. The FCC decided on an English-style auction but with a twist: the identity of the bidders was kept secret to avoid retaliatory bidding or collusion to keep prices down. The auctions broke all records, and the approach has been widely copied.

STABLE

ECONOMIES CONTAIN

THE SEEDS OF

INSTABILITY

FINANCIAL CRISES

IN CONTEXT

FOCUS
Banking and finance

KEY THINKER
Hyman Minsky (1919–96)

BEFORE
1933 American economist Irving Fisher shows how debt can cause depression.

1936 British economist John Maynard Keynes claims the financial markets have a larger role in the functioning of the economy than was previously thought.

AFTER
2007 Lebanese-American risk theorist Nassim Nicholas Taleb publishes *The Black Swan*, which criticizes the risk-management procedures of financial markets.

2009 Paul McCulley, former managing director of a large US investment fund, coins the term "Minsky moment" for the point at which booms bust.

The instability of economic systems has been debated throughout the history of economic thought. The view of classical economists, following in the tradition started by Adam Smith, is that an economy is always driven toward a stable equilibrium. There will always be disturbances that create booms and slumps—a pattern that is sometimes called the business cycle—but ultimately the tendency is toward stability with a fully employed economy.

The Great Depression of 1929 led some economists to examine business cycles in more detail. In 1933, US economist Irving Fisher described how a boom can turn to bust through instabilities caused by excessive debts and falling prices. Three years later John Maynard Keynes (p.161) questioned the idea that the economy is self-righting. In his *General Theory*, he developed the idea that an economy could settle into a depression from which it had little hope of escaping.

These works were the genesis of understanding the unstable nature of modern economies. In 1992, Hyman Minsky looked at the problem again in his paper "The

Pictured here after his arrest in 1910, Charles Ponzi ran investment scams in the US promising unrealistic returns. Minsky compared capitalist booms to Ponzi schemes, doomed to collapse.

Financial Instability Hypothesis." The paper suggested that the modern capitalist economy contains the seeds of its own destruction.

In Keynes's view the modern capitalist economy was different from the economy that had existed in the 18th century. The major difference was the role played by money and financial institutions. In 1803, the French economist Jean-Baptiste Say (p.75) gave a classical interpretation of the economy as essentially a refined barter system, in which people produce goods that they exchange for money, which is used to exchange for the goods they want. The real exchange is good for good: money is just a lubricant. Keynes argued that money does more than this: it allows transactions to occur over time. A firm could borrow money today to build a factory, which it hopes will generate profit that can be used to pay back the loan and the interest in the future. Minsky pointed out that it is not

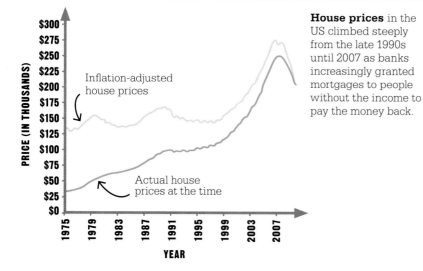

House prices in the US climbed steeply from the late 1990s until 2007 as banks increasingly granted mortgages to people without the income to pay the money back.

Inflation-adjusted house prices

Actual house prices at the time

only firms that are part of this process. Governments finance their national debts, and consumers borrow large sums to buy cars and houses. They too are part of the complex financial market that funds transactions over time.

Merchants of debt

Minsky argued that there was a second big difference between modern and pre-capitalist economies. He pointed out that the banking system does not merely match lenders with borrowers. It also strives to innovate in the way it sells and borrows funds. Recent examples of this include financial instruments called collateralized debt obligations (CDOs), which were developed in the 1970s.

CDOs were made by pooling different financial assets (loans) together, some high-risk, others low-risk. These new assets were then cut up into smaller sections to be sold. Each section contained a mix of debts. In 1994, credit default swaps were introduced to protect these assets by insuring them against the risk of default. Both of these innovations encouraged the supply of loans into the financial system, which increased the supply of liquidity, or money, into the system. Minsky concluded that these innovations meant that it was no longer possible for a government to control the amount of money in its economy. If the demand for loans was there, the financial markets could find a way to meet it.

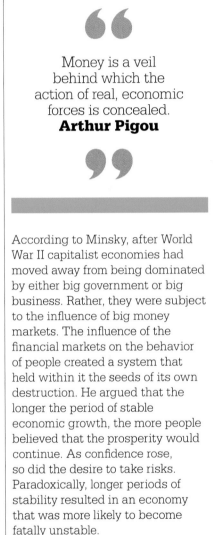

Money is a veil behind which the action of real, economic forces is concealed.
Arthur Pigou

According to Minsky, after World War II capitalist economies had moved away from being dominated by either big government or big business. Rather, they were subject to the influence of big money markets. The influence of the financial markets on the behavior of people created a system that held within it the seeds of its own destruction. He argued that the longer the period of stable economic growth, the more people believed that the prosperity would continue. As confidence rose, so did the desire to take risks. Paradoxically, longer periods of stability resulted in an economy that was more likely to become fatally unstable.

Minsky explained the pathway from stability to instability by looking at three different types of investment choices that people can make. These can be simply illustrated by looking at the way houses are bought. The safest decision is to borrow an amount that allows the person's income to repay the interest on the loan and also the original value of »

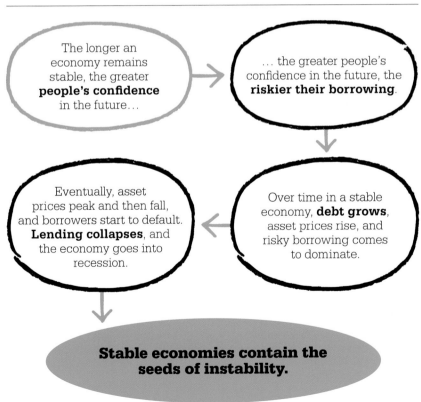

The longer an economy remains stable, the greater **people's confidence** in the future…

… the greater people's confidence in the future, the **riskier their borrowing**.

Over time in a stable economy, **debt grows**, asset prices rise, and risky borrowing comes to dominate.

Eventually, asset prices peak and then fall, and borrowers start to default. **Lending collapses**, and the economy goes into recession.

Stable economies contain the seeds of instability.

During a period of stability, confidence in the future grows, which leads people to make increasingly risky investments. This causes an asset price bubble, which will eventually burst.

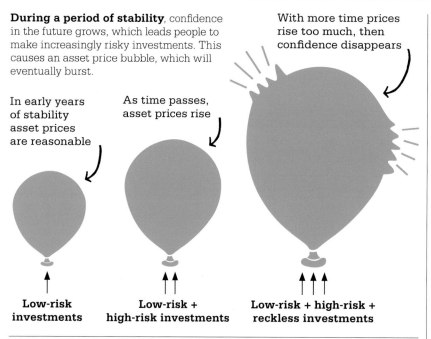

In early years of stability asset prices are reasonable

As time passes, asset prices rise

With more time prices rise too much, then confidence disappears

Low-risk investments

Low-risk + high-risk investments

Low-risk + high-risk + reckless investments

the loan over a period of time. Minsky called these hedge units, and they create little risk for the lender or borrower. If people felt more confident about the future, they might buy a larger interest-only mortgage, where their income could pay back the interest on the loan but not the loan itself. The hope would be that a stable period of positive economic growth would increase demand so that the value of the house would be greater at the end of the period than at the start. Minsky called these people speculative borrowers.

As time passed, if stability and confidence continued to last, the desire to take greater risks would encourage people to buy a house for which their income could not even pay the interest, so that the total level of debt would increase, at least in the short run. The expectation would be that house prices would rise fast enough to cover the shortfall in the interest repayments. This third type of investment would create the

greatest amount of instability in the future. Minsky named this third type of investor Ponzi borrowers after Charles Ponzi, the Italian immigrant to America who was one of the first to be caught running the financial scam that now bears his name. "Ponzi schemes" attract funds by offering very high returns. Initially, the con men use new investors' money to pay the dividends. In this way they can maintain the illusion that investment is profitable and attract new customers. However, soon the scheme collapses due to its failure

to meet the high level of returns that were promised. Investors in such schemes are likely to lose a large proportion of their money.

Housing bubble

The recent history of the US housing market is an example of how an economy that has had a long period of stability creates within itself the conditions for instability. In the 1970s and 80s the standard mortgage was sold in a way that made sure that the interest and the capital could be paid off, in what Minsky viewed as hedge units. However, by the end of the 1990s a sustained period of growth had pushed house prices up, persuading an increasing number of people to use interest-only mortgages as they speculated that prices would continue to rise. The financial system then began to supply a whole array of "Ponzi"-style mortgage deals to borrowers who had incomes so low that they could not afford to pay even the interest on the loan—these were the "subprime" mortgages. The monthly shortfall was to be added to their total debt. As long as house prices continued to rise, the value of the property would be worth more than the debt. As long as new people kept entering the market, prices kept rising. At the same time the finance industry that sold the mortgages bundled them up and sold them on to other banks as assets that would deliver a stream of income for 30 years.

The end of the game arrived in 2006. As the US economy stalled,

An agent shows a couple around a home. In the US housing boom banks were lending on the expectation of rising prices. People who could not afford mortgages were encouraged to buy.

> The peculiar
> behavioral attributes
> of a capitalist economy
> center around the
> impact of finance
> upon system behavior.
> **Hyman Minsky**

incomes fell, and the demand for new houses weakened. As house price increases began to slow, the first of an increasing number of defaults was triggered since borrowers saw their debts grow rather than shrink. Rising numbers of repossessed houses came onto the market, and prices tumbled.

In 2007, the US economy reached what has become known as the "Minsky moment." This is the point at which the unsustainable speculation turns into crisis. The collapse of the housing market left banks with enormous debts and, since no one knew who had bought the toxic mortgage debt, institutions stopped lending to each other. As a result banks began to fail, most famously Lehmann Brothers in 2008. As Minsky had foretold, a near-catastrophic collapse of the financial system beckoned because a period of stability had generated enormous levels of debt that created the conditions for enormous instability.

The three possible actions taken to halt the fatal instability, and the problems associated with making these corrections, had also been predicted by Minsky.

First, the central bank could act as the lender of last resort, bailing out the failing banking system. Minsky saw that this might further increase instability in the system in the future because it would encourage banking firms to take greater risks, safe in the knowledge that they would be saved.

Second, the government could increase its debt to stimulate demand in the economy. However, even governments have problems financing debts in times of crisis. Third, the financial markets could be subject to stricter regulation.

In 2009, financier Bernard Madoff was convicted of the largest Ponzi scheme fraud in history. He took more than $18 billion from investors over the course of 40 years before the scheme collapsed.

Minsky strongly believed that, in the long run, this was necessary. However, the speed at which innovation takes place in the money markets would make increased regulation very difficult.

For Minsky financial instability is key to explaining modern capitalism. Money is no longer a veil that hides the real workings of the economy; it has become the economy. His ideas are now drawing increasing attention. ∎

Hyman Minsky

An economist of the political Left, Hyman Minsky was born in Chicago to Russian-Jewish immigrant parents who had met at a rally to honor Karl Marx (p.105). He studied mathematics at Chicago University before switching to economics. Minsky had a vision of a better world and yet was equally fascinated by the practical world of commerce, and worked as an adviser and director of an American bank for 30 years.

After a period overseas with the US army during World War II he returned home to spend most of his working life as a professor of economics at Washington University.

An original thinker and natural communicator, Minsky made friends easily. Academically, he was more interested in the idea than mathematical rigor. The notion that pervades all his work is the flow of money. During his lifetime, partly by choice, he remained on the margins of mainstream economic thought, but since his death, and particularly since the crash of 2007–08 that he predicted, his ideas have become increasingly influential. Married with two children, he died of cancer in 1996, aged 77.

Key works

1965 *Labor and the War against Poverty*
1975 *John Maynard Keynes*
1986 *Stabilizing an Unstable Economy*

BUSINESSES PAY MORE THAN THE MARKET WAGE
INCENTIVES AND WAGES

IN CONTEXT

FOCUS
Markets and firms

KEY THINKERS
Joseph Stiglitz (1943–)
Carl Shapiro (1955–)

BEFORE
1914 During a recession US car manufacturer Henry Ford announces that he is doubling the pay of his workers to $5 a day.

1920s British economist Alfred Marshall suggests the idea of efficiency wages.

1938 The Fair Labor Standards Act introduces a minimum wage in the US.

AFTER
1984 Carl Shapiro and Joseph Stiglitz suggest that efficiency wages discourage shirking.

1986 US economists George Akerlof and Janet Yellen suggest social reasons for paying efficiency wages, such as boosting morale.

US economists Carl Shapiro and Joseph Stiglitz contend that firms pay what must be more than the market wage because there is always a core of unemployed workers. They explain this with the idea of "efficiency wages." Employers choose to pay over the market wage because it is worth their while—they get more from their employees this way.

This situation arises because of market "imperfections." Employers cannot observe their workers' effort

Workers build the Model T motorcar on Henry Ford's revolutionary assembly line in 1913. One of Ford's insights was to realize that his own workers should also be his best customers.

without cost (a problem that economists call "moral hazard"). Because of this, Shapiro and Stiglitz argue that efficiency wages cut "shirking." If workers knew they would be right back in a job as soon as they got fired, they might be tempted to slack on the job. The higher wages and the knowledge that dismissal might lead to long-term unemployment increases the cost of losing a job and will make workers less likely to shirk.

Employers also cannot observe their workers' ability without cost, and efficiency wages might help to attract better applicants. Other explanations include the employer's desire to boost morale and minimize turnover (the higher the wage, the easier it is to hold on to workers and avoid costly retraining). High wages may also keep workers healthy enough to do a good job. This is particularly important in developing countries. Efficiency wages can further explain why firms don't cut wages if demand falls: if they did, their best workers might quit. ■

See also: Supply and demand 108–13 ▪ Depressions and unemployment 154–61 ▪ Market information and incentives 208–09

REAL WAGES RISE DURING A RECESSION
STICKY WAGES

IN CONTEXT

FOCUS
The macroeconomy

KEY THINKER
John Taylor (1946–)

BEFORE
1936 John Maynard Keynes argues that government intervention can pull economies out of recessions.

1976 Thomas Sargent and Neil Wallace argue that rational expectations make Keynesian macroeconomic policies useless.

AFTER
1985 Greg Mankiw suggests that "menu costs"—the cost to a firm of making price changes—may cause price stickiness.

1990 US economist John Taylor introduces the "Taylor rule," showing that central banks should run active monetary policies to stabilize the economy.

Keynesian economics (pp.154–61) assumes that wages in money terms tend not to fall: they are "sticky" and respond only slowly to changing market conditions. When a recession hits and prices fall, the real value of wages therefore increases. Firms then demand less labor, and unemployment rises.

The new Keynesian economists, such as US economist John Taylor, attempt to explain this stickiness. In the 1970s the introduction of rational expectations (pp.244–47) undermined Keynesian economics. There could be no persistent unemployment because wages would fall and government policies to boost the economy wouldn't work. New Keynesian thinking showed that even with rational expectations, unemployment might linger and government policy could be effective. This was because wage stickiness could coexist with rational individuals.

Taylor and US economist Greg Mankiw argue that prices may be sticky due to so-called "menu costs"—the costs of making changes, such as printing new price lists. Stickiness can also be caused by labor contracts, in which wages are fixed for a time. Individual behavior and rationality were absent from early Keynesian models. The new Keynesian economists placed their Keynesian conclusions on some firmer theoretical foundations. ∎

> If you were going to turn to only one economist to understand the problems facing the economy, there is little doubt that the economist would be John Maynard Keynes.
> **Greg Mankiw**

See also: Depressions and unemployment 154–61 ∎ The Keynesian multiplier 164–65 ∎ Rational expectations 244–47 ∎ Incentives and wages 302

FINDING A JOB IS LIKE FINDING A PARTNER OR A HOUSE
SEARCHING AND MATCHING

It is usually easy to decide where to buy bread or soap. There are many supermarkets, and they are easy to find. But what about locating a particular make of used car or an antique musical instrument? According to the classical view of the market—where supply and demand always balance—buyers and sellers find each other immediately, without cost, and have perfect information about the prices of all goods and services. However, anyone who has tried to find a used car—or a new house or partner—knows that it rarely works like this in reality.

Search frictions

Markets are said to have "search frictions" when buyers and sellers do not automatically find each other. Economists have gradually developed "search theory" to investigate these frictions. One of the theory's main focuses has been on job searches and unemployment.

The classical model of the labor market assumes a labor supply schedule (the number of workers willing to work at a given wage) and a labor demand schedule (the number of jobs offered at a given wage). When the wage for each

Online dating agencies are markets where people are both buyers and sellers. Individuals cannot search indefinitely so they will work most effectively if they search within a range.

schedule matches, supply equals demand and the market is in equilibrium. So how can it be that at any one time there are many workers looking for jobs and employers looking for workers?

In the 1960s US economist George Stigler argued that the "one wage" market used by classical economists would only occur where there is no cost for information about wages offered or sought. In any market where products (such as jobs) are all different, searching

See also: Free market economics 54–61 ▪ Depressions and unemployment 154–61 ▪ Rational expectations 244–47 ▪ Sticky wages 303

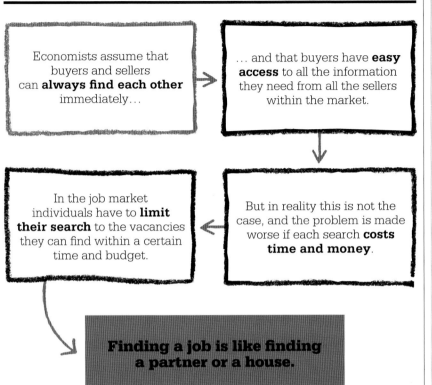

Economists assume that buyers and sellers can **always find each other** immediately…

… and that buyers have **easy access** to all the information they need from all the sellers within the market.

But in reality this is not the case, and the problem is made worse if each search **costs time and money**.

In the job market individuals have to **limit their search** to the vacancies they can find within a certain time and budget.

Finding a job is like finding a partner or a house.

Global unemployment

While many people now work in well-paid, satisfying jobs, unemployment is persistently high in some parts of the world. Moreover, the market in jobs is shifting, and good jobs are vanishing even in richer parts of the world.

In March, 2012, nearly half of Spaniards and Greeks under 25 were jobless, and unemployment in South Africa was running at nearly 30 percent. Even in the US, employment climbed above 9.1 percent. This appears to counteract the argument that there are always jobs for those prepared to take lower wages. US economist Edmund Phelps argues that globalization is a big factor in this because jobs created in richer countries tend to be in "non-tradable" sectors such as government and healthcare, while tradable jobs (such as phone-making) have moved to countries such as China and the Philippines, where wages are generally low. Resolving problems like these is one of the chief concerns for economists today.

In 2011, thousands of Spaniards calling themselves *los indignados* (the indignant), marched to Brussels to protest against an unemployment rate of 40 percent.

costs money. The greater the search costs, the wider the range of wages for a similar job will be. People looking for work realize that wages differ between employers and have to decide how far and how long to search. Stigler's research showed that to conduct an optimal search, workers should reject any wage lower than their "reservation wage" (the lowest they are willing to accept), but accept any offer above it. This model—of drawing a line at an acceptable level—works for searching in any market, even dating agencies.

In 2010, economists Peter Diamond, Dale Mortensen, and Christopher Pissarides were jointly awarded the Nobel Prize for their work on search and matching theory.

Diamond found that even a tiny increase in the cost of searching leads to an increase in price of the goods. Buyers are reluctant to pay for a second or third search, so if price rises are small in the place they are searching, sellers know that buyers will not notice because they are not comparing them with the results of other searches.

Searching and matching theory has implications for the efficient design of unemployment benefits. Benefits without conditions might reduce incentives for job seekers to search and to accept job offers. But those that are designed in a way that encourages searching might help to improve the efficiency of labor markets. ∎

THE BIGGEST CHALLENGE FOR COLLECTIVE ACTION IS CLIMATE CHANGE

ECONOMICS AND THE ENVIRONMENT

IN CONTEXT

FOCUS
Economic policy

KEY THINKERS
William Nordhaus (1941–)
Nicholas Stern (1946–)

BEFORE
1896 Swedish scientist Svante Arrhenius predicts a doubling of atmospheric carbon dioxide will produce a 9–11°F rise in global surface temperature.

1920 British economist Arthur Pigou proposes levying taxes on pollution.

1992 The United Nations Framework Convention on Climate Change is signed.

1997 The Kyoto Protocol is ratified; by 2011 more than 190 countries sign up to it.

AFTER
2011 Canada retracts from the Kyoto Protocol.

E conomic development and prosperity since the Industrial Revolution have come about through technology, largely driven by fuels such as coal, oil, and gas. It is increasingly clear, however, that this prosperity comes at a cost—not only are we fast depleting these natural resources, but burning fossil fuels pollutes the atmosphere. A growing body of evidence points to emissions of greenhouse gases, in particular carbon dioxide (CO_2), as a cause of global warming, and the consensus now among scientists worldwide is that we risk devastating climate change unless emissions are cut quickly and drastically.

See also: Provision of public goods and services 46–47 ▪ Demographics and economics 68–69 ▪ External costs 137 ▪
Development economics 188–93 ▪ The economics of happiness 216–19

The Industrial Revolution that
began about 150 years ago has led
to countries burning large amounts of
fossil fuels. These emissions create a
"greenhouse effect" in the atmosphere.

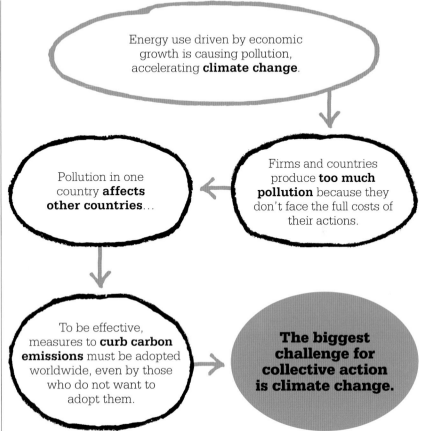

Energy use driven by economic
growth is causing pollution,
accelerating **climate change**.

Firms and countries
produce **too much
pollution** because they
don't face the full costs of
their actions.

Pollution in one
country **affects
other countries**…

To be effective,
measures to **curb carbon
emissions** must be adopted
worldwide, even by those
who do not want to
adopt them.

**The biggest
challenge for
collective action
is climate change.**

The implications are as much
economic as environmental, but
both economists and governments
are divided on the measures that
should be taken. Until recently,
many have argued that the costs
of combating climate change are
more damaging to economic
prosperity than the potential
benefits. Some continue to dispute
the evidence that climate change
is human-made, while others argue
that global warming could even be
beneficial. A growing number now
accept that the issue is one that
must be addressed, and economic
solutions have to be found.

The economic facts
In 1982, US economist William
Nordhaus published *How Fast
Should We Graze the Global
Commons?*, looking in detail at
the economic impact of climate
change and possible solutions. He
pointed out that certain features of
the climate problem make it unique
in terms of finding economic
solutions: the long time scale,

the uncertainties involved, the
international scope of the problem,
and the uneven distribution of
benefits and costs across the globe.
    In 2006, the UK government
commissioned a report by British
economist Nicholas Stern on
the economics of climate change.
The Stern Review was unequivocal
in its findings; it presented sound
economic arguments in favor
of immediate action to reduce
greenhouse gas emissions. Stern
estimated that the eventual cost
of climate change could be as much
as 20 percent of GDP (gross
domestic product, or total national
income), compared with a cost of

around 1 percent of GDP to tackle
the problem if action was taken
promptly. In 2009, Nordhaus
estimated that without intervention,
economic damages from climate
change would be around 2.5
percent of world output per year by
2099. The highest damages would
be sustained by low-income
tropical regions, such as tropical
Africa and India.
    The question was no longer
whether we could afford to cut
emissions, but whether we could
afford not to, and how this could
best be achieved. There are
strong arguments for government
intervention: the atmosphere can »

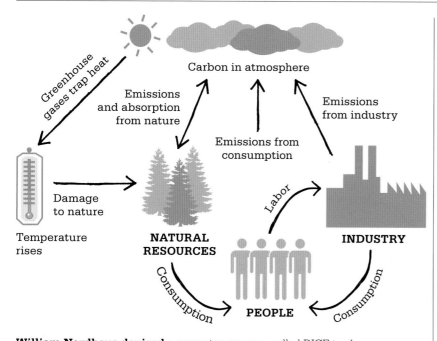

William Nordhaus devised a computer program called DICE to show how the elements of climate change interact, and where the ecological and financial costs lie. This financial modeling system allows governments to factor in their current consumption, resources, and needs, and weigh up the costs and benefits—to them and the Earth—of the choices available.

be considered in economic terms as a public good (pp.46–47), which tends to be undersupplied by markets; pollution can be seen as an externality (p.137), where the social costs of an action are not reflected in prices and so are not fully borne by the person taking it. For these reasons Stern described climate change as the greatest market failure ever experienced.

Unequal nations

The first hurdle for economists such as Nordhaus and Stern was to convince governments to introduce measures that would be harmful to their economies in the short run but would mitigate more damaging consequences in the long run. The second was to find the most efficient way of enforcing an emissions policy. Not all governments were easily persuaded. The more developed economies, which are mainly in temperate areas, are not likely to suffer the worst consequences of a rise in global temperatures. The likely changes in climate will hit poorer countries much harder. This means that, in many cases, the countries with the greatest incentive to mitigate the effects of climate change are those that are producing the least pollution.

The worst polluters, such as the US, Europe, and Australia, have been reluctant to accept that governments should impose expensive policies. Even if they did, the pollution is not restricted to their land masses. The problem is global and demands collective action on a global scale.

The need for collective action was first noted at a U.N. "Earth Summit" in 1992, which called for all its members to curb their emissions of greenhouse gases. Many governments have developed environmental policies and strategies for implementing those policies. Regulation in the form of punishments, such as fines for excessive production of pollutants, is one solution, but it is difficult to set emissions quotas that are fair to all businesses concerned. The fines are also difficult to enforce.

Another option, which was first suggested by British economist Arthur Pigou in 1920, is the imposition of taxes on pollution (p.137). Levying taxes on firms that emit greenhouse gases, and on energy suppliers and producers for the amount of carbon they release into the atmosphere, would act as a disincentive to pollute. Taxes on fossil fuels would discourage their excessive consumption. Pigou's idea is to make individuals face the full social costs of their actions, to "internalize" the externality.

Carbon-trading schemes

Pollution can be viewed as a market failure because normally there is no market for it. Economists suggest that if there was, the socially optimal

> Price-type approaches like harmonized taxes on carbon are powerful tools for coordinating policies and slowing global warming.
> **William Nordhaus**

Hurricane Katrina destroyed much of New Orleans in 2005. The cost of the damage, estimated at $81 billion, focused worldwide attention on the economic effects of climate change.

amount of pollution would be emitted because polluters would face the full costs of their actions. Therefore, another proposed solution to the climate problem is to create a market for pollution through emissions trading. This involves a government (or, in some cases, a number of governments working together) determining an acceptable level of, for example, CO_2 emissions, and then auctioning permits to firms whose business involves the discharge of carbon dioxide. The permits are tradable, so if a firm needs to increase its emissions, it can buy permits from another that has not used its quota. This kind of plan has the advantage of rewarding the firms who cut their emissions and can then sell their surplus permits. It can discourage firms from exceeding their quotas and having to buy extra permits. However, the total amount of emissions remains the same and is controlled by a central authority.

The Kyoto Protocol

While emissions trading programs are certainly a step in the right direction, the problem needs to

be tackled globally to avert the risk of climate change. However, international agreements such as the Kyoto Protocol have failed to achieve universal ratification. In 1997, 141 countries took part in discussions, but by 2012 only 37 countries had agreed to implement its targets for greenhouse gas emissions. The US has consistently rejected the terms of the agreement, and Canada pulled out in 2011. Even those countries that pledged to curb their emissions have often failed to meet their reduction targets. Developed countries such as the US and Australia argue that it would be too harmful to their economies; developing economies such as China, India, and Brazil argue that they should not have to pay for the pollution caused by the West (even though they themselves are fast becoming major polluters). On the other hand more eco-advanced nations, such as Germany and Denmark, agreed to reduction targets of more than 20 percent.

Economic modeling

Economists have devised various models for studying the economic impact of climate change, such as Nordhaus's Dynamic Integrated model of Climate and the Economy (DICE), first presented in 1992 (see opposite). This links together CO_2 emissions, the carbon cycles, climate change, climatic damages, and factors affecting growth.

Most economists now agree that climate change is a complex problem with the potential to cause serious long-term damage. The solution is far from obvious, but in 2007, Nordhaus said that he believed the secret to success lies not in large, ambitious projects, such as Kyoto, but in "universal, predictable, and boring" ideas, such as carbon taxes. ∎

India's growing needs

India's growth rate for 2012 was predicted to be 7–8 percent for the year. The country's business leaders are aware that if this rate of growth continues, there will be a huge energy shortage. The fear is that the shortfall will be met by the use of low-cost "dirty" coal and diesel fuel, so efforts are being made to increase efficiency while also encouraging the use of renewable energy products, using solar, wind, and geothermal technologies.

Economists hope that renewable energy forms, together with nuclear energy (judged to be a "clean" energy provider) can combine to meet all of India's growing needs. However, so far the renewable energy forms, such as solar, are not commercially viable industries on a large scale. This means that they will need a short-term boost from state subsidies to expand. This is provided for in India's ambitious National Action Plan on Climate Change, introduced in June, 2008.

Solar panels capture sunlight in the Himalayas in northern India. Solar power may be an efficient source of renewable energy in India, where sunshine is intense.

GDP IGNORES WOMEN
GENDER AND ECONOMICS

G ross domestic product (GDP) is the most commonly cited economic statistic. It provides a summary measure of the economic activity taking place within a country over a whole year—and appears to relate directly to important factors such as household incomes or the rate of employment. However, for all its prominence in economic debates, GDP is subject to considerable problems.

The problems and limits of GDP center on how it is calculated and what it includes. Measuring GDP relies on the collection of data relating to economic transactions. The principle behind it is that everything bought and sold in a year should be registered by GDP. Government statisticians conduct in-depth surveys to measure this figure. However, everything bought and sold in a nation is not exactly equivalent to all the economic activity that takes place. Nor does the eventual figure necessarily capture much of what people might value about a country. For example, an environmentalist would say that

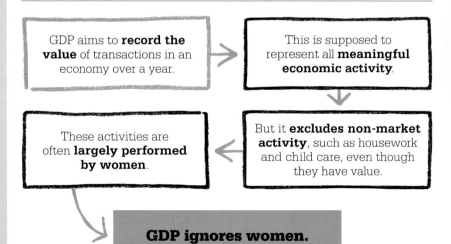

GDP aims to **record the value** of transactions in an economy over a year.

This is supposed to represent all **meaningful economic activity**.

But it **excludes non-market activity**, such as housework and child care, even though they have value.

These activities are often **largely performed by women**.

GDP ignores women.

See also: Measuring wealth 36–37 ▪ Economics and tradition 166–67 ▪
The economics of happiness 216–19 ▪ Social capital 280

Many kinds of work are performed mostly by women, including child care. They are vital to the economy but do not count toward GDP because they are not recorded in the paid economy.

GDP does not allow for the depletion of natural resources. Deforestation generally adds to GDP, assuming the lumber is sold. But a potentially irreplaceable natural resource is being consumed, and GDP gives no indication of this. Similarly, if an economic activity produces pollution, GDP would count only the products sold and ignore the undesirable side effects, such as loss of biodiversity or worsened public health.

Women's work

There are other difficulties with the figure arrived at in calculating GDP. In her influential 1988 book *If Women Counted*, Marilyn Waring, a one-time New Zealand politician, argued that GDP systematically underreports the work performed by women. Women account for a great bulk of the work performed in households across the world, as well as most child care and care for the elderly. This work is clearly economically necessary, because it helps to ensure the reproduction of the labor force, for example. But in the vast majority of cases it is not paid, and so does not enter into the calculation of GDP.

Excluding women

The accounting differences involved in calculating economic output can be highly arbitrary, treating essentially equivalent work very differently. Cooking is "economically active" when food is sold, but "economically inactive" when it is not. The only distinction here is the presence or absence of a market transaction, but the activity is identical. One will act to exclude women, while the other will not.

There is, then, a huge implicit gender bias in national accounts, and the true economic value of work performed by women is systematically underestimated in our conventional accounting systems. Waring went further to argue that the standard international system for calculating national income, the United Nations System of National Accounts (UNSNA), is an example of "applied patriarchy:" in other words an attempt by the male economy to exclude women in a way that acts to reinforce gender divisions globally.

Waring's criticisms, and those of other feminist economists, have helped to shape arguments over the future of national income accounting. Current debates on how to account for well-being and the development of broader social measures of economic progress indicate a growing desire to move beyond the constraints and limitations of GDP as a measure of worth. ▪

Marilyn Waring

One of New Zealand's first female members of Parliament, Marilyn Waring was born in 1952. She was promoted by the National Party Prime Minister Robert Muldoon to become chair of the Public Expenditure Committee in 1978. She later fell out with the government, threatening to vote in favor of an opposition motion banning nuclear weapons and nuclear power from New Zealand in 1984. Muldoon called a general election in response, which the National Party lost.

After Parliament Waring pursued her interests in farming and economics. In 2006, she became Professor of Public Policy at the Auckland University of Technology, where she has continued to research the measurement of areas excluded by conventional economics.

Key work

1988 *If Women Counted: A New Feminist Economics*

We women are visible and valuable to each other, and we must, now in our billions, proclaim that visibility and that worth.
Marilyn Waring

COMPARATIVE ADVANTAGE IS AN ACCIDENT
TRADE AND GEOGRAPHY

IN CONTEXT

FOCUS
Global economy

KEY THINKER
Paul Krugman (1953–)

BEFORE
1817 David Ricardo says that countries have comparative advantages due to physical factors.

1920s and 1930s Eli Heckscher and Bertil Ohlin argue that capital-abundant countries export capital-intensive goods.

1953 Wassily Leontief finds an empirical paradox: the US, a capital-abundant country, has relatively labor-intensive exports, in violation of existing trade theories.

AFTER
1994 Gene Grossman and Elhanan Helpman analyze the politics of trade policy, examining the effect of lobbying on the level of protection given to firms.

E conomists used to believe that nations traded with each other because they were different: tropical countries sold sugar to temperate countries, temperate ones exported wool. Some countries were better at producing certain things—they had a "comparative advantage" because of their weather or soil.

However, there is good reason to believe that this is not the whole story. In 1895, Catherine Evans from Dalton, Georgia, was visiting a friend and noticed a homemade bedspread. Inspired, she made a similar one and began to teach others. Soon, textile firms sprung up, creating a carpet industry that came to dominate the market. This contradicted the usual explanation of international trade, since Georgia has no comparative advantage for making carpet.

Quirk of history
In 1979, US economist Paul Krugman proposed a new theory that allowed for the influence of accidents of history, such as an

Regions that for historical reason have a head start as centers of production will attract even more producers.
Paul Krugman

industry arising from a chance event in Georgia. He observed that a lot of trade goes on between similar economies. Production has economies of scale: the initial outlay for a car plant means that costs are lower the more cars are made. Either country could make cars, but once one starts, it builds up a cost advantage that is hard for the other to erode. So a region may end up dominating trade in a good due purely to quirks of history. ∎

See also: Protectionism and trade 34–35 ▪ Comparative advantage 80–85 ▪ Economies of scale 132 ▪ Market integration 226–31

LIKE STEAM, COMPUTERS HAVE REVOLUTIONIZED ECONOMIES
TECHNOLOGICAL LEAPS

Economic growth is powered by innovation and invention. Some innovations are incremental, while others are revolutionary. A better drill may be one of many small innovations by which economies gradually become more productive. The discovery of electricity, however, was truly revolutionary, and over the last two centuries it has transformed economies, enabling the use of new types of machines. Recently, economists have started to think about these leaps. US economists Timothy Bresnahan and Manuel Trajtenberg call electricity a "general purpose technology." A better drill helps builders; electricity makes all firms more productive. However, the positive effects of such revolutionary advances can take time to be felt.

Exploiting new technology
In the late 1980s US economist Robert Solow (p.225) thought that he had found a paradox: the proliferation of information and communication technology (ICT) didn't seem to have had an obvious impact on productivity. During the Industrial Revolution the spread of steam power was surprisingly slow: it took time for it to become cost-effective and for firms to reorganize in order to use it. ICT has taken hold more quickly, but it has still taken time to spread. Solow's paradox is resolved by the fact that the full benefits of general purpose technologies take time to arrive. ■

By the 1980s computers had revolutionized the way that many of us work. However, it can take years for such fundamental changes to be reflected in increased productivity.

See also: The emergence of modern economies 178–79 ▪ Institutions in economics 206–07 ▪ Economic growth theories 224–25

WE CAN KICK-START POOR ECONOMIES BY WRITING OFF DEBT
INTERNATIONAL DEBT RELIEF

IN CONTEXT

FOCUS
Growth and development

KEY THINKER
Jeffrey Sachs (1954–)

BEFORE
1956 The Paris Club, a grouping of creditor nations, was established to facilitate debt relief between individual countries.

AFTER
1996 The IMF and World Bank launch the Heavily Indebted Poor Countries (HIPC) initiative to give debt relief and initiate policy reform in poor countries.

2002 Seema Jayachandran and Michael Kremer argue that countries may not be legally liable for "odious" debts incurred by corrupt regimes.

2005 G8 countries agree to write off $40 billion of debt under the Multilateral Debt Relief Initiative (MDRI) as part of the Gleneagles summit.

Debt in poor countries has grown so large that they **cannot afford** to service the debt and invest in growth.

→

Many of the loans were made by rich countries to **corrupt governments**.

↓

Canceling the loans will enable poor countries to invest in growth.

←

The loans should **not have been made** in the first place.

↓

We can kick-start poor economies by writing off debt.

In the last few decades of the 20th century the world's poorest countries piled up a staggering amount of debt, which grew from $25 billion in 1970 to $523 billion in 2002.

By the 1990s it was clear that there was a debt crisis. No heavily indebted African nation had ever prospered. Indeed, most were in such dire economic straits that they could not even service their debts without terrible suffering, let alone make the investments needed to climb out of the vicious cycle of economic decline. Campaigns for debt cancellation intensified.

Many campaigners took a moral stance, criticizing the negligent or self-interested role of the rich countries and institutions such as the World Bank and International Monetary Fund (IMF), which had made many of the loans. Campaigners argued that since

See also: International trade and Bretton Woods 186–87 ▪ Development economics 188–93 ▪ Dependency theory 242–43 ▪ Asian Tiger economies 282–87 ▪ Speculation and currency devaluation 288–93

> Shall we let the children of Africa and Asia die of curable disease, prevent them from going to school, and limit their opportunities for meaningful work—all to pay off unjust and illegitimate loans made to their forefathers?
> **Desmond Tutu**
> **South African archbishop (1931–)**

rich countries had made these loans either to buy support in the Cold War or to secure contracts for their own companies, they had an obligation to lift the debt. US economist Michael Kremer took a legal line. He said that since many debts were incurred by corrupt regimes to feather their own nests, they could be considered "odious." This would mean that countries have no legal obligation to repay them. The World Bank, for instance, continued to lend to former dictator Mobutu Sese Seko in Zaire (now the Democratic Republic of Congo), even after an IMF representative pointed out that he was stealing the money. Many of South Africa's debts were borrowed by the apartheid regime, considered by many not to have been a legitimate government.

Others, such as Jeffrey Sachs, gave an economic argument. Sachs argued that canceling debt and increasing aid could kick-start growth in poor countries. Such was the appeal of these arguments that the G8 countries (the eight largest economies in the world) agreed to write off over $40 billion in 2005. Another American, William Easterly, argues that debt relief rewards poor policies and corruption by recipient countries. Many criticize the free market reform programs that are made a condition for relief, which may damage the economic prospects of the countries receiving the relief.

Interestingly, the debt crisis has now shifted from the less developed world to the once-flourishing countries of Europe. Here, similar free market austerity measures are being pushed through—but, crucially, without the debts being canceled. ∎

In South Africa, high debts were incurred by the apartheid regime. Many argue that the debts from the apartheid era should be canceled since the government was not legitimate.

Jeffrey Sachs

One of the world's most controversial economists, Jeffrey Sachs was born in Detroit, Michigan, in 1954. He first came into the public eye in 1985 with a plan to help Bolivia deal with hyperinflation. The plan came to be called "shock therapy" and centered on making the country easily accessible to foreign business. This meant opening up the Bolivian market, ending government subsidies, eliminating import quotas, and linking the Bolivian currency to the US dollar. Inflation was indeed brought under control, and Sachs became known as a global economic troubleshooter. He was on hand in 1990 to shift Poland out of communism with breakneck privatization and did the same in Russia in the early 1990s. In the 2000s Sachs turned his attention to global development issues, arguing that, with the right interventions—including aid and microloans—extreme poverty could be eradicated in 20 years.

Key work

2005 *The End of Poverty*

PESSIMISM CAN DESTROY HEALTHY BANKS

BANK RUNS

IN CONTEXT

FOCUS
Banking and finance

KEY THINKERS
Douglas Diamond (1953–)
Philip Dybvig (1955–)

BEFORE
1930–33 One third of all US banks fail, leading to the creation of the Federal Deposit Insurance Corporation (FDIC) to insure depositors' money.

1978 US economic historian Charles Kindleberger publishes a landmark study of bank runs, *Manias, Panics, and Crashes: A History of Financial Crises*.

AFTER
1987–89 At the peak of the decade-long US savings and loan crisis, US bank failures rise to a level of 200 per year.

2007–09 Thirteen countries across the world experience systemic banking crises.

uring the Great Depression of the early 1930s some 9,000 US banks failed—a third of the total. However, it was not until the 1980s that economic theory came to grips with basic questions such as why banks exist, and what causes a bank run— where depositors panic and rush to withdraw their money from banks they think are at risk of failing. The article that started the debate was *Bank Runs, Deposit Insurance, and Liquidity*, written in 1983 by US economists Douglas Diamond and Philip Dybvig. They showed that even healthy banks can suffer from a bank run and go bust.

Liquid investments
Diamond and Dybvig made a mathematical model of an economy to demonstrate how bank runs occur. Their model has three points in time—such as Monday, Tuesday, and Wednesday—and assumes that there is only one good or product available to people, which they can consume or invest.

Each person starts off with a certain amount of the good. On Monday people can do two

If any bank fails, a general run upon the neighbouring banks is apt to take place, which if not checked in the beginning by a pouring into the circulation of a very large quantity of gold, leads to extensive mischief.
Henry Thornton
UK economist (1760–1815)

things with their good: they can store it, in which case they get back the same amount on Tuesday to consume; or they can invest it. If they choose to invest the good, which is only possible on Monday, they will receive much more of it back on Wednesday. However, if they cash in the investment early on Tuesday, they will receive

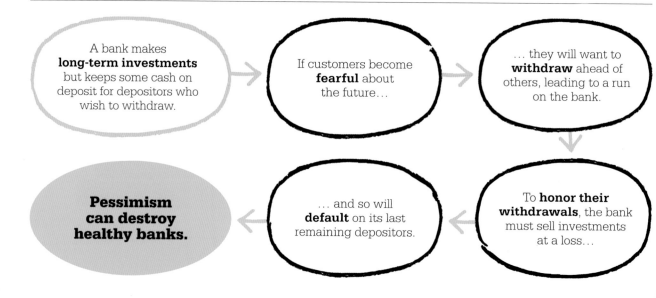

A bank makes **long-term investments** but keeps some cash on deposit for depositors who wish to withdraw.

If customers become **fearful** about the future…

… they will want to **withdraw** ahead of others, leading to a run on the bank.

To **honor their withdrawals**, the bank must sell investments at a loss…

… and so will **default** on its last remaining depositors.

Pessimism can destroy healthy banks.

Bank

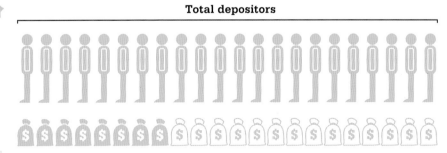

Banks only keep a relatively small percentage of their deposits in cash reserves. If all a bank's depositors turn up to demand their money back on the same day, only those at the front of the line will receive their money.

Total depositors

Total amount on deposit

Amount held in cash deposit

less than they invested. These investments, which are made for a set period, are what is known as "illiquid" investments. This means that they cannot easily be transformed into ready cash, as liquid assets can.

Patient and impatient

Diamond and Dybvig assume there are two types of people: patient people, who want to wait until Wednesday, when they can consume more, and impatient people, who want to consume on Tuesday. However, people do not discover which type of person they are until Tuesday. The decision that people face on Monday is how much to store and how much to invest. The only uncertainty in the model is whether these people are patient or impatient. Banks might have a good idea about probabilities: in general, 30 percent of people might prove to be impatient and 70 percent patient. So it is possible that people will store and invest amounts that

reflect these proportions. But whatever people choose, it will never be the most efficient outcome overall because impatient people should never invest, and patient people should not store anything. A bank can solve this problem. We can think of a bank in this model as a place where people all agree to pool their goods and share risks. The bank gives people a deposit contract and then itself invests and stores the goods in bulk.

The deposit contract offers a higher return than storage and a lower return than investment, and allows people to withdraw their goods from the bank on either Tuesday or Wednesday with no penalty. Having pooled people's goods, the bank, knowing the share of patient and impatient people, can then store enough of the good to cover the needs of impatient people and invest enough to cover the wants of patient people. In the Diamond–Dybvig model this is a more efficient solution than people could reach independently

because with large numbers, the bank can do this in a way that the individual cannot.

On Tuesday the bank has illiquid assets—the patient people's investment that will reap a return on Wednesday. At the same time it has to pay the impatient people their deposits right away. Its ability to do this is the reason for its existence. »

> A bank run in our model is caused by a shift in expectations, which could depend on almost anything.
> **Douglas Diamond Philip Dybvig**

A panicking crowd is held back by police outside a German bank in 1914. The declaration of war had caused pessimism among savers, leading to a number of bank runs.

Diamond and Dybvig showed that this property also makes the bank vulnerable to a run. A run occurs when, on Tuesday, patient people become pessimistic about what they will receive from the bank on Wednesday, and so withdraw their deposits on Tuesday. Their actions mean that the bank must sell investments at a loss; it will not have the resources to pay all of its patient and impatient customers, and those later in the line will not receive anything. Knowing this, customers become eager to be at the front of the line.

Pessimism can arise out of concerns about investments, other people's withdrawals, or the bank's survival. Crucially, this allows for the possibility of a self-fulfilling bank run even if the bank is sound. For instance, suppose that on Tuesday I believe that other people are going to withdraw their deposits—I then decide to do so as well because I fear that the bank may fail. Then suppose that many other people think in the same way that I have. This itself can cause a run on the bank, even if the bank would otherwise be able to meet its obligations today and tomorrow. This is an example of what economists call "multiple equilibrims"—more than one outcome. Here there are two outcomes: a "good" one in which the bank survives and a "bad" one in which it is sunk by a run. Where we end up may depend on the people's beliefs and expectations rather than the true health of the bank.

Preventing bank runs

Diamond and Dybvig showed how governments could alleviate the problem of bank runs. Their model was partly a defense of the US's system of federal deposit insurance, under which the state guarantees the value of all bank deposits up to a specified amount. Introduced in 1933, this system reduced bank failures. In March, 1933, President Franklin D. Roosevelt also declared

A modern bank run

In September, 2007, the first serious British bank run since 1866 took place. Northern Rock, Britain's eighth-largest bank, was a fast-growing mortgage lender. To expand its business, it had become over-reliant on "wholesale" funding—funding provided by other institutions—rather than personal deposits. When wholesale financial markets froze on August 9, 2007, a gradual, unseen wholesale run began. At 8:30 p.m. on Thursday, September 13, BBC Television News reported that the UK central bank, the Bank of England, would announce emergency liquidity support the next day.

It emerged later that Mervyn King, the Governor of the Bank of England, had opposed a rescue offer by Lloyds, another British bank. King had suggested that central bank support might reassure depositors. However, this reassurance did not happen, and a run on personal deposits began over the internet that evening. Under Britain's deposit insurance program, deposits above $3,300 (£2,000) were not fully insured, and the next day, long lines formed outside Northern Rock branches. The run ended the following Monday evening after the government announced a guarantee for all deposits.

> By the afternoon of March 3, scarcely a bank in the country was open to do business.
> **Franklin D. Roosevelt**

In 1933, President Roosevelt signed an act that guaranteed bank deposits. Bank runs were reduced, but some believe that such deposit guarantees increase risk taking.

a national bank holiday to prevent people from withdrawing their savings. Alternatively, the central bank can act as the "lender of last resort" to banks. However, there is often uncertainty about what the central bank will do. Deposit insurance is ideal, because it ensures that patient people will not participate in a bank run.

Alternative views

There are alternative explanations for the existence of banks. Some focus on banks' investment role. The bank can gather and keep private information about investments, choosing between good and bad investments, and reflect this private information efficiently through the returns it offers to savers. It can offer a return to depositors that is only possible if it carries out its monitoring role well.

In 1991, US economists Charles Calomiris and Charles Kahn published an article that took issue with the Diamond–Dybvig view. They argued that bank runs are good for banks. In the absence of deposit insurance, depositors have an incentive to keep a close eye on how well their bank performs. The

threat of a run also provides an incentive to the bank to make safe investments. This is one side of so-called "moral hazard" (pp.208–09). The other side is that managers will take riskier decisions than they would if there were no deposit insurance. The problem of moral hazard became apparent in the 1980s US savings and loan crisis, when mortgage lenders were allowed to make riskier loans and deposit insurance was enhanced. US bank failures rose.

Recent crises

It is hard to prove which of these two views about bank runs is correct, since in practice neither explanation can be isolated. There are many forms of moral hazard in a bank. A shareholder may encourage risk taking because all he can lose is his investment. A bank employee, offered bonus incentives, may take risks because all that is at stake is a job. One commonly proposed solution to moral hazard is tougher regulation.

Recent bank crises have usually begun with investment losses. Banks are forced to sell assets to reduce their borrowing. This leads to further falls in asset prices and further losses. A run on deposits follows, which can spread to other banks to become a panic. If the whole banking system is affected, it is called a systemic banking crisis. In the 2007–08 crisis, runs occurred despite the system of deposit insurance. A large part of the recent crisis took place institutions that are not regulated as banks, such as hedge funds, but were doing much the same as a bank: borrowing for short terms and lending for long terms.

Many countries strengthened their deposit insurance policies during the financial crisis that began in 2007–08. This is understandable, since bank failures can have a devastating effect on the real economy, breaking the connection between people with savings and people who need to invest. The moral hazard argument is like fire prevention, in that it is concerned with protecting the economy from a future crisis. However, the midst of a crisis may not be the time to be talking about preventative actions. ∎

> In the history of modern capitalism, crises are the norm, not the exception.
> **Nouriel Roubini
> Stephen Mihm**

SAVINGS GLUTS ABROAD FUEL SPECULATION AT HOME
GLOBAL SAVINGS IMBALANCES

IN CONTEXT

FOCUS
Global economy

KEY THINKER
Ben Bernanke (1953–)

BEFORE
2000 US economists Maurice Obstfeld and Kenneth Rogoff raise concerns about the large US trade deficit.

2008 British historian Niall Ferguson describes a world of crisis because of overuse of credit.

AFTER
2009 US economist John B. Taylor argues against the existence of a savings glut.

2011 Economists Claudio Borio of Italy and Piti Disyatat of Thailand argue that it is wrong to think that global imbalances in savings triggered the financial crisis.

I n February, 2012, 111 million Americans watched the Superbowl on television. At halftime an advertisement for Chrysler cars was shown. It was to become a national talking point. "It's halftime in America, too," said the ad. "People are out of work and they're hurting… Detroit's showing us it can be done. This country can't be knocked down with one punch."

The unashamedly patriotic implication of the ad—to buy Chrysler because it would save American jobs—was in tune with the feeling among many Americans that the US had let economic power slip into foreign, especially

See also: Financial services 26–29 ▪ Economic bubbles 98–99 ▪ Market integration 226–31 ▪
Financial engineering 262–65 ▪ Financial crises 296–301 ▪ Housing and the economic cycle 330–31

Since the closure of plants such as this Chrysler factory in Detroit, the US has been running trade deficits, meaning that it has been importing more than it has been exporting.

Chinese, hands. It was this type of feeling that made the explanations of the 2008 global financial crisis offered by US Federal Reserve chairman Ben Bernanke so widely appealing. He had developed his argument from 2005 onward, before the crisis really hit, and his thesis focused on global imbalances in savings and spending.

Central to Bernanke's idea is America's balance of payments (BOP). A country's BOP is the account of all money transactions between that country and the rest of the world. If a country imports more than it exports, its trade balance is in deficit, but the books must still balance. The shortfall is made up in some other way—for

example, by funds from foreign investments or by running down central bank reserves. Bernanke pointed out that the US deficit rose sharply in the late 1990s, reaching $640 billion, or 5.5 percent of GDP, in 2004. Domestic investment remained fairly steady at this time, but domestic saving dropped from 16.5 percent of GDP to 14 percent between 1996 and 2004. If domestic savings fell yet investment remained steady, the deficit can only have been financed using foreign money.

The savings glut
Bernanke argued that the deficit was being funded by a "global savings glut"—an accumulation of savings in countries other than the US. For instance the Chinese, who have a huge positive trade surplus with the US, were neither putting all their American export earnings into investment at home

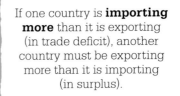

If one country is **importing more** than it is exporting (in trade deficit), another country must be exporting more than it is importing (in surplus).

The country in deficit must fund its imbalance, while the country in surplus can build up a **savings glut**.

The savings in the country in surplus are **borrowed in the country in deficit**, and this can fuel financial speculation.

Savings gluts abroad fuel speculation at home.

nor buying things; they were simply squirreling it away in savings and currency reserves. Bernanke highlights a number of reasons for the global savings glut besides Chinese frugality, including the rising oil prices and the building up of "war-chests" to guard against future financial shocks. »

Saving seems, at first sight, a prudent thing to do, a safeguarding of the future. However, savings in the global capitalist world is a mixed blessing. Any money that goes into savings is money lost to direct investment or consumer spending, but it doesn't just vanish. Bernanke's argument is that money from the savings glut overseas ended up flooding the financial markets of the US.

An abundance of money
All this money damped down interest rates and reduced the incentive for Americans and Europeans to save. With loan markets apparently awash with easy money, lenders bent over backward to offer deals. To meet the demand for outlets for the foreign cash, America's financial engineers came up with products such as collateralized debt obligations (CDOs), which packaged high-risk mortgages with lower-risk debts to make bonds that were given AAA credit ratings, meaning that they were rated very low-risk. Meanwhile, house prices boomed in two dozen countries, as even

In the longer term the industrial countries as a group should be running current account surpluses and lending… to the developing world, not the other way around.
Ben Bernanke

In the 1990s a new financial instrument called a collateralized debt obligation (CDO) was invented. High-risk mortgages were combined with low-risk bonds to create the illusion of low-risk debt. These debt obligations were central to the failure of the credit system in 2007–08.

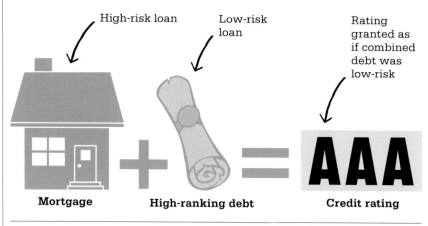

High-risk loan   Low-risk loan   Rating granted as if combined debt was low-risk

Mortgage   High-ranking debt   Credit rating

those on lower incomes were able to find a foot on the property ladder. Some of the mortgages granted to fund this boom—the so-called "subprime" mortgages in the US—were given to people who could not pay them back.

The crisis
In 2008, a cluster of subprime mortgage failures exposed how massively many financial institutions had invested many times more than the value of their capital. The Lehman Brothers investment bank collapsed in 2008, and many other financial institutions seemed in such great danger of going into meltdown that they had to be rescued by government bailout packages in most of the world's rich countries.

The simple thrust of Bernanke's message seemed to be that the financial crisis all came down to Chinese saving and American overspending. This was also the message in Niall Ferguson's *Ascent of Money* (2008), in which he analyzed the credit crunch and focused on the fated "Chimerica" —the symbiotic (or, as some saw it,

parasitic) link between China and the US. The notion appealed to many in American financial circles since it seemed to imply that it was the frugal Chinese who were to blame for the financial crisis.

Bernanke is adamant that it was Chinese cash that stoked American fires, though he argues that only a small portion went into high-risk assets. In 2011, he said, "China's current account surpluses were used almost wholly to acquire assets in the United States, more than 80 percent of which consisted of very safe Treasuries and Agencies."

The vanishing glut
Many economists have challenged Bernanke's theory. In the financial blog "Naked Capitalism," Yves Smith has suggested that the global savings glut is a myth, noting that global savings have stayed almost rock steady since the mid-1980s. US economist John B. Taylor argues that although there was increased saving outside the US, the decline in saving within the US meant that there was no global gap between

> I don't think
> that Chinese ownership
> of US assets is so
> large as to put our
> country at risk
> economically.
> **Ben Bernanke**

saving and investment—so the idea of a world awash with cheap cash is false.

Other economists point out that the current account deficits in the US and other countries amounted to much less than 2 percent of the money flow, so surely would have only a marginal affect. The savings glut theory also becomes harder to sustain when applied to Europe. Germany, for instance, in the years leading up to the 2008 crisis, was savings-rich. The savings glut theory would imply that German savers took up speculative financial arrangements in Ireland and Spain rather than put their money in institutions at home in Germany, which seems highly unlikely.

A "banking glut"?

Princeton University economics professor Hyun Song Shin has argued that the floods of speculative money chasing after mortgage securities came not from a savings glut but the "shadow" banking system—the complex variety of financial entities that fall outside the normal banking system, including hedge funds, money markets, and structured investment vehicles. European and American shadow banks were eager to find these securities and found them in Ireland and Spain as well as the US.

The markets played in by these shadow banks are dominated by derivatives. These are "financial instruments"—bets upon bets as to which way markets will go, underpinned by ingenious mathematical formulas. The charge here is that derivatives trading can encourage excessive risk-taking. It also creates a market in which financial institutions can make massive profits by betting on failures, including the failure of mortgage-backed securities.

The extra reserves of a savings glut might be irrelevant in this virtual casino. Indeed, the problem seems to have been that the banks were trading without sufficient cash backup. Bernanke points out that while Chinese and Middle Eastern buyers bought into American securities with funds from trade surpluses and oil exports, the European banks had to borrow money to buy in, leaving them exposed when the crisis hit.

Economists differ in their views about the trade imbalances that underlie the savings glut. Some have argued that the US trade deficit can be sustained, and that it would always be funded easily by foreign savings. Others worry about a hard landing for the US economy if capital flows were to dry up. Much of this has become a political issue between the US and China since US politicians have charged China with keeping its currency unfairly low in order to support its trade surplus. ∎

Ben Bernanke

Ben Shalom Bernanke was born and raised in South Carolina. In the early 1970s Bernanke went to Harvard University and then to the Massachusetts Institute of Technology, where he received a PhD in economics under the supervision of Stanley Fischer, future governor of the Bank of Israel.

Bernanke joined the US Federal Reserve in 2002. In 2004, he proposed the idea of the Great Moderation, which suggested that modern monetary policies had virtually eliminated the volatility of the business cycle. In 2006, Bernanke was made chairman of the Federal Reserve. His tenure as chairman of the Reserve has not been smooth, and he has been criticized for failing to foresee the financial crisis and for bailing out Wall Street financial institutions.

Key works

2002 *Deflation: Making Sure It Doesn't Happen Here*
2005 *The Global Saving Glut and the US Current Account Deficit*
2007 *Global Imbalances*

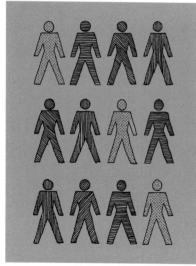

MORE EQUAL SOCIETIES GROW FASTER
INEQUALITY AND GROWTH

IN CONTEXT

FOCUS
Growth and development

KEY THINKERS
Alberto Alesina (1957–)
Dani Rodrik (1957–)

BEFORE
1955 US economist
Simon Kuznets publishes
*Economic Growth and Income
Inequality*, which concludes
that inequality is a side effect
of growth.

1989 US economists Kevin
Murphy, Andrei Shleifer, and
Robert Vishny claim income
distribution affects demand.

AFTER
1996 Italian economist
Roberto Perrotti claims that
there is no link between lower
taxes and higher growth.

2007 Spanish economist
Xavier Sala-i-Martin argues
that growing economies have
reduced inequality.

Wealth is divided **inequitably** through society.

⬇

Those without accumulated capital become **dissatisfied**...

⬇

... and call for more **redistributive policies** from the government.

⬇

But redistribution is paid for through **higher taxes** on accumulated capital...

⬇

... and higher taxes **slow economic growth**.

⬇

More equal societies grow faster.

For much of the 20th century economists asked themselves how economic growth affects people's incomes. Does growth increase or decrease income inequality? In 1994, Italian economist Alberto Alesina and Turkish economist Dani Rodrik turned the question on its head. They wondered how income distribution affects economic growth.

Alesina and Rodrik examined two factors in their model: labor and capital (accumulated wealth). They argued that economic growth is fueled by growth in total capital, but government services are funded by a tax on capital. This means the higher the taxes on accumulated wealth, the less incentive there will be to accumulate capital, and the lower the growth rate of the economy will be.

Those whose income derives mostly from accumulated capital prefer a lower tax rate. On the other hand an individual who has no accumulated wealth, and whose income derives entirely from his labor, tends to prefer a higher tax rate. This will provide him with public services and allows for a better redistribution of accumulated wealth.

See also: The tax burden 64–65 ▪ The emergence of modern economies 178–79 ▪ Social choice theory 214–15 ▪
Economic growth theories 224–25 ▪ Taxation and economic incentives 270–71

> The greater the
> inequality of wealth
> and income, the higher the
> rate of taxation, and
> the lower growth.
> **Alberto Alesina
> Dani Rodrik**

The tax rate is set by governments, which react to popular concerns. Even a dictatorship cannot ignore the popular will, due to the fear of being overthrown. For this reason the tax rate is set with the aim of pleasing as many people as possible—that is, the rate preferred by the median voter (the person at the exact middle of the spectrum of voters' views). According to Alesina and Rodrik's logic,

if the distribution of capital and accumulated wealth is shared equally through society, the median voter will be relatively rich in capital and will therefore demand a modest tax rate, which will not impede growth. If, however, there are large inequalities in wealth, with much of the accumulated capital being concentrated in a small elite, the majority will be poor and will demand a higher tax rate, which would stifle growth. Alesina and Rodrik argue that the more economic equality there is in any society, the higher the growth rate of its economy will be.

Growth and equality

Alesina and Rodrik's explanation is not the whole story. Some people think that the two economists have misidentified cause and effect. Spanish economist Xavier Sala-i-Martin (1962–), for instance, claims that economic growth has fueled a diminishing rate of income inequality across the globe. The World Bank has argued that the reduction of poverty

worldwide—which can help to lessen inequality—is due mainly to economic growth. On the other hand slower-developing countries, such as many in Africa, have suffered from decades of little or no growth. This has hurt living standards and impeded poverty reduction; the poorest lag behind, and inequality persists. ∎

Nordic countries such as Sweden seem to contradict Alesina and Rodrik's conclusions. They combine high tax with high living standards and the world's smallest equality gap.

Alberto Alesina

Alberto Alesina was born in 1957, in the northern Italian town of Broni. He studied economics and society at Boccini University in Milan, graduating with distinction in 1981. He went on to complete his M.A. and PhD in the economics department at Harvard. After completing his studies in 1986, he became a full professor at Harvard in 1993 and was chairman of the economics department from 2003 to 2006.

Alesina has published five books. His work straddles politics and economics and focuses especially on the economic and political systems of the US and Europe. He has achieved wide recognition for drawing attention to the influence of politics over economic matters.

Key works

1994 *Distributive Politics and Economic Growth* (with Dani Rodrik)
2003 *The Size of Nations* (with Enrico Spolaore)
2004 *Fighting Poverty in the US and Europe: A World of Difference* (with Edward Glaeser)

EVEN BENEFICIAL ECONOMIC REFORMS CAN FAIL

RESISTING ECONOMIC CHANGE

IN CONTEXT

FOCUS
Economic policy

KEY THINKERS
Dani Rodrik (1957–)
Daron Acemoğlu (1967–)

BEFORE
1989 British economist John Williamson uses the term "Washington Consensus" for the first time (see box, opposite).

2000 South African economist Nicolas van de Walle documents the failure of IMF-backed "structural adjustment" reforms in Africa.

AFTER
2009 US economists Douglass North, John Wallis, and Barry Weingast propose a new approach to reform based on societies' responses to the problem of violence.

2011 Reform packages in Europe following the 2008 financial crisis run into opposition.

Reform is designed to kick-start an economy and benefit a whole population through the transformation of institutions. One might think that reforms that benefit the economy would be welcomed and carried through. However, sometimes there is substantial resistance to reform, even from those who might eventually benefit. In order to "fix" an economy and return it to growth, it is necessary to remove the inefficiencies within the economic system. This can be difficult if the country is run by an unaccountable political class for its own benefit, as is often the case in the developing world.

Reform and influence
Turkish economists Dani Rodrik and Daron Acemoğlu have pointed out that when powerful groups

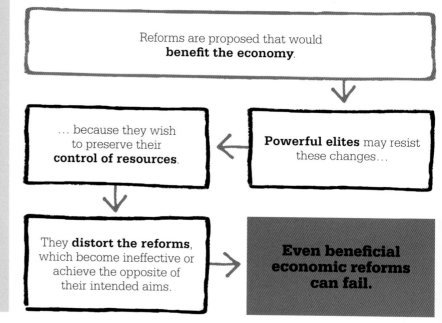

Reforms are proposed that would **benefit the economy**.

Powerful elites may resist these changes…

… because they wish to preserve their **control of resources**.

They **distort the reforms**, which become ineffective or achieve the opposite of their intended aims.

Even beneficial economic reforms can fail.

> Policies that work do become popular, but the time lag can be long enough for the relationship not to be exploitable by… reformers.
> **Dani Rodrik**

expect to see their privilege disappear as a result of economic reform, they may use their influence to introduce economic policies that redistribute income or power to themselves. Alternatively, they may distort policies so that measures are not implemented effectively. Acemoğlu has argued that this often happens when political elites are highly unaccountable, so there are limited checks and balances on their actions. Reforms typically fail in these cases because they tend not to address these deeper political constraints. However, in countries with highly accountable leaders, the benefits of reforms may already have been reaped. For these reasons reforms are most effective in "intermediate countries," where reforms are likely to have significant and positive results, and at the same time the political elites are not dominant enough to derail them.

Winners and losers

However, there are also problems when introducing reform into intermediate societies. When economic reform is proposed, it is often not clear who the winners and losers of the reform will be. This discourages people from accepting the measures, even where there would ultimately be more winners than losers. There may be a bias toward maintaining the status quo; individuals like to protect what they already have and minimize the risk of losing out. If a beneficial economic reform is

Sani Abacha seized power in Nigeria in 1994. His corrupt dictatorship was above the jurisdiction of the courts, which allowed his family to appropriate more than $2.2 billion from state funds.

proposed but shelved due to lack of popular support, politicians and economists may later propose it again in the belief that it will benefit the economy and society. However, without new, supportive information a society may well reject the measure again. On the other hand if beneficial reform is implemented despite a lack of popular support and goes on to create more winners than losers, it often goes on to gain popular support and is not repealed.

Most attempts at reform focus on measures designed to change "formal" institutions such as courts and voting systems. Their success depends on whether underlying "informal" institutions and surrounding politics support them. Without this, reforms of laws and constitutions are unlikely to change much. ▪

The Washington Consensus

The term Washington Consensus was first coined in 1989 by British economist John Williamson to refer to the package of free market economic reforms prescribed to developing countries in crisis during the 1980s.

These policies aimed to move the state-run economies of Latin America and post-socialist Eastern Europe toward the privatized free market. They focused on privatization of state enterprises, liberalization of domestic and international trade, the introduction of competitive exchange rates, and balanced fiscal (tax) policies.

The Washington Consensus was discredited in the 1990s. Reforms were said to have been implemented with little sensitivity to the differing political constraints evident in such a diverse group of countries. In Africa, in particular, dynamic markets raise the poorest out of poverty.

THE HOUSING MARKET MIRRORS BOOM AND BUST
HOUSING AND THE ECONOMIC CYCLE

IN CONTEXT

FOCUS
The macroeconomy

KEY THINKER
Charles Goodheart (1936–)

BEFORE
1965 US economist Sherman Maisel is the first to explore the effects of residential investment on the economy.

2003 US economists Morris Davis and Jonathan Heathcote conclude that housing prices are related to the overall state of the economy.

AFTER
2007 US economist Edward Leamer argues that housing construction trends are an early warning of recession.

2010 US mortgage-lenders Fannie Mae and Freddie Mac are delisted on the New York Stock Exchange after lowering underwriting standards during the subprime crisis (offering mortgages to those unable to repay).

Movements in the housing market are a reflection of "boom and bust" cycles in the wider economy. These are the periods where an economy's real output reaches its highest and lowest levels during the business cycle, which moves through periods of contraction and expansion, usually over periods of between three and seven years.

There are many reasons why residential investment is high in periods of economic growth. There are more jobs available, and a booming economy leads a greater number of people to think about buying their own home. At the same time mortgage lenders begin to relax their lending requirements, making buying easier, so more houses are sold. As this happens, the rising demand means that house prices rise. Those who sell are able to pay off large mortgages in full. House builders continue to invest in further housing stock to profit from the higher prices.

House prices are often relatively resilient, meaning that they do not change quickly in response to factors that could influence them. This is one of the reasons housing is seen as such a good investment,

A new housing development expands across farmland in the state of Washington during the boom period of the early 2000s. Building was fueled by lax mortgage-lending standards.

and rather than prices adjusting downward, they can remain stable even when the volume of sales falls.

Signs of a recession
Although house prices are usually resilient, they have been known to stagnate; the accompanying decline in residential investment is often the first indicator that a recession is about to occur. In more developed countries the housing market has begun to decline before each major recession of the last 50 years. The housing market recovers only when consumers are confident

See also: Boom and bust 78–79 ▪ Economic bubbles 98–99 ▪ Supply and demand 108–13 ▪ Testing economic theories 170 ▪ Financial crises 296–301

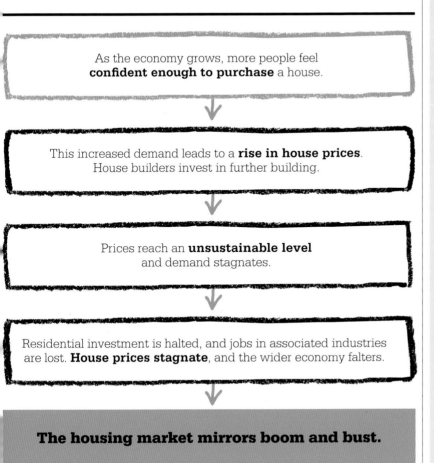

As the economy grows, more people feel **confident enough to purchase** a house.

⬇

This increased demand leads to a **rise in house prices**. House builders invest in further building.

⬇

Prices reach an **unsustainable level** and demand stagnates.

⬇

Residential investment is halted, and jobs in associated industries are lost. **House prices stagnate**, and the wider economy falters.

⬇

The housing market mirrors boom and bust.

that the value of their houses will rise. This confidence rises in step with an improving economy. As residential sales begin to return to a normal level, residential investment increases, providing jobs and further fueling a return to economic growth.

Economists have analyzed the relationship between the housing market and the overall economy and believe that by studying the levels of investment in housing, it is possible to accurately forecast recessions and recoveries. In their 2006 book *Housing Prices and the Macroeconomy*, British economists Charles Goodheart

and Boris Hofmann showed that there is a correlation between economic performance and housing prices. They claim that by following appropriate policies in the future, it should be possible to strongly mitigate, or even avoid, the worst effects of a recession.

Unfortunately, this was not the case with the housing "bubble" that burst in the US in 2008. Here, rapid financial innovations created instability in mortgage financing that led to unwarranted consumer confidence and an unsustainable boom. The housing market was the cause of the eventual bust. ■

Irresponsible lending in the housing market

The economic crash of 2008 owed much to the liberalization of the mortgage market and irresponsible lending by banks. At first, lenders enforced strict requirements on borrowers, lending only to those who could cover both the interest and repayments on the base amount that had been lent. However, as the economy improved, mortgages were offered to those who could afford to pay only the interest payments. These people were relying on an increase in their income or in the price of their home to pay off the balance of their loan.

In the US lenders then began to offer mortgages to people who did not earn enough even to cover the interest payments—these loans could only be serviced with strong growth in house prices and income. When the economy faltered and borrowers began to fail to pay back their loans, the whole economy collapsed.

During the wave of bank foreclosures that followed the 2008 financial crisis, boarded up homes such as this one in New Jersey became a common sight.

DIRECTORY

This book examines some of the most important ideas in economic thought, from its earliest beginnings to the evolution of political economy and the wide-ranging subject as we know it today. In doing so it inevitably looks at the ideas and achievements of major economists such as Adam Smith, John Maynard Keynes, and Friedrich Hayek. However, there are, of course, many other economists who have made important contributions, often in more than one area of study, and who deserve more than a passing mention. The thinkers discussed in the following pages have all played a part in establishing economics as a vital subject in modern industrial society, making sense of complexity, and expanding our understanding of economic activity in the world today.

JEAN-BAPTISTE COLBERT
1619–1683

Although born into a family of merchants in Rheims, France, Jean-Baptiste Colbert chose a career in politics rather than commerce. He rose to become Finance Minister to Louis XIV in 1665, and brought in measures to end political corruption. He also reformed the tax system, introduced policies to boost French industry and encourage overseas trade, and instituted improvements to the French infrastructure.
See also: The tax burden 64–65

PIERRE DE BOISGUILBERT
1646–1714

A French aristocrat, Pierre Le Pesant, sieur de Boisguilbert, pursued a career in law. He was a magistrate, then judge, and in 1690 became the *bailie*—the King's representative in charge of administration and justice for the city of Rouen, a post he held until his death in 1714. Seeing the effect of tax on the local economy, he opposed the tax system introduced by Jean-Baptiste Colbert. He believed that production and trade generated wealth, and proposed a reform of taxes to encourage freer trade.
See also: The tax burden 64–65

YAMAGATA BANTO
1748–1821

One of the most respected scholars of the city of Osaka, Japan, Yamagata Banto was also a money-exchange merchant. Along with others in the Kaitokudo School of Osaka, he introduced Western ideas of rationalism to Japanese institutions, helping to end Japan's feudal society, which had until then been built on Confucian ideas. Banto's multi-volume *Yume no shiro* ("Instead of Dreams") was critical of the old system, which he saw as dominated by the "age of gods," and proposed a rational, scientific approach to the social, political, and economic structure of modern Japan, founded on industry and trade.
See also: Comparative advantage 80–85

HENRI DE SAINT-SIMON
1760–1825

Claude Henri de Rouvroy was born into a noble family in Paris, France, but rejected his rightful title of "comte" because he advocated a form of socialism. His views were influenced by seeing the new society created in the US after the American Revolution. He argued that poverty could be eliminated through cooperation and technological innovation, and that education would remove the greed that drove people to seek social privilege and exploit others. His work influenced socialist thinkers of the 19th century, notably Karl Marx (p.105).
See also: Marxist economics 100–05

FRIEDRICH LIST
1789–1846

Friedrich List started his career as a civil servant in his hometown of Reutlingen, Germany, and rose quickly to high office. However, in 1822 he was imprisoned for his

views on reform, and escaped to France and then England. He emigrated to the US, becoming the US consul in Hamburg and then Leipzig. In 1843, he founded a newspaper to air his views on a "National System," whose expanded customs union could unite all of Germany. Ill health and financial problems dogged his final years, and he committed suicide in 1846.
See also: Comparative advantage 80–85

JOSEPH BERTRAND
1822–1900

The son of a French writer of popular science, Joseph Bertrand showed a precocious aptitude for mathematics from an early age. In 1856, he became a professor at the École Polytechnique in Paris. He made his name in the fields of number theory and probability, and opposed the theory of oligopoly described by his compatriot Antoine Augustin Cournot (p.91), proposing instead an alternative model of price competition.
See also: Effects of limited competition 90–91

CARL MENGER
1840–1921

One of the founders of the Austrian School of economics, Carl Menger was born in Galicia, now in Poland. His *Principles of Economics* (1871) outlined his theory of marginality (goods derive their value from the worth of each additional unit), which became key to the Austrian School's thinking. While professor of economics at the University of Vienna, he wrote the *Method of the Social Sciences*, which marked the final split from the German Historical School, which was based on 19th-century romantic ideals.
See also: Economic liberalism 172–77

LUJO BRENTANO
1844–1931

Born in Bavaria, Germany, Lujo Brentano earned doctorates in both law and economics. In 1868, he made a trip to Britain with the statistician Ernst Engel (p.125) to study trade unionism, and his ideas were influenced by the experience. A member of the German Historical School, Brentano nonetheless challenged many of its theories, arguing for social reform, human rights, and state responsibility for public welfare. His influence was particularly evident in the formation of the social market economies.
See also: The social market economy 222–23

EUGEN VON BÖHM-BAWERK
1851–1914

A founder of the Austrian School of economics, Eugen von Böhm-Bawerk was born in Brünn, Austria (now in the Czech Republic). He studied law at the University of Vienna and had a successful academic and political career, twice serving as Minister of Finance in the 1890s, during which he was able to put his frugal budget-balancing ideas into practice. His critiques of Marxist economics and theories of interest and capital were highly influential, especially on his students Joseph Schumpeter (p.149) and Ludwig von Mises (p.147).
See also: Central planning 142–47

FRIEDRICH VON WIESER
1851–1926

Friedrich von Wieser was born in Vienna. Like his brother-in-law Eugen von Böhm-Bawerk, he originally studied law but switched to economics after reading Carl Menger's work. After working for some years as a civil servant, in 1903 he succeeded Menger as professor in Vienna. His first major contribution was in value theory, in which he was influenced by Léon Walras (p.120) and Vilfredo Pareto (p.131), and he is credited with coining the term "marginal utility" (the satisfaction gained from each additional unit). He then turned his attention to applying economic theory to sociology, devising the important theory of social economy and its idea of opportunity cost.
See also: Opportunity cost 133

THORSTEIN VEBLEN
1857–1929

Famous as a maverick among US economists, Thorstein Veblen was the son of Norwegian immigrants who lived on a farm in Minnesota. His unconventional background gave him an outsider's view of US society, which led him to reject the conventional wisdom of his teachers. He developed a new institutionalist approach that combined sociology and economics. In 1899, he published *The Theory of the Leisure Class*, which introduced the idea of "conspicuous consumption" and criticized the inefficiency and corruption of the capitalist system and its "parasitic" business class.
See also: Conspicuous consumption 136

ARTHUR PIGOU
1877–1959

Born in Ryde, Isle of Wight, Arthur Pigou studied history at Cambridge University, UK, where he developed an interest in economics and met Alfred Marshall (p.110). After graduating, Pigou lectured at Cambridge until the outbreak of World War I, taking over Marshall's professorship in political economy in 1908. He is best known for the "Pigouvian taxes" he devised to offset externalities (costs or benefits that "spill over" onto third parties).
See also: External costs 137

NIKOLAI DMITRIYEVICH KONDRATIEV
1892–1938

Brought up in a peasant family near Kostroma, Russia, Nikolai Kondratiev studied economics at the University of St. Petersburg, then worked for the government. When Tsar Nicholas II was ousted in 1917, Kondratiev was a member of the Revolutionary Socialist Party and was made Minister of Supply. A month later, the provisional government was overthrown and Kondratiev returned to academic life. He developed a theory of 50- to 60-year cycles in capitalist economies, now known as Kondratiev waves. In 1930, his ideas fell out of favor. He was arrested, and executed eight years later.
See also: Boom and bust 78–79

RAGNAR FRISCH
1895–1973

Born in Christiana, Norway, Ragnar Frisch was a pioneer in the use of mathematics and statistics in economics. He coined the terms econometrics, microeconomics, and macroeconomics. He initially trained as a goldsmith, intending to join the family firm, but then studied economics and mathematics in France and England. In 1932, he founded the Oslo Institute of Economics, and in 1969 he became the first recipient of the Nobel Prize in Economic Sciences with his colleague Jan Tinbergen.
See also: Testing economic theories 170

PAUL ROSENSTEIN-RODAN
1902–85

Born into a Polish-Jewish family in Austrian-ruled Kraków, Rosenstein-Rodan began as a member of the Austrian School of economists. In 1930, he fled anti-Semitism in his homeland for London, where he lectured at the London School of Economics. In the 1940s his interest moved to development economics, and he proposed what came to be known as the "Big Push" theory. After World War II he moved to the US, working for the World Bank and as an adviser to the governments of India, Italy, Chile, and Venezuela.
See also: Development economics 188–93

JAN TINBERGEN
1903–1994

Joint winner of the first Nobel Prize in Economic Sciences with Ragnar Frisch in 1969, Dutch theorist Jan Tinbergen initially studied mathematics and physics, then began to apply scientific principles to economic theory and, in so doing, laid the foundations for the new field of econometrics. He worked as an adviser to the League of Nations and the Dutch Central Bureau of Statistics, where, in 1936, he developed a new national macroeconomic model. It was later adopted by other governments.
See also: Testing economic theories 170

RICHARD KAHN
1905–1989

Richard Ferdinand Kahn was born in London to German parents and gained a degree in physics at Cambridge University, UK, before switching to economics, obtaining an honors degree in one year under the supervision of John Maynard Keynes (p.161). At the age of 25 he made his name with an article describing the multiplier, a building block of Keynesian economics. A practical economist, he advised the British government during World War II before returning to Cambridge University, where he taught until his retirement in 1972.
See also: The Keynesian Multiplier 164–65

RAGNAR NURKSE
1907–1959

Born in Käru, Estonia (then part of the Russian Empire), Ragnar Nurkse studied law and economics at the University of Tartu. He continued his studies in Scotland and then Vienna. In 1934, Nurkse began working as a financial analyst for the League of Nations, which influenced his interest in international and development economics. After World War II he moved to the US,

teaching at Columbia and Princeton universities. With Paul Rosenstein-Rodan (p.336) he established the modern field of development economics, and was an advocate of the "Big Push" theory.
See also: Development economics 188–93

JOHN KENNETH GALBRAITH
1908–2006

Born in Ontario, Canada, John Kenneth Galbraith studied economics in Canada and the US. He later taught at Cambridge University, UK, where he was greatly influenced by John Maynard Keynes (p.161). During World War II he was deputy head of the US government Office of Price Administration, but his advocacy of permanent price controls led to his resignation in 1943. He worked as a journalist, academic, and economic adviser to President John F. Kennedy and gained a popular readership in 1958 with his book *The Affluent Society*.
See also: Conspicuous consumption 136

GEORGE STIGLER
1911–91

Greatly influenced by Frank Knight (p.163), his PhD supervisor at Chicago University, George Stigler went on to become a leading member of the Chicago School of economists, working with his friend and contemporary Milton Friedman (p.199). Known for his research into the history of economic thought, he also worked in the field of public choice theory (analysis of government behavior), and was one of the first to explore

the field of information economics. In 1982, he won the Nobel Prize.
See also: Searching and matching 304–05

JAMES TOBIN
1918–2002

James Tobin was born in Illinois and is popularly known today for the so-called "Tobin tax" that he devised to discourage speculation in currency transactions. Tobin is better known to economists as an advocate of Keynesian economics and for his academic work on investment and fiscal (tax) policy. Tobin went to Harvard University in 1935, where he met John Maynard Keynes. In 1950, he took up a teaching post at Yale, remaining there for the rest of his life. As a consultant to the Kennedy administration he helped to shape US economic policy throughout the 1960s, and in 1981 he won the Nobel Prize.
See also: Depressions and unemployment 154–61 ▪ The Keynesian multiplier 164–65

ALFRED CHANDLER
1918–2007

Born in Delaware, Alfred Chandler graduated from Harvard University in 1940. After serving in the US Navy in World War II he wrote his PhD thesis on management structures, based on documents left to him by his great-grandfather, the financial analyst Henry Varnum Poor. From the 1960s on he focused his attention on managerial strategy and the organization of large corporations. He wrote a large number of books, and his 1977 work, *The Visible*

Hand, won the Pulitzer Prize. The book described the rise of large-scale corporations as a "second industrial revolution."
See also: Economies of scale 132

ROBERT LUCAS
1937–

One of the most influential economists of the Chicago School of economics, Robert Lucas is also one of the founders of new classical macroeconomics. He studied at Chicago University and has been a professor there since 1974. He overturned Keynesian ideas, and his research into rational expectations (the idea that because people make well-informed, rational decisions, their actions can alter the intended course of government policy) influenced monetary policy during the 1980s.
See also: Rational expectations 244–47

EUGENE FAMA
1939–

A third-generation Italian-American, Eugene Fama was the first in his family to go to college. He initially studied French but became fascinated by economics. He was awarded a scholarship to study for a PhD at the University of Chicago, where he has taught ever since. He is best known as the originator of the efficient market hypothesis, which says that in any market with many, well-informed traders, the price reflects all the available information. He is also known for demonstrating the correlation between market efficiency and equilibrium.
See also: Efficient markets 272

KENNETH BINMORE
1940–

British academic Kenneth Binmore is a mathematician, economist, and game theorist. His work has pioneered the integration of traditional economics with new mathematical techniques and the use of experiments. He has developed theories of bargaining behavior and theories in the field of evolutionary game theory.
See also: Competition and cooperation 273

PETER DIAMOND
1940–

US economist Peter Diamond graduated in mathematics from Yale University, then studied economics at the Massachusetts Institute of Technology (MIT), where he has taught for most of his career. He is best known for his research into social insurance and has acted as a government adviser on Social Security policy. His later work on search and matching theory in the labor market led to him sharing the 2010 Nobel Prize with Dale Mortensen and Christopher Pissarides (p.339).
See also: Searching and matching 304–05

MICHAEL TODARO
1942–

US economist Michael Todaro graduated from Haverford College in Pennsylvania, then spent a year in Africa with his mentor, Professor Philip Bell, which inspired a passion for development economics. His 1967 PhD thesis formed the basis of a theory of migration in developing countries and set out what became known as the Todaro paradox. He worked for the Rockefeller Foundation in Africa and the Population Council in New York before taking up a permanent professorship at New York University.
See also: Development economics 188–93

ROBERT AXELROD
1943–

US economist and political scientist Robert Axelrod has taught for most of his career at the University of Michigan, which he joined in 1974. He is best known for his contribution to the theories of cooperation and complexity. His exploration of the "Prisoner's dilemma" in his book *The Evolution of Cooperation* (1984) showed that a "tit for tat" strategy could generate cooperative behavior in hostile and friendly situations. Axelrod has advised the United Nations, World Bank, and the US Department of Defense on promoting cooperation between countries.
See also: Competition and cooperation 273

MICHAEL SPENCE
1943–

Michael Spence's father was based in Ottawa during World War II, and although actually born in New Jersey, Spence was brought up in Canada. He studied philosophy at Princeton University, but then switched to economics for his PhD at Harvard University. He has spent most of his career teaching at the universities of Harvard and Stanford. His work has focused mainly on information economics (how information affects an economy) and the idea of "signaling" information indirectly (such as when a job hunter "signals" his or her ability for a certain job through academic qualifications). In 2001 he won the Nobel Prize with George Akerlof (p.275) and Joseph Stiglitz for his work on asymmetric (unbalanced) information in markets.
See also: Market uncertainty 274–75

JOSEPH STIGLITZ
1943–

One of the most influential (often controversial) economists of his generation, Joseph Stiglitz was born in Indiana to a family that he says "liked to debate political issues." He has held professorships at several prestigious universities in the US and the UK, served as an adviser to Presidents Clinton and Obama, and was Chief Economist for the World Bank. He made his name in the 1970s for his work on the economics of information (how information affects an economy), for which he was a joint winner of the 2001 Nobel Prize. In the 1990s he was a critic of the Washington Consensus (p.329), especially as applied to developing countries.
See also: Incentives and wages 302

ALICE AMSDEN
1943–2012

Described as a "fearless" economist, Alice Amsden focused on the development and industrialization of emerging economies. A graduate of Cornell University, she studied for her PhD at the London School of Economics, and then worked at the World Bank and the Organization for

Economic Cooperation and Development (OECD), while also holding high-level academic posts. In 2009, she was appointed to a three-year seat on the United Nations. She is especially remembered for her challenges to conventional ideas of globalization, through books such as *The Rise of "The Rest"* (2001).
See also: Asian Tiger economies 282–87

ROBERT BARRO
1944–

US economist Robert Barro originally studied physics, but then switched to economics at the PhD level. He has taught at many universities in the US and is honorary dean of the China Economics and Management Academy at the Central University of Finance and Economics in Beijing. Barro was a leading figure in the formation of the new classical macroeconomics and first drew attention in 1974 with his theories on the effect of present borrowing and future taxation. His later work has focused on the influence of culture on political economy.
See also: Borrowing and debt 76–77

CHRISTOPHER PISSARIDES
1948–

Born in the Greek-Cypriot village of Agros, Christopher Pissarides studied for a degree in economics at the University of Essex, UK. He then earned a PhD at the London School of Economics in 1973, where he has been on the staff since 1976. His most significant contribution has been in the field of searching and matching theory in the labor market, and unemployment. In the

1990s he developed a model of job creation and destruction with Dale Mortensen. He and Mortensen, along with Peter Diamond, were awarded the 2010 Nobel Prize for their analysis of markets.
See also: Searching and matching 304–05

PAUL KRUGMAN
1953–

Winner of the Nobel Prize in 2008 for his analysis of trade patterns, US economist Paul Krugman is known for his pioneering work in international trade and finance, and for his analysis of currency crises and fiscal (tax) policy. He has held many university teaching posts and worked as an economic adviser to the Reagan administration during the 1980s but is considered Left-leaning, politically. In the 1990s he developed an approach to the analysis of international trade that is now known as new trade theory.
See also: Trade and geography 312

DANI RODRIK
1957–

Born in Istanbul, Turkey, Dani Rodrik moved to the US for his university studies. Now Professor of International Political Economy at Harvard University, his main fields of interest are international and development economics. He has worked as a consultant for many international organizations, including the Centre for Economic Policy Research, the Center for Global Development, and the Institute for International Economics.
See also: Market integration 226–31 • Resisting economic change 328–29

HA-JOON CHANG
1963–

Born in South Korea, Ha-Joon Chang is a leading critic of mainstream economics. He graduated from the National University in Seoul before moving to the UK to gain a PhD from the University of Cambridge, where he continues his research. Chang has acted as a consultant to several United Nations agencies, the World Bank, the Asian Development Bank, and a number of national government agencies and NGOs. He criticizes conventional development policies as espoused by the World Bank, and his book, *23 Things They Don't Tell You About Capitalism* (2010) helped to popularize aspects of alternative economics.
See also: Asian Tiger economies 282–87

RENAUD GAUCHER
1976–

A graduate in psychology, history, and geography as well as economics, French thinker Renaud Gaucher has sought to integrate elements of the social sciences into economic thinking and take a more holistic approach. He has examined the psychology of money and behavioral economics from the point of view of positive psychology, with an emphasis on the "economics of happiness," following the research of economists such as Richard Easterlin, and considering its place in policies for development and climate change.
See also: The economics of happiness 216–19

GLOSSARY

Absolute advantage The ability of a country to produce a product more efficiently than another.

Aggregate The total amount; for instance, aggregate demand is the total demand for goods and services in an economy.

Asymmetric information An imbalance of information; for instance, buyers and sellers may have more or less information about the product than each other.

Austrian School A school of economics founded by Carl Menger in the late 19th century. It attributes all economic activity to the actions and free choice of individuals and opposes all forms of government intervention in an economy.

Balance of trade The difference in value of a country's imports and exports over a given time period.

Bankruptcy A legal declaration that an individual or a firm cannot repay their debts.

Barter system A system of exchange in which goods or services are exchanged for one another directly without the use of a medium of exchange, such as money.

Bear market A period of decline in the value of shares or other commodities.

Behavioral economics A branch of economics that studies the effects of psychological and social factors on decision making.

Bond An interest-bearing form of loan used to raise capital. Bonds are issued as certificates by the bond issuer (such as a government or firm) in return for a sum of money; the bond issuer agrees to repay the borrowed sum plus interest at a fixed date in the future.

Bretton Woods system A system of exchange rates agreed upon between the world's major industrial nations in 1945. It tied the value of the US dollar to gold, and the value of other currencies to the US dollar.

Budget A financial plan that lists all planned expenses and incomes.

Budget constraint The limit on the goods and services that a person can afford.

Bull market A period when the value of shares or other commodities increase.

Business cycle An economy-wide fluctuation in growth that is characterized by periods of expansion (boom) and periods of contraction (bust).

Capital The money and physical assets (such as machines and infrastructure) used to produce an income. A key ingredient of economic activity, along with land, labor, and enterprise.

Capitalism An economic system in which the means of production are privately owned, firms compete to sell goods for a profit, and workers exchange their labor for a wage.

Cartel A group of firms that agree to cooperate in such a way that the output of a particular good is restricted, and prices are driven up.

Central bank An institution that manages a country's currency, alters money supply, and sets interest rates. It may also act as a lender of last resort to banks.

Central planning A system of centralized government control of an economy, where decisions regarding production and allocation of goods are made by government committees.

Chaos theory A branch of mathematics that shows how small changes in initial conditions can cause larger effects later on.

Chicago School An avidly free market group of economists—linked to the University of Chicago—whose ideals of market liberalization and deregulation became mainstream in the 1980s.

Classical economics An early approach to economics developed by Adam Smith and David Ricardo, focusing on the growth of nations and free markets.

Collusion An agreement between two or more firms not to compete so they can fix prices.

Command economy An economy in which all aspects of economic activity are controlled by a central authority, such as the state. Also called a planned economy.

Commodity A general term for any product or service that can be traded. Often used in economics to refer to raw materials that are always of approximately the same quality and can be bought in bulk.

Communism A Marxist economic system in which property and the means of production are collectively owned.

Comparative advantage The ability of a country to produce a product relatively more efficiently than another country, even if the other country is more efficient overall.

Competition Competition arises when two or more producers attempt to win the business of a buyer by offering the best terms.

Consumption The value of goods or services purchased. Individual buying acts are aggregated by governments to calculate a figure for national consumption.

Credit crunch A sudden reduction in the availability of credit in a banking system. A credit crunch often occurs after a period in which credit is widely available.

Debt A promise made by one party (the debtor) to another (the creditor) to pay back a loan.

Default The failure to repay a loan under the terms agreed.

Deficit An imbalance. A trade deficit is an excess of imports over exports; a government budget deficit is an excess of spending over tax revenues.

Deflation A fall in the price of goods and services over time.

Deflation is associated with periods of economic stagnation.

Demand The amount of goods and services that a person or group of people are willing and able to buy.

Demand curve A graph showing the amount of a product or service that will be bought at different prices.

Dependency theory The idea that resources and wealth flow from poor countries to rich countries in such a way that the poor countries are unable to develop.

Depreciation A decrease in the value of an asset over time, caused by wear and tear or obsolescence.

Depression A severe, long-term decline in economic activity in which output slumps, unemployment rises, and credit is scarce.

Diminishing marginal returns A situation in which each extra unit of something produces successively smaller benefits.

Duopoly A situation in which two firms have control over a market.

Economic liberalism An ideology claiming that the greatest good is achieved when people are given the maximum personal freedom to make choices over consumption. Economic liberalism advocates a free market economy.

Economy The total system of economic activity in a particular country or area, comprising all the production, labor, trade, and consumption that take place.

Elasticity The sensitivity of one economic variable (such as demand)

to another (such as price). Prices of products may be elastic or inelastic.

Entrepreneur A person who undertakes commercial risk in the hope of making a profit.

Equilibrium A state of balance within a system. In economics, markets are in equilibrium when supply equals demand.

Eurozone Countries within the European Union that have formed a monetary union. They all use the same currency, the euro, and monetary policy is controlled by the European Central Bank.

Exchange rate The ratio at which one currency can be exchanged for another. An exchange rate is the price of a currency in terms of other currencies.

Externality A cost or benefit from any economic activity that is felt by a person not directly involved in that activity and is not reflected in price.

Factors of production The inputs used to make products or services: land, labor, capital, and enterprise.

Fiat money A form of money that is not backed by a physical commodity such as gold, but gains its value from the confidence people have in it. The world's main currencies are fiat money.

Fiscal policy A government's plans for taxes and spending.

Free market economy An economy in which decisions about production are made by private individuals and companies on the basis of supply and demand, and prices are determined by the market.

Free trade The import and export of goods and services without tariffs or quotas being imposed.

Game theory The study of strategic decision making by interacting individuals or firms.

GDP See *gross domestic product.*

Globalization The free flow of money, goods, or people across international borders; increased economic interdependence between countries through the integration of goods, labor, and capital markets.

GNP See *gross national product.*

Gold standard A monetary system in which a currency is backed by a reserve of gold and can theoretically be exchanged on demand for a quantity of gold. No country currently uses the gold standard.

Good Something that satisfies the desire or requirement of a consumer; normally used to refer to a product or raw material.

Great Depression A period of worldwide economic recession from 1929 to the mid-1930s. It started in the US with the Wall Street Crash.

Gross domestic product (GDP) A measure of national income over the course of a year. GDP is calculated by adding up a country's entire annual output, and it is often used to measure a country's economic activity and wealth.

Gross national product (GNP) The total value of all goods and services produced in one year by domestic-owned businesses, whether those businesses operate within the country or abroad.

Hyperinflation A very high rate of inflation.

Inflation A situation in which the prices of goods and services in an economy are rising.

Interest rate The price of borrowing money. The interest rate on a loan is generally stated as a percentage of the amount per year that must be repaid in addition to the sum borrowed.

International Monetary Fund (IMF) An international organization set up in 1944 to supervise the post-war exchange rate system, later moving into the provision of finance to poor countries.

Inverse relationship A situation in which one variable decreases as another increases.

Investment An injection of capital aimed at increasing future production, such as a new machine or training for the workforce.

Invisible hand Adam Smith's idea that as individuals pursue their own interests in the market, it leads inevitably to the collective benefit of society, as if there were some guiding "invisible hand."

Keynesian Multiplier The theory that an increase in government spending in an economy produces an even greater increase in income.

Keynesianism A school of economic thought based on the ideas of John Maynard Keynes, advocating government spending to pull economies out of recession.

Laissez-faire A French term meaning "let it do," which is used to describe markets free from government intervention.

Liquidity The ease with which an asset can be used to buy something without this causing a reduction in the asset's value. Cash is the most liquid asset since it can be used immediately to buy goods or services, with no effect on its value.

Macroeconomics The study of the economy as a whole, looking at economy-wide factors such as interest rates, inflation, growth, and unemployment.

Marginal cost The increase in total costs caused by producing one more unit of output.

Marginal utility The change in total utility, or satisfaction, that results from the consumption of one more unit of a product or service.

Market failure Where a market fails to deliver socially optimal outcomes. Market failure may be due to lack of competition (such as a monopoly), incomplete information, unaccounted costs and benefits (externalities), or lack of potential private profit (as with public goods).

Mercantilism A doctrine that dominated Western European economics during the 16th and 18th centuries. It stressed the importance of government control over foreign trade to maintain a positive balance of trade.

Microeconomics The study of the economic behavior of individuals and firms.

Mixed economy An economy in which part of the means of production is owned by the state and part of it is owned privately, combining aspects of planned economies and market economies. Strictly speaking, nearly all economies are mixed economies, but the balance can vary widely.

Monetarism A school of economic thought that believes that the primary role of government is to control the money supply. It is associated with US economist Milton Friedman and conservative governments of the 1970s and 80s.

Monetary policy Government policies aimed at changing the money supply or interest rates in order to stimulate or slow down the economy.

Monopoly A market in which there is only one firm. Monopoly firms generally produce a low output, which they then sell at a high price.

Neoclassical economics The dominant approach to economics today. It is based around supply and demand and rational individuals, and is often couched in mathematical terms.

New classical macroeconomics A school of thought within macroeconomics that uses forms of analyses that are based entirely on a neoclassical framework.

Nominal value The cash value of something, expressed in the money of the day. Nominal prices or wages change due to inflation, so cannot be usefully compared across different time periods (a wage of $50 would not buy the same amount of goods in 1980 and 2000).

Oligopoly An industry with only a few firms. In an oligopoly there is a danger that firms may form cartels to fix prices.

Pareto efficiency A situation in which no change can be made in the allocation of goods to make someone better off without making somebody else worse off. Named after Vilfredo Pareto.

Perfect competition An idealized situation in which buyers and sellers have complete information and there are so many different firms producing the same product that no individual seller can influence the price.

Phillips curve A mathematical graph illustrating the supposed inverse relationship between inflation and unemployment.

Planned economy
See *Command economy.*

Price The quantity of payment, in money or goods, given by a buyer to a seller in return for a good or service.

Protectionism An economic policy aimed at restricting international trade, in which a country imposes tariffs or quotas on imports.

Public good Goods or services, such as street lighting, that will not be provided by private firms.

Quantitative easing The injection of new money into an economy by a central bank.

Real value The value of something measured in terms of the amount of goods or services they can buy.

Recession A period during which an economy's total output decreases.

Shares Units of ownership in a company; also known as equities.

Social market The economic model developed in West Germany following World War II, characterized by a mixed economy in which private enterprise is encouraged, but government intervenes in the economy to ensure social justice.

Stagflation A period of high inflation, high unemployment, and low growth.

Sticky wages Wages that are slow to change in response to market conditions.

Supply The amount of a product that is available to buy.

Supply curve A graph showing the amount of a product or service that sellers will produce at different prices.

Surplus An imbalance. A trade surplus is an excess of exports over imports; a government budget surplus is an excess of tax revenues over spending.

Tariff A tax imposed on imports, often to protect domestic producers from foreign competition.

Tax A charge imposed on firms and individuals by governments. Its payment is enforced by law.

Utilitarianism A philosophy that claims that choices should be made so happiness will increase for the greatest number of people.

Utility A unit used to measure the satisfaction, or happiness, gained from consuming a product or service.

INDEX

D

E

F

ACKNOWLEDGMENTS

Dorling Kindersley would like to thank Niyati Gosain, Shipra Jain, Payal Rosalind Malik, Mahua Mandal, Anjana Nair, Pooja Pawwar, Anuj Sharma, Vidit Vashisht, and Shreya Anand Virmani for design assistance; and Lili Bryant for editorial assistance.

PICTURE CREDITS

The publisher would like to thank the following for their kind permission to reproduce their photographs:

(Key: a-above; b-below/bottom; c-center; f-far; l-left; r-right; t-top)

20 Getty Images: Barcroft Media (bc). **23 Alamy Images:** The Art Gallery Collection (tl). **Getty Images:** The Bridgeman Art Library (tr). **24 Getty Images:** AFP (cr). **25 Getty Images:** Nativestock / Marilyn Angel Wynn (br). **27 Corbis:** Bettmann (tr). **28 Dorling Kindersley:** Judith Miller / The Blue Pump (tr). **Getty Images:** John Moore (bl). **29 Getty Images:** Jason Hawkes (br). **31 Library Of Congress, Washington, D.C.:** (tr). **33 Getty Images:** Universal Images Group / Leemage (tl). **35 Getty Images:** AFP / Fred Dufour (tr). **37 Alamy Images:** The Art Archive (bl). **Getty Images:** Hulton Archive (tr). **38 Corbis:** Heritage Images (br). **42 Corbis:** The Gallery Collection (tc). **43** *Tableau Économique*, 1759, François Quesnay (bl). **44 Alamy Images:** The Art Gallery Collection (bl). **45 Getty Images:** Hulton Archive (tr). **47 Corbis:** Bettmann (tr); Hemis / Camille Moirenc (tl). **53 Corbis:** Godong / Philippe Lissac (tr); John Henley (bl). **56 The Art Archive:** London Museum / Sally Chappell (bl). **Corbis:** Johnér Images / Jonn (tr). **58 Getty Images:** The Bridgeman Art Library (b). **60 Corbis:** Robert Harding World Imagery / Neil Emmerson (bl). **61 Corbis:** Justin Guariglia (tl). **Library Of Congress, Washington, D.C.:** (tr). **63 Corbis:** Sebastian Rich (br). **65 Corbis:** The Art Archive / Alfredo Dagli Orti (tr). **Dreamstime.com:** Georgios Kollidas (bl). **67 Corbis:** Tim Pannell (tl). **Getty Images:** AFP (br). **68 Getty Images:** Paula Bronstein (bc). **69 Corbis:** Bettmann (tr). **71 Getty Images:** Bloomberg (tr). **73 Getty Images:** Bloomberg (bl). **Library Of Congress, Washington, D.C.:** (br). **75 Corbis:** National Geographic Society (bc). **Library Of Congress, Washington, D.C.:** (tr). **77 Corbis:** EPA / Simela Pantzartzi (cr). **79 Getty Images:** Archive Photos / Lewis H. Hine (tl). **83 Corbis:** Bettmann (br). **84 Corbis:** Imaginechina (tl). **Getty Images:** Hulton Archive (bl). **85 Corbis:** Cameron Davidson (bc). **95 Getty Images:** Hulton Archive / London Stereoscopic Company (tr); **Science & Society Picture Library** (bl). **97 Corbis:** Bettmann (tl). **Getty Images:** Per-Anders Pettersson (br). **98** *Flora's Mallewagen*, c.1640, Hendrik Gerritsz. Pot (bc). **102 akg-images:** German Historical Museum, Berlin (tr). **103 Getty Images:** Science & Society Picture Library (bl). **104 Corbis:** Michael Nicholson (tl). **105 Corbis:** Bettmann (tr). **Getty Images:** CBS Photo Archive (bl). **110 Alamy Images:** INTERFOTO (bl). **112 Getty Images:** Yawar Nazir (bl). **113 Getty Images:** AFP (tl). **115** *Popular Science Monthly*, volume 11, 1877 (tr). **117 Corbis:** EPA / Abdullah Abir (tr); Imaginechina (tl). **120 Alamy Images:** INTERFOTO (bl). **Dreamstime.com:** Ayindurdu (tr). **122 Getty Images:** Jeff J. Mitchell (tr). **124 Corbis:** Cultura / Frank and Helena (cr). **125 Alamy Images:** INTERFOTO (tr). **129 Getty Images:** Bloomberg (tr); Taxi / Ron Chapple (bl). **131 Library Of Congress, Washington, D.C.:** (tr). **132 Getty Images:** Photographer's Choice / Hans-Peter Merten (bc). **135 Getty Images:** Bloomberg (tr); Hulton Archive (bl). **136 Library Of Congress, Washington, D.C.:** (bc). **139 Getty Images:** Hulton Archive (bl); SuperStock (tl). **141 Corbis:** Viviane Moos (br). **Getty Images:** Hulton Archive (tl). **145 Getty Images:** De Agostini Picture Library (tr). **147 Corbis:** Bettmann (bl). **Courtesy of the Ludwig von Mises Institute, Auburn, Alabama, USA. 149 Corbis:** Bettmann (tr); Rolf Bruderer (bl). **156 Getty Images:** Hulton Archive (cr). **157 Getty Images:** Gamma-Keystone (tr). **159 Corbis:** Bettmann (tr). **160 Getty Images:** Ethan Miller (bl). **161 Corbis:** Bettmann (tr); Ocean (tl). **163 Corbis:** Paulo Fridman (cr). **165 Corbis:** Xinhua Press / Xiao Yijiu (tc). **167 Corbis:** Macduff Everton (bc). **Library Of Congress, Washington, D.C.:** (tr). **168 Dreamstime.com:** Gina Sanders (bc). **169 Corbis:** Dennis Degnan (br). **171 Corbis:** Darrell Gulin (br). **175 Corbis:** Reuters / Korea News Service (br). **177 Corbis:** Hulton-Deutsch Collection (tr). **Getty Images:** Bloomberg (tl). **179 Corbis:** Heritage Images (tr). **Getty Images:** AFP (bl). **181 Getty Images:** The Agency Collection (bl); Hulton Archive / Express Newspapers (tr). **186 Corbis:** Hulton-Deutsch Collection (bc). **187 Corbis:** Reuters (br). **192 Corbis:** Gideon Mendel (tl). **193 Corbis:** Reuters / Carlos Hugo Vaca (br). **Getty Images:** Photographer's Choice / Wayne Eastep (bl). **195 Getty Images:** AFP / Gabriel Duval (bl). **198 Library Of Congress, Washington, D.C.: U.S.** Farm Security Administration / Office of War Information / Dorothea Lange (t). **199 Corbis:** Bettmann (tr); Hulton-Deutsch Collection (tc). **201 Corbis:** Reuters (tl). **Getty Images:** Brad Markel (br). **203 Getty Images:** Dorothea Lange (cr). **205 Getty Images:** The Agency Collection / John Giustina (bl); Archive

Photos / Bachrach (tr). **207 Getty Images:** Andreas Rentz (tc). University of Nebraska-Lincoln: (tr). **209 Corbis:** Bettmann (bl); Stuart Westmorland (tl). **211 Corbis:** Imaginechina (bc). Getty Images: AFP (tr). **213 Getty Images:** Chris Hondros (bc). **215 Getty Images:** The Bridgeman Art Library (tr). **217 Corbis:** Blend Images / Sam Diephuis / John Lund (tr). **218 Corbis:** Christophe Boisvieux (br). **219 Corbis:** Nik Wheeler (tr). **223 Corbis:** SIPA / Robert Wallis (tr). **225 Corbis:** Sygma / Ira Wyman (bl). **Getty Images:** AFP / Frederic J. Brown (tr). **228 Corbis:** The Gallery Collection (cr). **229 Getty Images:** Science & Society Picture Library (br). **230 Corbis:** EPA / Udo Weitz (br); Imaginechina (tl). **233 Corbis:** Peter Turnley (tr). Courtesy Professor János Kornai. **236 Dreamstime.com:** Artemisphoto (tr). **239 Corbis:** Reuters (tr). **Digital Vision:** (bl). **240 Corbis:** Lawrence Manning (bl). **241 Corbis:** Tim Graham (tr). **243 Corbis:** EPA / George Esiri (tl). **245 Corbis:** Cultura / Colin Hawkins (tr). **246 Getty Images:** Photolibrary / Peter Walton Photography (tl). **247 Corbis:** EPA / Justin Lane (bl). **249 Dreamstime.com:** Ivonne Wierink

(t/Urn); Zoommer (t/Balls). **253 Corbis:** George Hammerstein (tr). **254 Corbis:** Sygma / Regis Bossu (tr). **Getty Images:** Bloomberg (bl). **257 Getty Images:** AFP / Tony Karumba (tr); Jeff Christensen (bl). **263 Corbis:** Robert Essel NYC (br). **264 Getty Images:** Glow Images, Inc. (tl). **265 Dreamstime.com:** Zagor (br). **267 Dreamstime.com:** Digitalpress (br). **269 Getty Images:** Paula Bronstein (tr). **271 Corbis:** John Harper (tr). **273 Getty Images:** Konstantin Zavrazhin (br). **275 Corbis:** Big Cheese Photo (tr). **Getty Images:** Dan Krauss (bl). **277 Corbis:** Reuters / Wolfgang Rattay (bl). **Getty Images:** Lisa Maree Williams (tl). **278 Corbis:** Frans Lanting (bc). **279 Corbis:** Louis K. Meisel Gallery, Inc. (br). **281 Corbis:** Ocean (cr). **285 Corbis:** Bettmann (tl). **Dreamstime.com:** Leung Cho Pan (br). **286 Corbis:** Justin Guariglia (tl). **287 Corbis:** Topic Photo Agency (br); Xinhua Press / Xu Yu (bl). **291 Corbis:** Reuters / Philimon Bulawayo (tr). **293 Corbis:** Xinhua Press / Guo Lei (br). **295 Corbis:** Hemis / René Mattes (br). **298 Corbis:** Bettmann (tr). **300 Getty Images:** The Image Bank / Stewart

Cohen (bc). **301 Corbis:** Reuters / Shannon Stapleton (tr). **302 Corbis:** Bettmann (bc). **304 Corbis:** Images.com (cr). **305 Corbis:** EPA / Mondelo (br). **307 Getty Images:** UpperCut Images / Ferguson & Katzman Photography (tl). **309 Corbis:** Eye Ubiquitous / David Cumming (br). **Getty Images:** Helifilms Australia (tl). **311 Getty Images:** Stone / Bruce Ayres (tl). **313 Corbis:** Roger Ressmeyer (bc). **315 Corbis:** EPA / Kim Ludbrook (cr). **Getty Images:** WireImage / Steven A. Henry (bl). **320 Library Of Congress, Washington, D.C.:** George Grantham Bain Collection (tl). **321 Corbis:** Bettmann (tc). **323 Getty Images:** Archive Photos / Arthur Siegel (tc). **325 Getty Images:** Mark Wilson (tr). **327 Corbis:** Robert Harding World Imagery / Duncan Maxwell (cr). **Getty Images:** Bloomberg (bl). **329 Getty Images:** AFP / Issouf Sanogo (tr). **330 Getty Images:** Stone / Ryan McVay (cr). **331 Corbis:** Star Ledger / Mark Dye (br)

All other images © Dorling Kindersley.

For more information see:
www.dkimages.co.uk